"When the dust settles on current political divisions, clear-eyed historians will see the occupant of the White House as an American revolutionary. Donald Trump's revolution was to unapologetically restore a nation's pride, resurrect its power, and unleash its engines of prosperity and opportunity. These achievements were made possible because Trump established a new standard for American leadership: *put America and its people first*. As a leader, be an American patriot and rally your people to its cause. The indefatigable Robert Spencer has written a primer for the new era that Trump has made possible. His new book, *Rating America's Presidents*, rejects the self-flagellations of the academic left and proposes a Trumpian standard for judging the forty-five individuals who have occupied the Oval Office. Where left-wing historians have rated America's presidents on how faithfully they adhere to left-wing biases, Spencer has re-evaluated America's leaders by the only standard that should count: have they advanced the interests of their country and the welfare of its citizens? *Rating America's Presidents* is itself a revolutionary act."

—**DAVID HOROWITZ**, author, *Radical Son*

"Robert Spencer has applied a cogent, clearly-explained standard for rating the presidents: 'How good were they for America?' His rankings are consistent, fair, and in my view, appropriate (we might differ strongly about Old Hickory, whom I think was a long-term disaster for the United States, but that's just me). No list that has anyone but Washington as number one should ever be considered, and appropriately that's where Spencer has him. Likewise, Lincoln rates a ten as 'great for America.' Agree with his ratings or not, no one can say that Spencer has been flippant or casual in his effort to portray all presidents in light of the single issue of how they made America greater."

—**LARRY SCHWEIKART,** author of *A Patriot's History of the United States* and *Reagan: The American President*

"One thing virtually every American can agree on is that every ranking of American presidents is a reflection of the values of the person or persons making those rankings. So, if you share the left-wing values of the vast majority of academics and journalists, you will certainly be pleased with how highly Woodrow Wilson and Barack Obama, to cite but two examples, are ranked. But if you believe, as I do, that these were two of the worst presidents in American history, where do you go for a knowledgeable ranking of the presidents? Here is the answer: Robert Spencer's *Rating America's Presidents*. It offers a new assessment based on the only criterion that matters: who did good for America? Given the author's credentials and the subject matter, this is an important and enjoyable book."

—**DENNIS PRAGER** is a nationally-syndicated radio talk host, syndicated columnist, and president of Prager University, the largest conservative video site in the world. He is also a *New York Times* bestselling author of ten books, including most recently the first two volumes of *The Rational Bible*, a five-volume commentary on the Torah

"The problem with so many presidential rating and ranking lists— typically based around polls of college professors—is not just that they are biased. The most recent Republican president is almost always given the lowest marks, of course. No, the deeper problem is that they revolve around flawed, or in many cases, no criteria at all. Spencer's evaluation of our presidents is quite different. He instead goes by the simple question: 'Who preserved, protected, and defended the Constitution of the United States?' Readers will find that *Rating America's Presidents* provides an enlightening perspective based on who fulfilled that simple, but essential presidential oath."

—**JARRETT STEPMAN,** columnist for *The Daily Signal* and author of *The War on History: The Conspiracy to Rewrite America's Past*

"American students are usually taught to remember names and dates, but rarely get asked to critically evaluate past presidents. Here, Spencer does that in a way never-before-seen. A must-read for students—students of history."

—**JACK POSOBIEC,** correspondent and host for One America News Network and author of *Citizens for Trump: The Inside Story of the People's Movement to Take Back America*

"A magnificent work; thorough, impressive, robust, not to mention eminently readable. Spencer has the brain the size of a small planet, and it shows. His groundbreaking analysis of our presidents is a must-read, and should be on the bookshelves of every home, classroom, and library."

—**NICK ADAMS,** author of *Trump and Churchill: Defenders of Western Civilization* and *Retaking America: Crushing Political Correctness*

"We've all taken sides in the fight about the best and worst presidents at some point, and going forward, this book is a necessary weapon in your truth arsenal."

—**BUCK SEXTON,** conservative radio host, political commentator, author, and former intelligence officer with the Central Intelligence Agency

"Robert Spencer's greatest contribution to the public debate has always been intellectual rigor and fearlessness in resisting facile orthodoxy. In *Rating America's Presidents*, he makes his cynosure President Donald Trump's guiding tenet: The duty of America's president is, simply, to put America's interests first. His effort to apply the same metrics to every chief executive in history will raise progressive hackles, rankle Republicans of a globalist bent, and hearten today's populist conservatives. Wherever one fits on the spectrum, none can deny that this book is thoroughly researched and forcefully argued—the Spencer we've come to know, has proved himself invaluable."

—ANDREW C. MCCARTHY, *New York Times* bestselling author

ALSO BY ROBERT SPENCER

Confessions of an Islamophobe

The History of Jihad: From Muhammad to ISIS

The Palestinian Delusion:
The Catastrophic History of the Middle
East Peace Process

RATING
AMERICA'S
PRESIDENTS

ROBERT
SPENCER

BOMBARDIER
B O O K S

A BOMBARDIER BOOKS BOOK
An Imprint of Post Hill Press
ISBN: 978-1-64293-535-6
ISBN (eBook): 978-1-64293-536-3

Rating America's Presidents:
An America-First Look at Who Is Best, Who Is Overrated, and Who
Was An Absolute Disaster
© 2020 by Robert Spencer
All Rights Reserved

Obama photo on cover by Elizabeth Cromwell

Post Hill Press
New York · Nashville
posthillpress.com

Published in the United States of America

This book is dedicated with love and respect to all Americans who are grateful to live in this extraordinary land.

TABLE OF CONTENTS

INTRODUCTION

HOW CAN WE KNOW WHO WAS A GREAT PRESIDENT AND WHO WASN'T?

When one attempts to evaluate the success or failure of the various presidents of the United States, the first question is this: By what criteria should each one be judged?

There have been at least twenty such surveys of historians, rating the presidents of the United States from "Great" down to "Failure" since 1948. There are some variations, but these surveys stand out more for their remarkable unanimity than for their differences. Most of them agree that America's greatest presidents were George Washington, Abraham Lincoln, and Franklin D. Roosevelt, with Woodrow Wilson, Harry Truman, and Theodore Roosevelt usually rounding out the top tier. At the bottom, we generally find Ulysses S. Grant, Warren G. Harding, and Richard Nixon.

These surveys don't generally reveal the assumptions and biases of the participating historians, but they're clear enough:

while some presidential rankings are based simply on whether the occupant of the White House got things done and fulfilled his promises, all too many historians, in accord with most of the academic world today, have generally favored presidents who were big-government statists and globalists. They dislike presidents who lowered taxes, protected American workers, and favored a small federal government that left the American people and the world as free as they possibly could.

In accord with the priorities and perspectives of contemporary historians, in May 2019, Northwestern University's Center for the Study of Diversity and Democracy surveyed 113 academics on their views of fourteen modern presidents (from FDR through Trump), rating them on the basis of their leadership ability and commitment to "diversity and inclusion." At the top were Franklin Roosevelt, Barack Obama, Lyndon Johnson, Bill Clinton, and John F. Kennedy. Donald Trump was, of course, at the bottom.

If the academics responsible for this survey were aware of FDR's opposition to civil rights legislation, as he feared it would alienate his Southern Democrat supporters, or of the disastrous results of Lyndon Johnson's Great Society in America's inner cities, or of Barack Obama's consistent tendency to fan, rather than soothe, racial tensions, they showed no sign of it. In any case, that survey is a good encapsulation of how modern-day historians see the presidents and American history.

Meanwhile, a Siena College Research Institute "Presidential Expert Poll" in 2010 graded the chief executives on a number of criteria, including party leadership, communication ability, relations with Congress, court appointments, handling of the economy, domestic and foreign policy accomplishments, and even integrity, imagination, and luck. The top five were again similar to those who topped many other polls: Franklin D. Roosevelt, Theodore Roosevelt, Abraham Lincoln, George Washington, and Thomas Jefferson.

Likewise, a C-SPAN survey of historians in 2017 evaluated them on the basis of criteria that included public persuasion, crisis leadership, economic management, moral authority, and whether or not the president in question "pursued equal justice for all." Yet again, the top five were largely predictable: Abraham Lincoln, George Washington, Theodore Roosevelt, and Franklin D. Roosevelt, with one surprise, Dwight D. Eisenhower.

Gauging recent presidents on the basis of popularity, the media company Morning Consult in February 2017 polled registered voters, asking them to rate the best and worst presidents since World War II. The top five: Reagan, Obama, JFK, Bill Clinton, and Donald Trump. Some of the same names appeared among the bottom five: Trump, Obama, Nixon, George W. Bush, and Bill Clinton. It's likely that these voters made their choices based on their view of current political controversies.

Most of the criteria used in these various surveys are deeply flawed. A president may have been wildly unpopular in his day and yet still have done what was good, right, and necessary. And while "diversity" may be a laudable goal to which to aspire, history is full of societies that were actually weakened, not strengthened, when they took in large populations of unassimilated immigrants. Nor are party leadership, communication ability, good relations with Congress, court appointments, handling of the economy, and the like necessarily indicators of a great or good president. A president may have accomplished a great deal, but if all his accomplishments took the country in the wrong direction, we would have been better off without him in the White House.

New criteria are needed—or, more precisely, old criteria. In fact, what is needed is the oldest criterion of all for judging the success and failure of various presidents: Were they good for America and Americans, or were they not?

This is the guiding criterion that George Washington, Thomas Jefferson, John Adams, and Founding Fathers who were not presidents, such as Alexander Hamilton, would likely use when judging the occupants of the White House up to the present day. The president's primary job is clear from the oath of office that every president recites in order to assume office, and it isn't to provide health care for illegal aliens, or to make sure that Somalia isn't riven by civil war, or to make sure America is "diverse." It is simply this: "I do solemnly swear (or affirm) that I will faithfully execute the Office of President of the United States, and will to the best of my ability, preserve, protect and defend the Constitution of the United States."

So what makes a great president? Preserving, protecting, and defending the Constitution of the United States. Or, to put it even more simply, a great president is one who *puts America first.*

Nowadays this point is hotly controverted. In Donald Trump's inaugural address on January 20, 2017, he declared:

"From this day forward, a new vision will govern our land. From this moment on, it's going to be America First.... We will seek friendship and goodwill with the nations of the world— but we do so with the understanding that it is the right of all nations to put their own interests first."[1] In response, neoconservative commentator William Kristol tweeted: "I'll be unembarrassedly old-fashioned here: It is profoundly depressing and vulgar to hear an American president proclaim 'America First.'"[2]

Eight months later, at the UN General Assembly, Trump explained that his guiding principle was simple common sense: "As President of the United States, I will always put America first, just like you, as the leaders of your countries will always, and should always, put your countries first."[3]

Indeed. As Trump continued, "All responsible leaders have an obligation to serve their own citizens, and the nation-state remains the best vehicle for elevating the human condition."[4]

Yet Kristol was not alone in his disgust that the president would use this phrase and make it the principal focus of his presidency. The idea that "all responsible leaders have an obligation to serve their own citizens" primarily, rather than those of the world at large, has been out of fashion since World War II, and in many ways since World War I. It has been mislabeled, derided, and dismissed as "isolationism," a fear or unwillingness to engage with the wider world, even

---

1   "Inaugural Address: Trump's Full Speech," CNN, January 21, 2017.

2   William Kristol (@BillKristol), Twitter, January 20, 2017.

3   "Full Text: Trump's 2017 U.N. Speech Transcript," Politico, September 19, 2017.

4   Ibid.

as it is becoming increasingly interconnected and interdependent. But it does not necessarily mean that America will withdraw from the world; it only means that in dealing with the world, American presidents will be looking out primarily for the good of Americans.

The term "America first" has also been associated, quite unfairly, with racism and anti-Semitism. The founding principles of the republic, notably the proposition that, as the Declaration of Independence puts it, "all men are created equal, and endowed by their Creator with certain unalienable rights," shows that putting America first has nothing to do with such petty and irrational hatreds.

In fact, the Founding Fathers and every president up until Woodrow Wilson took for granted that the president of the United States should put his nation first and would have thought it strange in the extreme that this idea should even be controversial.

That will therefore be the principal criterion of the evaluations of the presidents in this book: Did he put America first? Was he good for Americans? Or did he leave us in a worse, poorer, more precarious, or more dangerous position than we were in before he assumed office?

The controversial nature of Donald Trump's policies and personality as well as decades of conditioning have made many people suspicious of the phrase "America first," but what should an American president put first if not the interests of his people? Even internationalism was originally sold to the American people as being the best course to follow for the protection of America and its people.

Today there is more reason to revisit and embrace the "America first" principle than there has been in a century. Socialism and nationalism have found favor among some Americans since before the First World War. Nowadays, however, although the entire Democratic Party is embracing socialism, it is still massively discredited as a political philosophy. Its sister ideology, internationalism, is facing more opposition today than it has since before World War II.

Accordingly, it's time the assumptions of the likes of William Kristol and the modern historians who rate presidents were challenged. This is all the more important to do in light of the fact that several generations of American children have now been raised to despise the Founding Fathers as racist slave owners and to consider American history to be one long record of racism, imperialism, and oppression.

Americans need to recover an appreciation of their history and for the heroes of that history. This book, therefore, rates the presidents not on the basis of criteria developed by socialist internationalist historians, but on the basis of their fidelity to the United States Constitution and to the powers, and limits to those powers, of the president as delineated by the Founding Fathers.

This criterion upends much of the conventional wisdom. John Tyler, Ulysses S. Grant, and Warren G. Harding, generally ranked as among the worst presidents, here come out near the top. Woodrow Wilson and Franklin D. Roosevelt, usually ranked near the top, fall to the bottom. This criterion reveals that Donald Trump, who was rated the worst president ever in one recent survey and the third-worst in another, is actually, after just three years in office (as of this writing), one of the greatest presidents the United States has ever had, if not the very best. And Barack Obama, who is rated in the top twenty in four polls and in the top ten in another, is actually the most damaging and disastrous president this nation has ever had.

This is not simply the author's personal preference. This is the inevitable result if one examines the U.S. presidents while holding in mind the nature of the presidency as explained in the Constitution. The nation's founding document is quite spare in its description of the president's duties. He shall be, it says, "Commander in Chief of the Army and Navy of the United States," and "have Power to grant Reprieves and Pardons for Offences against the United States." He "shall have Power, by and with the Advice and Consent of the Senate, to make Treaties, provided two thirds of the Senators present concur; and he shall nominate, and by and with the Advice and Consent of the Senate, shall appoint Ambassadors, other public Ministers and Consuls, Judges of the supreme Court, and all other Officers of the United States, whose Appointments are not herein otherwise provided for...[and] he shall from time to time give to the Congress Information of the State of the Union, and recommend to their Consideration such Measures as he shall judge necessary and expedient."[5]

Those who believe the president should be much more proactive about climate change or the price of prescription drugs may be shocked to learn the fact, but that's pretty much it. The underlying assumption of this delineation of his duties is that he will be working to protect and defend the interests

---

5   U.S. Constitution, art. 2, secs. 2 and 3.

of America and Americans. On that basis, the presidents are judged in this book.

If George Washington or Thomas Jefferson were alive today, I don't think it terribly hubristic to say that they would largely agree with my evaluations. After all, I'm using the criteria they formulated.

ONE

GEORGE WASHINGTON

Pendleton's Lithography, Library of Congress[6]

---

6   Gilbert Stuart, *George Washington, First President of the United States* [1828?],
     photograph, Pendleton's Lithography, Library of Congress, https://www.loc.
     gov/item/96523313/.

Full name: George Washington

Lived: February 22, 1732–December 14, 1799

Presidency: April 30, 1789–March 4, 1797

Party: Federalist. Washington actually rejected party affiliation and warned against the formation of political parties. But in practice, he favored the group that came to be known as the Federalists, who supported a strong federal government, over the Democratic-Republicans, who favored a more decentralized model of governance.

Evaluation: Great for America

Rating: 10

What qualified him to be president

George Washington had a long career in public service, beginning in the Virginia Regiment during the French and Indian War (1754–1763). He was commander in chief of the Continental Army that fought for independence against Great Britain and secured it definitively in 1783. In the course of his service, he amassed a remarkable reputation for personal probity.

Nevertheless, Washington was not simply a war hero who won the presidency on the strength of his military achievements. He was also a delegate to the Continental Congress, which drafted and approved the Declaration of Independence, and later, he was deeply involved in the formulation of the U.S. Constitution. By 1789, he was so revered for his rectitude, valor, and integrity, as well as his unswerving loyalty to the cause of American independence, that he had earned the title "Father of His Country" and the agreement of virtually every public figure that he should serve as the nation's first president.

In fact, his popularity outstripped that of the new government itself, such that some were won over to supporting it solely because Washington would be heading it. The mythology that quickly surrounded Washington after his death, with the famous incidents of his honesty and courage that every schoolchild used to know (chopping down the cherry tree, crossing the Delaware, etc.), began to develop during his lifetime.

Those days are long gone. About the only thing today's schoolchildren learn about Washington and the other Founding Fathers is that they owned slaves; this is undoubtedly true, but in this, they were not singular. Slavery had been taken for granted as an acceptable practice in all the societies of the world, and most people during the time of the American founding believed the same way. Washington, in fact, was unusual among his contemporaries in growing progressively uneasy with the practice, although as president, he considered it necessary to maintain the legality of the "peculiar institution" in light of the fact that the Southern states clung to it so tenaciously, and he did not see any way to discard it without sacrificing national unity. In a will he drafted six months before he died, he ordered his own slaves to be freed.

Slavery is undoubtedly a moral evil, but to condemn outright all those who engaged in it at a time when its evil was by no means taken for granted and was often hotly contested is to manifest a historical ignorance and chronological triumphalism that transposes twenty-first century attitudes and assumptions onto ages in which such views would have been largely or completely foreign.

How he won

No one else was even seriously considered to become the new nation's first president. Washington remains the only person to be elected unanimously—twice—to the office. The popular vote at that time was insignificant; the electors (some, but not all, of whom were themselves chosen by popular vote) of every state, then, as now, chose the president. The choice in both 1789 and 1792 was widely hailed. One newspaper wrote of "what has never happened before in any part of the globe; above three millions of people, scattered over a country of vast extent, of opposite habits and different manners, all fixing their hopes on the same man, and unanimously voting for him only, without the intervention of force, artifice, plan, or concert."[7]

Notable accomplishments as president and events of his presidency

1. *Establishing the Cabinet, the federal judicial system, and more.* Washington's administration set the parameters for who the president of the United States was and how he was to behave, and thus became the model for all other presidencies.

---

7   Paul F. Boller, *Presidential Campaigns: From George Washington to George W. Bush* (New York: Oxford University Press, 2004), loc. 87, Kindle.

2. *Putting down the Whiskey Rebellion.* In 1794, a group of frontier farmers in Pennsylvania protested against what they considered to be an onerous tax burden on the whiskey they produced and rebelled against federal authority. Washington was reluctant to use force but ultimately decided that there was no other way to curb the rebellion; in doing so, he established the authority of the new government as a force to be respected.

3. *Staying neutral regarding the French Revolution and in the war between France and Great Britain in 1793.* To have married its fortunes either to those of France or Britain only a few years after the Constitution had been adopted could have been disastrous for the new nation; Washington wisely kept the nation out of the war and worked to ensure that the horrific excesses of the French Revolution were not exported to America. With the Jay Treaty of 1794, he normalized relations with Britain, thereby relieving a great deal of the pressure on the new government.

4. *Instituting a protective tariff,* thus allowing nascent American industries to grow and prosper.

5. *Voluntarily leaving office.* Washington was a wealthy American who entered politics out of a sense of patriotism and civic duty. When he had completed his job, he left: one of Washington's most important achievements was not so much what he did in office, but the fact that he left it, rather than holding onto it as long as he could. This became a point of honor for Washington's successors for 150 years; Jefferson, Madison, Monroe, Jackson, Grant, and Cleveland all served two full terms in office, as did Washington. All of them

followed his example in vacating the office and not seeking a third term (although Grant sought unsuccessfully to return to the White House after a four-year absence). No president until Franklin D. Roosevelt either would or could break Washington's precedent, and the Twenty-Second Amendment to the Constitution, ratified in 1951, ensured that no president would do so thereafter.

6. *Farewell address.* On September 19, 1796, Washington issued what has come to be known as his farewell address, a document that presidents and all politically involved Americans would do well to study closely. In it, he expatiated on the virtues of the American union remaining united, briefly explaining why it was in the best interests of every section to remain united with the others. He declared: "Citizens, by birth or choice, of a common country, that country has a right to concentrate your affections. The name of American, which belongs to you in your national capacity, must always exalt the just pride of patriotism more than any appellation derived from local discriminations. With slight shades of difference, you have the same religion, manners, habits, and political principles."[8]

Later in the address, Washington again emphasized the importance of maintaining national unity. He said that the union of the American states provided "an exemption from those broils and wars between themselves, which so frequently afflict neighboring countries not tied together by the same governments," and which, he said, "opposite foreign alliances,

---

8   George Washington, "Farewell Address" (speech, September 19, 1796), Avalon Project, Yale Law School, https://avalon.law.yale.edu/18th_century/washing.asp.

attachments, and intrigues would stimulate and embitter."[9] He declared: "The great rule of conduct for us in regard to foreign nations is in extending our commercial relations, to have with them as little political connection as possible."[10]

What made his presidency great for America

George Washington generally ranks as the greatest or very nearly the greatest president in American history, and in this case, the ranking is justified: Washington, being the first president, is the paradigmatic chief executive, whose administration established the pattern for all the presidencies that followed. His presidency set the standard for what the American presidency could and should be, and not solely because he was the first person to occupy the office; the histories of the nations of the world are full of first chief executives who were not and never could be the political and moral exemplars of what the occupants of their office should be.

In an age when the five richest counties in the country are all in northern Virginia, the home of legions of Washington bureaucrats, it is useful to recall that George Washington, although a wealthy man in his day, did not fatten at the public trough.[11] He had to borrow $600 ($17,500 in today's dollars) to pay off his debts and cover his travel to New York City and related expenses (the city of Washington did not yet exist)

---

9 Ibid.
10 Ibid.
11 Gaby Galvin, "The 10 Richest Counties in the U.S.," U.S. News & World Report, December 6, 2018.

for his first inauguration in 1789.[12] When he left office eight years later, he was by no means a rich man: his public service, unlike that of so many politicians today, did not enrich him.

The importance of Washington's voluntarily leaving office cannot be overstated. It was a sign of a certain degeneration of the American body politic that what had been a virtue and a hallmark of honest republican government, a voluntary safeguard against dynasties and demagogues, became a legal requirement, an element of morality that had to be legislated. Today, when the nation's wealthiest areas are concentrated around Washington, D.C., and congressmen and senators cling to power for decades if they can, often becoming millionaires in the process and creating their own private fiefdoms, the nation could benefit greatly from a few public servants who actually lived up to that term, and emulated Washington in relinquishing power instead of staying in office as long as they possibly can, more for their own benefit than anyone else's.

What Washington said in his farewell address about Americans having the "same religion, manners, habits, and political principles" is, of course, no longer true, and many, if not most, Americans would not consider it even desirable. Yet Washington was not entirely wrong or simply expressing a parochial eighteenth-century outlook when he said it. It is no accident that the supporters of socialism and internationalism today have worked so hard to flood America with people of different religions, manners, habits, and political principles. The United States today is made up of people of

---

12   James Thomas Flexner, *Washington: The Indispensable Man* (Boston: Little, Brown, and Company, 1969), 215.

many different backgrounds and perspectives, yet if there is not some basic agreement on the way the government should be organized and society ordered, some core union of values, then the nation will continue to fragment into mutually hostile camps, as it has been doing for quite some time now. While Washington's statement will be seen by most today as an assumption of "white supremacism" and "xenophobia," in fact, it contains an important kernel of wisdom: without some point of unity, a common polity will fracture and dissolve. Today, we see this happening before our very eyes.

Meanwhile, Washington's words about avoiding entangling alliances have been derided or approached with condescension particularly since World War II, during and after which the establishment of an organization of the nations of the world was taken for granted as being necessary to prevent another world war. Even today, after the singular failure of the United Nations to maintain peace in so many areas of the world or deal honestly with human rights abuses worldwide, many, if not most, still assume that "foreign alliances, attachments, and intrigues" do not "stimulate and embitter" but make the nation stronger.

There is, however, considerable evidence to the contrary at this point. The UN, of which the United States taxpayers are by far the largest funder, is and has for years been little more than an organ of the Organization of Islamic Cooperation, relentlessly aiding and supporting enemies of the United States, issuing condemnations of an American ally, Israel, and ignoring the actual human rights abuses of Islamic states and authoritarian regimes. The U.S. was bogged down in a war in

Iraq for years and is still involved in a war in Afghanistan, the longest in American history; neither war had a clear purpose, goal, or end point—let alone one that furthered American interests. The idea that the U.S. must keep its troops in other countries indefinitely in order to prevent jihad terror attacks will ultimately prove untenable, as jihadis operate on all inhabited continents, and the U.S. cannot put troops in every country in the world.

What's more, "nation-building," in particular the George W. Bush/Barack Obama effort to plant democracies in Muslim countries so that they would no longer pose a threat to the U.S., is a foredoomed endeavor; elections in most Muslim countries would lead largely to the victory of adherents of Islamic law, who would then oppress their own people and be inveterately hostile to the United States.

Modern American presidents would have been wiser to find other ways to contain the spread of jihad terrorism and prevent the entry of jihad terrorists into the United States. Had they heeded Washington's advice, they would have done so.

Washington also warned against "those overgrown military establishments which, under any form of government, are inauspicious to liberty, and which are to be regarded as particularly hostile to republican liberty." An "overgrown military establishment," seeking to justify its own existence, will recommend military intervention where cooler heads will recognize that it is neither necessary nor desirable.

That is the situation we are in today. The United States does indeed face many threats; however, in numerous ways, our resources are not adequately deployed to meet them. This is because, all too often, military force has been resorted to as a panacea when it wasn't fit for purpose. This is by no means to say that military force should never be resorted to; however, even President Dwight Eisenhower, after commanding the Allied forces against the Nazis during World War II, warned against the "military-industrial complex." In this, he was echoing his first predecessor. Washington wisely saw the dangers to a free society of the military gaining too much power, and modern politicians should read and ponder his words.

TWO

JOHN ADAMS

Pendleton's Lithography, Library of Congress [13]

---

13   Gilbert Stuart, *John Adams, Second President of the United States* [1828?], photograph, Pendleton's Lithography, Library of Congress, https://www.loc. gov/item/96522259/.

Full name: John Adams
Lived: October 30, 1735–July 4, 1826
Presidency: March 4, 1797–March 4, 1801
Party: Federalist
Evaluation: Harmful for America but Also Did Some Good
Rating: 4

What qualified him to be president

John Adams was a renowned patriot with a long list of credentials, going back to his leadership of the opposition to the Stamp Act of 1765. He gained a reputation for immense integrity even, or especially, when he took the wildly unpopular step of becoming the defense attorney for the British soldiers accused of perpetrating the Boston Massacre. They were, he argued, as entitled to legal representation as anyone else, and the consequences of denying such representation to them could be catastrophic for the restive colonists.

Adams was later a member of the Continental Congress, and during the Revolutionary War, he was sent to France, along with Benjamin Franklin, to cultivate an alliance with the French against the British. After the war was won, he became the new nation's first ambassador to Great Britain. When Adams was elected president, he had served two terms as George Washington's vice president, which gave him something of the patina of heir apparent, although he had nothing approaching Washington's stature. In 1796, when he ran for president, no one had a record of service that surpassed that of Adams, and few even equaled it.

How he won

By 1796, the party divisions that Washington had sought to avoid were fully formed. Washington's vice president, Adams, ran against the Father of His Country's former secretary of state, Thomas Jefferson. Adams's faction, known as the Federalists, favored a strong central government, although they never imagined the modern-day behemoth in Washington. Their opponents, the Republicans, also known as Democratic-Republicans (not to be confused with today's Republican Party), preferred a decentralized system featuring strong state governments and a weaker federal government, so as to guard against tyranny.

Adams was not the nationally unifying war hero that Washington had been. In sharp contrast to Washington, he was unpopular personally, albeit respected professionally. Alexander Hamilton said he was "petty, mean, erratic, egoistic, eccentric, jealous, and had a mean temper."[14] But a small majority of the electors of the day were willing to put aside their distaste for his abrasive personality in order to vote for the man whom Washington clearly favored to succeed him; he squeaked by Jefferson, 71 to 68. By the provisions of the Constitution, amended soon afterward, since Adams's political antagonist Jefferson was the second-highest vote-getter, he became vice president. It was not an auspicious basis for the new administration.

---

14   "John Adams—Obnoxious and Disliked," World History, March 25, 2019.

Notable accomplishments as president and events of his presidency

1. *Avoiding war with France.* The Adams administration was consumed for virtually its entire duration with a controversy over whether it would commit the United States to war with France. The Democratic-Republicans, with their dislike of central government, detested the British monarchy and favored France, which was ruled at the time by revolutionaries who had been inspired by America's example in freeing itself from British rule.

The French had aided the Americans in their quest for independence, and to many of the Founding Fathers, including Thomas Jefferson, the French revolutionaries looked as if they were expressing the same desire for freedom that had animated the American Revolution. The Federalists, however, were horrified at the news of the escalating excesses and atrocities of the French Revolution and preferred the British. Their view seemed to be borne out when the French began seizing American ships on the pretext that they were certainly heading for British ports; the Americans began arresting French sympathizers, and the calls for war grew shrill.

Adams tried negotiations, but when three French diplomats asked the American government for a massive loan, in effect a bribe in exchange for peace, the talks went sour. Representative Robert Goodloe Harper of South Carolina enunciated what became a national rallying cry: "Millions for defense, but not one cent for tribute!"[15] Adams informed

---

15   Burton Stevenson, ed., *The Home Book of Quotations: Classical and Modern,* 10th ed. (New York: Dodd Mead, 1984), 63.

Congress, although he withheld the names of the French envoys, referring to them only as X, Y, and Z. What came to be known as the XYZ Affair dominated the rest of the Adams administration, with the Federalists clamoring for war with France.

Adams, however, put America first. He recognized that the new nation was in no position for such a war. It was enough to deal with the intermittent clashes between French and American ships, which came to be known as the Quasi-War, and even as the president beefed up the U.S. military, he managed to avoid what would have been a costly and possibly catastrophic all-out war. Satisfied, Adams proposed his own epitaph: "Here lies John Adams, who took upon himself the responsibility of the peace with France in the year 1800."[16]

2. *The Alien and Sedition Acts.* In 1798, the Federalist-controlled Congress passed these two acts, the first of which restricted immigration and allowed for the deportation of non-citizens who were considered a threat to the well-being of the United States. The Sedition Act, meanwhile, criminalized the "writing, printing, uttering or publishing" of "any false, scandalous and malicious writing or writings against the government of the United States, or either house of the Congress of the United States, or the President of the United States, with intent to defame the said government, or either house of the said Congress, or the said President, or to bring them, or either of them, into contempt or disrepute; or to excite against them, or either or any of them, the hatred of the good

---

16   David Jacobs and Robert Rutland, "John Adams: Following in the Footsteps," in *American Heritage: The Presidents*, ed. Michael Beschloss (New World City, Inc., 2000), 44, iBooks.

people of the United States, or to stir up sedition within the United States."[17] The law set as penalties a fine of up to $2,000 ($40,000 in today's inflated currency) and two years in prison.

While controversy raged over the act, the Adams administration set about enthusiastically to enforce it. Congressman Matthew Lyon of Vermont got four months in an unheated Vermont prison cell and a $1,000 ($20,000 today) fine for saying that the Adams administration was demonstrating "an unbounded thirst for ridiculous pomp, foolish adulation, and selfish avarice."[18] Benjamin Franklin Bache, editor of the opposition newspaper *Aurora*, was arrested for criticizing "the blind, bald, crippled, toothless, querulous Adams" but died before his case went to trial.[19]

Virginia resident James Callender wrote in his book *The Prospect before Us* that Adams was a "repulsive pedant, a gross hypocrite and an unprincipled oppressor" and "in private life, one of the most egregious fools on the continent."[20] The former claims were arguably true, at least in regard to the Sedition

---

17   United States Congress, "An Act in Addition to the Act, Entitled 'An Act for the Punishment of Certain Crimes against the United States' " July 14, 1798, Avalon Project, Yale Law School, http://avalon.law.yale.edu/18th_century/sedact.asp.

18   Terri Diane Halperin, *The Alien and Sedition Acts of 1798: Testing the Constitution* (Baltimore: JHU Press, 2016); Phillip I. Blumberg, *Repressive Jurisprudence in the Early American Republic: The First Amendment and the Legacy of English Law* (New York: Cambridge University Press, 2010), 107.

19   Douglas Alan Cohn, *The President's First Year: None Were Prepared, Some Never Learned—Why the Only School for Presidents Is the Presidency* (Lanham, MD: Rowman & Littlefield, 2016), 27.

20   Alexander Young and Thomas Minns, *The Defence of Young and Minns, Printers to the State, Before the Committee of the House of Representatives [in Answer to the Accusation of Having Published a Libellous Article on T. Jefferson's Character. in the "New England Palladium"], with an Appendix, Containing the Debate, Etc.* (Boston: Gilbert & Dean, 1805), 20.

Act, even if the latter one wasn't. Callender also declared that Adams's administration was "one continual tempest of malignant passions" and that "the grand object of his administration, has been to exasperate the rage of contending parties, to calumniate and destroy every man who differs from his opinions."[21] Callender's claim was vindicated, but not in a manner he likely welcomed: he was sentenced to nine months in prison and given a $200 fine ($4,000 today).[22]

Also fined $200, and given a two-month sentence, was printer Anthony Haswell, who reprinted sections of *Aurora*, charging that the Adams administration considered Tories, "men who fought against our independence, who shared in the destruction of our homes, and the abuse of our wives and daughters," to be "worthy of the confidence of the government."[23]

In November 1798, a Massachusetts resident named David Brown led a group in setting up a liberty pole reading, "No Stamp Act, No Sedition Act, No Alien Bills, No Land Tax, downfall to the Tyrants of America; peace and retirement to the President; Long Live the Vice President"—that is, Jefferson, a vociferous critic of the Sedition Act. Brown was fined $450 ($9,000 today) and sentenced to eighteen months in prison.[24]

---

21   John Davison Lawson, *American State Trials: A Collection of the Important and Interesting Criminal Trials Which Have Taken Place in the United States, from the Beginning of Our Government to the Present Day: with Notes and Annotations*, vol. 10 (St. Louis: Thomas Law Book Company, 1918), 837.

22   David Barton, *The Jefferson Lies: Exposing the Myths You've Always Believed About Thomas Jefferson* (Nashville: Thomas Nelson Inc., 2012), 17.

23   Phillip I. Blumberg, *Repressive Jurisprudence in the Early American Republic: The First Amendment and the Legacy of English Law* (New York: Cambridge University Press, 2010), 107.

24   Geoffrey R. Stone, *Perilous Times: Free Speech in Wartime from the Sedition Act of 1798 to the War on Terrorism* (New York: W. W. Norton & Company, 2004), 64.

3. *Relinquishing office voluntarily to a successor from the opposing party.* George Washington's casting as Cincinnatus, the Roman farmer who assumed power by popular demand in the Roman Republic during a time of crisis, and then relinquished that power voluntarily when the trouble was past, wasn't entirely as selfless as it appeared. He refused to run for a third term and hadn't wanted to run for a second not wholly because he meant to establish a precedent for the peaceful relinquishing of power, but also because he was so disheartened by attacks from the press and the infighting in his administration between Secretary of State Thomas Jefferson and Secretary of the Treasury Alexander Hamilton.

However, the Cincinnatus precedent was reinforced by Washington's successor. Like the first president, one of the most important things the second president did as chief executive was voluntarily leave the presidency. Adams's leaving office was even more significant for the life of the nation than Washington's was, because Adams's successor was of the opposing party.

Why his presidency was harmful for America but also did some good

Adams's avoidance of war was wildly unpopular with his own party, whose leaders were horrified at the news coming out of France. The Jeffersonians, meanwhile, were appalled that the possibility of war with France was even on the table. Both sides blamed Adams.

In response, President Adams allowed his personal failings to get the better of him. For John Adams was not only abrasive and certain of the rightness of his own views; he was also impossibly self-important. Pennsylvania senator William Maclay recorded instances of Adams's conceit as vice president, noting that Adams was fond of pomp and titles, which made him suspect among the zealously anti-aristocratic magistrates of the young republic (behind his back, several senators mocked the roly-poly Adams as "His Rotundity"). Maclay noted that "before debate on any issue could begin, the Vice President insisted on addressing to the chamber a lecture on the constitutional responsibilities of the Senate. During debate, he was arbitrary and prejudiced in his decisions regarding who could and who could not participate. Before a vote could be taken, he would, like a schoolmaster talking to children, summarize the issue, or his own interpretation of it, and unhesitatingly instruct the Senators how to vote."[25] He added: "God forgive me for the vile thought, but I cannot help thinking of a monkey just put into breeches when I see him betray such evident marks of self-conceit."[26]

Such a man was not likely to bear criticism easily, and John Adams didn't. The Sedition Act made a mockery of the First Amendment's guarantee of the freedom of speech. Yet although it was clearly unconstitutional, the principle of judicial review, the idea that the Supreme Court could declare laws unconstitutional, had not yet been established, and so there was quite a bit of disagreement about what could or should be done.

---

25   Ibid.
26   Ibid.

The Kentucky and Virginia legislatures passed bills (written anonymously by Adams's critics Thomas Jefferson and James Madison) declaring the Sedition Act unconstitutional; the New Hampshire legislature, however, disagreed, issuing a statement objecting "that the state legislatures are not the proper tribunals to determine the constitutionality of the laws of the general government; that the duty of such decision is properly and exclusively confided to the judicial department."[27]

The controversy over whether the states could reject laws passed by the federal government was not resolved until the Civil War.

The Sedition Act was the law of the land until March 3, 1801, the date specified in the bill itself for its expiration.[28] Its foremost foe, Thomas Jefferson, became president the next day and pardoned those who were still in prison on Sedition Act charges. Their fines were repaid. Long afterward, in its ruling on *New York Times Co. v. Sullivan* in 1964, the Supreme Court stated: "Although the Sedition Act was never tested in this Court, the attack upon its validity has carried the day in the court of history."[29] Indeed.

John Adams's record as president wasn't all bad. He kept us out of an unnecessary war that could have been disastrous. And he helped establish a cardinal principle of the American

---

27   James Madison, *The Debates in the Several State Conventions: On the Adoption of the Federal Constitution, as Recommended by the General Convention at Philadelphia, in 1787*, vol. 4 (Philadelphia: J. B. Lippincott Company, 1901), 539.

28   United States Congress, "An Act."

29   "Text of the Supreme Court's Opinion in Libel Case Against the *New York Times*," *New York Times*, March 10, 1964.

republic. If a man less upright and visionary than John Adams had been in the White House and defeated for reelection in 1800 by a member of the opposition, the peaceful transfer of power may never have taken place.

All of this would give John Adams a place among the nation's great, or at least good, presidents were it not for the Sedition Act, which tips history's scales decisively against him.

THREE

THOMAS JEFFERSON

Pendleton's Lithography, Library of Congress[30]

---

30   Gilbert Stuart, *Thomas Jefferson, Third President of the United States*, ca. 1825, photograph, Boston, Pendleton's Lithography, Library of Congress, https://www.loc.gov/item/96523332/.

Full name: Thomas Jefferson
Lived: April 13, 1743–July 4, 1826
Presidency: March 4, 1801–March 4, 1809
Party: Democratic-Republican
Evaluation: Good for America but Also Did Some Harm
Rating: 7

What qualified him to be president

Thomas Jefferson had been the Democratic-Republicans' nominee for president in 1796, and by 1800, he was still the faction's foremost figure and the most popular choice to go up against John Adams again. He had been secretary of state in the Washington administration and vice president in the Adams administration (a peculiar situation made possible by the stipulation that the second-highest vote-getter became vice president), making 1800 the only election in which a sitting vice president ran against a sitting president.

His career before that was no less illustrious. As a delegate to the Continental Congress, he wrote the Declaration of Independence, becoming renowned for his rhetorical skill while setting forth for all time the principles upon which the nation was founded. After that, he was a delegate to the Congress of the Confederation, the representative body of the states before the Constitution was adopted. He also served as governor of Virginia and U.S. minister to France.

Who but Jefferson had the stature to challenge Adams for the presidency? Few among the Democratic-Republicans thought anyone did. The problem was that one of them was a former senator from New York with national ambitions and scant reverence for Jefferson: Aaron Burr.

How he won

John Adams was never popular, even among his supporters. The Quasi-War with France and his refusal to declare war outright led to Adams being widely despised within his own party; the Alien and Sedition Acts led to his being disliked by nearly everyone else.

Nonetheless, the 1800 campaign was hotly contested and stands out as notably acrimonious even now from the vantage point of two hundred more years of acrimonious campaigns. In those days, the candidates themselves did not campaign, but others more than took up the slack. The Federalist *Hartford Courant* sounded the alarm about the consequences of electing the deist Jefferson president: "Murder, robbery, rape, adultery and incest will all be openly taught and practiced, the air will be rent with the cries of the distressed, the soil will be soaked with blood, and the nation black with crimes."[31] A Federalist leaflet invoked the bloody excesses of the French Revolution: "Can serious and reflecting men look about them and doubt that if Jefferson is elected, and the Jacobins get into authority, that those morals which protect our lives from the knife of the assassin—which guard the chastity of our wives and daughters from seduction and violence—defend our property from plunder and devastation, and shield our religion from contempt and profanation, will not be trampled upon and exploded?"[32]

Jefferson's supporters gave this right back, calling Adams's presidency "one continued tempest of *malignant* passions."[33]

---

31   Boller, loc. 176.
32   Ibid.
33   Boller, loc. 190.

They claimed that he planned to marry off one of his sons to a daughter of British King George III and start an American monarchy. That was one of the milder charges; Adams's wife Abigail lamented that during the 1800 campaign, enough "abuse and scandal" was published "to ruin and corrupt the minds and morals of the best people in the world."[34]

Jefferson and Burr, who was the second man on the Democratic-Republican ticket, each received seventy-three electoral votes; Adams got sixty-five, and Adams's Federalist running mate Thomas Pinckney garnered sixty-four. In those days, the two factions each put up two candidates and electors would vote for two, with the understanding that one was running for president and the other for vice president, although this was not explicit. The Federalists had Alexander Hamilton to ensure that at least one Federalist elector would vote for Adams but not the Federalists' second candidate, to ensure that Adams would become president if elected. The Democratic-Republicans, however, has made no such provision to ensure that Jefferson and Burr wouldn't get the same number of electoral votes. They did, each receiving seventy-three, while Adams got sixty-five.

Jefferson was supposed to be the presidential candidate, so Burr was widely expected to step aside. Instead, Burr enraged everyone by refusing to concede; the election accordingly went to the House of Representatives, which chose Jefferson. Burr, like Jefferson before him, becoming the vice president of the man he had challenged, but this time from within the president's own party. Burr's contesting of the presidency led to

---

34   Boller, loc. 198.

Thomas Jefferson's harboring everlasting enmity against him. The consequences of that would leave a blot on the Jefferson administration.

Notable accomplishments as president and events of his presidency

1. *The Louisiana Purchase.* In 1803, for the price of $15 million ($341 million today), or three cents an acre, Jefferson bought the Louisiana Territory from France. This enormous territory stretched from the modern-day state of Louisiana all the way northward to Canada and westward to present-day Idaho; the purchase more than doubled the size of the United States. Jefferson also paved the way for the settlement of the territory, which was largely wilderness, by sending the explorers Meriwether Lewis and William Clark to explore it and map it out.

2. *Cutting the budget and reducing the national debt.* Jefferson believed in small government and had charged Adams with unlawful arrogation of power. As president, he remained true to his principles, slashing the federal budget in half and paying off a significant amount of the national debt. When he took office on March 4, 1801, the national debt was $83 million ($1.7 billion today); when he left the White House eight years later, it was $57 million (now $1.2 billion).

3. *The Barbary War.* From practically the moment that the American states won independence, the Barbary (Berber) states of Algiers, Tunis, and Tripoli targeted the new nation's ships. In 1784, Muslim pirates from neighboring Morocco captured the American ship *Betsey* and took its crew hostage,

demanding that the new nation pay tribute to avoid future such incidents. The Americans, newly independent and having neither the resources nor the desire to get involved in a war with the Barbary states, paid the tribute. But once it had been established that the Americans would give in to the jihadis' demands, those demands grew. In 1795, a payment to Algiers of nearly $1 million ($22.5 million today) comprised 16 percent of federal revenue for that year.

The situation grew even worse in 1801, when the Bashaw of Tripoli demanded $220,000 ($5 million) up front and $25,000 ($568,000) each year from the United States. Jefferson, operating according to the principle of "Millions for defense, but not one cent for tribute," opted instead to go to war. Emerging victorious against the Barbary states in 1805 (and again in a second war in 1815, when James Madison was president), the United States freed itself from paying tribute and established itself as a nation that should not be trifled with.

4. *Judicial review.* On February 24, 1803, the Supreme Court decision *Marbury v. Madison* established the principle of judicial review, that is, the idea that courts could find laws unconstitutional and accordingly strike them down. The case involved whether Secretary of State James Madison could lawfully refuse to allow William Marbury, one of John Adams's "midnight judges"—one of the numerous judges Adams appointed just hours before his term expired—to take his seat. The court ruled that he could. Jefferson and his supporters were enraged.

5. *Prosecutions for sedition.* Jefferson's opposition to the Alien and Sedition Acts did not stem from a notable

commitment to the freedom of speech. President Jefferson regarded the First Amendment as merely stipulating that the federal government would not restrict free discourse; the states, he believed, were perfectly free to do so. On February 19, 1803, when he was the object of furious attacks in the press, Jefferson wrote, "I have...long thought that a few prosecutions of the most eminent offenders would have a wholesome effect in restoring the integrity of the presses. Not a general prosecution, for that would look like persecution: but a selected one."[35] He supported state actions against several of his political opponents for their criticisms.

6. *The Embargo Act.* Britain and France continued to war with each other and prey upon American shipping. Jefferson knew that war with either one could be disastrous for the new nation, and so rejected all calls for war from Americans who looked upon these outrages to American ships with wounded pride. The Embargo Act, forbidding American ships to take cargo to Europe and closing American ports to all foreign ships, was meant instead to compel the belligerents, faced with the loss of American trade, to pledge to stop their attacks on American ships. But the new nation didn't have that much economic clout: Britain and France went on as before, and it was the American economy that went into a tailspin, which lasted well into the Madison administration.

---

35   Jon Meacham, *Thomas Jefferson: The Art of Power* (New York: Random House, 2012), 405.

How his presidency was good for America but also did some harm

In these days when breathtakingly bloated budgets and out-of-control federal spending are taken for granted to the extent that even the advocates of small government and fiscal responsibility try only to slow down the pace of government growth, rather than actually reverse it, Jefferson's precedent in reducing the federal debt and balancing the budget is valuable. He also gave the American economy, as well as the national morale, a shot in the arm by successfully pursuing war against the Barbary pirates, ending the humiliating practice of paying tribute to them. However, he effaced his good work in this area and threw a wrench into the American economy in 1807 with the Embargo Act. He vastly overestimated the importance of American products to Britain and France, and thereby did damage to the American economy that took years to repair. Even worse, in enforcing the act, Jefferson abandoned his long-held principle of a limited federal government, becoming instead a strong advocate of centralization.

The Louisiana Purchase is one of the most important events in American history; the good that was made possible because of it is incalculable. Territorial acquisitions have fallen out of favor in our hypersensitive modern world, even when all concerned parties are participating voluntarily. However, without the Louisiana Purchase, the United States of America never would have been able to expand to the Pacific, and almost certainly would never have become a great power. While many modern leftists may think that would have been a better outcome, the expansion of the United States from the

Atlantic to the Pacific has certainly brought with it political stability, which has, in turn, enabled economic prosperity and allowed the American republic to become a model of good government for nations the world over. The Louisiana Purchase also removed what could have become a serious source of trouble for the new nation: the port of New Orleans, at the mouth of the Mississippi River, someday falling into the hands of a hostile foreign power.

The downside is the precedent the Purchase set. Jefferson proclaimed himself what would be called today a "strict constructionist," determined to govern within the limits of the Constitution's explicit delineation of the powers of the president. But the Constitution was silent about the acquisition of territory; it didn't forbid the president from making land purchases, but it didn't give him permission to do so, either. The Tenth Amendment stipulated that "the powers not delegated to the United States by the Constitution, nor prohibited by it to the States, are reserved to the States respectively, or to the people," but this was not enough to serve as a guideline for the acquisition of territory: Would the states have to agree to the purchase? How many? Would agreement have to be unanimous, or would two-thirds or a simple majority suffice? Or would the people have to decide in a plebiscite?

There simply was no clear constitutional provision for what Jefferson had done; the strict constructionist accordingly planned to ask for an amendment to the Constitution. He wrote: "Our peculiar security is the possession of a written Constitution. Let us not make it a blank paper by construction."[36] But he was soon dissuaded: his friends and political allies argued that a constitutional debate would take too long, giving France's Napoleon time to change his mind on the sweetheart deal, and would offer an opportunity to the Federalists to accuse Jefferson of the same executive overreach of which he had accused Adams. Jefferson agreed; the Senate approved the Purchase without a constitutional amendment, and that was that.

In 1803, this sequence of events appeared to Jefferson's supporters to be a responsible exercise of power, enabling a tremendous boon to the United States. From the standpoint of over two hundred years later, however, Jefferson not only greatly strengthened the nation, but set the precedent for numerous presidents who succeeded him to ignore the Constitution and assume powers it had not accorded to them. Adams's Alien and Sedition Acts were challenged right at the beginning on constitutional grounds; the Louisiana Purchase was not, and thus served as an even more insidious model.

Jefferson and the Democratic-Republicans overreached again in their furious reaction to *Marbury v. Madison*. To be sure, the principle of judicial review has been outrageously misused in recent years by leftist judges who enforce by judicial fiat what leftist politicians could not win at the ballot box. However, the principle itself is sound. Jefferson's party, however, furious that the decision had gone against it, vindictively initiated impeachment proceedings against Supreme Court Justice Samuel Chase, who had committed no misdeeds.

---

36   Stefan Lorant, *The Glorious Burden: The American Presidency* (New York: Harper & Row, 1968), 74.

His crime was that he was a Federalist on the high court, as was Chief Justice John Marshall, who was to be the next impeachment target. But Chase survived in a narrow vote, and Jefferson sighed that impeachment was "a farce which will not be tried again."[37]

If only that had been true. Instead, the use of impeachment as a political tool would recur in American history and become, in the late twentieth and twenty-first century, a tool all too commonly used.

The attempted impeachment of Chase was not Jefferson's only vindictive act, either. His endorsement of state proceedings against his political opponents made his opposition to Adams's Sedition Act appear self-serving and hypocritical. He tried to resolve this contradiction in his second inaugural address on March 4, 1805, defending enforcement of the laws "provided by the State against false and defamatory publications." However, he added, "since truth and reason have maintained their ground against false opinions in league with false facts, the press, confined to truth, needs no other legal restraint; the public judgment will correct false reasonings and opinions, on a full hearing of all parties; and no other definite line can be drawn between the inestimable liberty of the press and its demoralizing licentiousness. If there be still improprieties which this rule would not restrain, its supplement must be sought in the censorship of public opinion."[38] Certainly libel and defamation were not afforded

37   Lorant, 71.
38   Thomas Jefferson, "Second Inaugural Address" (speech, March 4, 1805), Avalon Project, Yale Law School, https://avalon.law.yale.edu/19th_century/jefinau2.asp.

First Amendment protection, but most, if not all, of the political writers who were prosecuted for them during the Jefferson administration were critics of the president.

Although Jefferson had praised Burr during the contested election of 1800, he may not have been being completely honest in that case, either. In 1805, already under a cloud for having shot Alexander Hamilton dead in a duel the previous year, Burr leased a large tract of land in present-day Louisiana from the Spanish government. Since the Louisiana Purchase, it was not at all clear that Spain actually owned the land to lease it, but Burr, heedless of such niceties, began trying to attract American settlers to his territory. His goal remains unclear but appears simply to have been to try to make some money. Some of Burr's detractors, however, told Jefferson that the former vice president planned to establish his own western state and challenge the authority of the United States. Although there was virtually nothing concrete to back up this charge, Jefferson took it seriously and had Burr charged with treason and relentlessly pursued. Burr was tried in 1807 in a court presided over by Chief Justice Marshall. But the case against Burr was weak, so weak that he was quickly acquitted for lack of evidence. He was apparently only brought to trial in the first place because the Sage of Monticello wanted to settle a score. Another negative precedent was set.

All in all, the strict constructionist Jefferson became one of the most activist of presidents. But his authorship of the Declaration of Independence is reason enough in itself to warrant Jefferson's inclusion on Mount Rushmore. As president, his acquisition of the Louisiana Territory, his fiscal responsibility, and his facing down of the Barbary pirates only buttress the case for his inclusion, with Washington, Lincoln, and Theodore Roosevelt, in that most imposing and enduring of all presidential monuments. Without his illustrious pre-presidential record, however, Jefferson might have been compared unfavorably to other occupants of the White House when the figures were chosen for that pantheon.

FOUR

JAMES MADISON

Pendleton's Lithography, Library of Congress[39]

---

39   Gilbert Stuart, *James Madison, Fourth President of the United States* [1828?], photograph, Pendleton's Lithography, Library of Congress, https://www.loc. gov/item/96522271/.

Full name: James Madison
Lived: March 16, 1751–June 28, 1836
Presidency: March 4, 1809–March 4, 1817
Party: Democratic-Republican
Evaluation: Did Little Good but Not Much Damage
Rating: 5

What qualified him to be president

While he lacked the mythical aura of Washington and Jefferson and even the stature (literally as well as in terms of the public respect he commanded; he stood barely five feet tall), however grudging, of Adams, James Madison had an outsized impact upon the new nation. He was the principal architect of the United States Constitution, earning him the sobriquet "Father of the Constitution." Madison also proposed a series of amendments to the new Constitution, so as to make clear certain rights of the American people that were not to be infringed, including the freedom of speech, the freedom of the press, and the right to bear arms. These amendments, owed largely to Madison, became the Bill of Rights.

For decades, Madison was one of the foremost figures of American politics. After serving in the pre-Constitution Congress of the Confederation, writing many of the *Federalist Papers*, which explained the founding principles of our government, and then framing the Constitution itself, he spent eight years as a member of the House of Representatives and then eight more years as secretary of state in the Jefferson administration. The popular Jefferson wanted Madison to succeed him. There was little question that he would.

How he won

The Federalists, whose base had shrunk considerably while Jefferson was president, could do nothing to stop Madison in 1808. By 1812, however, Madison had grown so unpopular that a breakaway Republican, New York Governor DeWitt Clinton, established an unofficial coalition with the remaining Federalists (who declined to endorse him officially, fearing that such an endorsement would hurt his chances) and came close to unseating the Father of the Constitution. Madison won with 128 electoral votes to Clinton's 89; if Pennsylvania or Virginia had gone to Clinton, he would have been president.

Notable accomplishments as president and events of his presidency

1. *The War of 1812.* In his first inaugural address, Madison vowed "to cherish peace and friendly intercourse with all nations having correspondent dispositions; to maintain sincere neutrality toward belligerent nations; to prefer in all cases amicable discussion and reasonable accommodation of differences to a decision of them by an appeal to arms."[40]

These noble aspirations, however, proved impossible to fulfill, albeit not for want of trying. Britain, still embroiled in war with France, began to feel the pinch of the Embargo Act (which was repealed three days before Madison took office on March 4, 1809) and its successor, the Non-Intercourse Act, which allowed American trade with all nations except Britain

---

40　James Madison, "First Inaugural Address" (speech, March 4, 1809), Bartleby, https://www.bartleby.com/124/pres18.html.

and France. Within a month of Madison's taking office, Britain and the United States reached an agreement, which just as quickly fell through when the Americans would not agree to allow the British to seize American ships found to be engaging in trade with France. Hostile incidents increased; the British even armed the Indians who raided American settlements in the Northwest Territory.

The national honor had to be defended. The war, however, was widely unpopular and was derided in New England (which suffered an invasion by British troops) and elsewhere as "Mr. Madison's War."[41] It was largely because of the war's unpopularity that Madison was nearly defeated in the 1812 election.

2. *Reestablishing the Bank of the United States.* Madison had always opposed the idea of a national bank. But the War of 1812 led Madison to see the necessity for a controlling financial institution that would put the nation's finances in order. The second Bank of the United States was chartered near the end of his second term.

3. *Defining the role of the First Lady.* The title of First Lady was not then in general use, but it was Madison's wife Dolley who was the first wife of a president to be the nation's First Lady in the sense that would become customary. She also was one of the first upon whom the title itself was bestowed, although this was long after she left the White House. Upon her death in 1849, President Zachary Taylor eulogized her as "our first lady for half a century."[42]

---

41   J. C. A. Stagg, *Mr. Madison's War: Politics, Diplomacy, and Warfare in the Early American Republic, 1783–1830* (Princeton, NJ: Princeton University Press, 1983).

42   Roger Matuz, *The Presidents Fact Book* (New York: Black Dog & Leventhal, 2017), 77.

The wives of presidents before Madison had held social events at the White House, but it was Dolley who made presidential events a centerpiece of society, in the new city that was the nation's capital, and the Executive Mansion a center of art and culture for the entire nation. Mrs. Madison was outgoing and vivacious, qualities her husband decidedly lacked, and her popularity helped his image.

Dolley was not, however, universally popular. The Madison administration became the first to be subject to congressional harassment over minutiae when Dolley spent forty dollars ($650 today) on an imported mirror for the White House. The indignant Republicans of the Senate opened an investigation, which ended up costing $2,000 ($32,000).

Why his presidency did little good but not much damage

The War of 1812 lasted until the end of 1814 and didn't work out as well for either side as each had hoped. The British took Detroit and burned it down; in August 1814, in one of the most bitter humiliations the nation has ever endured, they seized Washington as well. They burned down the Capitol and didn't stop there. They forced the commander in chief to flee his own capital city and suffer the burning of the Executive Mansion.

Dolley was awaiting President Madison's arrival for dinner at the White House after he had met with his commanders; instead, the British broke through the American defenses before he arrived. Dolley wrote in panic to her sister: "Mr. Madison comes not; may God protect him! Two messengers covered with dust come to bid me fly; but I wait for him."[43] Soon word came from Madison that she should get out of the White House and waste no time in doing so. The Madisons met in Virginia, while British soldiers in the White House ate their meals. The next day, those soldiers put the White House to the torch. In New England, where the war hit the local economy hard, there was even talk of secession, so as to allow the region to extricate itself from the devastation wrought by Mr. Madison's War.

But the war wasn't working out very well for the British, either. They suffered reverses in New York State. The Americans also captured and burned Toronto, and at Baltimore in September 1814, they stopped the advance of the British forces that had taken Washington. It was during the battle of Baltimore that a young lawyer and poet named Francis Scott Key saw, after a night of British bombardment, that our flag was still there and wrote a poem about it that soon afterward was set to music and came to be known as "The Star-Spangled Banner."

The British were still at war with France, and many viewed the war with the United States as an unnecessary distraction, especially after Napoleon abdicated in April 1814. Britons began to chafe under the tax burden the war necessitated. In December 1814, the Treaty of Ghent ended the war and restored the prewar status quo: territories that each side had captured were returned, and the Americans didn't even win a declaration from the British that they would leave their shipping alone, although since the war with France was over,

---

43 Vincent Buranelli and Robert A. Rutland, "James Madison: The Nation Builder," in *The American Heritage Illustrated History of the Presidents*, 73.

this was a moot point. On January 8, 1815, after the treaty had been concluded but before news of it reached New Orleans, American forces under the command of General Andrew Jackson won a smashing victory over the British that did a great deal to assuage American anger over the British affronts to the young nation's sovereignty.

The mere act of holding out against the most powerful military force in the world established the United States as a nation whose sovereignty had to be respected. The very fact that the federal government even continued to exist after the British capture of Washington was achievement enough. Having suffered politically for the start of Mr. Madison's War, Madison benefited from its reasonably successful conclusion, which most Americans counted as a victory. Still, Madison didn't have much else positive to show for eight years in the White House. Like Jefferson, under the pressure of expediency, he began to abandon the principles that he had held throughout his political life before becoming president. He had been a forceful and articulate Republican, an opponent of a strong federal government, which he considered tantamount to opening the door to tyranny. The pressures of the war, however, led him to adopt a number of what had previously been considered to be Federalist positions.

Jefferson had proclaimed grandly during his first inaugural address that "we have called by different names brethren of the same principle. We are all Republicans, we are all Federalists."[44] It was Madison, however, who would do more

---

44   Thomas Jefferson, "First Inaugural Address" (speech, March 4, 1801), Avalon Project, Yale Law School.

to make this bipartisanship not a matter of mere words, but an actual policy. Above all, he adopted the Federalist position on the vexed question of a Bank of the United States. Such a bank, a private corporation, had been established during the Washington administration in 1791, but its charter expired in 1811 when a vote to renew it was narrowly defeated: the Senate vote was a tie, and Madison's vice president, George Clinton, voted against the bank.

The Bank's advocates contended that it was necessary to put the nation's finances in order; its foes, including Madison, argued that it was an unconstitutional power grab by the federal government. It was also dangerous, then as now, to turn power over the public funds to an oligarchy of private financiers; the possibility for corruption, and for a de facto second government developed by buying favors until large enough to challenge the government of the United States, was immense. Nonetheless, it was the Bank's great foe, Madison, whose signature brought the Bank of the United States back to life.

Jefferson had had to strengthen the U.S. military and take other measures that he had previously opposed in order to meet the challenges he faced as president. But Madison, whose administration actually was against the Bank before it was for it, became by that flip-flop the first president to oppose a measure before taking office that he ended up implementing as chief executive. It was inevitable that one president or another would be the first to do this, but that doesn't change the fact that Madison has the dubious distinction.

Still, the nation had faced a severe threat to its continuing independence and had survived. Whether or not this had to do with Madison's leadership was highly debatable, but no less an authority than John Adams was ready to give the president credit. In the last days of Madison's presidency, John Adams wrote to Thomas Jefferson: "Notwithstanding a thousand faults and blunders, his administration has acquired more glory, and established more union, than all his three predecessors, Washington, Adams, and Jefferson, put together."[45]

---

45   Noah Feldman, *The Three Lives of James Madison: Genius, Partisan, President* (New York: Random House, 2017), 616.

FIVE

JAMES MONROE

Pendleton's Lithography, Library of Congress[46]

---

46   Gilbert Stuart. *James Monroe, Fifth President of the United States* [1828?], photograph, Pendleton's Lithography, Library of Congress, https://www.loc.gov/item/96523417/.

Full name: James Monroe
Lived: April 28, 1758–July 4, 1831
Presidency: March 4, 1817–March 4, 1825
Party: Democratic-Republican
Evaluation: Good for America but Also Did Some
Harm
Rating: 7

What qualified him to be president

"Although not possessed of remarkable talents," wrote Martin Van Buren of James Monroe, "he passed through an almost unequalled number of responsible public employments without leaving a stain upon his character."[47]

Monroe was the last president from among the Founding Fathers, fighting as a young man in the Continental Army. Emanuel Leutze's renowned 1850 painting *Washington Crossing the Delaware* depicts young Monroe in the boat holding the American flag right behind a resolute Washington; Washington praised Monroe for his bravery during this campaign.

During the Washington administration, Monroe served as minister to France, getting the appointment when he was just thirty-five. Then he served three years as governor of Virginia before Thomas Jefferson sent him back to France to help negotiate the Louisiana Purchase; Jefferson then sent him to London

---

47   Martin Van Buren, *The Autobiography of Martin Van Buren*, ed. John C. Fitzpatrick (Washington, D.C.: Government Printing Office, 1920), chapter XIII, loc. 1863, Kindle.

as the U.S. minister to Britain. He was Madison's secretary of state, but when the British burned down the Capitol and the White House, Madison appointed him secretary of war, and for four months in late 1814 and early 1815, he was both. As the 1816 election approached, he was seen as Madison's heir apparent. The outcome was never really in doubt.

How he won

By 1816, the Federalists had lost four straight presidential elections. The Fourteenth Congress, elected in 1814, consisted of 26 Republicans and 12 Federalists in the Senate, and 117 Republicans with 65 Federalists in the House. In the 1812 presidential election, the Federalists didn't even field a candidate (although they backed rogue Republican DeWitt Clinton, who did better than the Federalist candidates in the two previous elections).

In 1816, the Federalists went back to putting up a Federalist—this time New York Senator Rufus King—against Monroe. But once again, with Madison riding a wave of popularity after the War of 1812, the outcome for his heir apparent was never in doubt. It was the "Era of Good Feelings," a time of national unity when the idea was widespread that political parties were a threat to that unity and needed to be transcended. And four years later, in 1820, with "the Era of Good Feelings" in full swing, the Federalists were almost completely a spent force. Monroe ran unopposed, although one elector cast his vote for Secretary of State John Quincy Adams so that Washington would remain the only president elected unanimously.

Notable accomplishments as president and events of his presidency

1. *Trying to put an end to partisan politics.* Following in the footsteps of Jefferson and other prominent politicians of the era, Monroe was determinedly nonpartisan, writing that "the existence of parties is not necessary to free government."[48] Monroe went beyond simple criticism of party politics, acting to eliminate political parties altogether as a feature of the American public square. As president, he supported several key Federalist policies, including a Bank of the United States, and appointed Federalists to some key positions, although, at this point, the Federalist Party was so moribund that nearly everyone of prominence in public life was a Republican. Monroe intended to make the Federalist Party unnecessary altogether by adopting some of its positions and thus removing the very reason for its existence. But the massive, big-tent Democratic-Republican Party that was thus created quickly splintered into factions of its own that ultimately became new political parties, bringing to naught Monroe's attempts to make political factionalism a thing of the past.

2. *The Missouri Compromise.* Tension over slavery was as old as the republic itself. Thomas Jefferson included a denunciation of slavery in his first draft of the Declaration of Independence, only to have it removed in the interests of national unity. During the "Era of Good Feelings," this tension came to a head for the first time. When the territory of Missouri petitioned for statehood in 1819, abolitionists, a growing force

---

48   James MacGregor Burns, *The Vineyard of Liberty, 1787–1863: The American Experiment* (New York: Open Road Media, 2012), 257.

in American politics, were alarmed at the prospect of another slave state joining the Union. Representative James Tallmadge of New York introduced amendments to Missouri's proposed state constitution, restricting slavery there.

The resulting controversy was intense. Missouri's constitution became the pretext for a divisive national debate about slavery that resulted in the Missouri Compromise of 1820. Missouri was admitted as a slave state, and Maine, which had hitherto been part of Massachusetts, was admitted as a free state; slavery was rendered illegal in United States territories north of the 36°30 parallel, with the exception of Missouri, which was north of that line and remained a slave state. This made official the nation's division into free states and slave states.

Monroe had little to do with any of this, but just as he reaped the political dividends of the War of 1812, the Missouri Compromise was a considerable factor in his near-unanimous reelection. War and disunion had been staved off; the Era of Good Feelings would continue.

2. *The Monroe Doctrine.* In his annual message to Congress on December 2, 1823, Monroe stated (in the words of his secretary of state, John Quincy Adams) that "the occasion has been judged proper for asserting, as a principle in which the rights and interests of the United States are involved, that the American continents, by the free and independent condition which they have assumed and maintain, are henceforth not to be considered as subjects for future colonization by any European powers."[49]

---

49   James D. Richardson, ed., *A Compilation of the Messages and Papers of the Presidents*, vol. II, part 1 (New York: Bureau of National Literature, Inc., 1897), loc. 4991, Kindle.

This was originally intended to be a statement of support for the newly independent states of Central and South America, for which Monroe had considerable sympathy: "with the Governments who have declared their independence and maintained it," said Monroe, "and whose independence we have, on great consideration and on just principles, acknowledged, we could not view any interposition for the purpose of oppressing them, or controlling in any other manner their destiny, by any European power in any other light than as the manifestation of an unfriendly disposition toward the United States."[50]

This was a quid pro quo: in the same speech, Monroe declared that the U.S. would not interfere with colonies of the European states. "We owe it, therefore, to candor and to the amicable relations existing between the United States and those powers to declare that we should consider any attempt on their part to extend their system to any portion of this hemisphere as dangerous to our peace and safety. With the existing colonies or dependencies of any European power, we have not interfered and shall not interfere."[51]

3. *Treaty with Britain.* The U.S. and Britain have been the closest of friends and allies for so long now that it is hard to imagine a time when Americans were deeply suspicious of the elder nation and worried that it might try yet again to reassert its control. The Monroe administration did a great deal to allay those suspicions and set the two nations on the

---

50   Ibid.
51   Ibid.

path to lasting amity with treaties in 1817 and 1818 fixing and demilitarizing the U.S./Canada border.

4. *Acquisition of Florida.* Continuing in the tradition of the Louisiana Purchase, the Adams-Onís Treaty of 1819 brought Florida into the Union and solidified the peace and security of the United States by eliminating Spain as a rival of the young nation in North America. As part of the treaty, however, the U.S. ceded part of the Louisiana Purchase to Spain—the part comprising the modern-day state of Texas. This, like other key events of the Monroe administration, spelled trouble for the future.

5. *Internal improvements.* The question of whether the federal government should spend money to improve the nation's infrastructure had been controverted from the beginning of the republic, with Republicans maintaining that such a use of federal money was unconstitutional and represented a dangerous expansion of federal power. But Monroe, as part of his efforts to obliterate political divisions, made the Federalist issue of internal improvements his own. The Supreme Court ruled in *Gibbons v. Ogden* in 1824 that the Commerce Clause of the Constitution, which gave the federal government the authority "to regulate Commerce with foreign Nations, and among the several States, and with the Indian Tribes," allowed the federal government to make these improvements.[52]

---

52   United States Constitution, art. 1, sec. 8, cl. 3.

Why his presidency was good for America but also did some harm

James Monroe's presidency is marred by initiatives that did not have the effects intended and caused or contributed to considerable harm for the nation long after his presidency. The Supreme Court's use of the Commerce Clause to declare the use of federal funds for internal improvements constitutional opened the door to abuse of the Commerce Clause to justify initiatives the Founders never remotely envisioned. And the great efforts during the Monroe administration to heal the nation's divisions over slavery only ended up making them worse.

The Missouri Compromise headed off a possible civil war in 1820, but otherwise it did little good and a great deal of harm. Obviously civil war was not postponed indefinitely, and the compromise only exacerbated and solidified the tensions between the sections that led ultimately to that war. All it essentially did was kick the can down the road, leaving the solution to the vexed question of slavery to future generations. Could Monroe have healed the nation's deep division over slavery with strong and decisive action? Probably not, but there is no doubt that he, like all his successors up to Abraham Lincoln, made no attempt to come to grips with the deeper problem slavery posed, and find a lasting solution beyond political compromises that were inherently temporary and unstable. The question would preoccupy the minds of the greatest Americans in public life for decades, and no one hit on any way to resolve it definitively.

Nonetheless, if there had been a decisive and visionary leader in the White House in 1820, it would have been considerably easier to excise the evil of slavery without bringing on civil war than it would be in 1860. Monroe, a slave-owning Virginian, had little, if any, interest in doing that. He was, however, a member of the American Colonization Society, which advocated freeing slaves and sending them to West Africa. This aim was partially realized in the creation of the nation of Liberia; that nation's capital was named Monrovia in honor of the American president. However, most black Americans refused to go, as conditions in Africa were harsh and uncertain. The American Colonization Society, like the Missouri Compromise, would not settle the issue of slavery. As Thomas Jefferson, who was considerably alarmed by the virulence of the Missouri debate, said: "We have the wolf by the ears, and we can neither hold him, nor safely let him go."[53]

The Monroe Doctrine was not intended by Monroe, or understood at the time, to be an encompassing statement of principle or policy. Nor was it a warning that European colonial adventurism in Latin America would be met with military force. The United States was not strong enough for that. Monroe's warning was essentially a dead letter, at least at first. If Britain had decided to establish colonies in Central or South America, or if Spain had reasserted its control over its former colonies, there was nothing that the United States could have done during Monroe's presidency. The Doctrine only had any teeth at all at first because the British decided to honor it and back it with their formidable navy, as a safeguard

---

[53]   Burns, 263.

against European adventurism in Latin America. The Monroe Doctrine, however, became a foundational American policy, the justification for numerous interventions in Latin America, and the paradigm for justifying other interventions elsewhere.

In that sense, the Monroe Doctrine's legacy, like that of President Monroe himself, is ultimately not one that American patriots should view with pride. Out of it grew the internationalism that ultimately left American interests behind and placed the nation's resources at the service of forces that not only did not put America first, but scoffed at the very idea that America should ever do that. To be sure, this was a development that would have shocked and horrified James Monroe.

SIX

JOHN QUINCY ADAMS

Library of Congress[54]

---

54   J. P. A. Healy, *J.Q. Adams*, ca. 1898, photograph, Library of Congress, https://www.loc.gov/item/96523419/.

Full name: John Quincy Adams
Lived: July 11, 1767–February 23, 1848
Presidency: March 4, 1825–March 4, 1829
Party: Democratic-Republican/National Republican/
    Whig
Evaluation: Did Little Good but Not Much Damage
Rating: 5

What qualified him to be president

Brusque and candid like his father, John Quincy Adams was not known for his personal diplomacy, but he was an accomplished diplomat. At the age of twenty-seven, he was appointed by George Washington to be U.S. minister to the Netherlands; he subsequently served as U.S. minister to Prussia, Russia, and Britain. In between the appointments to Prussia and Russia, he served five years as a senator from Massachusetts. He was Monroe's secretary of state for nearly eight years, during which time he wrote the Monroe Doctrine.

Adams was also the most learned of presidents, maintaining an extensive library that contained books on a wide variety of issues. In those days, it was possible to speak with candor and without incident in ways that are thoroughly stigmatized today; Adams demonstrated a keen awareness of a threat that his father had faced and that would strike at the United States much later as well. He wrote that Muhammad, the prophet of Islam, had "spread desolation and delusion over an extensive portion of the earth" and that he had "poisoned the sources of human felicity at the fountain, by degrading the condition of the female sex, and the allowance of polygamy;

and he declared undistinguishing and exterminating war, as a part of his religion, against all the rest of mankind."[55]

Adams noted that "the precept of the koran [sic] is, perpetual war against all who deny, that Mahomet is the prophet of God. The vanquished may purchase their lives, by the payment of tribute; the victorious may be appeased by a false and delusive promise of peace; and the faithful follower of the prophet, may submit to the imperious necessities of defeat: but the command to propagate the Moslem creed by the sword is always obligatory, when it can be made effective. The commands of the prophet may be performed alike, by fraud, or by force."[56]

Were Adams to make these observations today, he would be driven out of public life and hounded to such an extent that he would not even be able to appear in public without protests. But in his own day, these statements were taken for granted as manifestly true. Adams remains the most forthright of our chief executives on the ongoing threat of Islamic jihad.

A man who was genuinely dedicated to public service for the common good, not to public service as a means of lining his pockets, Adams served in the House of Representatives from Massachusetts for nearly seventeen years after his presidency; his death came shortly after he collapsed on the floor of the House. He opposed slavery throughout his political career. As a congressman in 1841, he emulated his father's defense of the British soldiers who fired at Americans in the Boston

---

55   Joseph Blunt, *The American Annual Register for the Years 1827–8–9* (New York: E. & G. W. Blunt, 1830), 269.

56   Ibid., 274.

Massacre by taking up a widely unpopular cause simply because he believed it right to do so: he joined the defense team in *United States v. The Amistad*, the trial of a group of Africans who were being taken to slavery but revolted and took over the ship that was transporting them. The seventy-three-year-old Adams defended them for four hours before the Supreme Court; the Africans were freed.

How he won

He didn't. The election of 1824 was anything but a mandate for Adams, and while he ultimately emerged as the victor, his victory was so tainted that his presidency was effectively crippled from the start. The Democratic-Republican Party now included virtually every politician of significance and had split into factions of its own. The congressional caucus that had chosen Jefferson, Madison, and Monroe bypassed Adams, whom many considered to be Monroe's heir apparent since he had served as secretary of state, as had Madison and Monroe before him. Instead, the caucus picked a candidate who stood for the old Republican principles of strict adherence to the Constitution and a weak federal government: William Crawford, who had been a senator from Georgia, minister to France, and secretary of war and secretary of the treasury in the Monroe administration.

The caucus, however, didn't have the influence in 1824 that it had enjoyed in previous years. Those who favored the positions that had initially been identified with the Federalists, including a strong federal government that funded internal improvements, the Bank of the United States, and high tariffs to protect American industry, were Adams and the speaker of the House, Henry Clay of Kentucky. Then there was General Andrew Jackson, the hero of the Battle of New Orleans in the War of 1812 and, more recently, a senator from Tennessee. Jackson had genuine popular support, which was increasingly important, as more and more states were choosing electors by popular vote. No one, however, knew exactly where Jackson stood on the issues. Adams, whom Jackson would soon count among his bitterest political enemies, actually supported him for vice president, albeit with a quip about Jackson's volatile character: "The Vice-Presidency was a station in which the General could hang no one, and in which he would need to quarrel with no one."[57]

Everyone in this race, like everyone for the first century and a half of the republic, had an America-first agenda. So there was nothing like the modern-day division of candidates on that score, and voters didn't have to ask themselves which candidate was less likely to sell America's interests to the highest international bidder. What's more, the positions that were truly best for America in the long run were distributed across factional lines; the Adams party held to some, and the Jackson party to others. The gargantuan growth of the federal government today and its increasing interference in the daily lives of its citizens make one long for the era when politicians were determined not just to pay lip service to the idea of limiting its power. One need not acquiesce in that unrestrained and continually growing power in order to accept

---

57   William J. Cooper, *The Lost Founding Father: John Quincy Adams and the Transformation of American Politics* (New York: Liveright, 2017), 208–209.

the Supreme Court's declaration of the constitutionality of using federal funds for internal improvements as based on the Commerce Clause; nor does this require one to endorse the later abuse of that clause. The Bank placed control of the public funds in private hands, which was never wise, as it risked the possibility of an elected clique, rather than the people, setting the national agenda; we are seeing the consequences of that in other contexts today.

The tariff issue divided the sections of the country. What tariff rates are best for America differ in various times and circumstances. Before the Civil War, the North generally preferred high tariffs in order to protect its nascent industries; the agrarian South, on the other hand, called for low tariffs so it could sell its cotton in Europe without an undue tax burden. Reasonable high tariffs protected wage-earning American laborers from competition from slaves and virtual slaves in other nations; the South, since its economy was built on slavery, didn't see this as a problem. Thus, high tariffs become more clearly an America-first position after the Civil War, when slavery no longer was any part of America. In the 1824 election and for some time thereafter, a voter's position on this issue would be largely determined by the region of the country in which he lived.

Quite aside from these issues was the question of Jackson's fitness for office; for no previous candidate had this been as much of an issue as it was for the renowned general in 1824. Jackson was widely considered to be unsuitable to be president, as he had little political experience. Clay sneered, "I cannot believe that killing 2,500 Englishmen at New Orleans qualifies for the various, difficult, and complicated duties of the Chief Magistracy."[58] Nevertheless, the election results had Jackson leading the field, winning ninety-nine electoral votes, with eighty-four for Adams, forty-one for Crawford, and thirty-seven for Clay. As none of the candidates had a majority, the election went to the House of Representatives, where the choice was between the three top vote-getters. Clay threw his support to Adams, who prevailed. Adams, as president, then chose Clay as the secretary of state, which was reasonable in light of their agreement on key issues. But Jackson and his supporters charged Adams and Clay with making a "corrupt bargain" to secure the presidency for Adams. Jackson raged: "So you see the Judas of the West [Clay] has closed the contract and will receive his thirty pieces of silver. Was there ever witnessed such bare faced corruption in any country before?"[59]

So it was that the presidency of John Quincy Adams, a man who was distinguished throughout his long political career for his integrity, was tainted from beginning to end by charges of corruption and venality. Adams entered the White House under a cloud that never dissipated. In his inaugural address, Adams appealed to the goodwill of the American people: "Less possessed of your confidence in advance than any of my predecessors, I am deeply conscious of the prospect that I shall stand more and oftener in need of your indulgence."[60] He didn't get it.

---

58   Paul E. Teed, *John Quincy Adams: Yankee Nationalist* (New York: Nova Science Publishers, Inc., 2006), 94.

59   Ibid., 97.

60   John Quincy Adams, "Inaugural Address" (speech, March 4, 1825), Avalon Project, Yale Law School.

The occupants of the White House aren't the only ones who set precedents regarding the American presidency. Sometimes their opponents set them. The savaging of John Quincy Adams in 1825 and thereafter was not, unfortunately, the last time a presidency would be attacked in such a manner despite the paucity of evidence to support the charges.

Notable accomplishments as president

1. *Treaties with Indian tribes.* In his first annual message to Congress in December 1825, Adams laid out a bold plan for internal improvements, some of which necessitated making peace with the Indian tribes of the West. He noted that an act of Congress of March 3, 1825, the last day of the Monroe administration, had "authorized treaties to be made with the Indians for their consent to the making of a road from the frontier of Missouri to that of New Mexico, and another act of the same date provided for defraying the expenses of holding treaties with the Sioux, Chippeways, Menomenees, Sauks, Foxes, etc., for the purpose of establishing boundaries and promoting peace between said tribes."[61] He also invoked an act of Congress of March 3, 1824, calling for the making of plans to build roads and canals.

Although he couched both of these as Monroe-era initiatives upon which he was simply following through, he had been their principal architect as secretary of state. He was savaged in the press as being too easy on the Indians, who had

---

61   John Quincy Adams, "First Annual Message" (speech, December 6, 1825), UVA Miller Center.

not ceased unprovoked and vicious attacks upon American settlers. The myth of the noble Native Americans cruelly and unjustly mistreated by racist Americans had not yet been invented, and most Americans were deeply frightened by the brutality of the Indians and the unpredictability of their attacks. The governors of Georgia, Alabama, and Mississippi came out strongly against his attempts to conclude treaties with the Indians that would deal fairly with both sides.

Meanwhile, Adams's calls in his first message to Congress for the establishment of a national university and national observatory came to nothing, as his legion of foes among the press and in Congress derided him as a tyrant with monarchal aspirations. With the tone deafness that he shared with his father, he warned in that address that adherence to public opinion could conflict with what was good for the nation, which he compared unfavorably to the authoritarian societies of Europe: "While foreign nations less blessed with that freedom which is power than ourselves are advancing with gigantic strides in the career of public improvement, were we to slumber in indolence or fold up our arms and proclaim to the world that we are palsied by the will of our constituents, would it not be to cast away the bounties of Providence and doom ourselves to perpetual inferiority?"[62]

Adams's constituents, as it turned out, had the same desire not to be palsied by his will.

2. *The tariff bill of 1828.* Vice President John C. Calhoun of South Carolina, who by this time supported Jackson, oversaw the introduction of a tariff bill that set high taxes on both the

---

62   Ibid.

import of manufactured goods that the South needed and on the export of the raw materials that the South produced. It also set high rates on imported raw materials that New England's industries needed for production.

Calhoun's plan was to present a tariff bill that would be so unpalatable not just to the South, but to New England, that the two sections would unite in voting it down, in the face of support from the Mid-Atlantic and Western states. Then the Jacksonians could blame Adams for its defeat and champion themselves as the "friends of domestic industry," an honor that otherwise would likely have gone to Adams, as the candidate from the most industrialized area of the country.[63] But the plan went awry: the proponents of the bill argued that any measure that benefited American industry was good for all Americans, and while Southerners in the House and Senate voted overwhelmingly against it, enough New Englanders were swayed by that argument to vote for it. Adams duly signed it as an expression of the will of the people.

Why his presidency did little good but not much damage

True to his lifelong seriousness of character and strong work ethic, Adams worked hard throughout his presidency, but he faced too much determined, even fanatical, opposition to be able to accomplish much. Emblematic of the obstacles

---

63   F. W. Taussig, *The Tariff History of the United States*, 5th ed. (New York: G. P. Putnam's Sons, 1910), 80.

Adams faced was the tariff bill of 1828, which was essentially an elaborate scheme to ensure his defeat in the presidential election later that year. Because of this "Tariff of Abominations," prices sharply increased, and Adams's political fate was sealed. Riding a wave of anger over this tariff bill, and fanning suspicions that Adams was a corrupt pol who made a backroom deal with Clay to get into the White House in the first place, Jackson, the "friend of industry," defeated him in a landslide.

SEVEN

ANDREW JACKSON

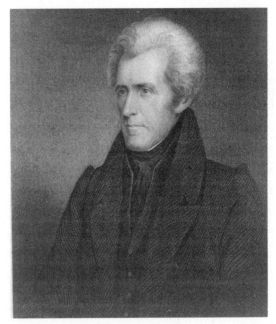

Library of Congress[64]

---

64   James Barton Longacre, *Andrew Jackson / Drawn from Life and Engraved by J.B. Longacre*, [1815–1845?], photograph, Library of Congress, https://www.loc.gov/item/96523440/.

Full name: Andrew Jackson
Lived: March 15, 1767–June 8, 1845
Presidency: March 4, 1829–March 4, 1837
Party: Democratic
Evaluation: Very Good for America
Rating: 8

What qualified him to be president

Four of the first six presidents were aristocratic slave owners from Virginia; the other two were anti-slavery aristocrats from Massachusetts who were father and son. By 1828, there was a widespread sentiment in the growing country that it was ruled by oligarchies whose interests did not necessarily coincide with those of the common people. In the election of that year, the common people put their candidate in the White House: the first populist president, Andrew Jackson.

Jackson had a thinner résumé, at least in regard to holding elective office, than any previous occupant of the White House. He was a renowned general and the hero of the War of 1812, as well as of campaigns against hostile Indians. "I am not a politician," he declared, and could make a substantial case for the claim.[65] His political experience consisted of nine and a half months in the House of Representatives at the end of the Washington administration and beginning of the Adams administration, another nine and a half months nearly a quarter of a century later as territorial governor of Florida, and two and a half years as a senator from Tennessee.

---

65   Boller, loc. 571.

But for many of his supporters, the fact that he had not served a long tenure in Congress, or as secretary of state, the office that most early heirs apparent occupied, was what made him appealing. Jackson was the first candidate to run as a Washington outsider, coming in to clean up the place, and, in particular, to turn out the man who had not wanted to be "palsied by the will of our constituents."

How he won

In 1828, Jackson's supporters were anxious to reverse the result of the 1824 election, which they believed had been stolen from them by the "corrupt bargain" between Adams and Clay. But the 1828 election was more than that as well. Jackson's supporters saw it as a contest between "the democracy of the country, on the one hand, and a *lordly purse-proud* aristocracy on the other." Adams partisans considered it a defensive action against "the howl of raving Democracy."[66]

This disdain for democracy is jarring to many people today who assume, without looking too deeply into the matter, that the United States is a democracy. However, the disdain reflects a common understanding of the antebellum period. While the highest officials of the United States routinely call the country a democracy today, and glory in that designation, the U.S. is actually a republic, in which the people entrust their representatives with various responsibilities and governing authority. If the United States were a straight democracy, major decisions would be made by plebiscite. In the early days

---

66   Boller, loc. 559.

of the American republic, when most education was in the classics, many educated people had a dim view of democracy, equating it with mob rule and unrestrained demagoguery, in line with Plato's view of it in *The Republic* as a degenerate form of government, leading inevitably to tyranny. Others, however, then as now, had little regard for such distinctions and considered the nation a democracy: Jackson's supporters derided Adams for "habits and principles" that were "not congenial with the spirit of our institutions and the notions of a democratic people."[67]

Whatever else it was, the 1828 campaign was the dirtiest America had seen up to that point. Jackson's men portrayed Adams as an effete snob with monarchist tendencies; Adams's men countered with claims that Jackson was functionally illiterate. Some of Adams's supporters published one of the ugliest pieces of campaign literature ever produced, the notorious "Coffin Handbill," which charged Jackson with murder for executing six deserters during the war against the Creek Indians in 1813. Jackson's supporters noted that the executed men had tried to incite a mutiny among the American troops, but the Adams forces brushed this aside, saying that the handbill was essentially correct in its claim that Jackson took pleasure from putting people to death.

The attacks that really made Jackson enraged, however, were claims that his mother was a prostitute and that his wife Rachel was an adulteress, as she had married Jackson before being divorced from her first husband. The Jacksons had married in good faith, only to discover later that Rachel's

---

67   Boller, loc. 596.

husband had not actually obtained a divorce as expected; as soon as it came through, they married again. Rachel Jackson died in December 1828, shortly after the election, and Jackson was sure that the attacks of the Adams men had killed her.

Few of Jackson's supporters were aware of his personal tragedy when they flocked to Washington for his inauguration on March 4, 1829. His supporters, overjoyed at the accession to the presidency of a man of the people, thronged to the White House, where their boisterous behavior shocked the city's aristocracy. Supreme Court Justice Joseph Story lamented that "the reign of KING MOB seemed triumphant."[68]

Notable accomplishments as president and events of his presidency

1. *Removal of Indian tribes to the West.* Jackson advocated for the removal of the Indians from the settled areas of the United States, and their relocation in unsettled areas of the West. In May 1830, he signed the Indian Removal Act that made this recommendation the law of the land. This is today considered to be one of the black marks on his presidency and a shameful period in the history of the United States. This is a reasonable judgment, as this policy amounted to penalizing all Indians for the misdeeds of Indian warriors, and it led to untold suffering.

2. *Nullification controversy.* Enraged by the 1828 Tariff of Abominations, the state of South Carolina, prompted by its most prominent native, Vice President John C. Calhoun, called

---

68   Sean Wilentz, *The Rise of American Democracy: Jefferson to Lincoln* (New York: W. W. Norton & Company, 2006), 312.

a convention that declared that the 1828 tariff and another tariff law from 1832 "are unauthorized by the Constitution of the United States, and violate the true meaning and intent thereof, and are null and void, and no law."[69] The convention also declared that any attempt by the federal government to enforce those laws or punish South Carolina for nullifying them would result in South Carolina leaving the Union.

Jackson was sympathetic to their opposition to the tariffs but absolutely unwilling to allow a state to override federal laws, which would, he maintained, lead to the dissolution of the Union. On December 10, 1832, Jackson issued a proclamation declaring that "the said ordinance prescribes to the people of South Carolina a course of conduct in direct violation of their duty as citizens of the United States, contrary to the laws of their country, subversive of its Constitution, and having for its object the destruction of the Union."[70] He warned the South Carolinians that they were veering close to treason and declared secession illegitimate, denying that the United States was "a mere league that may be dissolved at pleasure."[71]

Jackson asked Congress for a bill authorizing military force to make sure the tariff was enforced and got it. The controversy was defused when a compromise tariff was passed and South Carolina backed down, but the point had been made: the United States was one nation, not a compact of many, and the central government had the right and the authority to

---

69   Andrew Jackson, "Proclamation Regarding Nullification," December 10, 1832, Avalon Project, Yale Law School.
70   Ibid.
71   Ibid.

pass laws and enforce them. This point would have to be made again, amid much bloodshed, a few decades later. In our own age, there are some who still refuse to accept it.

3. *Negotiating treaties with foreign powers and maintaining neutrality*. When President John Quincy Adams had proposed sending an American delegation to a conference of the North, Central, and South American nations in Panama, Jackson opposed the idea and echoed Washington in stating: "The moment we engage in confederations, or alliances with any nation, we may from that time date the down fall [sic] of our republic."[72] As president, Jackson held to this principle, while settling problems that had continued for decades: after several years of protracted negotiations and a good deal of public grandstanding, the government of France paid $5 million ($136.5 million today) in damages to the United States for American ships it had seized. Jackson concluded similar arrangements with several other countries, as well as numerous trade agreements, without entangling the country in any commitments that would weaken its sovereignty.

4. *Killing the Bank*. President Jackson called the Bank of the United States a "monster," and denounced its "power and corruption."[73] He charged it with interfering in the political process and bribing elected officials and journalists with "loans" so that they would do its bidding. There was ample evidence for this. The *New York Courier and Enquirer*, which up until the 1832 election had opposed the Bank,

---

72   Robert V. Remini, *Andrew Jackson, Volume Two: The Course of American Freedom 1822–1832* (Baltimore: JHU Press, 2013), 131.

73   Ibid., 394–395.

received a substantial loan from it and suddenly became a vocal supporter of rechartering the Bank. The pro-Jackson *Washington Globe* accused pro-Bank senators George Poindexter of Mississippi and Josiah Johnston of Louisiana of accepting enormous bribes in return for their support of the Bank, and indeed, Poindexter had received from the Bank a $10,000 loan ($300,000 today) and Johnston one of $36,000 (over $1 million today). These were by no means the only loans the Bank gave to politicians.

Jackson warned that if the Bank, a "mere monied corporation," could use its money to buy politicians, "then nothing remains of our boasted freedom except *the skin of the immolated victim*."[74] He told his close friend and advisor Martin Van Buren: "The Bank, Mr. Van Buren, is trying to kill me, but I will kill it!"[75]

He did. The Bank's charter, the document that gave it the United States government's permission to exist, didn't expire until 1836, but in early 1832, the president of the Bank, Nicholas Biddle, applied for a new charter. His sole reason for doing this was to force Jackson to refuse to recharter the Bank; Biddle assumed that Jackson's opposition to the Bank would be unpopular and lead to his defeat in the upcoming election, and so he wanted to make sure the president committed publicly to this opposition during the campaign season.

Jackson duly vetoed a bill for rechartering the Bank in July 1832, whereupon Biddle poured massive amounts of

---

74   Ibid., 396–397.
75   Van Buren, loc. 12633.

money into the campaign of Jackson's opponent, Henry Clay. Clay campaigned on the issue of the Bank, but this issue did not prove as popular as he and Biddle had hoped. The American people saw Jackson as their champion against moneyed interests that were corrupting the body politic. Clay was resoundingly defeated, with 49 electoral votes against Jackson's 219.

5. *Paying off the national debt.* Remarkably, the Jackson administration remains the only one in American history to pay off the national debt completely.

6. *The spoils system.* James Monroe and John Quincy Adams, like Thomas Jefferson, had proclaimed that the era of party politics was over, and they worked to make good on their statements. Monroe pursued policies that helped to hasten the death of the Federalist Party, such as appointing Federalists to civil service positions. Owing their jobs to the Democratic-Republican president weakened their allegiance to their own party. But the idea of a big-tent party began to fall apart almost immediately. Andrew Jackson was elected president on promises to end the hegemony of a privileged aristocracy, and, to drain that swamp, he would need his own men in key positions. He removed a large number of civil service employees and replaced them with men of his own faction, which came to be known as the Democracy, or Democratic Party. (The Adams/Clay faction, meanwhile, was known as the Whigs, after the British party that opposed absolute monarchy; although they generally supported a strong federal government, they opposed what they characterized as the absolutism of "King Andrew" Jackson and, thus, took the name of the British proponents of constitutional monarchy.)

This came to be known as the spoils system, after the old adage "To the victor belong the spoils."

Why his presidency was very good for America

Much of what Jackson did was great, but not all of it. His payment of the national debt set an example of fiscal responsibility that has been forgotten in our enlightened age and that is all the more important and needed as a result. His opposition to the Bank destroyed the power of a moneyed elite that was manipulating politicians for its own ends. Here again, Jackson's example is salutary and instructive in an age when people of modest means get elected to Congress and walk away millionaires a few years later. His dealings with foreign powers were wise and sure-footed, and his handling of the nullification controversy was constitutionally sound, postponing a Civil War for thirty years. Unlike Monroe in the case of the Missouri Compromise, Jackson did not merely postpone the problem by failing to address the central issue of contention; instead, he laid out the basic principles by which the Union must and would be preserved. Abraham Lincoln's statements regarding the necessity to wage war to end the Southern rebellion could be extended footnotes to Jackson's statements on nullification.

The term "spoils system" is today practically synonymous with government corruption, but Jackson began it as a blow against corruption, preventing the establishment of an entrenched bureaucracy that would oppose the president. The administration of Donald Trump has made it clear that such a bureaucracy determined to thwart the president at every turn is a genuine concern; it is time for a reconsideration of the spoils system.

On the other side is Jackson's record regarding the Indians. It is noteworthy that he presented his Indian removal plan as beneficial not just for the Americans, but for the Indians as well. In his first annual message to Congress in December 1829, he said:

> The condition and ulterior destiny of the Indian tribes within the limits of some of our states have become objects of much interest and importance. It has long been the policy of government to introduce among them the arts of civilization, in the hope of gradually reclaiming them from a wandering life.[76]

Jackson pointed out that the endeavor to civilize the Indians was inconsistent with the practice of buying Indian land:

> This policy has, however, been coupled with another wholly incompatible with its success. Professing a desire to civilize and settle them, we have at the same time lost no opportunity to purchase their lands and thrust them farther into the wilderness. By this means they have not only been kept in a wandering state, but been led to look upon us as unjust and

---

76   Andrew Jackson, "First Annual Message to Congress" (speech, December 8, 1829), UVA Miller Center.

indifferent to their fate. Thus, though lavish in
its expenditures upon the subject, government
has constantly defeated its own policy, and the
Indians in general, receding farther and farther
to the west, have retained their savage habits.[77]

All this is jarring to modern ears. We are told today that the
idea that the Indians were not civilized and needed to be is
a racist assumption. We are told that to charge them with
"savage habits" is likewise ethnocentric and provincial. In the
1960s, 1970s, and thereafter, we were inundated with books
and films (such as *Bury My Heart at Wounded Knee*, *Little Big
Man*, *Dances with Wolves*, and many others) depicting the
Indians as innocent victims of American aggression and
imperialism; people who were naturally noble, generous,
and open-hearted were oppressed and killed wholesale by
rapacious, chauvinistic, sexually repressed white Europeans.

It makes for a good story and is a linchpin of the cultural
self-hatred that for decades now has been inculcated assi-
duously in American youth. But reality, as is always the case
when compared with propaganda, is more complicated. The
claim that Americans stole the land from the Indians is based
on the peculiar assumption that the migration of peoples, war,
and conquest, all of which are constants of human history, are
always illegitimate. If followed through, this principle would
roll back a great deal more than the European settlement of
North America.

---

77   Ibid.

What's more, the Indians were indeed waging a war. Jackson had ample reason to refer to the Indians' "savage habits," and if any of his hearers opposed his policy, it was not because they disputed that characterization. Indian raids aroused horror in American settlers for decades; U.S. Army Captain Robert G. Carter wrote of the victims of one raid years after Jackson's presidency that "their fingers, toes, and private parts had been cut off and stuck in their mouths, and their bodies, now lying in several inches of water and swollen or bloated beyond all chance of recognition, were filled full of arrows, which made them resemble porcupines. Upon each exposed abdomen had been placed a mass of live coals...One wretched man, Samuel Elliott, who, fighting hard to the last, had evidently been wounded, was found chained between two wagon wheels and, a fire having been made from the wagon pole, he had been slowly roasted to death—'burnt to a crisp.'"[78] Those who lived on the frontier in Jackson's day would not have found any of this unfamiliar.

Jackson's policy was not to respond in kind to the Indians, but to give them a place where they could flourish. "Our conduct toward these people," he said in his first message to Congress, "is deeply interesting to our national character. Their present condition, contrasted with what they once were, makes a most powerful appeal to our sympathies."[79] Noting that some tribes had died out altogether, he asserted that others would disappear also if they continued to live

---

78   S. C. Gwynne, *Empire of the Summer Moon: Quanah Parker and the Rise and Fall of the Comanche Tribe* (London: Constable, 2010), 5.

79   Jackson, "First Message to Congress."

among the Americans. "Humanity and national honor," he declared, "demand that every effort should be made to avert so great a calamity."[80] In order to "preserve this much-injured race," he called for "setting apart an ample district west of the Mississippi, and without the limits of any state or territory now formed, to be guaranteed to the Indian tribes as long as they shall occupy it, each tribe having a distinct control over the portion designated for its use."[81]

It is ironic that Jackson's solution is so derided today by the American Left, since it is eminently multicultural: instead of trying to make the Indians into Americans, Jackson proposed that they would have their land and their culture, separate from the land and culture of the Americans. Even the segregationist aspect of Jackson's plan is modern, for after having been banished from American life, segregation has returned: Wesleyan University, Brown University, MIT, Columbia University, Cornell, Oberlin College, and others, all bastions of multiculturalist orthodoxy, have established segregated dorms in the interest of allowing "marginalized" students to flourish.[82] They could have gotten the idea from a man they hate, Andrew Jackson.

Jackson's plan was popular but not without opposition. Its character of punishing all for the sins of a few repulsed even some of Jackson's supporters, including Davy Crockett, later an American hero at the Alamo and at that time a

---

80   Ibid.
81   Ibid.
82   Dion J. Pierre, "Demands for Segregated Housing at Williams College Are Not News," National Review, May 8, 2019.

congressman from Tennessee, who wrote that he opposed Jackson's "famous, or rather I should say his in-*famous*, Indian bill" from "the purest motives in the world."[83] He called it "a wicked, unjust measure," which he was determined to oppose despite the political cost.[84] He told Jackson's supporters, "I was willing to go with General Jackson in every thing that I believed was honest and right; but, further than this, I wouldn't go for him, or any other man in the whole creation; that I would sooner be honestly and politically d—nd, than hypocritically immortalized."[85] Accordingly, "I voted against this Indian bill, and my conscience yet tells me that I gave a good honest vote, and one that I believe will not make me ashamed in the day of judgment."[86] An indication of the popularity of Jackson's policy was the fact that Crockett lost his bid for reelection, whereupon he declared to those who had voted him out: "You may all go to hell and I will go to Texas."[87]

Jackson's Indian policy was understandable under the circumstances, but it was unjust as well. However, that makes his presidency a completely evil one only to the insufferable Manichaean moralists of the contemporary Left. His defeat of the forces of disunion (the Nullifiers) and of private oligarchies (the Bank), as well as his paying off of the national debt, make his presidency overall a beneficial one for Americans.

---

83   Davy Crockett, *A Narrative of the Life of David Crockett, of the State of Tennessee*, 2011, Project Gutenberg, 205.

84   Crockett, 205–206.

85   Ibid, 206.

86   Ibid.

87   Michael A. Lofaro and William C. Davis, "David Crockett," Texas State Historical Association, https://tshaonline.org/handbook/online/articles/fcr24.

EIGHT

MARTIN VAN BUREN

Library of Congress[88]

88   *Former President Martin Van Buren, Half-Length Portrait, Facing Right*, 1840–
      1862, photograph, Library of Congress, https://www.loc.gov/item/96522273/.

Full name: Martin Van Buren
Lived: December 5, 1782–July 24, 1862
Presidency: March 4, 1837–March 4, 1841
Party: Democratic
Evaluation: Did Good Things but Also Significant Damage
Rating: 6

What qualified him to be president

Martin Van Buren was the last sitting vice president before George H. W. Bush to be elected president, and, in a sense, he was the George H. W. Bush of his time: he served as vice president in the administration of a very popular president, and while he did not share that president's charisma or popularity, and was vastly different in temperament, he won election to the presidency based on the supposition that he would continue his predecessor's policies.

Also like Bush, Van Buren was not just the protégé of a great man; he was a dedicated public servant with a long and distinguished résumé of his own and a longstanding reputation for tact, diplomacy, and unusual cleverness in attaining his ends. (This earned him the nicknames "The Little Magician" and "The Red Fox of Kinderhook," after his hometown in New York. The political cartoonists, however, tended to call him "Matty.")

Van Buren served as a member of the New York State Senate for seven years and then as a U.S. senator from New York. He was also briefly governor of New York before Jackson tabbed him as his secretary of state, which he was for two years, until one of the oddest, most celebrated controversies in American history.

Van Buren was a master of the political game. As a senator, he once delivered an address on the tariff question that one of its hearers told one of Van Buren's friends was "a very able speech." But then, after a long pause, the man asked Van Buren's friend, "On which side of the Tariff question was it?"[89]

Peggy Eaton, the wife of Jackson's secretary of war, John Eaton, was rumored to be promiscuous and even to have been a prostitute; the wives of Vice President John C. Calhoun and other Cabinet members accordingly shunned her. This enraged Jackson, who correctly judged the controversy as a power play, an attempt to drive Eaton from his Cabinet and dictate whom he could and could not appoint. He stoutly defended Mrs. Eaton, but neither the women who ostracized Peggy Eaton nor their husbands were won over. Jackson appeared caught: he could fire Eaton, which would be a capitulation to Calhoun, or keep Eaton and remain vulnerable to charges that he was tolerating immoral behavior. Finally, the staunchly pro-Eaton Secretary of State Van Buren proposed a solution: he would resign, while Jackson would ask for the resignations of Eaton as well as all the anti-Eaton Cabinet members; in the end, the entire Cabinet except the pro-Eaton Postmaster General William Barry resigned. Jackson would be free to appoint his own men, and the moralists were disarmed.

Jackson followed this advice, and then gratefully nominated Van Buren to be U.S. minister to Britain. The Senate confirmation vote, however, was a tie. Vice President Calhoun, thinking he was administering the coup de grâce to a rival,

---

89   Van Buren, loc. 3200.

cast the deciding negative vote and said happily of Van Buren, "It will kill him sir. Kill him dead. He will never kick, sir. Never kick."[90] Van Buren was already in London and had to return home.

Calhoun was wrong. Van Buren did kick. The one whom the vote killed dead was not Van Buren, but Calhoun himself. When he heard about the vote, Jackson was enraged and cried out, "By the Eternal! I'll smash them!"[91] He told Van Buren, "The people will properly resent the insult offered to the Executive, and the injury intended to our foreign relations, in your rejection, by placing you in the chair of the very man whose casting vote rejected you."[92] Van Buren replaced Calhoun as vice-presidential candidate on the 1832 ticket of the Democracy.

He was just as masterful a politician as vice president. On one occasion, as Van Buren presided over the Senate, Henry Clay delivered an impassioned harangue about Jackson's tyranny, likening the president to "the worst of the Roman emperors" and emotionally appealing to Van Buren to intervene.[93] Van Buren left his seat and approached Clay as the senators watched agog, expecting the worst. But Van Buren merely asked Clay for "a pinch of his fine maccoboy snuff," defusing the tension; he and Clay became friends, although their political rivalry continued.[94]

---

90   Remini, 368.
91   Ibid., 369.
92   Ibid., 370.
93   Donald B. Cole, *Martin Van Buren and the American Political System* (Princeton, NJ: Princeton University Press, 2014), 251
94   Ibid., 252.

How he won

In the 1836 election, the Whigs couldn't settle on a single candidate. Instead, they ran several, hoping to force the election into the House of Representatives or, at the very least, that one of their men would emerge as their logical candidate for 1840. One of their 1836 presidential candidates, for example, was the renowned orator Senator Daniel Webster of Massachusetts. But the most popular Whig candidate in 1836 was General William Henry Harrison, a war hero from whom Van Buren would hear again. Even so, this time around, Jackson's mantle virtually assured Van Buren's election, and he won handily.

Notable accomplishments as president and events of his presidency

1. *The Panic of 1837.* After President Jackson refused to recharter the Bank of the United States, he placed federal funds in state banks, which had the benefit of not having the power to manipulate elected officials on the scale that the Bank did. However, they engaged in irresponsible land speculation and risky credit practices, which Jackson tried to curb in July 1836 with the Specie Circular, an executive order mandating that those who purchased land owned by the government, which was in plentiful supply after the removal of the Indians, had to pay in gold and silver, not paper money.

Jackson thought that requiring the Banks and those who were purchasing land to use gold and silver would lead them to be more responsible: rather than dealing freely in promissory notes, the land speculators would have to come up with hard currency. Jackson was trying to bring under control the inflation that had been caused by a superabundance of paper money in circulation.

The Specie Circular led, however, to money being in short supply, which in turn led banks to call in loans. Jackson, however, was out of office before the effects of these policies could be felt. It was Van Buren who had to endure their consequences. By the beginning of the Van Buren administration, Jackson's Specie Circular had sent the American economy into a depression, the Panic of 1837, which, like the War of 1812, lasted far longer than its designated year. Van Buren was blamed, and his presidency was doomed.

2. *Indian removal.* Van Buren continued Jackson's Indian removal policies. Although this initiative was generally popular, there was opposition. During the 1832 election, when the Indians were already being relocated and Van Buren was Jackson's running mate, his niece, whom Van Buren described as "a lady of remarkable intelligence and strength of character, and deeply imbued with religious feeling," told him, "Uncle! I must say to you that it is my earnest wish that you may lose the election, as I believe that such a result ought to follow such acts!"[95]

The philosopher-poet Ralph Waldo Emerson was moved in April 1838 to write to Van Buren, appealing for justice for the Cherokees. Of the plan to relocate them in the West he wrote:

> Such a dereliction of all faith and virtue, such a
> denial of justice, and such deafness to screams

---

95   Van Buren, locs. 5635, 5644.

for mercy were never heard of in times of peace and in the dealing of a nation with its own allies and wards, since the earth was made. Sir, does this government think that the people of the United States are become savage and mad? From their mind are the sentiments of love and a good nature wiped clean out? The soul of man, the justice, the mercy that is the heart's heart in all men, from Maine to Georgia, does abhor this business.[96]

Around the time this letter was written, the government was forcing about twenty thousand Cherokees and other Indians to move from the Southeast to West of the Mississippi along the "Trail of Tears." Over half of the Indians died along the way.

The injustice of the Indian removal policy haunts us to this day. Davy Crockett, Van Buren's niece, Ralph Waldo Emerson, and other opponents of the policy have been forgotten, and the myth has taken hold that a unanimous and inveterately racist white America connived to commit a genocide of the Native Americans, which was never the intention. Jackson and Van Buren responded to a genuine crisis with an ill-considered and excessive solution that remains a blot on the nation's history.

3. *Refusing to annex Texas.* On March 2, 1836, the Mexican province of Texas, to which a large number of American

---

96   Ralph Waldo Emerson to Martin van Buren, April 23, 1838, Bartleby, https://www.bartleby.com/90/1103.html.

settlers had moved, declared its independence from Mexico. The Texians, as they were known, quickly petitioned the U.S. government for annexation, and Jackson thought that was a capital idea, although he was not able to make it happen before he left office. Van Buren, although elected on the basis of the assumption that he would continue Jackson's policies, rejected the annexation request. He didn't want war with Mexico, or a massive slave state entering the Union and upsetting the delicate balance established by the Missouri Compromise. Since Americans made up the majority of the Texas population, however, the question of annexation would not go away; all Van Buren did was postpone it.

Why his presidency did good things but also significant damage

The Panic of 1837 ruined Van Buren's presidency, but it began just weeks after he took office and cannot justly be ascribed to any of his policies. Because the economic crisis overshadows everything else that happened during his administration, the good Van Buren did by *not* acting in some wrongheaded ways that have become familiar in the modern age, as well as the proposals he made that were not realized during his administration but were nonetheless sound and wise, have been overlooked.

President Van Buren is to be commended for not giving in to pressure during the Panic of 1837 to begin creating the gargantuan and out-of-control federal government that is a feature of our own age. The Whigs called upon him to use public funds for the relief of those who were suffering as a result of the Panic. Van Buren, they said, should initiate massive internal improvements that would call for labor and thereby reduce unemployment; in effect, they wanted what would be called a hundred years later a New Deal for the American people. There were even calls for a revival of the Bank of the United States, as its demise was often identified as the cause of all the trouble.

As a strict constructionist, however, Van Buren refused, considering such acts to be outside the scope of his constitutional powers; massive government "stimulus packages" to get the economy going would become fashionable only much later. Instead, Van Buren held to a laissez-faire policy and even relaxed regulations on businesses, so that they could rebound and the economy right itself. This paid off and ended the Panic in 1842, but, by then, Van Buren had already been voted out of the White House.

Van Buren tried to get to the root of the problem and repair matters once and for all with his proposal of an independent treasury, a government agency that would serve as the repository of federal funds and take banks out of the picture altogether. This would remove the government's funds from the reach of both the Bank's practice of buying politicians and the state banks' irresponsibility. But Van Buren failed to get this idea off the ground: the House of Representatives voted down the measure three times. It was finally adopted in 1840, only to be repealed when the Whigs took power in 1841. However, the Polk administration reestablished it in 1846, and it lasted until 1913, when the Federal Reserve replaced it.

The independent treasury did not create a government bank; the public funds were kept in the U.S. Treasury Building in Washington, as well as in sub-treasuries in other cities. Van Buren's independent treasury proposal was wisely framed as taking the public money out of private hands. This also was subject to abuse, of course, but it was intended to keep taxpayer funds subject to the discretion only of representatives chosen by the taxpayers and their appointed deputies, so that they could not be used, as those who had controlled the Bank of the United States had used them, to influence politicians and manipulate the public debate. The independent treasury would, Van Buren hoped, keep the buying of politicians to a minimum.

The Van Buren administration, however, was responsible for a great deal of damage in regard to the Indians. His amused recounting of his niece's reaction to his Indian policy shows him indifferent to the point of callousness to the Indians' plight. The removal of the Indians to the West was not a genocide; thousands of Indians died along the way not because of some deliberate intent to kill them, but because not enough effort was taken to ensure their survival. Van Buren didn't order this treatment, but he did nothing to stop it. As president of the United States at the time, he bore ultimate responsibility for it.

WILLIAM HENRY HARRISON

Library of Congress[97]

---

97   Charles Fenderich, *Wm. H. Harrison, President of the United States*, ca.
      1841, photograph, Washington City, D.C., Chas. Fenderich & Co, Library of
      Congress, https://www.loc.gov/item/96522278/.

Full name: William Henry Harrison
Lived: February 9, 1773–April 4, 1841
Presidency: March 4, 1841–April 4, 1841
Party: Whig
Evaluation: Did Little Good but Not Much Damage
Rating: None

What qualified him to be president

William Henry Harrison was primarily known as a military figure, the hero of the Battle of Tippecanoe over Tecumseh's Confederacy in 1811 and of the War of 1812. But he was not as implausible a presidential candidate as some other military candidates have been, as he had considerable political experience. For over a year during the elder Adams's administration, Harrison was a delegate from the Northwest Territory to the House of Representatives; then he served as governor of the Northwest Territory for twelve years. In 1816, he returned to Congress, this time as a representative from Ohio. He later served a three-year stint as a senator from Ohio. He resigned from the Senate in 1828 when John Quincy Adams sent him to South America as U.S. minister to Gran Colombia, where he served for a year and a half until Andrew Jackson recalled him for partisan reasons.

None of this, however, had anything to do with why he was elected president of the United States.

How he won

When his service in Gran Colombia ended in September 1829, Harrison returned to his farm in Ohio. He was not inclined, however, to remain a gentleman farmer for the rest of his life. In 1836, he was one of several Whig candidates for president and outpolled all the rest, making him the party's logical choice for 1840.

The Whigs were determined to get Harrison into the White House—not based on his public positions but rather upon the appeal of the persona they fashioned for him. Nicholas Biddle, the former president of the Bank of the United States and a powerful Harrison backer, directed in 1836 that the candidate should stay quiet about virtually everything: "Let him say nothing—promise nothing. Let no Committee, no Convention, no town meeting ever extract from him a single word about what he thinks now and will do hereafter. Let the use of pen and ink be wholly forbidden as if he were a mad poet in Bedlam."[98]

This advice went double for 1840. The Whig camp included those who favored the rechartering of the Bank of the United States, federal action to stimulate the economy, and a strong central government, but they also counted among their ranks opponents of all those positions, united only by their opposition of Jackson and Jacksonianism, and hence also of Jackson's protégé, Van Buren. The Whigs' lack of a clear message was compounded in 1840 by their choice of John Tyler, an anti-Bank states' rights advocate who had been a Democrat until

---

98   Boller, locs. 952–959.

he fell out of favor with Jackson by opposing the Force Bill. There was nothing unifying this motley group, and so the Whigs had to find an approach for the 1840 campaign that wouldn't expose their deep divisions on the issues.

In December 1839, the pro-Democrat *Baltimore Republican* inadvertently handed it to them. They derided Harrison as a simple man who was unfit for the presidency: "Give him a barrel of hard cider and a pension of two thousand a year and, my word for it, he will sit the remainder of his days in a log cabin, by the side of a 'sea-coal' fire and study moral philosophy."[99]

A presidential candidate who studied moral philosophy would be most welcome today, but it was the other part of the statement that gave the Whigs their main chance. They took the Democrats' 1828 strategy of portraying Andrew Jackson as a champion of the common man and took it to the next level. Harrison became Old Tippecanoe, the humble war hero, an ordinary man with simple tastes, content with a log cabin and a jug of hard cider. To this they contrasted a deeply unfair caricature of Martin Van Buren as an out-of-touch, champagne-drinking, cosseted aristocrat who had spent public funds on lavish furnishings for the White House. One political cartoon pictured Harrison greeting his visitors, Van Buren and his entourage. "Gentlemen," says Harrison, "you seem fatigued. If you will accept the fare of a log cabin, with a Western farmer's cheer, you are welcome. I have no champagne but can give you a mug of good cider, with some ham and eggs, and good clean beds. I am a plain backwoodsman.

---

99   Ibid., loc. 894.

I have cleared some land, killed some Indians, and made the Red Coats fly in my time."[100]

The Whigs held rallies, passed out hard cider, staged marches, and generally made the 1840 election into a party celebrating "Tippecanoe and Tyler Too."

This was all great fun, but it was also the sum of the Whigs' appeal to the American people. The Democrats were confounded. One Democrat editorialist vented his frustration: "In what grave and important discussion are the Whig journals engaged?... We speak of the divorce of bank and state; and the Whigs reply with a dissertation on the merits of hard cider. We defend the policy of the Administration; and the Whigs answer 'log cabin,' 'big canoes,' 'go it Tip, Come it Ty.' We urge the re-election of Van Buren because of his honesty, sagacity, statesmanship...and the Whigs answer that Harrison is a poor man and lives in a log cabin."[101]

No one was interested in appeals to reason. Old Tippecanoe ran the table, defeating Van Buren by 234 electoral votes to 60.

Notable accomplishments as president and events of his presidency

1. *Defending the prerogatives of the president*. Because he was not known for his political acumen, and no doubt also because of the circumstances of his election, Harrison at least twice in his brief tenure as president had to defend his prerogatives as the chief executive against advisors who would have been

---

100   Ibid., loc. 911.
101   Ibid., loc. 924.

happy to exercise the powers of president from behind the scenes. The first of these was the famed Whig senator and thrice-failed (his last run would come in 1844) presidential candidate Henry Clay, who was so demanding and dictatorial toward Harrison that the president had to tell him: "Mr. Clay, you forget that I am the President.... You use the privilege of a friend to lecture me. I take the same liberty with you—you are too impetuous. Much as I rely on your judgment, there are others whom I must consult...in many cases to determine adversely to your suggestions."[102]

Clay wasn't the last prominent politician to assert control over a sitting president; he wasn't even the last one during the vanishingly brief Harrison administration. The president chose a man, John Chambers, to be governor of the Iowa Territory; at a Cabinet meeting, however, Secretary of State Daniel Webster informed Harrison that the Cabinet had decided that the job should go to someone else. Harrison wrote on a piece of paper, handed the paper to Webster, and asked him to read it aloud. Webster read, "William Henry Harrison, President of the United States."[103] Harrison then declared, "William Henry Harrison, President of the United States, tells you, gentlemen, that, by God, John Chambers shall be governor of Iowa!"[104]

---

102   Lyon Gardiner Tyler, "The Annexation of Texas," *Magazine of American History*, vol. VIII, no. 6, June 1882, 379; Philip Weeks, *Buckeye Presidents: Ohioans in the White House* (Kent, OH: Kent State University Press, 2003), 36.

103   Weeks, 36.

104   Ibid.

Why his presidency did little good but not much damage

Harrison fell ill on March 25, 1841, just three weeks after taking office. On April 4, he died, having done virtually nothing as president. His campaign had far more enduring impact than his tenure. Martin Van Buren, whose distaste for the whole thing was understandable, overstated his case when he wrote in 1854: "The Presidential Canvass of 1840, and its attending occurrences, are at this moment, without reasonable doubt, subjects of regret with ninety-nine hundredths of the sober minded and well informed people of the United States."[105]

Van Buren was closer to the mark, however, when he added: "No one of that number can now hesitate in believing that the scenes thro' which the Country passed in that great political whirlwind were discreditable to our Institutions and could not fail, if often repeated, to lead to their subversion."[106]

Yet they would be repeated, again and again.

---

105   Van Buren, loc. 82.
106   Ibid., loc. 91.

TEN

JOHN TYLER

Library of Congress[107]

---

107   *President John Tyler, Half-Length Portrait, Facing Right,* ca. 1860, photograph,
       Library of Congress, https://www.loc.gov/item/96522383/.

Full name: John Tyler

Lived: March 29, 1790–January 18, 1862

Presidency: April 6, 1841–March 4, 1845

Party: Democratic until 1834, when he split with the
party over the nullification controversy and
Tariff of Abominations; Whig 1834–1841, when he
was expelled from the party for vetoing the Bank
of the United States; Democratic thereafter.

Evaluation: Very Good for America

Rating: 8

What qualified him to be president

The Whigs chose John Tyler for the vice-presidential spot in
1840 in hopes of attracting others who, like Tyler, were Democrats who had grown disenchanted over what they saw as
Jackson's high-handedness and trampling of states' rights. If
Whig solons had known that President Harrison would live
only a month beyond his inauguration, they would almost
certainly have picked someone else. John Quincy Adams, by
this time a Whig elder statesman, referred to him as "a political
sectarian, of the slave-driving, Virginian, Jeffersonian school,
principled against all improvement...No one ever thought of
his being placed in the executive chair."[108]

Tyler did not lack qualifications. He had been a member of
the House of Representatives, then governor of Virginia, and
after that a senator from Virginia. But most of this service had

---

108 Oliver Perry Chitwood, *John Tyler: Champion of the Old South* (New York:
American Historical Association, 1939), 207.

been as a member of the Democracy and acolyte of Andrew Jackson. He opposed the Bank of the United States, using federal funds for internal improvements, and high tariffs, all of which were central to the Whig program. His only quarrel with the Democrats had come over the nullification controversy; he thought that the states had every right to nullify federal laws.

Tyler's stance on nullification propelled him out of the Democracy and made him, he said, a "firm and decided Whig." The Whig name was taken from the British party that supported constitutional monarchy as opposed to royal absolutism; it began to be used in the South among Nullifiers who claimed Jackson was behaving like a tyrannical monarch.[109] However, Whig leader Henry Clay helped broker the compromise tariff that ended the nullification controversy, and the Whigs, incorporating many who had been Federalists, were not primarily known as a states' rights party.

What the Whigs were was an ideological muddle, united only by their opposition to Jackson and the Democrats. But states' rights advocates and foes of the Bank such as Tyler were decidedly a minority among them. Nor did Tyler seek a place on the party's ticket; he maintained during the campaign, "in the presence of my Heavenly Judge, that the nomination given to me was neither solicited nor expected."[110] The Whigs nominated him in order to broaden their base, and aware of the deep divisions among them, they didn't even try to put together a platform.

---

109   Lorant, 171.
110   Chitwood, 173.

How he became president

Tyler is remembered today, when he is remembered at all, as the second half of the slogan "Tippecanoe and Tyler Too," and that is about all he was during the campaign of 1840 as well. His campaign speeches shared the vagueness of the entire Whig endeavor; he spoke of "rescuing the country from the misrule of designing and ambitious men," that is, men he had counted as allies so recently that he avoided getting too specific about the wrongs they had committed.[111] The Whigs were aware of this as well, singing "We will vote for Tyler therefore/Without a why or wherefore."[112]

A month after the nation's first Whig president took office, the edge went off the Whigs' hard cider: the renegade Democrat Tyler was president of the United States.

Notable accomplishments as president and events of his presidency

1. *Settling the succession question.* When Harrison died, no one but John Tyler was sure of what should be done. The Constitution stipulated: "In Case of the Removal of the President from Office, or of his Death, Resignation, or Inability to discharge the Powers and Duties of the said Office, the Same shall devolve on the Vice President."[113] Some said that all this meant was that the vice president should discharge the president's

---

111   Ibid., 187.

112   Edward P. Crapol, *John Tyler, The Accidental President* (Chapel Hill: University of North Carolina Press, 2002), 18.

113   U.S. Constitution, art. 2, sec. 1, cl. 6.

duties until a new election could be held. Adams referred to him as "Acting President."[114]

Tyler, meanwhile, rejected the "Acting President" designation, and likewise refused to be addressed as "Vice President." He insisted that this meant that the vice president should become president in his own right, exercising the full powers of the presidency for the remainder of the president's term.

2. *Killing the Bank again.* With the Panic of 1837 widely blamed upon Jackson's refusal to recharter the Bank of the United States, the Whigs made persistent calls for the Bank's revival. With a Whig in the White House, Henry Clay, the Bank's foremost proponent, saw his chance, but Tyler was not an orthodox Whig; nor was he under Clay's thumb. He had never supported the Bank and made no secret of it, so it was not altogether surprising that he vetoed an attempt to revive it, as well as a second measure that Whig leaders in Congress fashioned after the first veto in an effort to find a version of the Bank that Tyler could accept.

Clay was enraged. In an attempt to pressure Tyler into submission, he engineered on September 11, 1841 the resignation of the entire Cabinet; only Secretary of State Daniel Webster, a rival of Clay's, stayed on. The Whigs expected Tyler to come crawling back and submit to Clay, accepting the Bank and more, or else see that he could not govern and resign the presidency. But Tyler stood firm. The Whigs accordingly, on September 13, 1841, expelled him from the party; Tyler remains the only sitting president to have been officially repudiated by his own party while in office.

---

114   Chitwood, 207.

Standing on his principles came at immense political cost for Tyler. Some of the Whigs in the House initiated an impeachment inquiry—the first attempt, but not the last, to use impeachment as a weapon to intimidate and discredit, if not remove from office, the man in the White House. Clay, however, although he despised Tyler, thought impeachment unwise, and the bill to begin an inquiry was defeated on January 10, 1843.

After so much antagonism with the Whigs, Tyler ultimately returned to the Democratic Party from which he had come and hoped it would nominate him for a term in his own right in 1844. But the Democrats shared the Whigs' distaste for political renegades, and he was never seriously considered. A third-party bid came to nothing; Tyler withdrew three months before the election.

3. *Defusing the Dorr Rebellion.* In Rhode Island, requirements that only large landowners could vote disenfranchised nearly the entire population of the state. In 1841, a group of those disenfranchised Rhode Islanders sought to remedy that by drawing up a new state constitution that gave the right to vote to nearly all white men (others remained disenfranchised) and naming their leader, T. W. Dorr, the new governor. However, the existing governor, Samuel King, did not step down or recognize the new constitution.

Both sides appealed to Tyler, who was caught between two unpalatable options: if he sided with King, he would be denying the popular will of most Rhode Islanders, but if he sided with Dorr, he would be acceding to subversion of the rule of law by an insurrectionist mob. As tensions rose and armed conflict looked likely, Tyler used that possibility to defuse the situation. He did not say anything about the suffrage question but stated unequivocally that "however painful duty...if resistance is made to the execution of the laws of Rhode Island by such force as the civil posse shall be unable to overcome, it will be the duty of this government to enforce the con stitutional guaranty."[115] The rebellion ran out of steam, and the situation was resolved peacefully; voter lists in Rhode Island expanded significantly in the election of 1844.

4. *The Webster-Ashburton Treaty.* The Webster-Ashburton Treaty of August 1842 between the U.S. and Britain settled longstanding disputes over the northern border of Maine and the Wisconsin Territory. These disputes had been quite tense over the years, and several times threatened to erupt in the war; the treaty quieted those tensions. Then, by invoking the Monroe Doctrine to warn the British not to interfere with the sovereignty of the Kingdom of Hawaii, he made it clear to the British that the treaty did not give them a free hand to meddle at the expense of American interests. The treaty also struck a strong blow for human rights by obliging both countries to act to end the transatlantic slave trade.

5. *Ending the Seminole War.* Toward the end of 1842, Tyler brought one of America's bloodiest conflicts with the American Indians, the Seminole War, to a close. He was unusual among the leaders of his day in wanting the Indians to be treated with justice and fairness. And rather than expelling them westward, as Jackson and Van Buren had done, he favored a policy of assimilating them into American society.

---

115   Ibid., 327.

For the most part, however, the Indians themselves were uninterested in this, and the impasse continued.

6. *Treaty with China.* In December 1844, the United States entered into a treaty of peace, amity, and commerce with China. When he heard that the particulars of the agreement had been concluded, Tyler was overjoyed. His wife recounted: "I thought the President would go off in an ecstasy a minute ago with the pleasant news."[116] This opening to the United States of the legendarily hermetic nation scrupulously followed Washington's directive: "The great rule of conduct for us in regard to foreign nations is in extending our commercial relations, to have with them as little political connection as possible."

7. *Annexing Texas.* Tyler, as a slave owner, did not share Van Buren's scruples about bringing the Republic of Texas into the Union as a slave state or, as one proposal had it, five slave states. Tyler was strongly in favor of annexation and sent his secretary of state, Abel P. Upshur, to negotiate a mutually acceptable agreement with President Sam Houston of Texas. By February 1844, the treaty's terms had been essentially agreed upon when Upshur and others were killed in a freak explosion aboard the U.S.S. *Princeton*; President Tyler was aboard, too, but his life was saved when he was detained below deck just before the disaster. His new secretary of state was John C. Calhoun, the nation's leading proponent of slavery. The choice of Calhoun galvanized abolitionist opposition to the annexation, and the whole process was derailed.

Still, Tyler hoped to ride the Texas issue into another term in the White House. The 1844 frontrunners, Van Buren and

---

116   Ibid., 332.

Clay, both opposed annexation, which Tyler thought gave him an opportunity to make the issue his own. The Democrats, however, denied him that opportunity by choosing the pro-annexation James K. Polk instead of Van Buren. Nonetheless, Tyler pressed on with annexation efforts and finally signed an annexation bill on March 1, 1845, three days before he left office.

In an ominous sign of what was to come, when news of the annexation reached the government of Mexico, it severed diplomatic relations with the United States. Mexico had never recognized the independence of Texas and considered the U.S. annexation of the Republic of Texas an encroachment upon its sovereignty.

Why his presidency was very good for America

By acting decisively and standing his ground on the legitimacy of his succession to the presidency, Tyler averted a constitutional crisis and provided a basis for the stability and continuity in the U.S. government upon the death of the president. The incentive to nullify an election by killing the president and forcing a new election was forever taken away. The Twenty-Fifth Amendment, adopted in 1967, 105 years after Tyler's death, codified the precedent he set when it stated: "In case of the removal of the President from office or of his death or resignation, the Vice President shall become President."[117] Tyler acted decisively again in the Dorr Rebellion, preventing armed conflict while strongly defending the rule of law.

---

117   U.S. Constitution, amend. 25, sec. 1.

Tyler's two vetoes of bills rechartering the Bank of the United States destroyed his presidency, but, like Jackson, with whom he had broken, John Tyler had saved America from the tyranny of an unelected elite class with the power to manipulate the political process. His opposition to the Bank was based primarily on his firm states' rights convictions, which ultimately led him, along with his positive view of slavery and loyalty to Virginia, to embrace the Confederacy. In November 1861, he was elected to the Confederate House of Representatives but died before he could take his seat. He is the only president of the United States to have been buried under the flag of a country other than the United States of America.

Nonetheless, even if Tyler had done the right thing for the wrong reasons, he prevented the revival of a dangerous source of corruption. Those who were so inclined would have to find other ways to buy senators and congressmen.

Tyler's support of the Webster-Ashburton Treaty was statesmanlike, for it helped calm the relationship between the former colonies and their mother country and set the two nations on the path to a lasting alliance. The ban on the transatlantic slave trade was farseeing coming from a slave-owning Southerner. Likewise far-seeing was his humane policy toward the Indians. And in the treaty with China, Tyler was operating on the principle of America first, opening up new trade possibilities without committing the nation to what could have proved to be a costly political alliance.

Tyler was less farseeing in pushing for the annexation of Texas. That annexation almost certainly would have happened

sooner or later, as the Republic of Texas was largely populated and governed by American settlers and had itself sought
annexation soon after winning its independence in 1836. Still,
Tyler's determination to ram annexation through over the
prudent objections of both Democrats and Whigs who rightly
saw that Texas would upset the balance between the free
states and slave states proved unwise. The admission of Texas
did indeed lead to more sectional strife, which ultimately
culminated in the Civil War. John Tyler, as a slaveholder, was
not the president to resolve once and for all the intractable
problem of some states considering legal, and even advocating
for, a practice that many in the other states considered to be
intrinsically evil. Maybe no one could have done it peacefully.
But John Tyler, like so many other presidents before and after
him, just postponed the problem.

ELEVEN

JAMES K. POLK

Library of Congress[118]

---

118   *President James K. Polk, Half-Length Portrait, Seated, Facing Right*, 1855–1865,
       photograph, Library of Congress, https://www.loc.gov/item/96522397/.

Full name: James Knox Polk
Lived: November 2, 1795–June 15, 1849
Presidency: March 4, 1845–March 4, 1849
Party: Democratic
Evaluation: Harmful for America but Also Did Some Good
Rating: 4

What qualified him to be president

James K. Polk had been a congressman from Tennessee for six years and speaker of the House for three of those years. He was so strong a supporter of President Jackson that he earned the nickname "Young Hickory," a counterpart to Jackson's "Old Hickory." In the House, he led Jackson's fight against the Bank of the United States, earning such wrath from the Bank's proponents that when Polk was in his last days as House speaker, Senator Henry Clay entered the House visitor's gallery to heckle him, shouting, "Go home, God damn you! Go home where you belong!"[119]

Polk did go home, where he served two years as governor of Tennessee. But he had national aspirations. As the 1844 presidential campaign loomed, Polk hoped that the Democrats would choose him as their vice-presidential candidate.

How he won

Polk was the first "dark horse" presidential candidate. As the Democratic National Convention began, it was generally

---

119   Lorant, 176.

assumed that former President Martin Van Buren would get the nomination for a third time. Old Tippecanoe was dead, and the Whigs were unlikely to come up with someone else they could propel into the White House by means of sheer ballyhoo. Nominating Van Buren in 1844 would be a way to redress the injustice of 1840.

The problem, however, was that Van Buren opposed the annexation of Texas, which made him unacceptable to the Southern pro-slavery delegates. They blocked his nomination, and the other contenders, who included Lewis Cass, the former secretary of war and ambassador to France; Van Buren's former vice president, Richard M. Johnson; and Pennsylvania senator James Buchanan, had even less support than Van Buren did, although Cass did begin to outpoll Van Buren on the convention's fifth ballot.

Finally, the convention turned to the strongly pro-annexation Polk, whom nobody had until then even considered to be a candidate. Meanwhile, the Whig candidate, Henry Clay, who was making his third try for the presidency, agreed with Van Buren on Texas, maintaining that "annexation and war with Mexico are identical" and claiming that significant popular opinion was against it: "Texas ought not to be received into the Union, as an integral part of it, in declared opposition to the wishes of a considerable and respectable portion of the Confederacy."[120] (In those pre-Civil War days, "the Confederacy" referred informally to the confederation of states that was the United States of America.)

---

120   Ibid., 173.

Clay, however, revealed that he knew Texas annexation was a popular issue when his son, smiling happily, came in to tell him whom the Democrats had chosen. Clay asked him, "Matty? Cass? Buchanan?" growing increasingly baffled as his son kept saying no. Clay finally asked, "Then who the devil is it?" When he heard it was Polk, Clay muttered, "Beat again, by God!" and poured himself a stiff drink.[121]

And he was. Polk ran an aggressive campaign centered on the slogans "All of Texas and all of Oregon" and "54°40' or fight." 54°40' was the latitude line marking the northern border of the Oregon Territory; the slogan indicated that in ongoing talks with Britain on the Oregon-Canada border, the United States would insist on the maximalist position and claim the entire territory. It would also annex Texas and demand the largest possible borders for the territory, claiming areas disputed with Mexico.

This program resonated with the American people, albeit not as decisively as the Democrats had hoped. Polk beat Clay with a plurality in the popular vote of only 39,000 and 170 electoral votes (to Clay's 105), exactly the same number as Van Buren had garnered in 1836.

Notable accomplishments as president and events of his presidency

1. *Bringing Texas into the Union.* Tyler had left Polk with a *fait accompli*, but there was still time when Polk took office for him to recall the messenger Tyler had sent to the Republic of

---

121   Ibid., 177.

Texas asking it to approve the annexation. Polk chose not to do so and instead went ahead with bringing Texas into the United States.

2. *The Mexican War and the acquisition of California and more.* Since Mexico had never recognized the independence of Texas, it saw the annexation of Texas as an act of war. Nevertheless, Mexico was much weaker than the U.S. and not disposed to start a war, even as the Americans demanded still more territory, claiming that the Texas/Mexico border was not the Nueces River, as Mexico insisted, but the Rio Grande River about thirty-five miles to the south. In this area were the trading post of Corpus Christi and the city of Laredo.

In April 1846, Mexican troops crossed the Rio Grande, which the Mexican government insisted was within Mexican territory. American troops moved to meet them, and a battle ensued in which eleven Americans were killed. Polk, accordingly, asserted in a May 11, 1846, message to Congress that the Mexican government, "after a long-continued series of menaces have at last invaded our territory and shed the blood of our fellow-citizens on our own soil."[122] It was war.

When that war ended with the signing of the Treaty of Guadalupe Hidalgo on February 2, 1848, Mexico was thoroughly defeated. The treaty fixed the U.S./Mexico border at the Rio Grande and ceded California, New Mexico, Arizona, and more to the United States in exchange for $15 million ($465 million today).

---

122   James D. Richardson, *A Compilation of the Messages and Papers of the Presidents*, vol. IV, part 3 (New York: Bureau of National Literature, Inc., 1897), loc. 1445, Kindle.

The Americans had fulfilled what many regarded as their Manifest Destiny to expand the American republic so that it stretched from the Atlantic to the Pacific Ocean.

3. *Settling the Oregon border.* Faithful to his campaign slogan "All of Texas and all of Oregon," President Polk was practically as belligerent toward Britain as he was toward Mexico, which was unwise in the extreme; Britain, after all, could fight back. At first, he insisted that the British cede to the United States all of the Oregon Territory, which then comprised not only the present-day states of Oregon and Washington, but also included the Canadian province of British Columbia up to just south of Alaska. However, as negotiations continued, it was clear that the British were never going to agree to this. Polk was ready to go to war with Britain, but cooler heads, alarmed at the prospect of the United States fighting both the British and the Mexicans at the same time, ultimately prevailed. Polk and the British finally agreed to partition the territory at the forty-ninth parallel, which remains the border to this day.

President Polk had succeeded in obtaining more than all of Texas and part of Oregon.

4. *Establishing the independent treasury system.* Polk revived Van Buren's idea of establishing an independent treasury to keep federal funds out of the control of private hands. Rather than depositing them in a new Bank of the United States or in state banks, the funds were kept in the U.S. Treasury in Washington and in sub-treasuries elsewhere. This was intended to forestall corruption, and it worked for decades, until other problems developed.

Why his presidency was harmful for America but also did some good

All the problems that Van Buren, Henry Clay, and other opponents of the annexation of Texas predicted would accompany its admission to the Union did indeed come to pass. They had warned that annexation would lead to war with Mexico, and it did.

That war, however, was begun by the United States, not by Mexico. That fact led two of Polk's successors to charge that the Mexican War was immoral and should never have been fought. Ulysses S. Grant, who fought in the Mexican War, stated in 1879: "I do not think there was ever a more wicked war than that waged by the United States on Mexico."[123] In 1885, he wrote in his famed *Memoirs* regarding the annexation of Texas that helped precipitate that war: "For myself, I was bitterly opposed to the measure, and to this day regard the war, which resulted, as one of the most unjust ever waged by a stronger against a weaker nation."[124]

Grant even saw the Civil War as divine judgment for the Mexican War: "The Southern rebellion was largely the outgrowth of the Mexican War. Nations, like individuals, are punished for their transgressions. We got our punishment in the most sanguinary and expensive war of modern times."[125]

---

123   James M. McPherson, "America's 'Wicked War,'" review of *A Wicked War: Polk, Clay, Lincoln, and the 1846 U.S. Invasion of Mexico*, Amy S. Greenberg, *New York Review of Books*, February 7, 2013.

124   Ulysses S. Grant, *Personal Memoirs of U.S. Grant*, vol. 1 (North Hollywood, CA: Aegypan Press, n.d.), 27.

125   Ibid., 28.

Abraham Lincoln was a Whig congressman while the war was raging; on December 22, 1847, he introduced into the House the "Spot Resolutions," taking issue with Polk's claim that Mexican forces had killed Americans within the United States and asking the president to specify at what spot they actually did so. Lincoln found the support for Polk's claims wanting, stating that the president could not deny and had not denied that the American troops had actually been the aggressors, and declared that "the war with Mexico was unnecessarily and unconstitutionally commenced."[126]

Lincoln's resolutions were ignored. President Polk never did specify where exactly on American soil American blood had been shed and, in fact, was basing his case on the assumption that the land between the Nueces and the Rio Grande was American soil, which was by no means settled at that point.

The fundamental problem with the Mexican War was not so much that it was a war of conquest as such. There have been wars of conquest throughout history, and as long as there are human beings, there will be more wars of conquest. Whether or not these are in every case morally evil, to roll them all back would require a mass migration of human beings that would make the India/Pakistan partition look like crossing the street. The problems lay in how the U.S. contravened some of its foremost principles in pursuing this war, as Grant and Lincoln articulated. They, and many other

---

126   Abraham Lincoln, "On the Mexican-American War" (speech, Washington, D.C., January 12, 1848), Modern Latin America, web supplement for 8th ed., https://library.brown.edu/create/modernlatinamerica/chapters/chapter-14-the-united-states-and-latin-america/primary-documents-w-accompanying-discussion-questions/abraham-lincoln-on-the-mexican-american-war-1846-48/.

Americans, considered an unprovoked, offensive war to be wrong in itself, ruled out for the United States by the principle that governments derive their just powers from the consent of the governed. Polk himself demonstrated his discomfort with waging an offensive war when he made his unverified claims about Mexicans having shed American blood on American soil.

What would have happened if the Mexican War had not taken place? It is always dangerous to speculate on what might have been; no one knows what would have been the consequences if the United States had not picked a fight with Mexico and taken Texas, California, and the rest. Perhaps Mexico would have reversed its earlier opposition and agreed to sell the territories. Perhaps war would have started in some other way. If the United States had never acquired these territories, it cannot be known whether it ever would have become a superpower and the leader of the free world; it is certainly hard to imagine the modern U.S. without them. Just one of these states—California—has the world's fifth-largest economy by itself. Polk's boldness did indeed result in great benefit for America.

But this benefit has come at a cost. The circumstances of the Mexican War have reverberated to the present day. Polk's goading of Mexico into war and the forced sale of a massive expanse of its territory created resentment that still festers today and is part of what makes the present-day problem of massive illegal immigration from Mexico so intractable; the government of Mexico is ill-inclined to be cooperative in American efforts to stop illegal aliens from crossing from Mexico into the former Mexican territories of Texas, New

Mexico, Arizona, and California. There are no doubt many Mexicans who still consider that territory to be theirs.

Polk also set an extremely negative precedent for the American waging of war. The Mexican War was the first, but unfortunately not the last, unnecessary and unprovoked war that the United States was to fight.

Van Buren and Clay were also correct that the annexation of Texas would aggravate the slavery question and divide the nation. Much of the escalation was due to a measure that Congressman David Wilmot of Pennsylvania introduced into the House on August 8, 1846, as an amendment to an appropriations bill for money to buy land from Mexico. Wilmot's amendment stipulated that "neither slavery nor involuntary servitude" would ever exist in "any territory from the Republic of Mexico by the United States, by virtue of any treaty which may be negotiated between them."[127] Even though it was never adopted, this "Wilmot Proviso" roiled the nation for years thereafter, right up until the Civil War. The division between those who believed slavery was a moral evil that should everywhere be eradicated and those who maintained that it was a just and even divinely ordained system was growing more heated and began to dominate American public discourse.

As Lincoln famously said later, a house divided against itself indeed could not stand, and the United States of America in the time between the Mexican War and the Civil War was most certainly a house divided.

---

127   David Wilmot, "Wilmot Proviso," August 8, 1846, Center for Legislative Archives, National Archives and Records Administration, https://www.archives.gov/files/legislative/resources/education/wilmot-polk/wilmot-proviso.pdf.

TWELVE

ZACHARY TAYLOR

Library of Congress[128]

---

128   Mathew B. Brady, *Zachary Taylor, Half-Length Portrait, Head in Profile to the Right*, 1844–1849, photograph, Library of Congress, https://www.loc.gov/item/2004664062/.

Full name: Zachary Taylor
Lived: November 24, 1784–July 9, 1850
Presidency: March 5, 1849–July 9, 1850
Party: Whig
Evaluation: Did Little Good but Not Much Damage
Rating: 5

What qualified him to be president

Zachary Taylor was a major general in the U.S. Army and a hero of the Mexican War. Unlike the Whig Party's last military candidate, William Henry Harrison, Taylor had no experience in elective office whatsoever when he became a presidential candidate. On September 27, 1847, Taylor wrote that he would not accept the presidential nomination "exclusively from either of the great parties which divide the country," for "the moment I done so [sic], I would become the slave of a party instead of the chief magistrate of the nation should I be elected."[129] However, he continued, with an imperfect grasp of spelling and grammar (which are rendered here as in the original):

> Without meddling with politics, or mixing myself up with political men in any way I have for many years considered the policy advocated by the whigs for the most part, more nearly assimelated to those of Mr Jefferson than those

---

129   Zachary Taylor to Dr. R. C. Wood, September 27, 1847, in *Letters of Zachary Taylor from the Battle-Fields of the Mexican War* (Rochester: University of Rochester, 1908), 134.

of the opponents which induced me to range myself on that side, & with these views I would have voted for Mr Clay at the last election, had I voted at all, which I have never done for any one of our chief magistrates since I entered the army or before, which is near forty years....[130]

Not only had Taylor never voted for a presidential candidate, he disapproved of the very act of voting for who should be president: "Could the present state of our national affairs have been forseen [sic], I believe that every man who loved his country more than party or office, would have done the same."[131]

After stating that he supported Whig policies, Taylor proceeded to state that he did not support a resurrection of the Bank of the United States, a cause dear to Whig hearts. The Bank, he said, was "dead, & will not be revived in my time."[132] He took a solidly middle-of-the-road stance on the tariff, saying it should be "increased only for revenue," which was not a ringing endorsement of the Whig support for high tariffs but was not a rejection of it either.[133] As for internal improvements, he said they would "go on in spite of presidential vetoes," which was again not an enthusiastic endorsement of the Whig position but still not a dissent.[134] As for the Wilmot Proviso, as president he would do nothing: it "must, or ought

---

130   Ibid.
131   Ibid.
132   Ibid.
133   Ibid.
134   Taylor to Dr. Wood, in *Letters of Zachary Taylor*, 135.

to be left to congress, the president has nothing to do with making laws, he must approve or veto them; when approved or passed by a majority of two thirds, his business is to see them proper executed."[135]

Taylor wrote firmly: "I would not be chief magistrate on any other terms than those which I have avowed; & have written to several political men to that effect."[136]

That was good enough for the Whigs, who were eager to recapture their magic of 1840.

How he won

Against Taylor the Democrats put up Senator Lewis Cass of Michigan, who defeated Martin Van Buren to obtain the nomination. Van Buren's anti-slavery position was unpalatable to Southern Democrats; Cass, by contrast, favored the principle of popular sovereignty, that is, allowing each state or territory to vote to allow or to outlaw slavery. When asked during the campaign about his position on slavery, Taylor responded that he owned three hundred slaves, and the South was satisfied with that answer; meanwhile, his statement on deferring to Congress made him acceptable to the North.

The campaign was somewhat lackluster, with Whigs attempting unsuccessfully to make Taylor into the second coming of Old Tippecanoe. But the enthusiasm of eight years before could not be recaptured. The principal excitement in the campaign was supplied by the old foe of Tippecanoe and

---

135   Ibid.
136   Ibid.

Tyler Too, Martin Van Buren, who ran as the candidate of the abolitionist Free Soil Party and took enough votes away from Cass in New York to tip the state to Taylor. If New York had gone for Cass, he would have been elected president.

Taylor seemed to be aware that Van Buren's third-party run would make all the difference for him, writing several weeks before the election: "If I am elected at all, it will be by a union of a portion of Whigs, Democrats & native votes."[137] President Polk was dismayed for the same reason. He charged that Taylor was "without political information and without experience in civil life," and was "wholly unqualified for the station, and being elected by the Federal party [that is, the Whigs] and the various factions of dissatisfied persons who have from time to time broken off from the Democratic party [that is, Van Buren and his followers], he must be in their hands, and be under their absolute control."[138]

As it turned out, he wasn't.

Notable accomplishments as president and events of his presidency

1. *Standing against the slave power.* Southern Whigs had supported Taylor because they believed that, as a slave owner himself, he would protect their interests. As president, however, Taylor could no longer maintain the ambiguity that had marked his campaign and made it clear that he was more

---

137   Taylor to Dr. Wood, October 19, 1847, in *Letters of Zachary Taylor*, 143.
138   Charles A. McCoy, *Polk and the Presidency* (Austin: University of Texas Press, 2014).

interested in preserving the Union than in favoring his own section of it.

This unfolded during the roiling controversies over what to do with the massive territories that had been obtained from Mexico. In 1848, gold was struck in California; the Gold Rush was on, and California's population skyrocketed. Taylor, in December 1849, asked Congress to admit California to the Union as a free state and New Mexico and Utah as territories, with their status on slavery undetermined.

Southerners were furious. Some Southern leaders threatened that the South would leave the Union if portions of California and New Mexico were not opened to slaveholders. But there was no significant slaveholding population in California, and it voted to ban slavery. Taylor accordingly warned, in his message to Congress of January 23, 1850, against adding "a condition to her admission as a State affecting her domestic institutions contrary to the wishes of her people."[139] The following month, Taylor met with Southern leaders who threatened secession unless they got their way; the old general responded: "If it becomes necessary I'll take command of the army myself and if you are taken in rebellion against the Union, I will hang you with less reluctance than I hanged the deserters and spies in Mexico."[140]

---

139   Zachary Taylor, "Message Regarding Newly Acquired Territories" (speech, January 23, 1850), UVA Miller Center, https://millercenter.org/the-presidency/presidential-speeches/january-23-1850-message-regarding-newly-acquired-territories.

140   John S. D. Eisenhower, *Zachary Taylor: The American Presidents Series: The 12th President, 1849–1850* (New York: Macmillan, 2008), 134.

Senator John C. Calhoun, the great champion of the slave-holding South, was unmoved. In a speech on March 4, 1850, that was read out by Senator James Murray Mason of Virginia, as Calhoun was too ill to read it himself, he again threatened secession: "The equilibrium between the two sections," Calhoun's speech stated, "in which the Government as it stood when the constitution was ratified and the Government put in action, has been destroyed."[141] This was because of the new territory acquired from Mexico: "The North is making the most strenuous efforts to appropriate the whole to herself, by excluding the South from every foot of it."[142] As a result, "the Southern States...cannot remain, as things now are, consistently with honor and safety, in the Union."[143]

Why his presidency did little good but not much damage

In this tense atmosphere, Senator Henry Clay and others began working on a compromise that would allow for the admission of California as a free state but mollify the South in other ways, notably by a harsh new Fugitive Slave Law that outraged abolitionists who encouraged slaves to run away from their masters and sheltered them when they did, as it required captured slaves to be returned to their masters.

---

141   John C. Calhoun, *Speeches of John C. Calhoun Delivered in the House of Representatives and in the Senate of the United States* (New York: D. Appleton, 1883), 544.

142   Ibid., 548.

143   Ibid., 543.

Clay's compromise also allowed voters in the new territories to decide whether or not they wanted slavery.

Taylor opposed this compromise and any possible extension of slavery into the Southwest, which he believed was unsuited to it. However, he would not live to see the controversy play out: on July 4, 1850, he attended festivities at the Washington Monument, where he ate large amounts of cherries and other fruits, washing them down with ice water and milk. He soon fell ill, and, on July 9, he died, with the unity of the nation hanging in the balance.

Rumors that enraged defenders of slavery had poisoned Taylor arose nearly a century and a half after his death, when Americans were more likely to believe that slaveholders, by dint of being slaveholders, were evil in every respect and would stop at nothing to preserve their power. These rumors were put to rest in 1991, when his body was exhumed and tests conducted. Taylor died wearied and dispirited, saying as he lay ill: "I should not be surprised if this were to terminate in my death. I did not expect to encounter what has beset me since my elevation to the Presidency. God knows I have endeavored to fulfill what I conceived to be an honest duty. But I have been mistaken. My motives have been misconstrued, and my feelings most grossly outraged."[144]

Many of his successors would face even worse.

---

144   James Harrison Kennedy, *The American Nation: Its Executive, Legislative, Political, Financial, Judicial, and Industrial History,* vol. 2 (Cleveland: Williams Publishing Company, 1888), 736.

THIRTEEN

MILLARD FILLMORE

Library of Congress[145]

---

145   Mathew B. Brady, *Millard Fillmore, Three-Quarter Length Portrait, Seated, Facing Left*, 1850–1874, photograph, New York, Library of Congress, https://www.loc.gov/item/96522448/.

Full name: Millard Fillmore
Lived: January 7, 1800–March 8, 1874
Presidency: July 10, 1850–March 4, 1853
Party: Whig
Evaluation: Did Little Good but Not Much Damage
Rating: 5

What qualified him to be president

In 1855, Oxford University offered Millard Fillmore an honorary degree. The former president declined, saying: "They would probably ask, 'Who's Fillmore? What's he done? Where did he come from?' And then my name would, I fear, give them an excellent opportunity to make jokes at my expense."[146]

He may have had a point. Before the Whig Party nominated him for vice president, he had served eight years in the House of Representatives, without attracting much notice. When he got the nomination, he was serving as comptroller of New York. The Whig ticket of 1848 featured two men with the least political experience of any major party ticket in American history.

How he became president

"Who's Fillmore?" indeed. Fillmore got the vice-presidential nod because he was from New York, which the Whigs knew they needed in order to win in 1848 (and that state actually did put them over the top, with a bit of help from Martin Van

---

146   Thomas Vinciguerra, "Why He Gets the Laughs," *New York Times*, March 18, 2007.

Buren). Fillmore was also an acceptable vice-presidential candidate because he was thought to be a strong supporter of Henry Clay, who had been frustrated in his presidential aspirations yet again when Zachary Taylor was nominated.

Notable accomplishments as president and events of his presidency

1. *The Compromise of 1850.* Unlike Tyler, the only other vice president up to that time who had assumed the presidency, Fillmore broke with his predecessor immediately. He asked for, and received, the resignations of Taylor's Cabinet members, who had accorded him scant respect. He filled his own Cabinet with supporters of Henry Clay's compromise, which was passed in September 1850. The Union was preserved—for another decade.

This was accomplished by giving both sides some of what they wanted, while not addressing the central issue underlying all the disagreements: whether slavery was immoral and should be illegal, or good and proper and should thus be preserved. The compromise stipulated that California would enter the Union as a free state, as Taylor had wished; also, slavery would be outlawed in the District of Columbia, and a border dispute between the state of Texas and the Territory of New Mexico was settled largely in favor of New Mexico, although Texas emerged larger than it had been in Clay's initial version of the compromise. It overrode New Mexico's territorial constitution that banned slavery and stipulated that New Mexico and the other new Territory of Utah could vote to allow or outlaw slavery; everyone knew that the vote was likely to go against the slaveholders, barring massive migration from the South.

The compromise also had the federal government take over Texas's $10 million debt ($314 billion today) and, above all, gave the South a harsh new Fugitive Slave Law that required officials in free states and in territories where slavery was outlawed to do all they could to locate and return escaped slaves to their owners, or face hefty fines for not doing so. Civilians could be forced to help find runaway slaves, and those who aided the runaways could be imprisoned.

2. *Refusing to annex Cuba.* Some Southerners believed they had been cheated out of their fair share of the lands taken from Mexico; Southerners as well as Northerners had fought in the Mexican War and deserved, they felt, equal representation in the division of its spoils. The South's Manifest Destiny, they concluded, lay not in the West but even farther South. Calls to acquire Cuba, at that time a Spanish colony, either by peaceable means or by force, and admit it to the Union as a slave state grew more insistent throughout Fillmore's presidency.

In his annual message to Congress of December 6, 1852, the president replied judiciously that he would consider Cuba's "incorporation into the Union at the present time as fraught with serious peril. Were this island comparatively destitute of inhabitants or occupied by a kindred race, I should regard it, if voluntarily ceded by Spain, as a most desirable acquisition. But under existing circumstances I should look upon its incorporation into our Union as a very hazardous measure. It would bring into the Confederacy a population of a different national stock, speaking a different language, and not likely to harmonize with the other members."[147] He also believed, almost certainly correctly, that it would upset the Compromise of 1850: "It would probably affect in a prejudicial manner the industrial interests of the South, and it might revive those conflicts of opinion between the different sections of the country which lately shook the Union to its center, and which have been so happily compromised."[148]

Why his presidency did little good but not much damage

Fillmore's warning that the acquisition of Cuba would be unwise because its population was linguistically and culturally different from Americans was entirely uncontroversial in 1852. It was taken for granted, and would be for over a century thereafter, that while immigrants to the United States were welcome, they were expected to assimilate and adopt American values. Cuba as a Southern state would all at once add a large, unassimilated, and culturally distinct population to the United States; the potential for strife of all kinds would have been enormous.

Fillmore's reservations were entirely reasonable; only a few years later, however, the former president would mount a third-party bid to return to the White House as the candidate of the American Party, which was actively nativist and

---

147   Millard Fillmore, "Third Annual Message" (speech, December 6, 1852), UVA Miller Center, https://millercenter.org/the-presidency/presidential-speeches/december-6-1852-third-annual-message.

148   Ibid.

anti-immigrant and proclaimed its "eternal hostility to Foreign and Roman Catholic influence."[149]

Fillmore's message to Congress was more measured, and his becoming the American Party standard-bearer was unfortunate. Nowadays, concern that immigrants assimilate and adopt American values is routinely conflated with nativism and general hostility to immigration as such; no one remembers Fillmore today, but his career trajectory does nothing to dispel this impression.

Meanwhile, President Fillmore was happy with the Compromise of 1850, stating happily that it was a "final settlement" of the slavery issue.[150] The Union, he thought, was saved. Fillmore had gotten the vice-presidential nomination because he was a Northern Whig, while Taylor was, most assumed, a Southern Whig. However, he was not an abolitionist, and with the compromise, Fillmore demonstrated that the preservation of the Union was more important to him than loyalty to any particular section. The problem was that nothing was actually settled. In those febrile times, Fillmore managed to dissatisfy everyone: instead of being happy with what they got, both Northerners and Southerners were enraged over what they didn't get.

Southerners were angered by the expansion of areas of the country where slavery was outlawed, which they saw as

---

149   "K. N. Ticket," ca. 1855, Ohio History Central, https://ohiohistorycentral. org/w/File:OHS_AL04131.jpg

150   Ron Gorman, "Kidnapped into Slavery: Northern States' Rights, Part 1," *Oberlin Heritage Center Blog*, December 19, 2013, http://www.oberlinheritagecenter.org/blog/2013/12/ kidnapped-into-slavery-northern-states-rights-part-1/.

upsetting the balance of power between free and slave states that had hitherto been maintained. Many also saw the Fugitive Slave Law as one that would never be enforced and was hardly equal compensation for the provisions of the compromise that favored the free states. They were right about the Fugitive Slave Law, as abolitionists were outraged at a law that required them to aid and abet what they considered to be a moral abomination.

No one except the most hardline abolitionists and Southern fire-eaters wanted to touch the moral issue. In his message to Congress on December 2, 1850, Fillmore declared that "the great law of morality ought to have a national as well as a personal and individual application."[151] But he was talking about foreign policy, not slavery. "In our domestic policy," he added, "the Constitution will be my guide, and in questions of doubt I shall look for its interpretation to the judicial decisions of that tribunal which was established to expound it and to the usage of the Government, sanctioned by the acquiescence of the country. I regard all its provisions as equally binding."[152] Not a word about morality.

Much as Fillmore tried, there was, at this point, no pleasing everyone. The nation was headed for civil war, and even though the Compromise of 1850 postponed that conflict for a decade, it was once again only an exercise in postponing the problem. Fillmore, like all the other presidents of the

---

151   Millard Fillmore, "First Annual Message" (speech, December 2, 1850), UVA Miller Center, https://millercenter.org/the-presidency/presidential-speeches/december-2-1850-first-annual-message.
152   Ibid.

period, including Abraham Lincoln initially, put preserving the Union over acting against the moral evil of slavery. Unless William Lloyd Garrison had been elected, the situation would likely have been the same no matter who was president.

Ultimately both ends were attained: the Union was preserved and slavery abolished, but only at the cost of a terrible war. Fillmore tried to stave off that war, but this only prolonged the contradiction that lay at the heart of a nation that cherished the principle that "all men are created equal" but held a sizable population in bondage. Jefferson had likely been correct in his initial draft of the Declaration of Independence: the time to abolish slavery was at the very beginning of the republic. But there may never have been a United States of America in that case, as the South would have gone its own way sooner rather than later. And Jefferson didn't grasp this nettle, either, when he was president for eight years.

There was no visionary in the days before the Civil War who could cut through this Gordian knot.

FOURTEEN

FRANKLIN PIERCE

Library of Congress[153]

---

153   *President Franklin Pierce, Three-Quarter Length Portrait, Seated, Facing Right, with Left Hand inside Vest*, 1855–1865, photograph, Library of Congress, https://www.loc.gov/item/96522460/.

Full name: Franklin Pierce
Lived: November 23, 1804–October 8, 1869
Presidency: March 4, 1853–March 4, 1857
Party: Democratic
Evaluation: Disastrous for America
Rating: 1

What qualified him to be president

Franklin Pierce was young (forty-seven) for a presidential candidate, he was handsome, he had served with distinction in the Mexican War and attained the rank of brigadier general, he had also been a congressman and a senator, and he was a friend of Nathaniel Hawthorne (who wrote his campaign biography, a decidedly uninspiring and thin addition to the celebrated author's oeuvre). What was there not to like about Franklin Pierce?

What's more, as the slavery issue continued to roil the country after the Compromise of 1850 was supposed to have put it to rest, Pierce had appeal for both sections: he was a "doughface," a Northerner who did not oppose slavery and objected to abolitionism. He wasn't initially a candidate for president in 1852, but the Democratic National Convention deadlocked. Neither the front-runner, Lewis Cass, who had narrowly lost to Taylor four years before, nor his principal challenger, Polk's secretary of state, James Buchanan, could garner enough support to put them over the top. Pierce didn't receive any votes at all until the thirty-fifth ballot and didn't win until the forty-ninth.

How he won

The Whigs, deeply split over slavery and other issues, rolled out for the third time a no-issue campaign featuring a war hero, Major General Winfield Scott, the commanding general of the U.S. Army. Like Taylor, Scott had never held elective office, and so made Pierce, with his limited time in Congress, look like the more experienced candidate. By this time used to Whigs running campaigns of ballyhoo and bluster, the Democrats were ready to operate on the same level, charging that Scott was a "weak, conceited, foolish, blustering disciple of gunpowder."[154] Pierce, said the Whigs, was a coward under fire in the Mexican War; he "tumbled from his horse just as he was getting into one fight...fainted and fell in the opening of a second...got sick and had to go to bed on the eve of a third, and...came pretty near getting into a fourth, missing it only by about an hour."[155] The Whigs also charged Pierce with alcoholism, calling him "the hero of many a well-fought bottle."[156]

That was the tenor of the entire campaign. The nation was sitting on a powder keg that no one wanted to address: the issue of slavery. The Whigs, even more divided than the Democrats, could muster none of the enthusiasm they had aroused for Harrison, or even for Taylor. Pierce trounced Scott after a campaign in which both candidates avoided the key issues splitting the country as much as they possibly could. The youngest president up to that time would take office; his failings, however, could not be ascribed to the callowness of youth.

---

154   Boller, loc. 1198.
155   Ibid., loc. 1206.
156   Joseph Cummins, *Anything for a Vote: Dirty Tricks, Cheap Shots, and October Surprises in U.S. Presidential Campaigns* (Philadelphia: Quirk Books, 2007), 86.

Notable accomplishments as president and events of his presidency

1. *The Kansas-Nebraska Act and Bleeding Kansas.* Senator Stephen A. Douglas of Illinois was the main architect of the principle of popular sovereignty, the idea that slavery would be approved or outlawed in the new territories of Utah and New Mexico by popular vote. Popular sovereignty became associated with him, and he thought he could use it to propel himself into the White House. At the deadlocked 1852 Democratic National Convention, he led the field on the thirtieth and thirty-first ballots, but his support faded after that. Two years later, he sought to add to his luster as a presidential candidate by applying the principle more broadly.

Douglas drafted the Kansas-Nebraska Act to establish new territories by those names in part of the land that had been acquired in the Louisiana Purchase and was still unorganized. He wanted them organized although they were sparsely populated because doing so would make it easier to route a transcontinental railroad through them. The act stipulated that Kansas and Nebraska would decide by popular sovereignty whether to allow slavery or not. Since both territories lay north of the 36°30' parallel, slavery should have been outlawed in both of them, according to the Missouri Compromise.

That should have been the end of the matter, with popular sovereignty definitively ruled out for Kansas and Nebraska. Instead, Douglas and his allies were determined to repeal the Missouri Compromise and won Pierce over to the idea that doing so would be the best way to bring peace to the nation once and for all over the slavery question. Slavery would be voted up or down in various states and territories, and all would be well.

Congress approved the Kansas-Nebraska Act, Pierce signed it, and all was not well. The fatal weakness of the principle of popular sovereignty immediately became obvious: proponents and foes of slavery rushed into Kansas and Nebraska in order to tip the vote in their direction. Armed conflict ensued and persisted throughout Pierce's presidency; "Bleeding Kansas" became a symbol of the intractability of the slavery issue and the absolute ineffectiveness of President Pierce.

In a message on the unrest in Kansas dated January 24, 1856, Pierce claimed that "serious and threatening disturbances in the Territory of Kansas" had been "speedily quieted without the effusion of blood and in a satisfactory manner."[157] However, he admitted that "disorders will continue to occur there, with increasing tendency to violence."[158] In a proclamation on Kansas issued on February 11, 1856, Pierce called on outsiders "to abstain from unauthorized intermeddling in the local concerns of the Territory," and warned that "any endeavor to intervene by organized force will be firmly withstood."[159]

---

157   Franklin Pierce, "Message Regarding Disturbances in Kansas" (speech, January 24, 1856), UVA Miller Center, https://millercenter.org/the-presidency/presidential-speeches/january-24-1856-message-regarding-disturbances-kansas.
158   Ibid.
159   Franklin Pierce, "Proclamation Addressing Disturbances in Kansas" (speech, February 11, 1856), UVA Miller Center, https://millercenter.org/the-presidency/presidential-speeches/february-11-1856-proclamation-addressing-disturbances-kansas.

Few paid any attention. Kansas continued to bleed. Three months after Pierce's proclamation, pro-slavery forces in Lawrence, Kansas, attacked free-staters, destroying the offices of two abolitionist newspapers and a hotel that abolitionists frequented. The Pierce administration did nothing and could do nothing. The sacking of Lawrence was emblematic of its failure.

Likewise emblematic of the outrageously overheated state of the public debate was an incident that unfolded on the floor of the Senate in May 1856. On May 19 and 20, Senator Charles Sumner of Massachusetts delivered a lengthy speech entitled "The Crime against Kansas." In it, he resorted to lurid imagery to make his case, saying: "Not in any common lust for power did this uncommon tragedy have its origin. It is the rape of a virgin Territory, compelling it to the hateful embrace of Slavery; and it may be clearly traced to a depraved longing for a new slave State, the hideous offspring of such a crime, in the hope of adding to the power of Slavery in the National Government."[160]

Sumner also mocked Senator Andrew Butler of South Carolina in terms that strongly hinted of the widespread belief among abolitionists that slaveholders were primarily interested in their female slaves for sexual use: "The senator from South Carolina has read many books of chivalry, and believes himself a chivalrous knight, with sentiments of honor and courage. Of course he has chosen a mistress to whom he has made his vows, and who, though ugly to others, is always

---

160   Charles Sumner, *The Crime against Kansas* (New York: John P. Jewett & Company, 1856), 5.

lovely to him; though polluted in the sight of the world, is chaste in his sight; — I mean the harlot Slavery."[161]

Southern honor was offended, and Southern honor would be avenged. On May 22, Congressman Preston Brooks of South Carolina, Butler's cousin, entered the Senate chamber and made for Sumner's desk. He told the senator: "Mr. Sumner, I have read your speech twice over carefully. It is a libel on South Carolina, and Mr. Butler, who is a relative of mine."[162] He began beating Sumner over the head with a heavy wooden cane and did not stop when Sumner began bleeding profusely and knocked his desk loose from the floor (it was bolted down) in an attempt to get away. Brooks didn't stop until he had broken his cane. He later recounted: "I...gave him about 30 first rate stripes. Towards the last he bellowed like a calf. I wore my cane out completely but saved the Head which is gold."[163]

Both men were hailed as heroes. Southerners inundated Brooks with canes to celebrate his attack and replace the one he had broken over Sumner's head. The cane was not the only thing that was broken. The Union was as well.

Why his presidency was disastrous for America

When Pierce was nominated for president, the story went around that a man in the candidate's hometown of Hillsborough, New Hampshire, was skeptical about his fitness for the job (spelling and grammar as in the original): "Wall, wall,

---

161   Ibid., 9.
162   Michael S. Green, *Politics and America in Crisis: The Coming of the Civil War* (Santa Barbara, CA: ABC-CLIO, 2010), 94.
163   Ibid.

dew tell! Frank Pierce for President! Neow Frank's a good fellow, I admit, and I wish him well, he made a good State's attorney, that's no doubt about that, and he made a far Jedge, thar's no denying that, and nobody kaint complain of him as a Congressman, but when it comes to the hull Yewnited States I dew say that in my jedgment Frank Pierce is a-goin to *spread durned thin*."[164]

The old New Englander was right. Pierce significantly reduced the national debt, but that is about the only positive accomplishment of his administration.

Northern politicians (and even some Southerners, including Senator Sam Houston of Texas, a former president of the Republic of Texas and the only former foreign head of state to take a seat in the U.S. Congress) were appalled at the repeal of the Missouri Compromise. Instead of calming the controversy over slavery, the Kansas-Nebraska Act made it rage more fiercely than ever.

There is no doubt that the Missouri Compromise was flawed. It was not remotely viable as a lasting solution to the problem of slavery, as it attempted to accommodate fundamentally incompatible views of the morality of the peculiar institution and enable people who thought slavery was evil to live in harmony side by side with people who thought abolitionists were evil. Nonetheless, it had prevented civil war from breaking out for three decades. Foes of slavery saw its repeal, and Pierce's approval of that repeal, as something even worse than a betrayal: it was a unilateral abrogation of the compact that had allowed the Union to continue to exist.

---

164   Boller, loc. 1216.

And so, it wouldn't for much longer. Bleeding Kansas was appalling enough in itself, as was Pierce's inability to bring the violence to a halt. But, for abolitionists, presidential perfidy compounded presidential impotence. There are two kinds of failed presidents: those who were effective in imposing unwise and destructive policies upon the country, and those who failed to deal adequately with a crisis, thus making it even worse. Franklin Pierce managed to be both.

FIFTEEN

JAMES BUCHANAN

Library of Congress[165]

---

165   *James Buchanan / Engraved by Permission, from the Original in the Possession of J.C. Buttre*, ca. 1860, photograph, Library of Congress, https://www.loc.gov/item/89707760/.

Full name: James Buchanan
Lived: April 23, 1791–June 1, 1868
Presidency: March 4, 1857–March 4, 1861
Party: Democratic
Evaluation: Disastrous for America
Rating: 0

What qualified him to be president

On paper, James Buchanan looked better qualified to be president of the United States than virtually everyone else in the country. He had been a member of the Pennsylvania House of Representatives and then, for ten years, a U.S. representative from that state. Andrew Jackson then sent him to Saint Petersburg as U.S. minister to Russia; when he returned, he served another ten years in Congress, this time in the Senate. He was secretary of state in the Polk administration and minister to Britain in the Pierce administration. He had tried for the Democratic Party's presidential nomination in 1844, 1848, and 1852.

In 1856, it was finally his turn, as the Democrats rejected Pierce's bid for renomination. The fact that Buchanan had been in London for most of the Pierce administration may have been what made him most attractive to the delegates much more than his long résumé: he hadn't had to take a stand on the Kansas-Nebraska Act.

How he won

By 1856, the Whig Party had collapsed under the weight of its contradictions. Buchanan and the Democrats faced the first presidential candidate offered by a new party, the Republicans, which anti-slavery forces, including former Whigs and even some Democrats, founded in Wisconsin in 1854. The Republican Party was not exactly national as the 1856 campaign began; its forthright anti-slavery stance made it anathema in the slaveholding states, where its first presidential candidate, the famous explorer and former senator John C. Frémont, did not appear on the ballot. In the North, the race was Buchanan versus Frémont, but in the South, it was Buchanan against the candidate of the nativist American Party (also known as "Know Nothings" after the answer they were instructed to give when questioned about the organization: "I know nothing."): former president Millard Fillmore.

Buchanan's election was a foregone conclusion, as his opposition was split between two candidates, and during the campaign, he was careful to ensure that he never, in the words of the *Richmond Enquirer*, "uttered a word which could pain the most sensitive Southern heart."[166] The South could thus be relied upon to fall in behind him, as could "doughface" Northerners who objected to abolitionism. At age sixty-five, Buchanan won the prize he had sought since he had been a much younger man, and the oldest president up to that point followed the youngest into the White House.

Still, Buchanan won only 45 percent of the popular vote, with Frémont garnering 33 percent and Fillmore 22 percent.

---

166   Boller, loc. 1243.

Frémont won no states south of Ohio; Buchanan won none north of his native Pennsylvania. It was a sign of worse to come. Buchanan would still have won in the Electoral College even if his opposition had united behind one candidate, but the message was clear: most voters did not think James Buchanan was the answer to the increasing divisions in the nation. And he wasn't.

Notable accomplishments as president and events of his presidency

1. *Endorsing popular sovereignty.* When Buchanan became president, the blood was still flowing in Kansas, a direct consequence of the principle of popular sovereignty. The problem wasn't putting slavery in Kansas up to a vote. Rather, it was the idea of voting on a principle that some considered a great moral evil and others thought to be a cornerstone of a well-ordered society as if it were akin to a proposal about the route for the new highway. It was inevitable that to influence the Kansas vote, people from other areas would stream into the territory, and that violence would break out.

Yet while it was still raging, during his inaugural address, Buchanan exclaimed: "What a happy conception, then, was it for Congress to apply this simple rule, that the will of the majority shall govern, to the settlement of the question of domestic slavery in the Territories."[167]

---

167   James Buchanan, "Inaugural Address" (speech, March 4, 1857), UVA Miller Center, https://millercenter.org/the-presidency/presidential-speeches/march-4-1857-inaugural-address.

2. *The Dred Scott decision.* On March 6, 1857, the Supreme Court, under the leadership of Chief Justice Roger B. Taney, published its infamous ruling in *Dred Scott v. Sandford*, a case that had been brought by Dred Scott, a slave who had been taken into free territory and argued that, as a result, he was now free. The court voted 7–2 against Scott. In his opinion, Taney wrote that blacks were a "subordinate and inferior class of beings" who "are not included, and were not intended to be included, under the word 'citizens' in the Constitution, and can therefore claim none of the rights and privileges which that instrument provides for and secures to citizens of the United States."[168]

Dred Scott, consequently, was not even eligible to sue, and "no word can be found in the Constitution which gives Congress a greater power over slave property or which entitles property of that kind to less protection that property of any other description." Thus, the Missouri Compromise, already a dead letter, was declared unconstitutional: "the act of Congress which prohibited a citizen from holding and owning property of this kind in the territory of the United States north of the line therein mentioned is not warranted by the Constitution, and is therefore void."[169] Congress could not prohibit slavery in any territory of the United States.

Buchanan strongly endorsed the decision. Since he and others who endorsed it styled themselves as strict constructionists, the Dred Scott decision has been used as Exhibit A

---

168 *Scott v. Sandford*, 60 U.S. 393, 404–405, Legal Information Institute, Cornell Law School, https://www.law.cornell.edu/supremecourt/text/60/393#writing-USSC_CR_0060_0393_ZO.

169 Ibid., 452.

of why faithful adherence to the letter of the Constitution is unwise and unjust, as it sanctions slavery. However, the Dred Scott decision itself was fundamentally incoherent. As Justice Benjamin Robbins Curtis noted in his dissent, blacks at the beginning of the republic had the right to vote in five states; how, then, could Taney declare that they were not and had never been intended to be citizens? (This was long before the idea became fashionable that non-citizens should vote in American elections and receive the fruit of American tax-payers' labor.) The other dissenting justice, John McLean, pointed out that by declaring that Scott was not a citizen and thus could not sue, the court was acknowledging it had no jurisdiction in the case and, therefore, could not rightly, and should not have, issued a ruling. It could also have been argued, once Curtis's point about blacks being citizens was granted, that slavery was outlawed, or the seeds of its outlawing were planted, by the First Amendment guarantees of freedom of speech and freedom of assembly. Slaves were restricted in both because of their status as slaves itself. If they were citizens, they had constitutional guarantees of both that would work against their status as slaves and ultimately require them to be freed.

But Buchanan had neither the wit nor the imagination to follow such a course, even if he had been inclined to do so.

2. *Pushing slavery on Kansas.* By this time, the Kansas Territory had two governments: one in Topeka that outlawed slavery and enjoyed the support of a majority of Kansans and another in Lecompton that was pro-slavery. When the Lecompton government sent a proposed pro-slavery state

constitution to Washington, Buchanan accepted it, despite the fact that he was committed to the principle of popular sovereignty and that slavery would almost certainly have been voted down in a free and fair election in Kansas. The president tried to win support for the Lecompton Constitution in Congress with a variety of favors and perks, but the House voted it down anyway. Buchanan kept pushing for Kansans to accept it, offering them all manner of inducements also, but they, too, voted it down. They didn't want slavery, no matter how determined President Buchanan was that they have it.

3. *Dithering about secession.* In late 1860 and early 1861, within weeks of the election of Republican Abraham Lincoln as president, seven Southern states seceded from the Union: South Carolina, Mississippi, Florida, Alabama, Georgia, Louisiana, and Texas. In his last annual message to Congress on December 3, 1860, Buchanan appeared to justify secession, stating: "The long-continued and intemperate interference of the Northern people with the question of slavery in the Southern States has at length produced its natural effects."[170] He lamented that "for five and twenty years the agitation at the North against slavery has been incessant" and exclaimed: "How easy would it be for the American people to settle the slavery question forever and to restore peace and harmony to this distracted country!"[171] All that was needed to do that, he said, was to allow the South "to be let alone and permitted to

170   James Buchanan, "Fourth Annual Message" (speech, December 3, 1860), UVA Miller Center, https://millercenter.org/the-presidency/presidential-speeches/december-3-1860-fourth-annual-message.

171   Ibid.

manage their domestic institutions in their own way."[172] Yet that, given what most in the North believed about slavery, was no longer possible.

Buchanan believed the South was right on constitutional grounds in the nation's grand dispute over slavery and suggested that it had a right to secede if its rights were not respected: "The Southern States, standing on the basis of the Constitution, have right to demand this act of justice from the States of the North. Should it be refused, then the Constitution, to which all the States are parties, will have been willfully violated by one portion of them in a provision essential to the domestic security and happiness of the remainder. In that event the injured States, after having first used all peaceful and constitutional means to obtain redress, would be justified in revolutionary resistance to the Government of the Union."[173]

Buchanan waffled. While denying that states had a right to secede from the Union, he added: "The right of resistance on the part of the governed against the oppression of their governments can not be denied," referring to the slaveholders, not the slaves, as the victims of that oppression.[174]

A month later, Buchanan declared in a statement on "Threats to the Peace and Existence of the Union" that "no State has a right by its own act to secede from the Union or throw off its federal obligations at pleasure," and that "the right and the duty to use military force defensively against those who resist the Federal officers in the execution of their

---

172   Ibid.
173   Ibid.
174   Ibid.

legal functions and against those who assail the property of the Federal Government is clear and undeniable."[175] But on January 9, 1861, when South Carolinians fired upon the ship he sent to reinforce the Union garrison at Fort Sumter, off the coast of Charleston, he did nothing.

Why his presidency was disastrous for America

Despite the hopeless failure of Pierce's presidency, Buchanan's was just more of the same, as if Democratic leaders thought that policies that had been proven not to work would somehow succeed if reapplied. Buchanan proved to be even more of a doughface than his predecessor, stocking his Cabinet with Southerners and doughfaces. Calling the principle of popular sovereignty a "happy conception" in his inaugural address as the blood was still warm on the ground was tone-deaf at very least. And as tensions over slavery continued to rise for the next four years, President Buchanan never had a better idea. In the first year of his presidency, an economic downturn, the Panic of 1857, hit the country. One of its causes was a drop-off in settlement of the territories by people from the free states and the consequent devaluation of Western land and railroad stock. The Dred Scott decision had contributed to making the territories less appealing to opponents of slavery. However, even the flagging economy did not lead Buchanan to change course.

---

175   James Buchanan, "Message on Threats to the Peace and Existence of the Union" (speech, January 8, 1861), UVA Miller Center, https://millercenter.org/the-presidency/presidential-speeches/january-8-1861-message-threats-peace-and-existence-union.

He thought, in fact, that the Dred Scott decision would settle the problem of slavery once and for all. It didn't. Instead, the Dred Scott decision increased the possibility that the violence of Bleeding Kansas would spread to all the territories of the West, for it held that while Congress could not prohibit slavery in the territories, once a territory became a state it could vote to outlaw slavery. The same rush of outsiders into various territories, and the same violence, that had torn Kansas apart, were now national prospects.

Buchanan should have denounced the Dred Scott decision's incoherence and declared it unenforceable. Instead, he kept pushing it even when it was clear that it was deepening, rather than healing, the divisions in the country. The formal dissolution of the Union that began while he was still president had been a very long time coming, but during his tenure in the White House, he did nothing to stave it off and a great deal to hasten it.

Buchanan was still president when the first seven Southern states left the Union, but his term would expire on March 4, 1861, and for the last months of his term, all he did was run out the clock. He did nothing to stop secession, arguing that it was not within his powers to do so, and simply handed off the problem to his successor. His failure to address this greatest of the nation's crises was the last in a series of mistakes and demonstrations of weakness that had characterized his presidency. This most qualified of presidential candidates turned out to be one of the most wholly unfit men ever to occupy the White House.

ABRAHAM LINCOLN

Library of Congress[176]

---

176   Alexander Gardner, *Abraham Lincoln, Head-and-Shoulders Portrait, Facing Front*, ca. 1900, photograph, Library of Congress, https://www.loc.gov/item/96522529/.

Full name: Abraham Lincoln

Lived: February 12, 1809–April 15, 1865

Presidency: March 4, 1861–April 15, 1865

Party: Whig in the 1840s; Republican from 1854; ran for reelection as president on the National Union Party ticket in 1864.

Evaluation: Great for America

Rating: 10

What qualified him to be president

Sometimes a man's qualifications to be president don't show in his résumé but in his character: his courage, his insight, and his ability to keep his head and manage a crisis. No one illustrates this better than Abraham Lincoln, who, before he was elected president of the United States, had served one term in the House of Representatives during the Polk administration and was a failed candidate for the U.S. Senate.

Lincoln was what many of his predecessors and successors were not: a penetrating and original thinker and something that is even more rare, a remarkable writer. In 1854, he had written brilliantly of the incoherence of slavery as a concept:

> You say A. is white, and B. is black. It is *color*, then; the lighter, having the right to enslave the darker? Take care. By this rule, you are to be slave to the first man you meet, with a fairer skin than your own. You do not mean *color* exactly? You mean the whites are *intellectually* the superiors of the blacks, and, therefore have

the right to enslave them? Take care again. By this rule, you are to be slave to the first man you meet, with an intellect superior to your own. But, say you, it is a question of *interest*; and, if you can make it your *interest*; you have the right to enslave another. Very well. And if he can make it his interest, he has the right to enslave you.[177]

It was his failed run for the U.S. Senate in Illinois in 1858 that established Lincoln as a national figure. When he received the nomination of the new Republican Party on June 16, 1858, Lincoln framed the conflict rending the nation in indelible terms: "'A house divided against itself cannot stand.' I believe this government cannot endure, permanently half *slave* and half *free*. I do not expect the Union to be *dissolved* — I do not expect the house to *fall* — but I *do* expect it will cease to be divided. It will become *all* one thing or *all* the other."[178]

No one else in those days had the vision or courage to go to the heart of the matter quite so directly. Lincoln continued to stress the immorality of slavery, a fact that few others dared to approach, in his subsequent debates with his opponent, Stephen A. Douglas, the champion of popular sovereignty. "Every sentiment he utters," Lincoln said in their debate at Knox College in Galesburg, Illinois, on October 7, 1858,

---

177 Abraham Lincoln, "Fragments on Slavery," April 1, 1854, Teaching American History, https://teachingamericanhistory.org/library/document/fragments-on-slavery/.

178 Abraham Lincoln, "House-Divided Speech" (June 16, 1858), Abraham Lincoln Online, http://www.abrahamlincolnonline.org/lincoln/speeches/house.htm.

"discards the idea that there is any wrong in slavery. Judge Douglas declares that if any community want slavery, they have a right to have it. He can say that, logically, if he says that there is no wrong in slavery; but if you admit that there is a wrong in it, he cannot logically say that anybody has a right to do wrong."[179]

Lincoln also insisted that the slaves were equal in dignity with all other human beings: "In the right to eat the bread without the leave of anybody else which his own hand earns, he is my equal and the equal of Judge Douglas, and the equal of every other man."[180]

Although Lincoln bested him in the debates, Douglas won the election. But Lincoln was on his way. The debates made him a serious contender for the 1860 election. On February 27, 1860, Lincoln gave a speech at the Cooper Union in New York City that further established his national prominence. In it, he maintained that nothing in the Constitution "properly forbade Congress to prohibit slavery in the federal territory" and, once again, brought the slavery issue to a fine point:

> If slavery is right, all words, acts, laws, and constitutions against it, are themselves wrong, and should be silenced, and swept away. If it is right, we cannot justly object to its nationality—its universality; if it is wrong, they cannot justly insist upon its extension—its enlargement. All they ask, we could readily grant, if we thought

179   Fergus M. Bordewich, "How Lincoln Bested Douglas in Their Famous Debates," *Smithsonian Magazine*, September 2008.
180   Ibid.

> slavery right; all we ask, they could as readily grant, if they thought it wrong. Their thinking it right, and our thinking it wrong, is the precise fact upon which depends the whole controversy.... Let us be diverted by none of those sophistical contrivances wherewith we are so industriously plied and belabored — contrivances such as groping for some middle ground between the right and the wrong.[181]

Against the moral waffling of Douglas, Buchanan and other proponents of popular sovereignty, this moral clarity shone out luminously.

Still, a great thinker and rhetorician did not necessarily make a great president. Compared to James Buchanan and his decades of public service and experience in numerous positions of responsibility, Lincoln looked almost wholly unqualified for the office he assumed at the nation's most perilous hour.

Yet if Buchanan had decided to run for reelection and won in 1860 instead of Lincoln, the Union would almost certainly have dissolved, and America would never have become a great nation and a champion of liberty and human rights. It was Lincoln who faced the crisis, defined its terms, endured the worst, and rode it out to the point where he could speak about a time to "bind up the nation's wounds."[182]

---

181   Abraham Lincoln, "Cooper Union Address" (speech, February 27, 1860), Abraham Lincoln Online, http://www.abrahamlincolnonline.org/lincoln/speeches/cooper.htm.

182   Abraham Lincoln, "Second Inaugural Address,"(speech, March 4, 1865), Avalon Project, Yale Law School, https://avalon.law.yale.edu/19th_century/lincoln2.asp.

When he was elected in 1860, however, that time couldn't have appeared more remote. In fact, many were certain that Lincoln was precisely the wrong man for the job. Just before Lincoln took office, the *Salem Advocate* from his home state of Illinois editorialized that "he is no more capable of becoming a statesman, nay, even a moderate one, than the braying ass can become a noble lion."[183] Lincoln's "weak, wishy-washy, namby-pamby efforts, imbecile in matter, disgusting in manner, have made us the laughing stock of the whole world."[184] The *Salem Advocate* argued, as critics of other presidents would do later, that the president embarrassed Americans before the world: "the European powers will despise us because we have no better material out of which to make a President."[185]

Edward Everett, the renowned orator, former senator and secretary of state, and, in 1860, the vice-presidential candidate for the Constitutional Union Party, wrote that Lincoln was "evidently a person of very inferior cast of character, wholly unequal to the crisis."[186] Congressman Charles Francis Adams, son of one president and grandson of another, sneered that Lincoln's "speeches have fallen like a wet blanket here. They put to flight all notions of greatness."[187]

---

183   "Evidence for The Unpopular Mr. Lincoln," American Battlefield Trust, https://www.battlefields.org/learn/articles/evidence-unpopular-mr-lincoln.
184   Ibid.
185   Ibid.
186   Ibid.
187   Ibid.

How he won

The election of 1860 showed that the divisions in the country revealed in the election of 1856 had only gotten worse. The Democrats, at their convention in Charleston, South Carolina, couldn't agree on a candidate; the party splintered into two factions, Northern and Southern. The Southern, pro-slavery Democratic nominee was Vice President John C. Breckinridge; his Northern counterpart was Douglas.

There was a fourth candidate as well. Some former Whigs calling themselves the Constitutional Union Party ran former Tennessee senator John Bell for president. The Constitutional Union Party offered no platform beyond a pledge to uphold the Constitution and laws, and it was determinedly neutral on the slavery issue.

But the time for neutrality was over. The nation was so divided that none of the four contenders were functionally national candidates at all. The 1860 race was between Lincoln and Douglas in the North, while in the South, it was Breckinridge versus Bell.

In that overheated time, the bland party of national unity, the Constitutional Union Party, carried only the border states of Virginia and Kentucky, plus Tennessee. The pro-slavery Breckinridge otherwise swept the slave states, with the exception of Missouri, which was the only state Douglas carried. Although he ran close to Lincoln in the popular vote, Douglas won no states in the North; neither did Breckinridge or Bell. Lincoln, meanwhile, won no states in the South and received less than 40 percent of the popular vote, but carried enough Northern states to put him in the White House.

Although Lincoln repeatedly stated that he would uphold the Constitution and laws of the United States, including those protecting slavery, the South considered the very idea of his presidency abhorrent. Slaveholders ignored the fact that Lincoln had repeatedly made it clear that he had no intention of challenging slavery, but in his inaugural address on March 4, 1861, with secession already a fact, he tried to reassure them yet again: "Apprehension seems to exist among the people of the Southern States that by the accession of a Republican Administration their property and their peace and personal security are to be endangered. There has never been any reasonable cause for such apprehension.... I have no purpose, directly or indirectly, to interfere with the institution of slavery in the States where it exists."[188]

Where it exists. Southerners, hyper-attentive at this point to any possible slight, knew what that meant: Lincoln favored outlawing slavery in the territories and had said as much directly at other times. This would, Southerners argued, upset the balance of the regions and limit the South's growth and power vis-à-vis the North. Lincoln's election to the presidency brought the long-simmering conflict to a head. Between that election and the inauguration of the first Republican president, seven states seceded from the Union.

President Lincoln was reelected in 1864, as the Civil War raged on, as the candidate of the National Union Party, a coalition of Republicans and pro-Union Democrats. Andrew Johnson, a former slaveholder and Unionist Democrat

---

188   Abraham Lincoln, "First Inaugural Address" (speech, March 4, 1861), Avalon Project, Yale Law School, https://avalon.law.yale.edu/19th_century/lincoln1.asp.

from the border state of Tennessee, was chosen as the vice-presidential nominee. With most of the states that formed their base outside the Union, the Democrats faced an uphill battle. They took a page from the old Whigs' book by nominating the closest thing they could get to a war hero, Major General George B. McClellan, who had been the commanding general of the U.S. Army and commander of the Army of the Potomac until his inaction and insubordination led Lincoln to cashier him despite his popularity.

Even the firing didn't dampen the enthusiasm of McClellan's following, which was made up of those who, like their hero, believed Lincoln to be unfit for the presidency. The Democrats, however, were as divided as they had been before the war: the party's platform called for an end to the war and peace with the South, while McClellan favored continuing the war until the South was defeated; he had to repudiate his own party's platform. The candidates' fortunes ebbed and flowed with the war, with Lincoln at one point certain he would lose; he made his Cabinet members sign a folded piece of paper that turned out to be a pledge that they would cooperate with the incoming administration.

The pledge turned out to be unnecessary. The Union forces' fortunes turned, and Lincoln was overwhelmingly reelected.

Notable accomplishments as president and events of his presidency

1. *Preserving the Union*. Over 150 years after its conclusion, the Civil War remains the costliest war the United States has ever fought, with more Americans killed than in any other

conflict. President Lincoln initially framed the imperative to fight this terrible war as his responsibility, delineated in his promise in the oath of office to "preserve, protect, and defend the Constitution of the United States."

However, this most incisive and insightful of thinkers also saw preserving the Union not simply as a matter of fidelity to his oath, much less as establishing the hegemony of the North over the South, as many Southerners maintained. Lincoln saw the conflict, in philosophical terms, as essential to the survival of the idea of republican, representative government: if any disaffected minority could leave a polity, then the very idea of majority rule was impossible, although the tyranny of the majority was also to be eschewed.

Jefferson Davis, who had been secretary of war during the Pierce administration and a senator from Mississippi, was chosen as president of the new nation the seceding Southern states hastily formed, the Confederate States of America. In his inaugural address on February 18, 1861, Davis said: "Our present condition, achieved in a manner unprecedented in the history of nations, illustrates the American idea that governments rest upon the consent of the governed, and that it is the right of the people to alter or abolish governments whenever they become destructive of the ends for which they were established."[189]

In his own inaugural address, Lincoln responded to this, although he did not mention Davis and may not at that

---

189   Jefferson Davis, "First Inaugural Address" (speech, February 18, 1861), Papers of Jefferson Davis, Rice University, https://jeffersondavis.rice.edu/archives/documents/jefferson-davis-first-inaugural-address.

time have known the contents of his Southern counterpart's address. Still, he answered Davis's point when he explained that on the question of the federal government's power to prohibit slavery in the territories and related issues:

> We divide upon them into majorities and minorities. If the minority will not acquiesce, the majority must, or the Government must cease. There is no other alternative, for continuing the Government is acquiescence on one side or the other. If a minority in such case will secede rather than acquiesce, they make a precedent which in turn will divide and ruin them, for a minority of their own will secede from them whenever a majority refuses to be controlled by such minority. For instance, why may not any portion of a new confederacy a year or two hence arbitrarily secede again, precisely as portions of the present Union now claim to secede from it? All who cherish disunion sentiments are now being educated to the exact temper of doing this.[190]

Consequently, he argued, "the central idea of secession is the essence of anarchy. A majority held in restraint by constitutional checks and limitations, and always changing easily with deliberate changes of popular opinions and sentiments, is the only true sovereign of a free people."[191]

---

190   Lincoln, "First Inaugural Address."
191   Ibid.

As he put it in his remarks on November 19, 1863, at the dedication of the national cemetery in Gettysburg, Pennsylvania, the site of a great Civil War battle, the war was being fought so that "government of the people, by the people, for the people, shall not perish from the earth."[192]

The nation, in its darkest hour, had the visionary leader it needed to articulate what was at stake and why its very existence was worth preserving. At the time, however, this was not universally realized. The *Harrisburg Patriot & Union*, in its account of the commemoration at Gettysburg, wrote: "We pass over the silly remarks of the President. For the credit of the nation we are willing that the veil of oblivion shall be dropped over them and that they shall be no more repeated or thought of."[193]

2. *Abolishing slavery.* Lincoln was indeed a visionary, but he was also a pragmatist. Although he considered slavery a moral evil, he did not initially take up arms against the Confederate States because of slavery, but to preserve and defend the Union. On August 22, 1862, he wrote to the influential abolitionist editor of the *New York Tribune*, Horace Greeley: "My paramount object in this struggle *is* to save the Union, and is *not* either to save or to destroy slavery. If I could save the Union without freeing *any* slave I would do it, and if I could save it by freeing *all* the slaves I would do it; and if I

---

192 Abraham Lincoln, "Gettysburg Address" (speech, November 19, 1863), Cornell University Library, https://rmc.library.cornell.edu/gettysburg/good_cause/transcript.htm.

193 Donald Gilliland, "Living on the Wrong Side of History? The *Harrisburg Patriot & Union*'s Notorious 'Review' of the Gettysburg Address," *Harrisburg Patriot-News*, November 14, 2013.

could save it by freeing some and leaving others alone I would also do that."[194]

At length, this proved impossible. On January 1, 1863, Lincoln issued the Emancipation Proclamation, declaring that "all persons held as slaves within any State or designated part of a State, the people whereof shall then be in rebellion against the United States, shall be then, thenceforward, and forever free."[195]

Here Lincoln the visionary and Lincoln the pragmatist met: this was not a blanket abolition of slavery, as it didn't touch the peculiar institution in the border states that had not seceded from the Union.

It was also more a matter of military strategy than of moral imperative. Leftist historian Howard Zinn claims that the Emancipation Proclamation was only issued in order to gain black manpower for hard-pressed Union armies; this is false, as Northern commanders did not at that time generally consider blacks fit for combat duty, and free slaves did not join the Union forces in any significant numbers. But the Proclamation was an attempt to sow unrest behind enemy lines and give the Southern states an inducement to end their rebellion: within the Union, they could presumably maintain the way of life they had left the Union to preserve, but outside the Union, they could not. That moment passed; the rebellion continued,

---

194   Abraham Lincoln to Horace Greeley, August 22, 1862, Abraham Lincoln Online, http://www.abrahamlincolnonline.org/lincoln/speeches/greeley.htm.

195   Abraham Lincoln, Emancipation Proclamation, January 1, 1863, Presidential Proclamations, 1791–1991, Record Group 11, General Records of the United States Government, National Archives, https://www.ourdocuments.gov/doc.php?flash=true&doc=34&page=transcript.

and the Emancipation Proclamation became the first step toward the total abolition of slavery in the United States.

The Proclamation did, however, have its critics. The *Chicago Times* decried it as "a monstrous usurpation, a criminal wrong, and an act of national suicide."[196] The *Crisis* of Columbus, Ohio, sounded the alarm: "We have no doubt that this Proclamation seals the fate of this Union as it was and the Constitution as it is.... The time is brief when we shall have a DICTATOR PROCLAIMED, for the Proclamation can never be carried out except under the iron rule of the worst kind of despotism."[197]

As fanciful as all that was, many believed it.

3. *Standing against anti-Semitism.* Major General Ulysses S. Grant, commander of the District of Tennessee, which comprised the states of Tennessee, Kentucky, and Mississippi, was irritated by black-market trading between Unionists and Confederates in his area, which he decided was largely being carried on by Jews. On December 17, 1862, Grant issued General Order No. 11, which read:

> The Jews, as a class violating every regulation of trade established by the Treasury Department and also department orders, are hereby expelled from the department within twenty-four hours from the receipt of this order.
>
> Post commanders will see to it that all of this class of people be furnished passes and required to leave, and any one returning after

---

196   "Evidence for the Unpopular Mr. Lincoln."
197   Ibid.

such notification will be arrested and held in confinement until an opportunity occurs of sending them out as prisoners, unless furnished with permit from headquarters. No passes will be given these people to visit headquarters for the purpose of making personal application of trade permits.[198]

This was an importation of Old-World anti-Semitism, blaming all Jews collectively for the deeds of a few, into the New World. Jewish leaders immediately appealed to President Lincoln, who acted quickly and ordered Grant to rescind the General Order, which he did less than a month after it was issued. On January 6, 1863, the General Order already rescinded, Lincoln received a Jewish delegation and assured them that he did not draw a distinction between Jews and non-Jews, and that "to condemn a class is, to say the least, to wrong the good with the bad."[199]

Why his presidency was great for America

Lincoln preserved the Union, and with it, he also preserved both constitutional rule and, as he had pointed out so eloquently, the very idea of representative government. Some charged, then and now, that he did so by, in effect, trampling

---

198   Ulysses S. Grant, General Order No. 11, December 17, 1862, Jewish Virtual Library, American-Israeli Cooperative Enterprise, https://www. jewishvirtuallibrary.org/order-no-11-judaic-treasures.

199   "Anti-Semitism in the United States: General Grant's Infamy," Jewish Virtual Library, American-Israeli Cooperative Enterprise, https://www. jewishvirtuallibrary.org/general-grant-s-infamy.

upon the Constitution and behaving like a despot. This argument rests primarily upon Lincoln's April 1861 suspension of habeas corpus, the right of a defendant to be brought before a judge or court rather than simply held indefinitely.

Lincoln knew that if Maryland, a slave state, left the Union and Washington, D.C., became surrounded by hostile territory, the war would be lost and secession accomplished. Accordingly, when angry mobs attacked federal troop transports in Baltimore and the state of Maryland asked Lincoln to remove Union troops from its territory, Lincoln ordered the suspension of habeas corpus in the areas of Maryland where the fervor to join the Confederacy was strongest. The Constitution gave Congress the authority to suspend habeas corpus "in cases of Rebellion or Invasion," but Congress was not in session at the time.[200] Lincoln justified his action by arguing that time was of the essence, and only the president could act quickly, in his role as commander in chief of the armed forces, to preserve the Union in this time of large-scale insurrection.

Lincoln was called a dictator and a tyrant for this. Yet he had not seized powers that were not in the Constitution; he had assumed, in a time of crisis, powers that the Constitution delegated to Congress. Congress later ratified his actions. That he had no intention of becoming the dictator and tyrant that his detractors accused him of being was clear from the many things he did *not* do that characterize the behavior of real dictators: he did not suspend habeas corpus indefinitely or universally; he did not profit personally from his actions; he did not issue a sweeping decree abolishing slavery in

---

200   U.S. Constitution, art. 1, sec. 9, cl. 2.

the Union, but instead asked Congress for a constitutional amendment that would phase slavery out extremely gradually, ending with the institution's extinction in 1900. He did not suspend the free press, which was often harshly critical of his actions, and he did not arrest his political opponents or suspend the 1864 presidential election (which, at one point, he was quite sure he would lose). He never even considered such measures. He did set a precedent for the growth of the power of the executive branch, but this precedent should never have been followed without a repetition of the conditions that led Lincoln to take the course he chose: a civil war.

Lincoln was also criticized for not asking Congress for a declaration of war before going to war with the Confederacy. But a centerpiece of his approach to the South was a refusal to accord it the recognition that belligerent states usually gave to their enemies; to do so would, he argued, be a tacit admission that the South was indeed an independent nation, which was the very claim he was going to war to contradict. The South, Lincoln said, was a region of the United States in rebellion against lawful authority. The Constitution did not require a declaration of war to put down an insurrection.

Abraham Lincoln was forced to articulate and defend the reasons for going to war and continuing the war after staggering losses on both sides; with his remarkable skills as a rhetorician, he articulated not only a justification for the war, but for representative government itself. In doing so, he was the first president to become the nation's spokesman, conscience, and philosophical guide. Many of his successors would attempt to emulate him, with varying degrees of success.

Lincoln also faced charges that he was too lenient to the secessionists. Late in 1863, he established a plan allowing states that had seceded to hold new elections and return to the Union if 10 percent of the voting population took an oath of loyalty to the United States and agreed to the abolition of slavery. The Radical Republican faction of Lincoln's party always deplored Lincoln's statement that if he could save the Union without freeing a single slave, he would do it, and they considered his "ten percent plan" too soft.

Although Lincoln shared their conviction that slavery was a moral evil, he took a more pragmatic approach than they were willing to take. This conflict would only come to a head after his death. Just over a month before he was murdered, Lincoln was still holding out hope for an amicable resolution to the nation's intractable conflict:

> With malice toward none; with charity for all; with firmness in the right, as God gives us to see the right, let us strive on to finish the work we are in; to bind up the nation's wounds; to care for him who shall have borne the battle, and for his widow, and his orphan—to do all which may achieve and cherish a just, and a lasting peace, among ourselves, and with all nations.[201]

Peace would come, but with plenty of malice and precious little charity.

---

201   Abraham Lincoln, "Second Inaugural Address" (speech, March 4, 1865), National Park Service, https://www.nps.gov/linc/learn/historyculture/lincoln-second-inaugural.htm.

SEVENTEEN

ANDREW JOHNSON

Library of Congress[202]

---

202   *Hon. Andrew Johnson, Half-Length Portrait, Facing Left,* 1855–1865, photograph, Library of Congress, https://www.loc.gov/item/96522530/.

Full name: Andrew Johnson
Lived: December 29, 1808–July 31, 1875
Presidency: April 15, 1865–March 4, 1869
Party: National Union/Democrat
Evaluation: Very Damaging for America
Rating: 2

What qualified him to be president

Andrew Johnson had been a U.S. senator from Tennessee and was serving during the Civil War as that state's military governor, but his primary qualification for replacing Vice President Hannibal Hamlin as Abraham Lincoln's running mate in 1864 was that he was a Democrat. He had even owned slaves, although he had freed them in 1863.

It was curious, to say the least, to have a Republican president running for reelection with a Democratic vice-presidential candidate, but in the political calculus of that tumultuous time, it made perfect sense. Worried about carrying the border states that had remained, albeit precariously, in the Union during the Civil War, the Republicans formed the National Union Party, which was meant to be a big-tent party comprising Republicans and Democrats who wanted to preserve the Union. Andrew Johnson's vice-presidential candidacy was a bid for the votes of Tennessee, Kentucky, Missouri, Maryland, and Delaware in an election that most thought would be extremely close.

How he became president

No one expected that the most momentous outcome of the 1864 election would be that Andrew Johnson would end up president of the United States just five weeks after Lincoln's second inauguration. Abraham Lincoln was the first president to be assassinated, and although there had been threats in the air for years, there had been no talk during the campaign of the possibility of Lincoln not serving out his term or of Andrew Johnson's fitness to be president. The still relatively new Republican Party would never have opted for its electoral success to be negated by an assassin's bullet; if Republican leaders had fully realized how much danger Lincoln was in, they would have renominated Hamlin for vice president or chosen some other reliable Republican.

By the time Johnson left office in 1869, there were no doubt many who wished that there had been those discussions about his suitability for the job.

Notable accomplishments as president and events of his presidency

1. *Reconstruction*. Lincoln had called for "malice toward none" and "charity for all," but none of those who followed in his wake could figure out how to deliver that, and most weren't even interested in trying.

The Radicals meant to secure equality of rights, including the right to vote, for the freed slaves. This was a laudable and charitable goal, but not everyone saw it as such at the time. Former slaveholders, the entire landed aristocracy of the South, regarded the prospect of blacks voting, and black elected officials, as a malicious infringement of their own rights. Their goal was to preserve the South's established order as much as possible in light of new realities, freeing the slaves but rendering them second-class citizens by denying them the franchise and placing other restrictions upon them.

Then there was the white working class in the South, which didn't think the freeing of the slaves was charitable at all, as the freedmen would be competing with white working-men for wage-paying jobs. President Johnson, who had come from this class, threw in his lot with it. He opposed the enfranchisement and equality of rights of blacks and simultaneously worked against the interests of the plantation aristocracy. In this, Johnson departed from Lincoln's course, as his martyred predecessor had favored civil rights for the freed slaves, albeit not on the sweeping and unlimited terms that the Radicals favored. In May 1865, Johnson granted amnesty to all ex-Confederates except those who owned property worth $20,000 ($300,000 today), that is, virtually the entire former ruling class.

President Johnson apparently thought that he could form a new coalition of working-class white Southerners with moderate Republicans and northern Democrats. The Radicals, however, were not about to acquiesce in the disenfranchisement of the freed slaves, which they viewed as a negation of the entire cause for which the war had been fought. Johnson, an unelected president, a former slave owner who was not even a member of their party and who was not carrying out the policies of his slain predecessor, became the focus of their hostility, which the president returned in kind.

This controversy engulfed and ultimately destroyed the Johnson presidency. On February 19, 1866, President Johnson vetoed a bill to extend the charter of the Freedmen's Bureau, a government agency providing aid for former slaves. Johnson explained that insufficient consideration was being given to "the ability of the freedmen to protect and take care of themselves."[203] He neglected to mention that powerful forces still existed that were determined to interfere with that ability.

Then, on March 27, 1866, he contradicted himself as he vetoed the Civil Rights Act, which granted American citizenship to the freed slaves and guaranteed them equality of rights under the law. Of the freed slaves he wrote: "Can it be reasonably supposed that they possess the requisite qualifications to entitle them to all the privileges and immunities of citizens of the United States? Have the people of the several States expressed such a conviction?" He himself had just five weeks before this expressed the conviction that they could "protect and take care of themselves."[204] If they could do that, why couldn't they be citizens?

Johnson also argued that the bill was an unconstitutional expansion of federal power but objected to it on racial grounds too: "The distinction of race and color," he wrote, "is by the bill made to operate in favor of the colored and against the white race."[205]

---

203   Andrew Johnson, "Veto Message on Freedmen and Refugee Relief Bureau Legislation" (speech, February 19, 1866), UVA Miller Center, https://millercenter.org/the-presidency/presidential-speeches/february-19-1866-veto-message-freedmen-and-refugee-relief.

204   Andrew Johnson, "Veto of the Civil Rights Act" (speech, March 27, 1866), UVA Miller Center, https://millercenter.org/the-presidency/presidential-speeches/march-27-1866-veto-message-civil-rights-legislation.

205   Ibid.

The Radicals were furious. The *Springfield Republican* denounced the veto, saying that protecting the civil rights of the freed slaves "follows from the suppression of the rebellion.... The party is nothing, if it does not do this—the nation is dishonored if it hesitates in this."[206] Congress overrode Johnson's veto of the Civil Rights Act, and the commanding general of the U.S. Army, Ulysses S. Grant, sent troops into the South to enforce the act.

In a bid to win popular support for his lenient Reconstruction policies, Johnson, in the run-up to the 1866 midterm elections, embarked on "the Swing around the Circle," a tour around the Northeast and Midwest. But "Andy's Trip," as political cartoonist Thomas Nast derisively dubbed it, soon became a disaster. Full of grandiosity and self-pity, Johnson likened himself to Christ and the Radical leaders to Confederates eager to tear the nation apart again. Johnson invited ridicule by starting every speech with "It is not for the purpose of making a speech that I now appear before you."[207] He allowed pro-Radical hecklers to draw him into verbal sparring matches. When someone called out, "Hang Jeff Davis!" Johnson was incredulous, responding, "Hang Jeff Davis? Hang Jeff Davis? Why don't *you* hang him?" and later, "Why don't you hang [Radical Republican leaders] Thad Stevens and Wendell Phillips?"[208] When taunted with cries of "Don't get mad,

---

206   Eric Foner, *Reconstruction: America's Unfinished Revolution* (New York: HarperCollins, 1988), 283.

207   Garry Boulard, *The Swing around the Circle: Andrew Johnson and the Train Ride that Destroyed a Presidency* (New York: iUniverse, 2008), 113.

208   Ibid., 115.

Andy!" he got all the angrier.[209] Admonished that his outbursts diminished the dignity of the presidency, he replied, "I don't care about my dignity."[210] He took General Grant with him, hoping to add the war hero's luster to his campaign, but Grant was cheered while Johnson was jeered, and the general, disgusted by Johnson's rhetoric, left the tour early.

Unsurprisingly, Andy's Trip came to nothing; the Radicals won decisive majorities in both houses of Congress, and were able to override future Johnson vetoes, which came at an unprecedented rate as the president continued to stand against the Radical program.

2. *The Tenure of Office Act and impeachment.* After the 1866 elections, President Johnson could do nothing to stop the Radical program except, as commander in chief of the armed forces, refuse military help to enforce it. For that, however, he needed the cooperation of Secretary of War Edwin M. Stanton, himself a Radical, and when that cooperation was not forthcoming, Johnson wanted to remove Stanton from office. To prevent Johnson from firing Stanton, the Radical Congress in 1867 passed (over Johnson's veto) the Tenure of Office Act, which required the Senate to approve the removal of any Cabinet officer.

The act was clear legislative overreach and was doubtful on constitutional grounds; in 1926, thirty-nine years after it had been repealed, the Supreme Court called it "invalid." Johnson fired Stanton, but Congress ordered him reinstated. Finally, on February 21, 1868, he fired Stanton again. Stanton

---

209   Lorant, 287.
210   Boulard, 116.

barricaded himself in his office, and Congress immediately began impeachment proceedings. Just three days later, the House voted 126–47 in favor of impeachment. In the Senate, the vote was 35–19 to convict Johnson and remove him from office; however, 36 votes, or two-thirds of the senators, were needed. Johnson's presidency was saved, and he served out the rest of his term. Nevertheless, this crippled his ability to accomplish anything else of significance.

3. *The Fourteenth Amendment* was adopted on July 9, 1868, over President Johnson's objections. Southern states had been pressured to approve it as a condition of being allowed to send their representatives to Congress. The amendment stipulated that "all persons born or naturalized in the United States, and subject to the jurisdiction thereof, are citizens of the United States and of the State wherein they reside."[211] This was meant to guarantee citizenship for freed slaves. It banned restricting the right to vote for men over the age of twenty-one "except for participation in rebellion, or other crime."[212] It also barred former Confederates from becoming senators or representatives, although it allowed the House to override this in particular circumstances.

4. *Buying Alaska*. Amid all the fury over Reconstruction, Johnson's secretary of state, William Seward, found the time to negotiate the purchase of Alaska from the Russian Empire for $7.2 million ($130 million today). While today it is considered horrifying that one country might purchase territory from another, no one thought that then; still, the purchase was

---

211 U.S. Constitution, amend. 14.
212 Ibid.

derided as "Seward's Folly," since few people in the United States at the time saw the land of Alaska as worth much. This is one achievement of Andrew Johnson's presidency—indeed, the only one—that looks better from the vantage point of a century and a half later than it did in its day.

Why his presidency was very damaging for America

Andrew Johnson's presidency was damaging for America largely because of things that others did, some long after he left office. The first section of the Fourteenth Amendment, with its stipulation that all citizens should enjoy "equal protection of the laws," has been used to justify practices that would have shocked and horrified those who framed it, who intended to frame it narrowly as addressing only slavery and the treatment of slavery in the post-Civil War era. They never dreamed of its being used to justify practices such as abortion (*Roe v. Wade*) and same-sex marriage (*Obergefell v. Hodges*). This, however, is more the fault of the method of interpreting the Constitution that became fashionable in the late twentieth and early twenty-first century, in which the plain words of the document could be freely bypassed in the interpreter's quest to make it say what he or she wanted it to say. Those who drafted it only wanted to protect and safeguard the rights of the freedmen.

Andrew Johnson opposed it, and this was just one of his many errors of judgment. For all his faults, however, or, more precisely, because of all his faults, he became a martyr for the principle of limited, responsible government and a victim of hyper-partisan politics. He was impeached for violating a law that was only passed to limit his power in the first place and that was an unconstitutional infringement upon the powers of the chief executive. He had committed no other "high crimes and misdemeanors," as the Constitution requires for impeachment.[213] If he had been a Radical Republican, the Tenure of Office Act never would have been passed, and he would not have been impeached.

The impeachment of Andrew Johnson is a disgraceful episode in American history, both in and of itself and for the precedent it set. For a considerable period, it stood alone as the single example of unscrupulous legislators using impeachment as a weapon against a president they loathed for political reasons rather than for any actual crimes. Nowadays it has become a veritable paradigm for the use of impeachment as a tool of partisan politics. Contemporary legislators who use impeachment as a political tool may never have had the audacity to make such a travesty of the constitutional system of checks and balances were it not for the precedent that the impeachment of Andrew Johnson set.

That was not, of course, Johnson's fault. Yet he was not blameless. The whole impeachment fiasco came about because President Johnson espoused policies that many quite rightly saw as negating the North's victory in the Civil War and relegating black Americans to a situation little different from the one they were in before the war, thus rendering null and void the supreme sacrifice so many had made. If Johnson had not resisted voting rights and other civil rights for the freed

---

213   U.S. Constitution, art. 2, sec. 4.

slaves, the Radicals never would have gone to war against him with such fury and descended to congressional overreach and impeachment.

Speaking in Philadelphia on September 8, 1866, Carl Schurz, a German immigrant, Missouri politician, and Radical Republican leader, articulated the Radicals' vision:

> Americans, the lines are drawn, and the issues of the contests are clearly made up.
>
> You want the Union fully restored. We offer it to you — a Union based upon universal liberty, impartial justice and equal rights, upon sacred pledges faithfully fulfilled, upon the faith of the Nation nobly vindicated; a Union without a slave and without a tyrant; a Union of truly democratic States...
>
> The reactionists, with their champion, Andrew Johnson, also offer you a Union — a Union based upon deception unscrupulously practiced, upon great promises treacherously violated, upon the National faith scandalously broken; a Union whose entrails are once more to be lacerated by the irrepressible struggle between slavery and liberty...[214]

---

214   Carl Schurz, "The Logical Results of the War" (speech, September 8, 1866), Wikisource, https://en.wikisource.org/wiki/The_Logical_Results_of_the_War.

Schurz had a point. Johnson enabled the restriction of black civil rights in the South at the time when they should have been guaranteed. The consequences of this continue to be felt, like the consequences of the Radicals' attempts to arrogate power. During the presidency of Andrew Johnson, there were no heroes, no one untainted in one way or another.

ULYSSES S. GRANT

Library of Congress[215]

---

215   Frederick Gutekunst, *Ulysses S. Grant, Lieutenant-General, U.S.A.*, ca. 1865, photograph, Philadelphia, Library of Congress, https://www.loc.gov/item/00652563/.

Full name: Hiram Ulysses Grant; Ulysses S. Grant from
    1839
Lived: April 27, 1822–July 23, 1885
Presidency: March 4, 1869–March 3, 1877
Party: Republican
Evaluation: Very Good for America
Rating: 8

What qualified him to be president

Hiram Ulysses Grant always hated his first name, reversing the order of his first and middle names until he enrolled in West Point in 1839 and was erroneously registered as Ulysses S. Grant. Rather than correct the record, the young man seized happily on the error. U.S. Grant was born.

Like Zachary Taylor, Ulysses S. Grant was a general, a war hero, and a man who had never held elective office before he was elected president of the United States. Also like Taylor, he had been largely apolitical before becoming a presidential candidate. The only time he had voted for president, he recalled, had been in 1856, when he voted for James Buchanan, because, he said, "I knew Frémont."[216]

Unlike Taylor, however, Grant had strong political convictions. As we have seen, he thought the Mexican War was unjust and had brought divine judgment upon the United States. He was also a strong Unionist; aside from the quip about Frémont, he explained why he had voted for Buchanan: "I preferred the success of a candidate whose election would

---

216   Lorant, 295.

prevent or postpone secession, to seeing the country plunged into a war the end of which no man could foretell. With a Democrat elected by the unanimous vote of the Slave States, there could be no pretext for secession for four years. I very much hoped that the passions of the people would subside in that time, and the catastrophe be averted altogether; if it was not, I believed the country would be better prepared to receive the shock and to resist it. I therefore voted for James Buchanan for President."[217]

The catastrophe was not averted, but Grant did more than perhaps any other man to bring it to an end. While General George B. McClellan found excuse after excuse for inaction instead of trying to take the Confederate capital of Richmond—and his successors were no better—Grant was decisive and successful. When he won a major victory at Shiloh in Virginia but faced calls for his removal over rumors that he was a drunkard and had been unprepared for the Confederate assault his troops ultimately repulsed, Lincoln responded: "Ah! You surprise me, gentlemen. But can you tell me where he gets his whiskey? Because, if I can only find out, I will send a barrel of this wonderful whiskey to every general in the army."[218]

On another occasion, Lincoln was more direct: "I can't spare this man. He fights."[219]

When Lincoln finally made him commanding general of the army in March 1864, Grant moved to do what other Union

---

217   Grant, 105–106.
218   "The President's Habeas Corpus Proclamation and the Act of Congress on the Subject," *New York Herald*, September 18, 1863, 6, Quote Investigator, https://quoteinvestigator.com/2013/02/18/barrel-of-whiskey/.
219   Matuz, 291.

commanders had shied away from doing: confronting and destroying the army of General Robert E. Lee, the Confederacy's foremost fighting force. Lee, whose reputation for strategic acumen was unmatched, himself observed: "I have carefully searched the military records of both ancient and modern history, and have never found Grant's superior as a general."[220]

Lee was right. On April 9, 1865, a little more than a year after Grant was made commanding general, he accepted the surrender of Lee's army. The bloodiest war in American history was over.

After the war, Grant demonstrated yet again that he was a man with a keen moral compass: he favored measures that would remove forever the possibility that the same strife could recur, including equality of rights for the freed slaves, and hence tended to side with the Radical Republicans.

His only experience in a non-military position of responsibility was his five months as acting secretary of war in the Johnson administration during the imbroglio over Edwin M. Stanton and the Tenure of Office Act. This ended in a bitter break with the president over Johnson's claim that he had reneged on a promise to stay in his post during the battle and whether Stanton could lawfully be removed without Senate approval.

That ugly incident did not overshadow the popular adulation he enjoyed as the conqueror of the South, the man who ended the Civil War; on the contrary, given the general animus toward Johnson, it only bolstered Grant's popularity.

---

220   Ibid.

How he won

Grant was the Republicans' unanimous choice for president at the convention in 1868. The Democrats nominated former New York governor Horatio Seymour and ran him on a platform calling for the "immediate restoration of all States to their rights in the Union under the Constitution," amnesty for all former Confederates, and "the regulation of the elective franchise in the States by their citizens."[221] That last point meant the right of white Southerners, chiefly former slaveholders and all Democrats, to restrict the freed slaves' right to vote. For good measure, the Democratic platform called the Reconstruction Acts "unconstitutional, revolutionary, and void."[222] A Seymour campaign badge proclaimed, "Our Motto: This is a White Man's Country; Let White Men Rule."[223]

Not as many people were enthralled with the man who had ended the Civil War as most people expected. The election was surprisingly close, demonstrating how deeply divided America still was and how much more interested people were in the question of how to order society in the post-Civil War era than in the fact that there had been a Civil War at all, and that this was the general who had won it. Grant won 53 percent of the popular vote, just over 3,000,000, which was 300,000 more than Seymour. The Republicans carried the former Confederate states of North Carolina, South Carolina,

---

221   Lorant, 301–302.

222   Ibid.

223   "Our Ticket, Our Motto: This Is a White Man's Country; Let White Men Rule," Schomburg Center for Research in Black Culture, Photographs and Prints Division, New York Public Library Digital Collections, ://digitalcollections. nypl.org/items/62a9d0e6-4fc9-dbce-e040-e00a18064a66.

Florida, Tennessee, and Mississippi; those states went into the Republican column because of the votes of 500,000 freedmen, whose right to vote all over the South was protected by the military. If the vote had been restricted to white Americans only, Seymour would have won the popular vote. The Democrats determined to redouble their efforts to end Reconstruction and take the right to vote away from the freed slaves who had just gained it; it was either that or electoral oblivion.

By 1872, however, even many influential Radical Republican leaders, including Carl Schurz and Charles Sumner, thought the job of Reconstruction was finished after the ratification of the Fifteenth Amendment, and considered the Grant administration incurably corrupt. They bolted from the Republican Party and formed a new party, the Liberal Republicans, calling for the withdrawal of troops from the South and low tariffs, and nominating the longtime Republican newspaper editor, Horace Greeley, to run against Grant. The Democrats, seeing that Grant was popular despite his administration's scandals and not wishing to split the anti-Grant vote, also nominated Greeley, despite the fact that he had been a vociferous critic of the Democratic Party for decades. Greeley, whom the polite considered an eccentric and the less polite a buffoon, was not a popular choice: the *New York Times* huffed that if "any one man could send a great nation to the dogs, that man is Mr. Greeley."[224] He wouldn't get a chance. It was a strange election, with Southern Democrats campaigning for a man who had denounced them strenuously and repeatedly and Republicans calling for the

---

224   Boller, loc. 1751.

defeat of a popular Republican president. In the end, Grant won decisively.

Notable accomplishments as president and events of his presidency

1. *Reconstruction*. In apologizing for and retracting his wartime General Order No. 11, expelling Jews from the states under his control, Grant declared: "The order was issued and sent without any reflection and without thinking of the Jews as a set or race to themselves, but simply as persons who had successfully...violated an order.... I have no prejudice against sect or race but want each individual to be judged by his own merit."[225] He worked hard to make up for the impression General Order No. 11 had given, becoming in 1874 the first president to visit a synagogue.

From the very beginning of his presidency, Grant showed a consistent commitment to the equality of rights of all people. In his first inaugural address, he called for the ratification of the Fifteenth Amendment, which stated: "The right of citizens of the United States to vote shall not be denied or abridged by the United States or by any State on account of race, color, or previous condition of servitude."[226]

Two weeks later, President Grant approved an act stipulating that the word "white" be struck from all requirements to hold office or serve as a juror in the District of Columbia. When Southern states resisted Reconstruction measures,

---

225   Jean Edward Smith, *Grant* (New York: Simon and Schuster, 2001), 465.
226   U.S. Constitution, amend. 15.

denied blacks the right to vote, and allowed the Ku Klux Klan to terrorize black populations, Grant sent federal troops to restore order and enforce the law. And in 1870, the Fifteenth Amendment was approved.

Grant's determination to protect the rights of the freed slaves made him extremely unpopular in the South, and increasingly in the North as well, as many Radicals considered the job of Reconstruction to be finished when black Americans had the right to vote and there was no chance of the Southern states rebelling again. The corruption of some Grant administration officials only made it all the more difficult for him to continue his Reconstruction program; in the minds of many, Reconstruction meant corrupt profiteers descending upon the South and despoiling it in the name of civil rights.

In the 1874 midterm elections, the Democrats won the House and further stymied Reconstruction efforts. Grant was committed to civil rights for the freed slaves, but he was increasingly the freedmen's only champion. The whole Reconstruction enterprise had become bogged down in corruption and partisan politics. The Civil Rights Act of 1875 forbade racial discrimination in places such as restaurants and public transportation. But here Grant faltered, not enforcing it because it was both the brainchild of his opponents among the Radicals and not what he had wanted, which was a law against violence intended to prevent people from voting. Grant's proposal was widely seen as yet more of his administration's corruption—simply an attempt to secure Republican votes in the South. The brief postwar period during which black Americans were able to vote and had their rights protected was drawing to a close.

2. *Attempting to acquire Santo Domingo.* Grant had a longstanding desire for the United States to acquire the Dominican Republic, which was then commonly known as Santo Domingo. This stemmed from his concern for civil rights for black Americans. Grant noted: "The present difficulty in bringing all parts of the United States to a happy unity and love of country grows out of the prejudice to color. The prejudice is a senseless one, but it exists."[227] A solution to this, he suggested, could be large-scale black emigration to a Santo Domingo annexed to the United States: "If two or three hundred thousand blacks were to emigrate to St. Domingo... the Southern people would learn the crime of Ku Kluxism, because they would see how necessary the black man is to their own prosperity."[228]

Grant emphasized that he was not advocating this emigration; he was merely suggesting it as a solution to the systematic denial of rights to freed slaves in the South. "I took it that the colored people would go there in numbers, so as to have independent states governed by their own race. They would still be States of the Union, and under the protection of the General Government; but the citizens would be almost wholly colored."[229] Santo Domingo, he asserted, was "capable of supporting the entire colored population of the United States, should it choose to emigrate."[230] However, once Santo Domingo was established as a haven for the freedmen, white

---

227   Ron Chernow, *Grant* (New York: Penguin, 2017), 676.
228   Ibid.
229   Ibid.
230   Ibid.

Southerners would want to discourage further emigration, for then the black man's "worth here would soon be discovered, and he would soon receive such recognition as to induce him to stay."[231]

On September 4, 1869, the president of the Dominican Republic signed a treaty approving the U.S. annexation of the country, which would be admitted to the Union as a territory, with statehood to follow. The Senate, however, voted the treaty down. Grant persisted, sending Frederick Douglass to Santo Domingo as part of a commission to study the matter; this commission returned with a report saying that most Dominicans favored annexation, but nothing came of it.

3. *Signing the Indian Appropriation Act.* Not only did Grant work to secure civil rights for black Americans; he also moved to heal relations with American Indians. This 1871 act established educational and medical programs for Indian communities.

4. *Avoiding new conflict with Britain.* It is unlikely that the United States would have gone to war with Britain so soon after the conclusion of the Civil War, but there was a great deal of anger in the country over the Confederate warships that British shipbuilders had constructed. The atmosphere was heated, with calls to annex Canada or extract massive punitive sums from the British or do both. Instead, Grant's secretary of state, Hamilton Fish, negotiated the Treaty of Washington in 1871, which submitted the dispute to international arbitration. The arbitrators awarded the U.S. $15.5

---

231   Ibid.

million ($295 million today), and the two nations' amicable relations were further cemented.

5. *Avoiding war with Spain.* In the 1870s, Cuba fought for independence from Spain and enjoyed widespread sympathy among Americans. In October 1873, the Spanish captured a private ship, the *Virginius*, which was carrying soldiers and ammunition to Cuba, and executed over fifty members of its American crew. Amid clamors for war, Fish again engaged in quiet negotiations, with Spain finally issuing a formal apology and returning the ship and the crewmembers who had not been executed.

6. *Greenbacks and corruption.* During the Civil War, the U.S. government had printed paper money, backed by neither gold nor silver, to cover its rapidly rising war debts. Grant attempted to curb inflation and restore some fiscal responsibility to the economy by phasing out the greenbacks and conducting the government's business in gold coins. He also maintained high tariffs to protect American workers and industries.

Railroad magnate Jay Gould and stockbroker Jim Fisk had personally advised Grant to take this course and were poised to take advantage. They bribed Assistant U.S. Treasurer Daniel Butterfield for inside information and proceeded to try to corner the gold market. In September 1869, Grant discovered their scheme and ordered his secretary of the treasury, George S. Boutwell, to sell $4 million in gold ($75 million today). This broke the power of the Gould/Fisk "Gold Ring," but it also caused the first Black Friday, an economic downtown that lasted into 1870. Grant, moreover, was accused of knowing about the Gold Ring's scheme and even of being part of it.

Another scandal came in 1872, when stockholders of the Union Pacific Railroad, which had been given government money to build a railroad line to the West Coast, gave the contract for construction of the railroad to another company they owned, Crédit Mobilier of America. This enabled them to control the entire construction process, and without outside observers seeing what was going on, they submitted massively inflated bills for the construction and pocketed the profits. Grant himself was not involved, but several Grant administration officials, including Vice President Schuyler Colfax, were implicated in this scheme, and the image of the administration was again tarnished.

The Panic of 1873 brought more economic trouble, which Congress hoped to cure simply by printing more money. But Grant held the line, vetoing the 1874 Inflation Bill, which would have mandated the printing of millions of greenbacks. Grant reasoned that the inflation would do the economy more harm than good in the long run, and he set the country on course to return to the gold standard; paper money would be promissory notes for various amounts of gold, not simply paper backed only by the good faith of the U.S. government.

President Grant was right in this, but he could not escape the impression of corrupt financial dealings. Even if he wasn't personally involved, his detractors argued, he was too lenient with his corrupt associates, of whom there were many. In 1875, Orville Babcock, his private secretary, was accused of being part of the "Whiskey Ring," the members of which were siphoning the revenues of whiskey taxes to their personal coffers. Secretary of the Treasury Benjamin Bristow confronted Grant with evidence of Babcock's guilt, but Grant refused to be convinced and even submitted a deposition at Babcock's trial. His friend was acquitted.

Accusations of cronyism and corruption intensified. Yet Grant maintained that he was in favor of the prosecution of the members of the Whiskey Ring. Throughout his presidency, despite numerous accusations, he was never found to have been fattening himself at the public trough. His besetting sin was a poor choice of subordinates.

Why his presidency was very good for America

As president, Ulysses S. Grant is a tragic figure. He had the best of intentions, better than most men who have held the office, but for a variety of reasons, not least because of his political inexperience and uncritical sense of personal loyalty, he was often unable to follow through on those intentions. Grant himself remarked: "It was my fortune, or misfortune, to be called to the office of chief executive without any previous political training.... Mistakes have been made, as all can see, and I admit, but it seems to me oftener in the selections made of the assistants appointed to aid in carrying out the various duties of administering the government."[232]

Grant's presidency is frequently classified as a failure, but failure is a relative term. There are presidents who were supremely effective at doing things that hurt the country; Grant was less than effective in doing things that would have greatly helped the country. Had he been able to fully implement and

---

232   Matuz, 296.

enforce his Reconstruction agenda, he would have gone down in history as one of the nation's greatest presidents, bridging and healing the racial divide that continues to be a source of strife. He failed, but he stands out in the Reconstruction period as one of the few who maintained his positions because it was the right thing to do, and tried to provide a pathway to a nation in which all men were truly created equal and endowed by their Creator with certain unalienable rights that the federal government was determined to do all it could to protect. That places him in the top tier among the presidents of the United States.

NINETEEN

RUTHERFORD B. HAYES

Library of Congress[233]

---

233 *President Rutherford B. Hayes, Half-Length Portrait, Seated, Facing Left,* 1877–1893, photograph, Library of Congress, https://www.loc.gov/item/96522533/.

Full name: Rutherford Birchard Hayes
Lived: October 4, 1822–January 17, 1893
Presidency: March 3, 1877–March 4, 1881
Party: Republican
Evaluation: Very Damaging for America
Rating: 2

What qualified him to be president

A one-term congressman and three-term governor of Ohio, not many people thought Rutherford B. Hayes was good presidential material as the 1876 campaign season began. The front-runner for the Republican nomination was Senator James G. Blaine of Maine, who had previously served as speaker of the House.

Blaine, however, was tainted by scandal: the Union Pacific Railroad had paid him $64,000 ($1.5 million) for some worthless stock in another railroad. It looked like a bribe, and Blaine only reinforced that impression when letters that he had written detailing the transactions surfaced. Blaine couldn't have looked guiltier when it came to light that one of them, written to a business associate named Warren Fisher, concluded: "Kind regards to Mrs. Fisher. Burn this letter."[234]

Another former Blaine associate, James Mulligan, had come forward with the letters. Blaine made matters even worse for himself when he asked Mulligan to meet him in a hotel room to discuss the letters. Mulligan agreed. During their meeting, Blaine asked Mulligan if he would let him see

---

234   Lorant, 383.

one of the letters for a moment to check a detail; the candidate then snatched them all out of a flabbergasted Mulligan's hand and ran out of the room. Blaine refused to turn over the letters, offering a sanitized version of events that many found unconvincing.

The Republican Convention turned instead to the relatively obscure Hayes, who had a reputation for probity and the advantage of being unconnected to any of the scandals of the Grant administration.

How he won

To counter Hayes, the Democrats nominated New York Governor Samuel J. Tilden. Tilden had begun to make a name for himself as a morally upright fighter against corruption back in the 1840s, as a member of the anti-slavery Democratic Party faction known as the "Barnburners" for their willingness to burn down the barn in order to rid it of rats—that is, split the party to stand on principle. He was a follower of Martin Van Buren and did indeed bolt the Democrats along with the Red Fox of Kinderhook to work for Van Buren's 1848 Free Soil presidential campaign. Later, Tilden's star rose in New York politics as an anti-corruption crusader, fighting against the corrupt Tammany Hall political machine.

Tilden was the Democrats' third straight candidate from New York (and McClellan before that was from New Jersey). With the South largely in their camp even during Reconstruction, the Democrats knew that it was the North they had to win to regain the White House. And while the Republicans "waved the bloody shirt," as they had in 1868 and 1872—that is, accused the Democrats of responsibility for the Civil War—the Democrats had an effective comeback as the party of clean government fighting against the corrupt party of Grant and Blaine.

It almost worked; actually, it may really have worked. Tilden won the popular vote by 250,000 votes over Hayes. He also seemed to have won the electoral vote, and hence the presidency. However, in three Southern states, South Carolina, Louisiana, and Florida, the Democrats and Republicans produced two separate popular vote tabulations, both claiming victory in each state. There was also a dispute about one elector in Oregon, where the Democratic governor had appointed a Democrat after a Republican elector resigned and the Republicans cried foul. At stake were twenty electoral votes. The undisputed tally had Tilden with 184 and Hayes with 165, so if Hayes were awarded all twenty of the disputed votes, he would win the presidency by one vote.

The dispute roiled the nation. No one was sure what to do, as the Constitution hadn't provided for such a contingency, and while the Republicans may have been engaged in voter fraud, the Democrats had almost certainly practiced voter suppression, preventing freedmen, who voted for the party that freed the slaves, from voting, or throwing out their votes uncounted. In 1878, a congressional investigation found evidence of Democratic attempts to bribe election officials. But it is unlikely that the Republicans weren't cheating as well.

Enraged Democrats charged that the Republicans were trying to steal the election. Some, crying "Tilden or Blood!," even threatened a new civil war if their candidate was not declared the victor.[235] Finally, Congress appointed a commission of seven Democrats, seven Republicans, and one independent to determine which votes to accept and which to reject. The independent, however, Supreme Court Justice David Davis, resigned to take a seat in the Senate; his replacement was a Republican, and the die was cast. On an 8–7 party-line vote, the Republican vote totals were accepted. Hayes was named "the duly elected President of the United States" on March 3, 1877, the day before the inauguration.

The Democrats accepted this, although they derided Hayes as "Rutherfraud" throughout his presidency.[236] Tilden took the news resignedly, saying: "I prefer four years of Hayes' administration to four years of civil war."[237] He withdrew from the field while maintaining the rightness of his cause: "I can retire to private life with the consciousness that I shall receive from posterity the credit of having been elected to the highest position in the gift of the people, without any of the cares and responsibilities of the office."[238]

One reason why the Democrats did not draw out the dispute or refuse to accept the commission's decision that Hayes had won was that they had driven a hard bargain: as a condition of their accepting Hayes's election, they demanded, and received, the withdrawal of federal troops from the South. Reconstruction was over, and with it died any semblance

---

235 Lorant, 338.
236 Matuz, 314.
237 Lorant, 342.
238 Charles Van Doren and Robert McHenry, eds., *Webster's Guide to American History: A Chronological, Geographical, and Biographical Survey and Compendium* (Springfield, MA: Merriam Webster, 1971), 276.

of equality of rights for black Americans. Republican "carpetbaggers" packed up their carpetbags and returned to the North; the South became a one-party state that replicated antebellum society, with blacks denied voting rights and discriminated against in numerous other ways.

Was the reinforcement of second-class status for the freed slaves and the end of any chance to make America a society in which all people truly enjoyed equality of rights worth it, so that the country could experience the presidency of Rutherford B. Hayes? No.

Notable accomplishments as president and events of his presidency

1. *Ending Reconstruction.* Grant began and Hayes finished the withdrawal of troops from the South, ending the Reconstruction period. In doing so, they enabled the creation of the "Solid South," which voted nearly unanimously Democratic in virtually every national, state, and local election for the next eighty years and systematically deprived black Americans of equality of rights.

2. *Advocating for civil service reform.* The Hayes campaign had touted him as a foe of corruption, and President Hayes duly set his sights on the spoils system, under which jobs in the federal government went to members of the president's party. This practice led to numerous incompetent people being placed in positions of responsibility. Hayes sought to remedy that by making civil service jobs based on merit rather than party affiliation.

Civil service reform, however, faced stiff opposition in Congress. Both parties benefited from the system in place, but the principal opposition came from the Republican New York Senator Roscoe Conkling, an influential power broker who was the leader of the Stalwarts, the supporters of the spoils system.

Unable to get a civil service bill passed, Hayes issued an executive order that forbade political parties to require federal officeholders to make contributions to them or work for them. When Hayes faced open defiance from a Stalwart named Chester A. Arthur, the Collector of the Port of New York, the president fired him, and then was unable to get Congress to confirm Arthur's designated replacement, Theodore Roosevelt, Sr., father of the future president.

Civil service reform would come to the federal government, but Hayes would not be the president to bring it. The president who finally achieved it was the man Hayes fired for resisting it, Chester Arthur.

3. *Standing for justice for Indians.* In February 1881, President Hayes wrote: "Nothing should be left undone to show the Indians that the Government of the United States regards their rights as equally sacred with those of its citizens. The time has come when the policy should be to place the Indians as rapidly as possible on the same footing as the other permanent inhabitants of our country."[239] By that time, however, he only had a month left as president. His record in actually bringing equal justice to American Indians is uneven.

---

239   United States Indian Claims Commission, *Indian Claims Commission Decisions, Volume 17* (Boulder, CO: Native American Rights Fund, 1978), 188.

Why his presidency was damaging for America

No one can know for sure what would have happened if federal troops had remained in the South after 1877. Many have represented the end of Reconstruction as the beginning of national healing from the wounds of the civil war, but that healing came only to one segment of the population. The continued discrimination against and disenfranchisement of a large section of the population was not good for America. It gave fuel to those who claimed that the ideals for which the nation stood were a sham, and it planted the seeds for future strife, as we are seeing today.

If the federal government had been consistent and thorough in its enforcement of the citizenship rights and voting rights of the freed slaves, perhaps national divisions would be healed by now. Even if strict enforcement of Reconstruction laws had not bound up the nation's wounds, the very act of that enforcement would have strengthened the United States' commitment to the high ideals upon which it was founded and made it abundantly clear that the lofty words of the Declaration of Independence about all men being created equal were not just empty rhetoric. Either outcome would likely have been better for America in the long run.

There is no doubt that those entrusted with enforcing Reconstruction in the South were often corrupt and unjust. But the endeavor should have been reformed, not ended altogether. Many have suggested that the brutality of Reconstruction itself gave rise to the Ku Klux Klan and the total disenfranchisement of the freed slaves as a reaction to its injustices, but the chronology doesn't bear that out: the Klan was founded in December 1865, when Reconstruction had barely begun.

In any case, instead of working to reform it and protect justice for all, the Republicans acquiesced to what the Democrats actively brought about: the reimposition of the South's racial caste system, which represented a resurgence of the slave power that had been defeated in the nation's bloodiest war. "The policy of the president," said a congressman named James A. Garfield, "has turned out to be a give-away from the beginning. He has nulled suits, discontinued prosecutions, offered conciliations in the South, while they have spent their time in whetting their knives for any Republican they could find."[240]

Ending Reconstruction would by no means be the last time that the Democrats were out front on a course of action that was decidedly harmful to America, and instead of resisting, the Republicans tamely played along.

---

240   Matuz, 315.

JAMES A. GARFIELD

Library of Congress[241]

---

241   *President James A. Garfield, Half-Length Portrait, Facing Right*, 1870–1881, photograph, Library of Congress, https://www.loc.gov/item/96522558/.

Full name: James Abram Garfield
Lived: November 19, 1831–September 19, 1881
Presidency: March 4, 1881–September 19, 1881
Party: Republican
Evaluation: Did Little Good but Not Much Damage
Rating: 5

What qualified him to be president

James A. Garfield was the first, and to this day remains the only, sitting congressman to be elected president of the United States. He was not initially a candidate for president in 1880, but his speech at the Republican National Convention nominating former Ohio senator John Sherman for president was so compelling that the convention turned to him on the thirty-sixth ballot after the two front-runners, former president Ulysses S. Grant and Maine Senator James G. Blaine, both proved too tainted by charges of corruption to be acceptable to a majority of delegates.

Garfield was a champion of civil service reform; to mollify the Stalwarts, or Republicans who favored the spoils system, the vice-presidential nod went to Chester Alan Arthur, the man whom Hayes had fired from his job as Collector of the Port of New York for ignoring Hayes's civil service reform executive order forbidding forcing federal officers to make campaign contributions. No one was concerned about this: Garfield was only forty-eight and in perfect health, and the Civil War, which led to the assassination of Lincoln, had been over for fifteen years.

How he won

In the 1880 presidential contest, Garfield faced Democratic candidates Winfield Scott Hancock for president and William H. English for vice president. The two candidates were virtually indistinguishable: both had been major generals in the Civil War and had served with distinction; both were proponents of civil service reform; and both had reputations as honest men, although the Democrats did all they could to portray Garfield as yet another corrupt politician on the take. Their chief point of attack was the fact that Garfield had been involved in the Crédit Mobilier scandal back in 1872, having accepted $329 ($7,150 today) from the company that he later paid back, saying it was a loan.

The Democrats ran with this, writing "329" everywhere in order to remind people of the scandal and Garfield's supposed corruption. The number was chalked on the walls and sidewalks of major cities and in virtually every other place where Democrats could be found. Apparently, Hayes's secretary of state, William Evarts, employed a Democrat among his domestic staff, for he found "329" scrawled on the headboard of his bed. Secretary of War Alexander Ramsey must have employed a Democrat as well: one morning at breakfast he saw that "329" was written on his napkin. The commissioner of agriculture, William Gates LeDuc, found a beet placed on his desk; on it was carved "329."

It didn't work. Garfield had never been charged or even credibly accused of any wrongdoing. He wrote: "There is nothing in my relation to the case for which tenderest conscience or the most scrupulous honor can blame me."[242] Most Americans seemed to agree; the Democratic charges didn't stick.

The Republicans, meanwhile, noticing that their opponents' major general had a more impressive war record than their major general, resorted to ridicule: they published a pamphlet entitled "A Record of the Statesmanship and Political Achievements of General Winfield Scott Hancock... Compiled from the Records," which consisted of nothing but blank pages.[243] They made an issue out of the Democratic platform's call for "a tariff for revenue only," arguing that high tariffs were necessary to protect American industries.[244] When Hancock tried to defuse the controversy by saying "the tariff is a local issue," the ridicule began anew.[245] Political cartoonist Thomas Nast drew Hancock asking an associate, "Who is Tariff, and why is he for revenue only?"[246]

Another controversy during the campaign was over the mass Chinese immigration into the West that the railroad companies were sponsoring. Both parties opposed it on the grounds that it put American workers at a disadvantage, as the Chinese immigrants worked for lower wages. The Democrats pledged that: "the toiling millions of our own people will be protected from the destructive competition of the Chinese, and

---

242   Candice Millard, *Destiny of the Republic: A Tale of Madness, Medicine, and the Murder of a President* (New York: Anchor Books, 2011), 68–69.

243   Boller, loc. 1960.

244   Edward B. Dickinson, official stenographer, *Official Proceedings of the National Democratic Convention* (Dayton, OH: Daily Journal Book and Job Rooms, 1882), 128.

245   Boller, loc. 1960.

246   Ibid.

to that end their immigration to our shores will be properly restricted."[247] The Republican platform likewise stated that:

> Since the authority to regulate immigration and intercourse between the United States and foreign nations rests with the Congress of the United States and the treaty-making power, the Republican party, regarding the unrestricted immigration of the Chinese as a matter of grave concernment under the exercise of both these powers, would limit and restrict that immigration by the enactment of such just, humane and reasonable laws and treaties as will produce that result.[248]

Nowadays such concerns would be dismissed as "racism," but neither party appealed to race in making their case; they presented their concern about mass Chinese immigration as stemming from a desire to protect the American worker. No one doubted that immigration could or should be restricted in the national interest. Opponents of restricting Chinese immigration, however, did claim that racism was what was behind the proposal.

On October 20, 1880, less than two weeks before the election, the Chinese immigration issue threatened to upend the entire Republican campaign. The Democrats published

---

247   Dickinson, 168.
248   Gerhard Peters and John T. Woolley, "Republican Party Platform of 1880," American Presidency Project, June 2, 1880, https://www.presidency.ucsb.edu/documents/republican-party-platform-1880.

a letter purportedly from Garfield, in which the candidate supposedly wrote that he opposed restrictions on Chinese immigration, as "individuals or Company have the right to buy labor where they can get it cheapest."[249] One Democratic organ that published the letter called it "Garfield's Death Warrant" and gleefully claimed that because of it, "A Prominent Republican Journal Deserts Garfield. And Hoists the Names of Hancock and English, the Glorious Leaders of the Democracy."[250]

Garfield dismissed the letter as a forgery, but it almost certainly cost him votes in the West. The election was extremely close: Garfield won the popular vote by only 1,898 votes, the smallest margin in any American presidential election, although his electoral margin over Hancock was more comfortable, 214 to 155.

In victory, Garfield felt an obscure sense of foreboding. "There is," he wrote, "a tone of sadness running through this triumph which I can hardly explain."[251]

Notable accomplishments as president and events of his presidency

1. *Calling for equal rights for black Americans.* In his inaugural address, Garfield declared: "The elevation of the negro

---

249   "Garfield's Death Warrant. That Letter in Which He Advocates an Extended Chinese Immigration—He Advises the Employer's Union of Lynn, Mass., 'That the Question of Employees Is Only a Question of Private and Corporate Economy'—Read, Workingmen," *Advertiser Extra*, October 20, 1880, Library of Congress, https://www.loc.gov/resource/rbpe.1600140b/?st=text.

250   Ibid.

251   Millard, 73.

race from slavery to the full rights of citizenship is the most important political change we have known since the adoption of the Constitution of 1787. No thoughtful man can fail to appreciate its beneficent effect upon our institutions and people.... No doubt this great change has caused serious disturbance to our Southern communities. This is to be deplored, though it was perhaps unavoidable. But those who resisted the change should remember that under our institutions there was no middle ground for the negro race between slavery and equal citizenship. There can be no permanent disfranchised peasantry in the United States. Freedom can never yield its fullness of blessings so long as the law or its administration places the smallest obstacle in the pathway of any virtuous citizen."[252]

Garfield pledged that "so far as my authority can lawfully extend they shall enjoy the full and equal protection of the Constitution and the laws," deplored the denial of voting rights to blacks, and called for a universal educational system that would be open to black as well as white children.[253] All of this was a bit too late, however, as with the withdrawal of troops from the South in 1877, the federal government had foreclosed upon any possibility of enforcing black voting rights and educational opportunities.

2. *Advocating for civil service reform.* Garfield believed that the spoils system was an unending source of government corruption and pushed for measures that would end it. When

---

252   James A. Garfield, "Inaugural Address" (speech, March 4, 1881), Bartleby, https://www.bartleby.com/124/pres36.html.
253   Ibid.

a scheme to steal the public revenues was discovered in the Post Office Department, President Garfield moved swiftly, firing those implicated and calling for the prosecution of anyone involved, no matter how high a position he occupied. Accompanying this was his insistence on adopting a merit-based system that would, he hoped, reduce corruption by removing federal offices from the realm of partisan politics. He did not live to see this come to fruition.

Why his presidency did little good but not much damage

Garfield had only been president for four months when, on July 2, 1881, he and Secretary of State James G. Blaine were walking through the Baltimore and Potomac Railroad Station in Washington, on their way to board a train to spend part of the summer in New Jersey, away from the heat of the capital. Just then, a man stepped up behind Garfield and fired his gun twice at the president, hitting him in the back and arm, and crying, "I am a Stalwart and now Arthur is President!"[254]

That man was Charles Guiteau, who has been described in so many history books as a "disappointed office seeker" that the label has practically become a Homeric epithet. A disappointed office seeker Guiteau undeniably was, but he was much more than that. After repeatedly pressing Chester Arthur for a chance to campaign for the Garfield/Arthur ticket during the 1880 campaign, Arthur relented, likely just to end his harassment, and Guiteau delivered his speech, "Garfield

---

254   Matuz, 344.

against Hancock," a single time. Guiteau thought he was owed a federal office as a result and had pestered White House officials repeatedly for a chance to see Garfield, who did meet with him at least once, and then Blaine in order to make his case for an appointment as consul to France.

Guiteau was, however, not an ordinary office seeker. He wanted a position in France but did not speak French. His sister recounted that in 1875, six years before the assassination, he had raised an axe to her with a look on his face "like a wild animal."[255] She explained: "I had no doubt then of his insanity. He was losing his mind."[256] In 1881, before the assassination, he also pressured Senator John Logan of Illinois for a federal job; Logan recounted: "I must say I thought there was some derangement of his mental organization."[257]

There was. As he bought a pistol and hatched his plan to murder Garfield, Guiteau wrote: "The Lord inspired me to attempt to remove the President in preference to someone else, because I had the brains and the nerve to do the work. The Lord always employs the best material to do His work."[258]

The wounds he gave to Garfield were not mortal, and the president lingered through the summer. This was, however, the age before sanitary practices were known to be necessary. On September 19, 1881, Garfield died of infections his doctors had given him in probing the wound.

---

255   Millard, 64.
256   Ibid.
257   Ibid., 124.
258   Ibid., 137.

At his trial, Guiteau stated that he was pleading "insanity, in that it was God's act and not mine. The Divine pressure on me to remove the president was so enormous that it destroyed my free agency, and therefore I am not responsible for my act."[259]

Guiteau was not a "disappointed office seeker" first and foremost; he was a madman. That he has gone down in history as the former rather than the latter can be attributed to attempts to discredit the spoils system and advance the merits of civil service reform. Although Guiteau thought that by elevating Arthur to the presidency he was protecting the spoils system, his crime had the opposite effect: national revulsion over the killing of Garfield made civil service reform the most pressing issue of the day. The time for that reform had come at last, even as the Stalwart Arthur took the oath of office.

---

259   Ibid., 274.

CHESTER A. ARTHUR

Library of Congress[260]

---

260   C. M. Bell, *Chester A. Arthur, President of the United States*, 1882, photograph, Library of Congress, https://www.loc.gov/item/96524270/.

Full name: Chester Alan Arthur
Lived: October 5, 1829–November 18, 1886
Presidency: September 20, 1881–March 4, 1885
Party: Republican
Evaluation: Very Good for America
Rating: 8

What qualified him to be president

Although Chester A. Arthur is forgotten today, his memory once shone brightly. Nearly a quarter-century after the death of the twenty-first president, the parents of the renowned twentieth-century bluesman known as Howlin' Wolf named him Chester Arthur Burnett. This was because Arthur was a champion of civil rights in an age when very few were.

In 1854, when he was twenty-five, Arthur joined the law firm of Erastus D. Culver, at which he formed part of a legal team that argued successfully for the freedom of any slaves that their owners brought to New York. Arthur also led the defense team for a black woman, Elizabeth Jennings Graham, who was not allowed to ride a New York City streetcar. The future president won the case, and New York City streetcars were desegregated, one hundred years before Rosa Parks, courtesy of Chester Arthur.

How he became president

Arthur had been quartermaster general of the New York Militia during the Civil War; after the war, he became a key cog in the political machine of New York political boss Roscoe

Conkling, an influential power broker in the Republican Party. In 1868, he became chairman of the New York City Republican executive committee and, in 1869, legal counsel to the New York City Tax Commission; his star continued to rise. In December 1871, President Grant appointed him Collector of the Port of New York. The *New York Times* wrote approvingly of the choice, saying of Arthur that "his name very seldom rises to the surface of metropolitan life and yet moving like a mighty undercurrent this man during the last 10 years has done more to mold the course of the Republican Party in this state than any other one man in the country."[261]

Collector of the Port of New York was a powerful and lucrative position. Arthur's annual salary was $50,000 ($1 million today), which was the same as the president's and almost seven times more than what Supreme Court justices made. New York was not just the most active port in the country, but in the entire world, and the customs duties collected there were the federal government's largest single revenue source, making Arthur one of the most powerful men in the country.

Arthur remained Conkling's man, hiring and firing employees at the Port of New York based on their Republican Party bona fides. Arthur became the focus of the controversy between the spoils system and civil service reform in 1878, when President Hayes fired him for ignoring Hayes's executive order forbidding the practice of requiring federal employees to make campaign contributions. Supporters of civil service

---

261 M. Scott Norton, *The White House and Education through the Years: U.S. Presidents' Views and Significant Educational Contributions* (Lanham, MD: Rowman & Littlefield, 2018), 57–8.

reform advocated, instead of making federal jobs subject to political patronage, for a merit-based system in which government employees could not be fired simply for being a member of the opposition party.

Instead of ending Arthur's political career, his firing by Hayes proved to be, for Arthur, a step to even greater things. In 1880, despite having held no elected office, Arthur was nominated for vice president as a sop to Conkling after James A. Garfield, a supporter of civil service reform, got the presidential nomination. Supporters of reform considered Arthur's presence on the ticket a sign that Republicans were simply not committed to cleaning up the corruption that the spoils system had enabled. For Arthur was not just a Stalwart; outside of Conkling himself, he was the most prominent exponent of the old system and a man who had stood for it at great personal cost.

Arthur's identification with the Stalwarts was so total that Garfield's assassin invoked him after shooting the president, proclaiming, "I am a Stalwart, and now Arthur is President!"

But contrary to the prevailing view then and now of the Stalwarts as corrupt and interested only in lining their pockets, Chester Arthur was a man of strong convictions. His misfortune was that in being faithful to those convictions, he gave the appearance of being disloyal to his longtime friends and political associates.

When he became president, Arthur proceeded to shock the entire nation, and especially his patron Conkling, by supporting civil service reform. His determination that he had a responsibility to do what Garfield would have done outweighed his commitment to the Stalwarts. He declared his support for civil service legislation, explaining that not he, but Garfield, had been elected president, and that he consequently had a responsibility to carry out his policies.

It was an unusual and courageous stand, but few were in the mood to hail Arthur as a paragon of moral integrity. Some, however, did realize what he was really made of. In 1884, Arthur sought the Republican nomination in his own right, but he was quite ill from Bright's disease, and many Republicans opposed his candidacy out of a belief that he had betrayed them. However, one of the speakers seconding Arthur's nomination for president at the Republican National Convention that year was Pinckney B. S. Pinchback of Louisiana, who during Reconstruction had been the first black man to serve as the governor of a state and had been elected to the U.S. Senate, although Senate Democrats prevented him from taking his seat. Pinchback called Arthur "a prudent, a safe and a reliable ruler," and demonstrated that Arthur's lifelong stand for the equality of rights of black Americans had not gone unnoticed.[262]

Notable accomplishments as president and events of his presidency

1. *Civil service reform.* On January 16, 1883, Arthur signed the Pendleton Civil Service Reform Act, which mandated that some employees of the government would be hired on the basis of written tests, not political affiliation, and forbade the firing of government employees for political purposes.

---

262   *Official Proceedings of the Republican National Convention: Held at Chicago, June 3, 4, 5 and 6, 1884* (Charles W. Johnson, 1903), 119–120.

2. *Restricting immigration.* President Arthur signed the Immigration Act of 1882, which excluded convicted criminals and other groups, including the insane and those unable to take care of themselves, from entering the United States. If he were president today, Arthur would be excoriated for this and accused of all manner of "hatred." He was, however, acting in the interests of the American people—putting America first and excluding those who would be a danger to the country or a drain upon its resources. While it would be nice for the United States to take in all the needy people of the world, to do so would overtax the nation's ability to care for them all and eventually overwhelm the country altogether; consequently, measures of this kind are sometimes necessary for the nation to continue and thrive, even if they appear heartless to modern sensibilities.

Under pressure from lawmakers, Arthur also signed the Chinese Exclusion Act of 1882, which was based on the proposition that large-scale Chinese immigration endangered American workers, as the Chinese would work for lower wages than the Americans would. However, many at the time believed that the whole controversy over Chinese immigration was really motivated by simple racism. An 1882 political cartoon depicted a Chinese man sitting forlornly outside the closed "Golden Gate of Liberty," next to a sign reading "Notice–Communist Nihilist–Socialist Fenian & Hoodlum Welcome but No Admittance to Chinamen."[263] Massachusetts Republican Senator George Frisbie Hoar said that the Chinese

---

263   *Frank Leslie's Illustrated Newspaper*, vol. 54, April 1, 1882, 96, Library of Congress, http://loc.gov/pictures/resource/cph.3b48680/.

Exclusion Act was "nothing less than the legalization of racial discrimination."[264]

Maybe it was. If proponents of the measure had really been primarily interested in protecting American wage earners, they could have found a way to devise a bill that did not exclude people based on their ethnicity. That they did not do so has given rhetorical ammunition ever since to those who oppose responsible restrictions on immigration: any and all such measures are now greeted with charges of nativism, racism, and xenophobia.

3. *Working for civil rights.* Perhaps demonstrating that his acquiescence to the Chinese Exclusion Act was not racially motivated, Arthur as president continued to stand for the equality of rights of all people before the law. He deplored the Democratic Party takeover of the South and worked with third parties in the South to try to build a coalition that would dislodge the Democrats from power and end the denial of civil rights to black Americans. This initiative failed, as did Arthur's request to Congress for new legislation to replace the Civil Rights Act of 1875, which the Supreme Court declared unconstitutional in 1883.

President Arthur had greater success on a smaller scale, when he intervened to order the freeing from prison of the black West Point Cadet Johnson Chesnut Whittaker, who had been railroaded, dishonorably discharged, and court-martialed in a case marred by racial bias.

---

264   Roger Daniels, *Asian America: Chinese and Japanese in the United States since 1850*, (Seattle: University of Washington Press, 2011), 54.

4. Outlawing polygamy. Consistent with his lifelong commitment to civil rights, President Arthur in 1882 signed the Edmunds Act, outlawing polygamy and barring polygamists from holding public office. This was a response to the growth of the Church of Jesus Christ of Latter-Day Saints in the Utah Territory; the Mormons would not ban polygamy until 1890, as a condition for Utah's becoming a state. The Edmunds Act was an important step toward recognizing the human dignity of women and stigmatizing the practice of treating them as commodities.

Why his presidency was very good for America

Chester Arthur demonstrated immense personal courage and honor in choosing to carry out the wishes of his slain predecessor rather than implement his own contrary agenda. His decision to do this effectively ended his political career, as he almost certainly knew it would, and yet he stood firm.

Whether his stance was entirely wise in the long run is a separate question. Historians take for granted that civil service reform was good for the country, and there has been no significant indication that it wasn't until quite recently, when a president has been thwarted in numerous endeavors by an army of unelected bureaucrats within the various departments and agencies of the government, who are determined to impede his agenda in every way possible.

The proponents of civil service reform never envisioned a situation in which deeply entrenched opponents of a sitting president in the FBI, the Justice Department, and elsewhere would be determined to destroy the president—or at very least make it impossible for him to carry out his policies—and could not be removed from their jobs because of civil service regulations.

Would not government work more smoothly, and the executive branch be able to operate more effectively in the way the Founding Fathers envisioned it would, if the president were able to clear out the employees of these agencies who opposed him and replace them with people more in line with his vision?

The spoils system has no defenders today and has had none for over a century. It should have more.

Nonetheless, when President Arthur signed the Pendleton Civil Service Reform Act, he meant to strike a blow for honest and good government, and to a large extent, he did. The deficiencies of the merit-based system for hiring and retaining government employees have come about through the abuse of that system to provide lifetime appointments for partisan hacks, but that practice did not begin until long after Arthur left the White House. His presidency is underrated and unappreciated.

TWENTY-TWO

GROVER CLEVELAND

Library of Congress[265]

---

265   *President Grover Cleveland, Half-Length Portrait, Facing Right*, ca. 1888,
       photograph, Library of Congress, https://www.loc.gov/item/96511406/.

Full name: Stephen Grover Cleveland
Lived: March 18, 1837–June 24, 1908
Presidency: March 4, 1885–March 4, 1889
Party: Democratic
Evaluation: Did Good Things but Also Significant
    Damage
Rating: 6

What qualified him to be president

In an age that was rife with political corruption, Grover Cleveland had a strong reputation for honest dealing. That propelled him into the White House and made him the only man to return there after having lost a bid for reelection. As mayor of Buffalo, New York, and later as governor of the state, Cleveland acquired a reputation for fiscal responsibility and unflinching opposition to corrupt officials.

That reputation gave him the Democratic Party's presidential nomination on the second ballot in 1884, as the Democrats, able to count on the Solid South but needing votes from the North, nominated their fourth candidate from New York in five elections.

How he won

Cleveland had such a sterling reputation in 1884 that when the Republicans nominated former senator and secretary of state James G. Blaine (on his third try for the prize), a group of influential Republicans bolted the party and declared their support for the Democratic candidate. The "Mugwumps," as they came to be known, refused to support a man whose name had become synonymous with corruption, and whom Democrats mocked in a famous chant, "Blaine, Blaine, James G. Blaine, the continental liar from the state of Maine."[266]

Republicans countered with what they hoped would be a death blow to Cleveland on the issue of personal character: they uncovered evidence that he had fathered an illegitimate son ten years before and paid child support to the child's mother. Contrary to the popular image of the Victorian age, however, this gained little traction; voters seemed more concerned with the candidates' behavior in positions of public responsibility than with their private lives, and that was bad news for James G. Blaine.

Still, the election looked to be very close, like those of 1876 and 1880. Blaine's campaign received a significant boost when Tammany Hall, the notorious New York Democratic political machine, quietly backed Blaine rather than Cleveland, although to those who wanted clean government, this only seemed to be new confirmation of Blaine's corruption and Cleveland's uprightness. Then, on October 29, 1884, just six days before the election, Blaine attended a rally in New York City in which the Reverend Samuel D. Burchard of the Murray Hill Presbyterian Church denounced the Democrats as the party of "rum, Romanism and rebellion."[267]

Rummies, Romanists, and rebels were furious, as were Democrats who resented their party being thus characterized. The Democrats gleefully took up the phrase, and Tammany's

---

266   Lorant, 383.
267   Lorant, 388.

endorsement was undone: Irish Catholics, who had been expected to vote for Blaine in high numbers, turned away from him in droves. Blaine lost New York State by just over a thousand votes, and with it, the presidency.

Notable accomplishments as president and events of his presidency

1. *Civil service reform.* Cleveland was the first Democratic president in twenty-four years, but he quickly dashed the hopes of Democrats assuming they would be in line for patronage jobs in the federal government: he announced that he would not fire Republican officials just because they were Republican, although, under pressure from members of his own party, he did retreat slightly from this stance, dismissing some Republican officials and replacing them with Democrats.

2. *Standing for constitutional limitations on government and against the welfare state.* On February 16, 1887, Cleveland vetoed "An Act to enable the Commissioner of Agriculture to make a special distribution of seeds in drought-stricken counties of Texas, and making an appropriation therefor."[268] Cleveland acknowledged that "a long-continued and extensive drought has existed in certain portions of the State of Texas, resulting in a failure of crops and consequent distress and destitution." However, he added: "I can find no warrant for such an appropriation in the Constitution, and I do not believe

---

268   Grover Cleveland, "Cleveland's Veto of the Texas Seed Bill,"
       February 16, 1887, WikiSource, https://en.wikisource.org/wiki/
       Cleveland's_Veto_of_the_Texas_Seed_Bill.

that the power and duty of the general government ought to be extended to the relief of individual suffering which is in no manner properly related to the public service or benefit."

The president concluded: "The people support the government, the government should not support the people." Such a notion would be jarring to many today, when it is widely taken for granted that government can and should provide all manner of services, and that its largesse should not be restricted even to citizens alone.

3. *Fighting for low tariffs.* High tariff rates protected American industries, rebuilding in the post-Civil War period, from competition with British industries at a time when Britain was an unmatched world power. However, high tariffs meant higher prices for consumers in the short term, as American businesses could not yet match the lower prices offered by their more established British competitors. Cleveland wanted tariff reduction but was unable to get it through Congress.

Why his presidency did good things, but also significant damage

President Cleveland's determination to destroy the spoils system and allow Republican officeholders to keep their job if their performance was satisfactory was in keeping with his reputation for fairness and incorruptibility and helped to burnish that reputation. Nobody foresaw at the time that it was the seed of the entrenched Washington bureaucracy that is accountable to no one and can impede the elected president's policies at will.

Another aspect of Cleveland's presidency that was good for America was his veto of the Texas Seed Bill. President Cleveland held the line against the gargantuan growth of governmental services, as well as of the government's power, that became a hallmark of the twentieth-century presidency. His vision was in keeping with the Founding Fathers' determination not to submit to tyrants and not to create a government that could become a tyranny. If that vision became current again today, Americans would once again be able to stop the advance of a tyranny.

Cleveland's resolve to lower tariffs, however, was not nearly as wise. In his last annual message to Congress of his first term, delivered on December 3, 1888, after he had already lost his bid for reelection, Cleveland decried the growing gap between rich and poor in America: "We find the wealth and luxury of our cities mingled with poverty and wretchedness and unremunerative toil.... The gulf between employers and the employed is constantly widening, and classes are rapidly forming, one comprising the very rich and powerful, while in another are found the toiling poor."[269]

Many other politicians would echo Cleveland's rhetoric over the years. His characterization may have been true, but it is more important as one of the earliest enunciations of the idea that it is the responsibility of the federal government to relieve the poverty of some American citizens. Cleveland's call for social justice was the beginning of the Democratic

---

269 Grover Cleveland, "Fourth Annual Message" (speech, December 3, 1888), UVA Miller Center, https://millercenter.org/the-presidency/presidential-speeches/december-3-1888-fourth-annual-message.

Party's downhill slide into large-scale state control, and of the ever-popular idea that the government must forever grow and become ever more intrusive into the citizenry's daily lives in a messianic attempt to end human misery.

The man who actually said these words was not able to act fully upon them. Nonetheless, all this was undeniably true; the question of what to do about it was less clear. President Cleveland called on Congress to cut taxes, which was eminently sensible, as in those days the government was running a surplus. He also called for lower tariffs, and, in doing so, he contradicted his declaration in the Texas Seed Bill veto a year earlier. Now Cleveland said that one who "proposes that the Government shall protect the rich and that they in turn will care for the laboring poor" actually "mocks the people." He added: "Any intermediary between the people and their Government or the least delegation of the care and protection the Government owes to the humblest citizen in the land makes the boast of free institutions a glittering delusion and the pretended boon of American citizenship a shameless imposition."[270]

So the government owed "care and protection" to the "humblest citizen in the land"—this from the man who had said: "I do not believe that the power and duty of the general government ought to be extended to the relief of individual suffering."

In his rhetoric about the gap between rich and poor, however, what Cleveland did not realize, as many others have failed to realize up to our own day, is that the government

---

270   Ibid.

need not protect the rich, but if it ends up hindering the rich and the ability to become rich, the poor will inevitably suffer, for it is the rich who run the businesses that employ the poor.

Low tariffs benefited consumers in the short run, but in Cleveland's time as today, insufficient attention was paid to the fact that prosperous American businesses were better for American consumers in the long run. Protected from competition from British industries, American industries were able to grow and provide more jobs for Americans. The high tariffs of the late nineteenth century were among the policies that paved the way for the golden age of American prosperity, when the United States became the world's strongest and most powerful economy.

In Cleveland's day, the benefit of high tariffs was not instant but became clear after he had left the White House. They helped to bring about an age of economic expansion and American inventiveness that resulted in the transformation of society by the phonograph, the light bulb, the automobile, and much more. American industries arose around these innovations that employed hundreds of thousands, if not millions, of Americans, and that may well not have survived competition from foreign companies that were able to undercut them. In refusing to go along unreservedly with his efforts to lower tariffs, Congress saved Cleveland from himself, and America from policies that would have caused harm well into the twentieth century. American workers, and the nation as a whole, benefited from the growth of American industry. In the labor controversies of the coming century, this fact was all too often overlooked.

TWENTY-THREE

BENJAMIN HARRISON

Library of Congress[271]

---

271   Geo Prince, *Benjamin Harrison, Three-Quarter Length Portrait, Seated, Facing Left, with Right Hand on Table*, 1888, photograph, https://www.loc.gov/item/96524264/.

Full name: Benjamin Harrison
Lived: August 20, 1833–March 13, 1901
Presidency: March 4, 1889–March 4, 1893
Party: Republican
Evaluation: Did Little Good but Not Much Damage
Rating: 5

What qualified him to be president

Benjamin Harrison came from a family of patriots and public servants. He was the grandson of a president, William Henry Harrison, and the great-grandson of a signer of the Declaration of Independence, who was also named Benjamin Harrison. His father, John Scott Harrison, was a congressman. During the Civil War, Harrison himself served as a colonel and as a commander of an Indiana brigade; he was honored with the grade of brevet brigadier general shortly before the war ended.

After the war, Harrison became active in the Indiana Republican Party, ran twice for governor of the state and lost both times. Then he served one term as a U.S. senator from Indiana and was defeated in his bid for reelection.

It was a thin résumé for a presidential candidate, to be sure, but when James G. Blaine withdrew his name from consideration for the 1888 Republican presidential nomination, Harrison's way was relatively clear. Senator John Sherman, the brother of Civil War General William Tecumseh Sherman, led in the early balloting at the Republican National Convention, but Harrison overtook him on the seventh ballot and won the nomination on the eighth, largely because he had a more impressive war record than Sherman and was from a state the Republicans needed to win, Indiana, while Sherman was from reliably Republican Ohio. He also lacked the defects that others had: he wasn't famously corrupt like Blaine or too closely identified with either the backers of the gold standard or of free silver or any other of the burning issues of the day.

How he won

The tariff was the big issue of the 1888 campaign, with Harrison campaigning on a pledge to protect American industries and President Cleveland calling for tariffs to be lowered so that American individual consumers could obtain lower-priced, foreign-made goods. The Republican platform declared: "We are uncompromisingly in favor of the American system of protection. We protest against its destruction, as proposed by the President and his party. They serve the interests of Europe; we will support the interests of America."[272] Republican marchers held aloft banners saying, "Cleveland Runs Well in England" and "We Are Not Going to Vote Away Our Wages."[273] They argued that lowering tariffs would mean the end of American prosperity.

This message didn't exactly resonate with the American voter, who was also hearing from the Democrats that low tariffs would mean low prices. In the end, Cleveland won the popular vote, but Harrison and his team managed to keep the Reverend Burchard of Rum, Romanism, and Rebellion fame

---

272   Lorant, 401.
273   Ibid., 404.

quiet and carry New York, which, once again, decided the election. Harrison also got help from Tammany Hall, which was as unwilling to endorse Cleveland in 1888 as it had been in 1884. Cleveland also boosted Harrison's chances by barely paying any attention at all to the campaign. In 1892, neither Tammany nor Cleveland would repeat what they did in 1888, and Harrison was out.

Notable accomplishments as president and events of his presidency

1. *The Dependent and Disability Pension Act.* The U.S. government after the Civil War was running a surplus. Civil War-era revenue collection measures had not been repealed, and federal spending had not expanded. Many in both parties thought it scandalous for the federal government to take and hold money from the people without using it. President Harrison on June 27, 1890, signed the Dependent and Disability Act, which provided pensions for Civil War veterans and quickly and substantially depleted the surplus.

2. *The Sherman Antitrust Act.* Signed by Harrison on July 2, 1890, the Sherman Antitrust Act, sponsored by his 1888 rival Senator John Sherman, was an attempt to protect American consumers by preventing the formation of monopolies that would control the market for various goods and set prices much higher than they would have been had the monopoly company been subjected to fair competition.

3. *The Sherman Silver Purchase Act.* Western farmers were burned with heavy debts that the Republican tariff policy would only make heavier, as it would lead to higher prices in

the short term. The Harrison administration tried to address this with the Sherman Silver Purchase Act, also the work of John Sherman. Harrison signed it into law on July 14, 1890, twelve days after the Sherman Antitrust Act. This act provided for the coinage of silver; since silver was cheaper and more plentiful than gold, there would be more money in circulation, prices would go up, and debts would be easier to pay.

4. *The McKinley Tariff.* President Harrison was true to his campaign promises regarding tariffs. On October 1, 1890, Harrison signed the Tariff Act of 1890, which was more commonly known by the name of its sponsor, Rep. William McKinley of Ohio. It was a kind of companion piece to the two Sherman Acts. The McKinley Tariff raised tariff rates prohibitively high on some goods, which led to higher prices, leading to widespread public dissatisfaction and undercutting the administration's America-first rhetoric: what good was protecting American industry if that protection didn't lead to the benefit not just of industrialists, but of American consumers?

5. *Standing for the civil rights of black Americans.* In his first annual message to Congress on December 3, 1889, Harrison said: "The colored people did not intrude themselves upon us. They were brought here in chains and held in the communities where they are now chiefly found by a cruel slave code. Happily for both races, they are now free. They have from a standpoint of ignorance and poverty—which was our shame, not theirs—made remarkable advances in education and in the acquisition of property."[274] However, "In many parts of our

---

274   Benjamin Harrison, "First Annual Message" (speech, December 3, 1889), UVA Miller Center, https://millercenter.org/the-presidency/presidential-speeches/december-3-1889-first-annual-message.

country where the colored population is large the people of that race are by various devices deprived of any effective exercise of their political rights and of many of their civil rights. The wrong does not expend itself upon those whose votes are suppressed. Every constituency in the Union is wronged."[275]

6. *Civil service reform*. Harrison, like Cleveland, was a strong supporter of hiring federal officials and keeping them in their jobs based on their merit, not party affiliation. In this, however, he ran into the same problem that befell Cleveland: members of his party had been out of power and wanted federal jobs when he became president. Harrison's refusal to make appointments based on party affiliation only managed to alienate many who would otherwise have been his supporters.

Harrison's personality didn't help. He undermined his own effectiveness by being famously aloof and cold. He disdained the day-to-day work of politics, the glad-handing, the act of making an effort to win others over, and in the end, this cost him.

Why his presidency did little good but not much damage

Harrison's administration had good intentions that it could not carry through. The Dependent and Disability Pension Act was a fine way to deplete the surplus while providing for penurious veterans; its implementation was marred, however, by several high-profile cases of officials skimming

---

275   Ibid.

off for themselves some of the money meant for the veterans, thereby dissipating the good will that the act might otherwise have created.

Even worse, President Harrison's ringing words in favor of equality of rights for blacks came to nothing; bills protecting black voting rights and funding schools blacks attended were never passed. The Solid South held firm.

Meanwhile, the Sherman Antitrust Act, Sherman Silver Purchase Act, and the McKinley Tariff were designed to solve both sides of a thorny problem: tariffs would protect American business from foreign competitors that could undercut their prices for the goods they manufactured, and the Sherman Antitrust Act would protect American consumers from businesses taking unfair advantage of a lack of competition.

However, the McKinley Tariff rates were too high, and the Sherman Antitrust Act was not immediately strong enough to counteract the Tariff's effects on American consumers. The Sherman Silver Purchase Act did lead to inflation, and while this may have indeed helped farmers with their debts, it didn't endear the administration to other Americans who had to deal with prices that were going even higher.

All this handed the Democrats an issue that gave them control of both houses of Congress in the 1890 midterm elections and returned Grover Cleveland to the White House in 1892. The McKinley Tariff obscured the benefit that would redound to American workers if American industries prospered; many industrialists didn't help their case by failing to provide adequate wages for their employees.

The Republicans failed to communicate convincingly the fact that protecting American industries would ultimately be good for all Americans, leading to the creation of new products and inventions that would redound to the benefit of society as a whole. Meanwhile, the Harrison administration did little to press American businesses to treat their workers more fairly.

It wouldn't be the last time that the Republicans were on the right side of an issue but were unable to communicate their message effectively. Harrison was, in many ways, the paradigm of the well-intentioned politician who is unable or unwilling to communicate his message effectively or gather the allies necessary to implement it.

TWENTY-FOUR

GROVER CLEVELAND

Library of Congress[276]

---

276   *Grover Cleveland*, ca. 1888, photograph, Library of Congress, https://www.loc.gov/item/2004667241/.

Full name: Stephen Grover Cleveland
Lived: March 18, 1837–June 24, 1908
Presidency: March 4, 1893–March 4, 1897
Party: Democratic
Evaluation: Did Good Things but Also Significant
      Damage
Rating: 6

What qualified him to be president

In 1892, Grover Cleveland was a candidate for president who had been president before. Cleveland pointed to his record as a president of honest government and fiscal responsibility and was able to compare this record favorably to that of Benjamin Harrison, whom he had defeated in the popular vote in 1888.

How he won

Harrison was not a popular or particularly successful president, but Cleveland had alienated many Democrats with his refusal to budge from his opposition to silver coinage, an issue that had large and growing support within the party. Orator and politician Robert Ingersoll quipped: "Each side would have been glad to defeat the other if it could do so without electing its own candidate."[277]

Both candidates ran on the tariff issue. The Republican platform reaffirmed the party's commitment to "the American doctrine of protectionism" and stated that "the prosperous

---

277   Boller, loc. 2197.

condition of our country" was due to the Republicans' "wise revenue legislation."[278] The Democrats countered this America-first message by charging in their own platform that "Republican protection" was "a fraud, a robbery, of the great majority of the American people for the benefit of the few."[279]

Class envy and class warfare continued to expand their influence in American politics. The Democrats successfully portrayed Harrison as an elitist, interested only in protecting American plutocrats at the expense of the working man. Abetting this impression was the defection of the traditionally Republican stronghold of the West to the People's Party, which called for free coinage of silver to aid the financial plight of farmers.

After two close elections, Cleveland was swept back into office again in 1892 by a comfortable margin. Cleveland won New York State, but even if he hadn't, for the first time since 1876, that state's choice was not decisive for the election.

Leaving the White House on March 4, 1889, at the conclusion of Cleveland's first term, the outgoing president's wife, Frances, told a caretaker, Jerry Smith: "Now, Jerry, I want you to take good care of all the furniture and ornaments in the house, for I want to find everything just as it is now when we come back again. We are coming back just four years from today."[280]

And so they did.

---

278   Ibid.
279   Ibid, loc. 2202.
280   Louis W. Koenig, "Grover Cleveland: The Law Man," in *The American Heritage Illustrated History of the Presidents*, ed. Michael R. Beschloss (New York: American Heritage, 2000), 271.

Notable accomplishments as president and events of his presidency

1. *Fighting for low tariffs.* During Cleveland's second term, the Democrats managed to get a bill lowering tariffs through, but only with numerous amendments that watered it down considerably. Still, it did reduce tariffs to some degree, and Cleveland let it become law, albeit without his signature. The fact that he did not endorse it wholeheartedly inspired considerable resentment within his own party, which was becoming bitterly split over economic issues.

2. *Holding the line on fiscal responsibility.* Cleveland's second term began with the Panic of 1893, a severe depression that lasted for several years and destroyed his popularity, although it had been brought on by his predecessor's policies, rather than by his. Cleveland was certain that among the chief causes of the Panic was the Sherman Silver Act of 1890, which allowed for coinage of silver in addition to gold. Silver was more plentiful and worth less than gold, so the coinage of silver led to more money in circulation and, consequently, to inflation.

Western and Southern farmers were happy with that inflation, as it enabled them to pay their debts with money that was worth less than the money they had borrowed; however, businesses suffered, and the higher prices hurt individual Americans. Cleveland resisted calls for drastic government action and pressed for repeal of the Sherman Silver Act, placing the nation's money supply on a firmer basis and combating the inflation. Nonetheless, the depression lasted for the whole of his second term, and Cleveland came under immense pressure.

In 1894, a labor activist named Jacob Coxey led a group of unemployed men, known as "Coxey's Army," in a march on Washington to demand government action: a massive public works program to help those without jobs. Coxey was widely dismissed as a crank and arrested. His "army" was dispersed, and nothing came of his demands until they became Democratic Party policy much later.

For years after Cleveland left the White House, Republicans invoked the miseries of his second term to warn Americans against electing another Democrat to the presidency. Many Democrats were no happier with Cleveland: the bitter controversy between advocates of the gold standard and those who called for the free coinage of silver led to a deep division in the Democratic Party that contributed a great deal to its defeat in 1896.

3. *Ending the Pullman Strike.* In July 1894, after a 25 percent pay cut, employees of the Pullman Palace Car Company in Chicago went on strike, led by the American Railway Union and its president, Eugene V. Debs. The strike was contentious and led to rioting in Chicago; the U.S. Post Office complained that the strikers had stopped delivery of the mail. Cleveland thundered, "If it takes the army and navy of the United States to deliver a postcard in Chicago, that card will be delivered."[281] He sent in troops to stop the strike.

That was not the end of anything but rather the beginning of a great deal. Labor, and its grievances and demands, had now become a force in American politics. Debs went on to

---

281   Koenig, "Grover Cleveland," 274.

become the most prominent American socialist of the early twentieth century.

4. *Rejecting the annexation of Hawaii.* In January 1893, a group made up largely of European and American business-men overthrew Hawaii's Queen Liliuokalani; the new government quickly requested annexation by the United States. Benjamin Harrison had already been defeated for reelection, but his administration didn't hesitate to negotiate a treaty before Cleveland returned to the White House, although the Senate didn't act upon it. However, Cleveland rejected annexation and withdrew the treaty, explaining to Congress on December 18, 1893, that "it appeared from the documents accompanying the treaty when submitted to the Senate, that the ownership of Hawaii was tendered to us by a provisional government set up to succeed the constitutional ruler of the islands, who had been dethroned, and it did not appear that such provisional government had the sanction of either popular revolution or suffrage."[282]

Why his presidency did good things but also significant damage

President Cleveland stood for honest government in rejecting the annexation of Hawaii, which would have considerably stretched the meaning of "United States of *America.*" The annexation would happen anyway in a few short years, but

---

282 Grover Cleveland, "President Cleveland's Message about Hawaii," December 18, 1893, American History from Revolution to Reconstruction and Beyond, http://www.let.rug.nl/usa/documents/1876-1900/president-clevelands-message-about-hawaii-december-18-1893.php.

Cleveland's words in his December 1893 message to Congress remained true: "The law of nations is founded upon reason and justice, and the rules of conduct governing individual relations between citizens or subjects of a civilized state are equally applicable as between enlightened nations."[283]

Those rules of conduct had certainly been transgressed in the case of Hawaii, as Cleveland also noted: "The lawful Government of Hawaii was overthrown without the drawing of a sword or the firing of a shot by a process every step of which, it may be safely asserted, is directly traceable to and dependent for its success upon the agency of the United States acting through its diplomatic and naval representatives."[284]

The problematic aspect of the annexation of Hawaii was not the contemporary idea that acquisition of territory is immoral in itself, but the fact that those in Hawaii who were negotiating the acquisition were hardly a representative government. Their seizure of power was reminiscent of the flooding of the Mexican province of Texas with American settlers, and those settlers' subsequent proclamation of an independent republic and request for annexation by the United States. Cleveland was right that "the United States in aiming to maintain itself as one of the most enlightened of nations would do its citizens gross injustice if it applied to its international relations any other than a high standard of honor and morality."[285] This standard is one of the things that have made America great.

---

283   Ibid.
284   Ibid.
285   Ibid.

On the negative side of the ledger, Cleveland presided over the beginning of labor strife that lasted for many decades. By 1894, when Coxey and his army marched on Washington, Cleveland seemed to have forgotten the "care and protection" that in 1888 he said the government owed to the "humblest citizen." Coxey's Army was dispersed, but the bitterness over the injustices of unrestrained monopolies remained. Massive corporations were indeed often unjust to workers. A political cartoon during the Pullman Strike depicted Pullman crushing a worker between two huge stones, one labeled "Low Wages," and the other "High Rents."[286] If employers would not deal justly with their employees, increasing numbers of Americans believed that it would benefit all Americans if they were legally compelled to do so.

Opponents of this idea countered that expanding federal power to check that of monopolies would simply substitute one massively powerful authority that could work its will unopposed for another. Throughout the twentieth century, evidence multiplied showing that these critics were correct. Yet in the twenty-first, monopolies emerged that were characterized by a disquieting willingness to restrict Americans' constitutional freedoms, particularly the freedom of speech; only the federal government had the ability to stop them, although little was done, and many who opposed the uncontrolled growth of federal power also opposed actions against these monopolies for that very reason. The proper balance had to be found. Over a century and a quarter later, it has still not been found.

---

286   "The Condition of Laboring Man at Pullman," *Chicago Labor Newspaper*, July 7, 1894, http://www.gompers.umd.edu/visual.htm.

TWENTY-FIVE

WILLIAM MCKINLEY

Library of Congress[287]

---

287   *William McKinley, Head-and-Shoulders Portrait, Facing Right*, ca. 1900,
       photograph, Library of Congress, https://www.loc.gov/item/96522569/.

Full name: William McKinley
Lived: January 29, 1843–September 14, 1901
Presidency: March 4, 1897–September 14, 1901
Party: Republican
Evaluation: Harmful for America but Also Did Some Good
Rating: 4

What qualified him to be president

As a congressman from Ohio, a position he held for thirteen years, William McKinley's crowning achievement was the adoption of the McKinley Tariff in 1890, which cemented his reputation as a defender of American industry, the engine of American prosperity. The Tariff made him a national figure and a presidential contender, and his ability to articulate and defend his principles made his star continue to rise. On October 4, 1892, by which time he was governor of Ohio, he ably made the case for high tariffs during a speech in Boston:

> Ah! But they say, if you had not the Protective Tariff things would be a little cheaper. Well, whether a thing is cheap or whether it is dear depends on what we can earn by our daily labor. Free trade cheapens the product by cheapening the producer. Protection cheapens the product by elevating the producer. Under free trade the trader is the master and the producer the slave. Protection is but the law of nature, the law of self-preservation, of self-development,

of securing the highest and best destiny of the race of man.[288]

McKinley explained how the chief beneficiary of protectionism was the American worker:

> We used to buy our buttons made in Austria by the prison labor of Austria. We are buying our buttons to-day made by the free labor of America. We had 11 button factories before 1890; we have 85 now. We employed 500 men before 1890, at from $12 to $15 a week; we employ 8,000 men now, at from $18 to $35 a week. The value of the output before 1890 was less than $500,000; it is $3,500,000 to-day.[289]

In 1894, McKinley campaigned for many Republican candidates during the midterm elections; by 1896, he was the Republican front-runner for the presidential nomination, particularly after former president Harrison declared that he was not interested in running again. At the Republican National Convention, McKinley was nominated on the first ballot.

How he won

While the Republicans were calmly nominating McKinley, the Democrats were going through a revolution. The Republican platform committed the party to the gold standard, which

---

288   Murat Halstead and Melville Phillips, *The Great Battle for Protection and Sound Money Led by Hon. Wm. McKinley* (Philadelphia: Edgewood Publishing Company, 1897), 253.

289   Halstead and Phillips, 254.

prevented the production of so much currency as to lead to inflation. A minority of Republicans and a significant majority of Democrats, however, supported the free coinage of silver, which would lead to inflation and thereby make it easier for farmers to pay off their debts. That rapidly rising prices were rendering the life savings of Americans essentially worthless did not trouble the silver advocates, who cloaked their case in the language of support for the plight of the common man.

President Cleveland supported the gold standard, but toward the end of his second term, he was deeply unpopular, and the silver forces among the Democrats were restive. At the Democratic National Convention, a handsome and vigorous thirty-six-year-old congressman from Nebraska named William Jennings Bryan electrified the delegates with a speech in favor of the free coinage of silver that is one of the most celebrated pieces of oratory in American history. "You come to us," Bryan declared, "and tell us that the great cities are in favor of the gold standard; we reply that the great cities rest upon our broad and fertile prairies. Burn down your cities and leave our farms, and your cities will spring up again as if by magic; but destroy our farms and the grass will grow in the streets of every city in the country."[290]

Bryan sounded notes of class warfare that would become ever more common in American politics: "We do not come as aggressors. Our war is not a war of conquest; we are fighting in the defense of our homes, our families, and posterity. We

---

290   William Jennings Bryan, "Cross of Gold Speech" (July 8, 1896), American History from Revolution to Reconstruction and Beyond, http://www.let.rug.nl/usa/documents/1876-1900/william-jennings-bryan-cross-of-gold-speech-july-8-1896.php.

have petitioned, and our petitions have been scorned; we have entreated, and our entreaties have been disregarded; we have begged, and they have mocked when our calamity came. We beg no longer; we entreat no more; we petition no more. We defy them!"[291] In conclusion, he thundered: "You shall not press down upon the brow of labor this crown of thorns, you shall not crucify mankind upon a cross of gold."[292]

In a frenzy of enthusiasm over this populist appeal, the Democrats nominated Bryan for president. This marked a sea change for the Democratic Party, as the party that had always favored a limited central government now began to advocate for a massive increase of federal control over the economy, under the cloak of a concern for the common man.

The campaign was a study in contrasts. With indomitable energy, Bryan traversed the country, making speeches that aroused a fervor among his supporters that was positively messianic. Those who loved him saw Bryan as the man who would lead them out of their poverty and despair to the promised land of earthly prosperity. One Bryan supporter in Kentucky expressed the sentiments of many when he wrote to the candidate, "I look upon you as almost a Prophet sent from God."[293]

McKinley was not nearly as exciting and wisely did not try to be. Advised to imitate Bryan and begin a hectic national speaking tour, McKinley declined: "I might just as well put up a trapeze on my front lawn and compete with some profession-

---

291   Ibid.
292   Ibid.
293   Michael Kazin, *A Godly Hero: The Life of William Jennings Bryan* (New York: Anchor, 2007), loc. 1920, Kindle.

al athlete as go out speaking against Bryan. I have to think when I speak."[294] The Republican candidate stayed at his home in Canton, Ohio, addressing supporters who gathered on his lawn from his front porch.

Although Bryan outdid him in passion, rhetorical skill, and the zeal of his following, in the end, McKinley's followers proved to be greater in number. The "Boy Orator of the Platte," with all his class rhetoric, alarmed businessmen large and small, and they turned out in force to affirm their support for sound money and protectionism. McKinley won with 271 electoral votes to Bryan's 176.

Bryan's following, however, was too invested in their hero to see this defeat as decisive. Bryan won the Democratic nomination again in 1900 and opposed McKinley's bid for a second term. Bryan tried to make an issue of McKinley's imperialism in fighting the Spanish-American War and taking control of so many former Spanish colonies, but few found this issue compelling. By this time, the country was enjoying a wave of prosperity due to the Republicans' America-first principles, and this time, the man whom many thought of as the hero of the workingman was beaten even more soundly, 292 to 155.

Notable accomplishments as president and events of his presidency

1. *The Spanish-American War.* Cuba, a Spanish colony, was fighting for its independence, and had the sympathy of many

---

294   Ibid., loc. 1570.

Americans who opposed colonial rule on principle. The American press, particularly silver baron William Randolph Hearst's *New York Journal*, began a push for war that McKinley resisted. He did, however, send the armored cruiser USS *Maine* to Havana harbor, where it stood as a silent indication of U.S. support for Cuban independence until February 15, 1898, when it sank in a massive explosion; 260 men were killed.

What exactly had happened to the USS *Maine* was unclear and remains controversial to this day. Initial reports called the explosion an accident, and the Spanish government of Cuba expressed sympathy and offered to help with the investigation. An American court of inquiry, however, found that the ship had been blown up by a mine. Hearst's *Journal* and other newspapers clamored all the more for war, exhorting Americans to "Remember the *Maine!*" and stirring war sentiment with reports of Spanish mistreatment of Cubans.

McKinley bowed to the pressure. The Spanish-American War began on April 21, 1898, and lasted less than four months; it resulted in the U.S. gaining control of the former Spanish colonies of Cuba, Guam, the Philippines, and Puerto Rico, made a war hero of Colonel Theodore Roosevelt, and set the stage for the twentieth century, when the United States became a major player on the international stage, and eventually the world's foremost power.

2. *Annexing Hawaii.* In April 1897, a month after he took office, President McKinley met with longtime Republican politician, diplomat, and strategist Carl Schurz, who urged him to resist calls to annex Hawaii. "Ah, you can be sure," McKinley assured Schurz, "there will be no jingo nonsense

under my Administration. You need not borrow any trouble on that account."[295]

However, the two men had vastly differing ideas of what exactly "jingo nonsense" was. Schurz considered all talk of the annexation of Hawaii to be that "jingo nonsense"; McKinley did not. Those who argued for annexation based their case on the proposition that the United States should get there first; as John Foster, who had served as secretary of state in the Benjamin Harrison administration, put it, "The ultimate fate of the islands, if they are not annexed by the United States, will be annexation by some of the other great powers."[296]

McKinley favored annexation for that reason and on the pretext that the Hawaiians could not govern themselves, although the Hawaiians themselves disagreed with that. The deposed Queen Liliuokalani came to Washington to lobby against annexation, armed with a petition against annexation that had been signed by over 21,000 of the 39,000 native Hawaiians. The annexation treaty failed to gain approval in the Senate, where many senators opposed it because they believed the statement in the Declaration of Independence that governments derive "their just powers from the *consent of the governed.*" However, almost immediately after the treaty was rejected, the Spanish-American War, with the Philippines as one of its theaters, broke out, and Hawaii suddenly became of immediate strategic importance. Congress approved the annexation treaty, and McKinley signed it into law on July 7, 1898.

---

295   Robert W. Merry, *President McKinley: Architect of the American Century* (New York: Simon & Schuster, 2017), 212.

296   Merry, 176.

3. *"Open Door Policy" with China and the Boxer Rebellion.* Much of the McKinley administration's embrace of imperialism was in pursuit of opening up new markets to American business and outflanking competition from the British, French, and others who were also vying for those markets. The acquisition of Hawaii and the establishment of the Philippines as an American protectorate confirmed the United States' place as an economic and political power in the Pacific region, contending with the British Empire for hegemony. President McKinley likewise advocated trade with China, and when the Boxer Rebellion targeted foreign interests in China in 1900, he acted swiftly, sending five thousand troops to China to protect the Americans there without bothering to get congressional approval first.

4. *High tariffs and the gold standard.* On July 24, 1897, less than five months after taking office, McKinley signed the Dingley Act, which raised tariffs on a number of commodities and effectively canceled Cleveland's lowering of tariff rates in 1894. With American industries protected, the economy began booming to such an extent that McKinley was able to make the prosperity his policies had brought to the nation a centerpiece of his 1900 presidential campaign, with slogans including "Four more years of the full dinner pail" and "Prosperity at Home. Prestige Abroad. Sound Money."[297] "Sound Money" referred to the gold standard rather than free coinage of silver, limiting the amount of money in circulation and preventing

---

297   Richard Pallardy, "United States Presidential Election of 1900," in *Encyclopaedia Britannica*, https://www.britannica.com/event/ United-States-presidential-election-of-1900.

inflation. Bryan made free silver coinage a focus of his campaign again in 1900, when the nation's prosperity had rendered it largely a dead issue.

Why his presidency was harmful for America but also did some good

The Spanish-American War brought the Philippines, Guam, Puerto Rico, and Cuba into the U.S. sphere of influence. The Philippines revolted against American rule almost immediately, but by 1902, the revolt was put down, and the nation was granted its independence in 1946. Cuba was given its independence almost immediately, but in the 1950s, Fidel Castro and his band of Communist rebels were able to exploit continuing American economic dominance in their revolutionary rhetoric. Guam and Puerto Rico remain American territories, with the latter remaining in the odd situation of being a Spanish-speaking entity with a Spanish-Caribbean culture within a larger Anglo-American nation.

All this set the United States on the path to becoming the world's policeman. Defending the American presence in the Philippines during the revolt, McKinley said: "Until Congress shall direct otherwise, it will be the duty of the Executive to possess and hold the Philippines, giving to the people thereof peace and order and beneficent government; affording them every opportunity to prosecute their lawful pursuits; encouraging them in thrift and industry; making them feel and know we are their friends, not their enemies, that their good is our aim, that their welfare is our welfare, but that neither their aspirations nor ours can be realized until our authority is acknowledged and unquestioned."[298]

The McKinley administration's intentions in the Philippines may indeed have been pure, but another negative precedent was set. If the Americans were in the Philippines in order to ensure their people enjoyed peace and order and beneficent government, was it likewise the responsibility of the United States to send troops elsewhere around the world where the people did not enjoy peace and order and beneficent government? The number of people who believed that the U.S. did indeed have such a responsibility would only grow throughout the twentieth century.

During his 1900 campaign, Bryan attacked the notion that it was up to the United States to provide beneficent government to countries that supposedly could not govern themselves. He warned, "A war of conquest would still leave its legacy of perpetual hatred, for it was God Himself who placed in every human heart the love of liberty. He never made a race of people so low in the scale of civilization or intelligence that it would welcome a foreign master."[299]

The history of the foreign adventures of the United States in the twentieth and twenty-first centuries abundantly proves that Bryan was right. Numerous interventions in other countries have provided ammunition to charges of imperialism and colonialism, despite the fact that the American government has never actually followed the path of European states in amassing colonies. The secular messiah

---

298   Merry, 364.
299   Kazin, loc. 2347.

Bryan was right that the United States was unwise to undertake messianic missions as a nation; it has never had and never could have the resources to solve all the world's problems and, particularly in the twenty-first century with the pointless excursions in Iraq and Afghanistan, has weakened itself while pursuing missions with no clear purpose or goal.

McKinley set another bad precedent by sending troops to China during the Boxer Rebellion without congressional approval. Congress should have but did not contest his doing so, and so this executive overreach would be emulated many times in the coming century and beyond, committing the United States to all manner of overseas ventures it would have been better off dealing with in other ways. The imperial presidency was born during the presidency of imperialism.

Despite the prosperity McKinley brought to the country, his age was still one of deep social unrest. The assassination of James A. Garfield in 1881 was one of the first political assassinations in an age in which they became distressingly common; McKinley's assassination in 1901 was one of the last of this period. His murderer, Leon Czolgosz, was a man of the Left, an anarchist and associate of the renowned activist Emma Goldman. After hearing Goldman (who actually advocated the assassination of rulers she thought unjust) speak about the injustices of American society, Czolgosz determined that "I would have to do something heroic for the cause I loved."[300] He traveled to Buffalo, where McKinley was appearing at the Pan-American Exposition, to kill the president.

---

300   Merry, 478.

The mood in Buffalo was ebullient. On September 5, 1901, the night sky lit up with words spelled out in fireworks: "Welcome President McKinley! Chief of Our Nation and Our Empire!"[301] Czolgosz shot the chief of the new empire the next day; he died eight days later. Goldman was not unhappy, charging that McKinley had "betrayed the trust of the people, and became the tool of the moneyed kings."[302] She charged that "he and his class had stained the memory of the men who produced the Declaration of Independence, by the blood of the massacred Filipinos."[303] With that, she demonstrated that in departing from the principle that governments derive "their just powers from the *consent of the governed*," McKinley gave fodder not just to the loyal opposition represented by Bryan, but to dark, sinister, and violent forces that were able to sway unstable minds such as that of Leon Czolgosz.

Emma Goldman also suggested that the assassination was justified: "Some people have hastily said that Czolgosz's act was foolish and will check the growth of progress. Those worthy people are wrong in forming hasty conclusions. What results the act of September 6 will have no one can say; one thing, however, is certain: he has wounded government in its most vital spot."[304]

---

301   Jessica Gunderson, *President McKinley's Killer and the America He Left Behind: The Assassin, the Crime, Teddy Roosevelt's Rise, and the Dawn of the American Century* (North Mankato, MN: Capstone, 2018), 5.

302   Emma Goldman, "The Tragedy at Buffalo," *Free Society*, October 1901, https://web.archive.org/web/20110927085715/http://ublib.buffalo.edu/libraries/exhibits/panam/law/images/tragedyatbuff.html.

303   Ibid.

304   Ibid.

This the-end-justifies-the-means rhetoric would become a staple of leftist discourse, particularly in the twenty-first century, when the Left in America grew more violent than it ever had before.

TWENTY-SIX

THEODORE ROOSEVELT

Library of Congress[305]

---

305   Pach Brothers, *Theodore Roosevelt, Three Quarter Length Portrait, Facing Front*, ca. 1904, photograph, Library of Congress, https://www.loc.gov/item/2009631526/.

Full name: Theodore Roosevelt
Lived: October 27, 1858–January 6, 1919
Presidency: September 14, 1901–March 4, 1909
Party: Republican
Evaluation: Harmful for America but Also Did Some Good
Rating: 4

What qualified him to be president

After Vice President Martin Van Buren succeeded Andrew Jackson as president in 1837, the vice presidency became the preserve of obscure men who were not generally considered presidential timber. The second spot was given to longtime party loyalists or men whose only obvious selling point was that they balanced the ticket geographically or appeased a party faction whose presidential candidate had lost the race for the nomination.

When McKinley's vice president, Garret A. Hobart, died in 1899, Republican Party leaders had to find the president a new running mate for 1900. Theodore Roosevelt, who would turn forty-two just ten days before the election, was chosen precisely because his political star was rising—so as to stop that ascent.

In May 1898, Roosevelt, who been a pivotal figure in New York politics since the early 1880s, resigned his post as assistant secretary of the navy to become second in command of a regiment known as the Rough Riders. Two months later, he became a national hero when he led a charge up San Juan Hill near the city of Santiago de Cuba, contributing to a decisive American victory. By the time he was nominated for vice president, he was governor of New York.

Republican Party bosses, notably McKinley's chief backer, Ohio Senator and Republican National Committee Chairman Mark Hanna, thought Roosevelt a reckless radical. Many Republican leaders agreed and thought that the best way to end Roosevelt's political career would be to make him vice president: the vice presidency was where promising careers in the public service died. Hanna disagreed, asking, "Don't any of you realize there's only one life between this madman and the presidency?"[306]

When Leon Czolgosz showed by killing McKinley how important such concerns really were, one prominent Republican is said to have exclaimed, "Now look, that damned cowboy is president of the United States."[307]

How he won

Most Americans loved "that damned cowboy"; Roosevelt was extraordinarily popular. He was as charming and charismatic as William Jennings Bryan, if not more so, and did not display any of the quasi-religious fanaticism of both Bryan and his followers that frightened off many from supporting the Democratic leader. Roosevelt's story of rising from his sickly,

---

306 Neil A. Hamilton, *Presidents: A Biographical Dictionary* (New York: Infobase Publishing, 2010), 214.

307 Most historians say that Ohio Senator and Republican National Committee Chairman Mark Hanna said this: Jeff Nilsson, "The Unexpected and Unwelcome Presidency of Teddy Roosevelt," *Saturday Evening Post*, September 14, 2017. Others say the speaker was New York Senator Thomas Platt: Murray Kempton, "That Damned Cowboy," *Spectator*, April 27, 1962, 5.

asthmatic childhood and becoming a champion of what he called "the strenuous life," as well as his heroics in Cuba and vivid personality, made him beloved as few presidents have been before or since.

In 1904, after maintaining American prosperity and increasing the nation's international influence during the balance of McKinley's second term, Roosevelt ran for president in his own right. The Democrats, after losing twice with Bryan, retreated from his populist zeal and nominated Judge Alton B. Parker of New York, who was as colorless as Bryan was fiery. The campaign featured no great discussions of burning issues. The Democrats presented Parker as the "Safe and Sane" candidate, as opposed to Roosevelt, who was, they implied, neither one. The American people chose excitement, resoundingly choosing to keep Roosevelt in the White House, with 336 electoral votes to Parker's 140.[308] Parker received substantially fewer popular and electoral votes than Bryan had in both of his losses.

Notable accomplishments as president and events of his presidency

1. *Trust-busting*. Roosevelt was determined to protect ordinary Americans from being victimized by massive corporations that, since they had monopolies on various commodities, could fix prices to maximize profits and squeeze the consumer. To help

---

308   Parker rides a "Safe and Sane" Democratic donkey hobbyhorse in William Allen Rogers' political cartoon "Czar Parker," *Harper's Weekly*, October 8, 1904, 1542–1543, https://elections.harpweek.com/1904/cartoon-1904-Medium. asp?UniqueID=39&Year=1904.

keep these corporations in check, President Roosevelt signed the Elkins Act in 1903 and the Hepburn Act in 1906, which vastly increased the power of the federal government to regulate corporations. Also in 1903, Roosevelt created the Cabinet-level Department of Commerce and Labor, which was meant to oversee corporations and control the growth of monopolies.

The Roosevelt administration also drastically stepped up enforcement of the Sherman Antitrust Act, initiating more than twice the number of prosecutions of various corporations than had the Harrison, Cleveland, and McKinley administrations combined. One of the chief targets, John D. Rockefeller's Standard Oil corporation, was broken up into thirty companies that competed with one another, making oil more affordable.

2. *Aiding labor in the Coal Strike of 1902.* Hand in hand with Roosevelt's actions against huge corporations was his intervention on behalf of striking coal miners in Pennsylvania. The strike began in May 1902 and dragged on for months, raising the prospect of large American cities going without coal, and hence without heat, through the winter. President Roosevelt sided decisively with the strikers, threatening to send federal troops to the coal mines to seize coal production from the owners of the mines who would not accede to the strikers' demands for fewer work hours and higher pay. When warned that such an act would be an unconstitutional seizure of private property, Roosevelt exclaimed, "To hell with the Constitution when the people want coal!"[309]

---

309   Bradley C. S. Watson, ed., *Progressive Challenges to the American Constitution: A New Republic* (Cambridge: Cambridge University Press, 2017), 196.

3. *The Pure Food and Drug Act.* In 1906, the socialist journalist Upton Sinclair published his novel *The Jungle*, an extended exposition of the claim that socialism was the answer for the working poor. The book contained a lengthy description of horrific conditions inside the meatpacking industry, which were based on Sinclair's investigation of conditions inside meatpacking plants. The book caused a sensation, leading Roosevelt to send investigators of his own into the plants; they confirmed much of what Sinclair had described. "Radical action," said Roosevelt, "must be taken to do away with the efforts of arrogant and selfish greed on the part of the capitalist."[310]

The result was the Meat Inspection Act and the Pure Food and Drug Act, establishing government regulations for meatpacking and the labeling of food products.

4. *Establishing national parks and forests.* Roosevelt established the United States Forest Service and oversaw the creation of numerous national parks, nature preserves, forests, national monuments, and more. The American Antiquities Act of 1906 gave the president the authority, "in his discretion, to declare by public proclamation historic landmarks, historic and prehistoric structures, and other objects of historic or scientific interest that are situated upon the lands owned or controlled by the Government of the United States." These were to be "confined to the smallest area compatible with proper care and management of the objects to be protected."

---

310   Erhan Simsek, *Creating Realities: Business as a Motif in American Fiction, 1865–1929* (Bielefeld, Germany: Transcript Verlag, 2019), 13.

5. *Attempting to raise taxes.* In keeping with his taste for a large, vigorous federal government, Roosevelt called for a federal income tax, despite the fact that the Supreme Court had ruled such a tax unconstitutional in 1895. In this, however, Roosevelt was stymied, which rarely happened.

6. *Officially appointing the United States the world's policeman.* Roosevelt was the first president to enunciate explicitly America's new role as the arbiter of international disputes, in what became known as the "Roosevelt Corollary" to the Monroe Doctrine. In his annual message to Congress on December 6, 1904, Roosevelt declared that "adherence of the United States to the Monroe Doctrine may force the United States, however reluctantly, in flagrant cases of such wrongdoing or impotence, to the exercise of an international police power."[311]

7. *Building the Panama Canal.* When Roosevelt articulated his Corollary in December 1904, he had already provided an indication the previous year of what kind of "wrongdoing or impotence" could result in American intervention. Roosevelt wanted to dig a canal in Central America to facilitate shipping by allowing for the easy passage of ships between the Atlantic and Pacific Oceans; up to this time they had had to go all the way around South America to get from one ocean to the other. He fastened upon Panama, a department of Colombia, as the best location for this canal, but the Colombian government rejected a proposed treaty that would have allowed

---

311   Theodore Roosevelt, "Annual Message for 1904" (speech, December 6, 1904), https://www.docsteach.org/documents/document/roosevelt-corollary-monroe-doctrine.

the U.S. to build the canal. Roosevelt then threw U.S. support behind Panamanian separatists, who secured Panamanian independence and immediately concluded a treaty with the United States for the establishment of the Canal Zone under American control and the building of the Panama Canal.

8. *Striking a blow against racial inequality.* Roosevelt was friendly with the black American educator Booker T. Washington. Just weeks after taking office, the new president invited Washington to dine with him at the White House. Many Southerners were enraged; Senator Ben Tillman of South Carolina said that Roosevelt's action would require Southern whites to kill a thousand blacks to remind them of their subservient place in society. Roosevelt was dismayed by the reaction, although from a political standpoint, he need not have let it trouble him: the Southern states were not going to vote for a Republican anyway. This was only forty years after the Civil War began and twenty-four after Reconstruction ended. Many Civil War veterans were still alive, and the memory of the Lost Cause burned bright in the South. Roosevelt never invited Washington to dinner again, although he did consult with him at the White House. In 1905, President Roosevelt visited the Tuskegee Normal and Industrial Institute for the Training of Colored Young Men and Women, which Washington had founded, and he served on its board of trustees.

Besides this, however, Roosevelt did little to challenge the institutionalized discrimination that the Democrats had established in the Southern states, which were, by this time, one-party Democratic fiefdoms.

Why his presidency was harmful for America but also did some good

President Roosevelt remarked: "My action on labor should always be considered in connection with my action as regards capital, and both are reducible to my favorite formula—a square deal for every man."[312] "Square Deal" became his administration's slogan. Today, when monopolies threaten the freedoms guaranteed by the U.S. Constitution as they never have before, Roosevelt's trust-busting looks prescient. In providing that square deal, however, Roosevelt greatly expanded the power and scope of the federal government, leaving middle- and working-class Americans vulnerable to a new tyranny from the very power that was saving them from the injustices of big business.

Roosevelt's exclamation "To hell with the Constitution when the people want coal!" was indicative of his overall approach to governing. It sounded good, as if he were willing to cut through all the red tape and get done what needed to be done for the good of the people. It appealed to people who admired his directness and decisiveness. But it left unanswered the question of what would protect those same people when their government got into the habit of ignoring the Constitution in order to act as the chief executive saw fit. Authoritarian regimes routinely couch their oppression in the language of service to the people as well. This is not to say that Roosevelt was any kind of authoritarian. But he opened

---

312   William R. Nester, *Theodore Roosevelt and the Art of American Power: An American for All Time* (Lanham, MD: Rowman & Littlefield 2019), 149.

the door to the good of the people being invoked as an excuse justifying all manner of abuses of power.

In both the coal strike and the controversy over *The Jungle*, Roosevelt based his expansion of the federal government on issues that enabled him to appear as the champion of the common folk. His big-government moves were intended to be genuinely for the good of the people, so that they couldn't be poisoned by unscrupulous meat-packers and frozen to death by callous coal mine owners who refused to let go of even the smallest bit of their massive profits for the public welfare. For their part, the common folk were generally pleased and grateful to their benefactor, without often considering the implications of these increases in government power. This was true despite the fact that the costs of meat inspections and proper labeling were borne by the consumer.

Throughout the twentieth century and the beginning of the twenty-first, many presidents and other politicians would follow Roosevelt's playbook, showing even less concern than he did for constitutional constraints on executive power. George W. Bush and Barack Obama, for example, seized nearly a billion acres and designated it parkland. This was over ten times more than all previous presidents combined had designated. They based their authority to do so on the Antiquities Act, despite the fact that it was limited to preserving historical landmarks, and declared that such tracts should be as small as possible. By the time of their presidencies, it had been abundantly established that a president need not be constrained by the letter of the law: "To hell with the Constitution," Bush and Obama might have said, "when the people want parks!"

Roosevelt's foreign policy was little better. The Roosevelt Corollary helped speed the U.S. on its way to becoming the world's policeman, leading to numerous disastrous international interventions, many of them self-defeating. In his 1904 annual message to Congress, Roosevelt stated: "In asserting the Monroe Doctrine, in taking such steps as we have taken in regard to Cuba, Venezuela, and Panama, and in endeavoring to circumscribe the theater of war in the Far East, and to secure the open door in China, we have acted in our own interest as well as in the interest of humanity at large."[313] Whether many of the interventions of the coming years were really in America's best interests is highly debatable.

President Roosevelt was a man of action. He couldn't be bothered with petty objections to his grand plans. Getting the Panama Canal built was a tremendous feat of imagination, daring, and diplomacy on Roosevelt's part. The canal was a boon not just to the United States, but to the world at large. As he had in the coal strike, he acted decisively, did what he thought was best, and let lesser men sort out the legal minutiae. "I took Panama and let Congress debate," he said later, "and while the debate goes on, the canal does too."[314] Exactly so.

Theodore Roosevelt was a grand fellow, a great man, a larger-than-life figure, and one of the few presidents who were bigger than the presidency. If Mount Rushmore celebrates the presidents who were big personalities, then Roosevelt

---

313   Roosevelt, "Annual Message for 1904."
314   Joseph Bucklin Bishop, *Theodore Roosevelt and His Time* (New York: Charles Scribner's Sons, 1920), 308.

richly deserves his place on it. He vigorously ushered the United States into what came to be known as the American Century, in large part because of his assertions of American power and authority on the world stage. At the same time, his personal charm and vigor, the appeal of his personality, and his good intentions should not be allowed to obscure all the negative precedents he set. While his good intentions cannot be doubted, neither, unfortunately, can the harmful and even dangerous aspects of the example he left for his successors.

TWENTY-SEVEN

WILLIAM HOWARD TAFT

Library of Congress[315]

---

315   *William Taft, Head-and-Shoulders Portrait, Facing Left*, ca. 1908, photograph, Library of Congress, https://www.loc.gov/item/96522628/.

Full name: William Howard Taft
Lived: September 15, 1857–March 8, 1930
Presidency: March 4, 1909–March 4, 1913
Party: Republican
Evaluation: Did Little Good but Not Much Damage
Rating: 5

What qualified him to be president

William Howard Taft's political career started and ended in the judiciary. In 1890, Harrison appointed him solicitor general of the United States, the Justice Department lawyer who represents the federal government in cases before the Supreme Court. Two years later, Taft became a judge of the U.S. Court of Appeals for the Sixth Circuit. He left the judicial sphere in 1901, when McKinley named him governor-general of the Philippines. Taft continued in that office for his friend Theodore Roosevelt, who then made him secretary of war in 1904; he was still in that position when he became the Republicans' 1908 presidential nominee. After being defeated for reelection in 1912, he was out of the public eye until 1921, when Warren G. Harding returned him to the judiciary, appointing him chief justice of the Supreme Court. He remained in that post until shortly before his death in 1930.

Taft's pre-presidential career somewhat resembles that of George H. W. Bush. Taft never held elected office before he was elected president, and while Bush served two undistinguished terms as a congressman from Texas, he spent the bulk of his career in appointed positions, making his name in them before he was elected to the vice presidency and then to the presidency. Both Taft and Bush were primarily Washington insiders, rather than politicians, and both became president as successors and political heirs of extremely popular presidents whose popularity they could not themselves attract or sustain.

Theodore Roosevelt was only fifty years old in 1908 and could easily have won another presidential election, but he had served out most of McKinley's second term and one term of his own, and believed at the time that the custom of presidents serving only two terms was salutary for the republic. He anointed Taft as his successor, and the Republican Party cheerfully went along.

How he won

The Democrats had gone the "Safe and Sane" route in 1904 and failed even more resoundingly than before to appeal to American voters. Thus, in 1908, they went back to being unsafe and insane, turning for a third time to William Jennings Bryan. Bryan was now the more or less undisputed leader of the Democratic Party, still only forty-eight years old but balding, paunchy, and generally appearing graver and less reckless than he had in 1896 and 1900.

Bryan made the slogan "Shall the people rule?" the cornerstone of his campaign.[316] He advocated a variety of measures designed to restrict the power of large corporations for the general welfare of the American people, although, as always, having "the people rule" meant having a massive federal government rule over the people. The only problem with this

---

316   Boller, loc. 2536.

approach is that the Roosevelt administration was renowned for its trust-busting, so it appeared that, in sharp contrast to his revolutionary campaigns of 1896 and 1900, Bryan was now offering an echo, not a choice. The American electorate loved Theodore Roosevelt, and since they couldn't vote for him again, they voted for his man Taft, who won by a margin almost as large as Roosevelt's in 1904, with 321 electoral votes to Bryan's 162.

Notable accomplishments as president and events of his presidency

1. *The Payne-Aldrich Tariff Act.* Taft entered the White House beholden to Roosevelt's "progressive" wing of the Republican Party, that is, the faction that favored expanded federal control over the economy and other aspects of American life, a political philosophy that was much in vogue in those days.

Taft wanted to give the progressives something they had long wanted: lower tariff rates that would in turn lead to lower prices. However, that would also hurt consumers in the long run by weakening the American businesses that employed them. He threw his support behind a bill that substantially lowered tariffs; it didn't go as far as the progressives wanted, but Taft explained that it was as good "as we can hope."[317] However, in the Senate, supporters of high tariffs piled on amendments that negated the tariff reductions and even raised tariff rates on some items.

---

317   Alan Brinkley, "William Howard Taft," in *The American Presidency*, Alan Brinkley and Davis Dyer, eds. (Boston: Houghton Mifflin, 2004), 289.

Taft said and did nothing, arousing the suspicions of the progressives who had backed his White House bid. When the bill as amended, the Payne-Aldrich Tariff Act, was passed, he signed it and said: "This is the best tariff bill the Republican party has ever passed, and therefore the best tariff bill that has been passed at all."[318]

Progressives felt betrayed. Taft had let down the people who put him in the White House.

2. *Corporate income tax.* President Taft gave the progressives at least one thing to cheer, a corporate income tax, as one of the many amendments to the Payne-Aldrich Tariff Act. All companies that earned more than $5,000 ($130,000 today) had to pay the tax; this immediately became a significant revenue source for the expanding federal government.

3. *Continuing Roosevelt's trust-busting.* Taft fell out of favor with progressives over the Payne-Aldrich Tariff Act, and they were not mollified by the fact that the Taft administration actually pursued more antitrust suits in four years than Roosevelt had in seven and a half. Roosevelt himself was unhappy when the Taft administration initiated an antitrust action against U.S. Steel over its purchase of the Tennessee Coal and Iron Corporation. When he was president, Roosevelt had approved this transaction, and he was furious that Taft was now challenging it. He accused Taft of "playing small, mean and foolish politics."[319]

That was actually the farthest thing from Taft's mind. He hadn't meant to do anything but carry out Roosevelt's

---

318   Ibid.
319   Lorant, 512.

program, which included trust-busting, and hadn't realized that U.S. Steel was off limits. As Roosevelt grew angrier, Taft grew more bewildered. Taft said plaintively to a friend of them both: "If only I knew what the President wanted"—that is, his predecessor—"I would do it, but you know that he has held himself so aloof that I am absolutely in the dark. I am deeply wounded, and he gives me no chance to explain my attitude or learn his."[320] He lamented that "a devoted friendship" was "going to pieces like a rope of sand."[321]

4. *Reorganizing and expanding the State Department.* Taft found the department he inherited from Roosevelt to be woefully ill-equipped to meet the challenges of the world Roosevelt had made and determined to remake it to fit the needs of the new era. "The truth is," he wrote, "the State Department does not cost the government as much money as the Govt. ought to spend to make it effective. It needs reorganization. It is organized on the basis of the needs of the Government of 1800 instead of 1900."[322] Taft affected that reorganization, establishing divisions devoted to dealing with various regions of the world.

5. *Dollar diplomacy.* In his last annual message to Congress on December 3, 1912, after he had already been defeated for reelection, Taft explained the guiding philosophy of his administration's foreign policy: "The diplomacy of the present administration has sought to respond to modern ideas of

---

320   Ibid.

321   Ibid.

322   Donald F. Anderson, *William Howard Taft: A Conservative's Conception of the Presidency* (Ithaca, NY: Cornell University Press, 2019), 68.

commercial intercourse. This policy has been characterized as substituting dollars for bullets. It is one that appeals alike to idealistic humanitarian sentiments, to the dictates of sound policy and strategy, and to legitimate commercial aims."[323]

Derided by Taft's many critics as "dollar diplomacy," this was the practice of giving loans and other financial enticements to governments in Latin America and elsewhere in order to help them achieve stability, rather than resorting to threats of arms. The Taft administration's efforts in this area were a resounding failure, causing considerable resentment in both Latin America and the Far East; in both regions, Taft's "idealistic humanitarian sentiments" looked more like bribes and attempts to gain openings for American business interests.

Why his presidency did little good but not much damage

Taft's presidency was destroyed by the dissatisfaction of the "progressives" who had gotten him elected. His first mistake was to ally himself with them and count on their support, for then as now, they were never going to be satisfied with someone who deviated even in the smallest way from their agenda. And the Payne-Aldrich Act was just part of how Taft enraged them. He also replaced Roosevelt's conservation-minded secretary of the interior, James R. Garfield (son of the slain president)

---

323   William Howard Taft, "Fourth Annual Message" (speech, December 3, 1912), UVA Miller Center, https://millercenter.org/the-presidency/presidential-speeches/december-3-1912-fourth-annual-message.

with Richard Ballinger, who was a corporate lawyer and not notably committed to preserving the environment. Ballinger was quickly kneecapped by accusations that he had conspired to deliver coal-rich public lands to a business associate; after an investigation, Taft sided with Ballinger, ultimately firing his accuser, U.S. Forest Service Chief Gifford Pinchot. But Pinchot and Garfield were progressives and close friends and allies of Roosevelt. The progressives were enraged anew, and Roosevelt grew increasingly hostile to his former friend.

It was unfortunate that the progressives had so much power. The "progressive" label reflected the assumption of this faction and its allies that they were marching in step with the inevitable progression of history, a notion derived from the Marxist/Hegelian determinist view of history and all too often uncritically accepted by the "progressive" movement's opponents. They also shared the Marxist conviction that a just society could best be achieved by massive state control of the means of production, although of course they did not go nearly as far as Marx did.

There was and is nothing genuinely progressive about progressivism. It was actually a rejection of the freedoms guaranteed in the Bill of Rights and an embrace of state power that inevitably led not to real progress, but to ever-increasing government control of the daily lives of citizens. Authoritarianism—in Fascist Italy, Nazi Germany, the Soviet Union, Communist China, and many other places—would be the bane of the twentieth century; progressivism was a softer version of the same impulse and put America on the same path as those countries, even if the progressives never got as far in the United States as they did elsewhere (or at least they haven't yet).

President Taft failed to please the progressives with the Payne-Aldrich Tariff Act and outraged them with the removal of Garfield and Pinchot, but he was very much a progressive himself. He certainly aided their agenda with his expansion of the State Department. He was undoubtedly correct that the State Department needed to be reorganized in accord with contemporary needs, but with his reorganization, the nation was well on its way to the gargantuan federal bureaucracy of today. While President Taft did not intend to create a behemoth of unaccountable functionaries, the growth of the federal government in the twentieth and twenty-first centuries is an object lesson in the law of unintended consequences.

That law was also at work in Taft's failed dollar diplomacy initiatives. Although they failed utterly to create new American allies or open up new markets for American industries, future administrations would frequently imitate them. The guiding principle was that America should invest in foreign countries to cultivate them as political allies and could win hearts and minds around the world by means of foreign aid. In some cases, this approach backfired embarrassingly, with that aid being funneled by supposedly friendly governments to America's enemies. But that never induced Washington politicians to stop the gravy train.

Fed up with what he represented as Taft's surrender to "the bosses and to the great privileged interests," Roosevelt challenged Taft for the Republican nomination in 1912.[324]

---

324   Lorant, 514.

Both candidates were to varying degrees "progressive," as was the Democratic Party, which was still dominated by Bryan, although the Democrats were not about to give him a fourth nomination. This was a fateful moment in American history, when progressivism became a powerful movement in American politics; its fortunes have waxed and waned ever since, but it has never left the political arena altogether. It has been the affliction of the second and third centuries of the American republic.

TWENTY-EIGHT

WOODROW WILSON

Library of Congress[325]

325 Pach Brothers, *Woodrow Wilson, Head-and-Shoulders Portrait, Facing Left*, ca. 1912, photograph, New York, Library of Congress, https://www.loc.gov/item/96522632/.

Full name: Thomas Woodrow Wilson
Lived: December 28, 1856–February 3, 1924
Presidency: March 4, 1913–March 4, 1921
Party: Democratic
Evaluation: Disastrous for America
Rating: 0

What qualified him to be president

Woodrow Wilson, for most of his career, was a professor, with an academic's certainty and a smug assurance about how the nation should be run. Then, three years after he entered politics, he was president of the United States, determined to make the world over the way he was certain it should be ordered. The nation, and the world, has not yet recovered.

Early in his academic career, Wilson displayed impatience with the American system of checks and balances. What America needed, he opined, was a strongman. In his 1885 book *Congressional Government: A Study in American Politics,* he lamented that "Congress must act through the President and his Cabinet; the President and his Cabinet must wait upon the will of Congress. There is no one supreme, ultimate head—whether magistrate or representative body—which can decide at once and with conclusive authority what shall be done at those times when some decision there must be, and that immediately."[326] This defect, he wrote, "in times of sudden exigency...might prove fatal."[327]

---

326   Woodrow Wilson, *Congressional Government: A Study in American Politics* (Boston: Houghton Mifflin, 1885), 283.
327   Ibid.

He was also an early advocate of the welfare state, calling for charitable obligations to be "made the *imperative legal duty of the whole*."[328]

All this would have remained within the realm of academic "progressive" theory had not Wilson decided to enter politics after serving as president of Princeton University from 1902 to 1910. He was elected governor of New Jersey, serving for two years and gaining a reputation as a reliable progressive. In a crowded Democratic field with William Jennings Bryan's shadow looming over all the candidates, he attracted attention as someone who could be counted upon to further the "progressive" agenda but was also palatable to the "Safe and Sane" faction. At a deadlocked Democratic National Convention, Wilson was nominated on the forty-sixth ballot.

How he won

The anger of Theodore Roosevelt and the progressive Republicans at William Howard Taft was the best thing that happened to the Democrats since Grover Cleveland was reelected twenty years before. Denied the Republican nomination, Roosevelt and his supporters bolted the Republican Party and created the Progressive Party, splitting the Republican vote and virtually ensuring the election of Wilson. The Democrat won in an electoral landslide that was illusory, since the popular votes that Roosevelt and Taft received, if they had been combined, would have won them enough states to result in a fifth

---

328   Robert M. Saunders, *In Search of Woodrow Wilson: Beliefs and Behavior* (Westport, CT: Greenwood Press, 1998), 13.

straight comfortable victory for the Republicans in both the popular and electoral votes. Wilson actually received fewer popular votes than Bryan had in 1908, but Bryan was facing a united opposition.

The progressives called for restrictions on campaign contributions, lower tariffs, a social insurance system akin to social security, and other expansions of government regulation and power. Bryan, now the Democratic Party's kingmaker, charged Roosevelt and the progressives with stealing ideas from the Democratic program. Roosevelt responded cheerfully: "So I have. That is quite true. I have taken every one of them except those suited for the inmates of lunatic asylums."[329] And maybe some of those as well.

Wilson was narrowly reelected in 1916, running against Charles Evans Hughes, a justice of the Supreme Court until he resigned to become the Republican presidential nominee. The Republicans were united this time around, although not altogether happily: Theodore Roosevelt derided Hughes as "the whiskered Wilson," despite the fact that, given the similarities between their political philosophies, Roosevelt himself could justly have been styled "the mustachioed Wilson."[330]

Wilson ran on the slogan "He Kept Us out of War," albeit with a pronounced affinity for Britain. The press savaged Hughes for pointing out that the British, as well as the Germans, had engaged in "improper interference with American commerce or with American mails" and calling for strict

---

329   Lorant, 523.
330   Lorant, 541.

impartiality.[331] Despite this, Hughes ran a strong campaign. On election night, the New York newspapers announced that Hughes had won. The candidate was staying in the Hotel Astor in New York City, on the roof of which a large lighted sign flashed the name of the winner: "HUGHES." The presumptive president-elect had gone to bed when the results in California began to turn; Wilson won the state, with its thirteen electoral votes, by fewer than four thousand votes, and with it the presidency. A reporter called Hughes's suite, only to be told that "the President has retired." The reporter responded, "When he wakes up, tell him he is no longer President."[332]

Wilson won reelection on a boast that he would render hollow just five months after the election.

Notable accomplishments as president and events of his presidency

1. *World War I.* The Great War began in August 1914. It was a complicated affair of Europe's web of alliances, and the parity of the two sides resulted in a much wider and longer conflict than anyone initially expected. Wilson did indeed keep us out of it at first. There was no reason to get in it. During the war, Germany and its allies never threatened the United States in any serious way, but Germany did sink passenger and merchant ships, hoping to cut off supplies to Britain and force it to surrender. After it sank the British ship *Lusitania* on May 7, 1915, and 128 Americans on board were killed, William

---

331   Ibid.
332   Lorant, 544.

Jennings Bryan, whom Wilson had appointed secretary of state, urged the president not to enter the war. He pointed out that the British were blockading German ports, causing large-scale starvation in Germany, and argued that the blockade was as bad or worse than the German operations against passenger ships.

Wilson, however, sent a letter of protest to the German government, warning it to stop targeting such ships, and Bryan resigned. Tensions cooled when Germany stopped targeting nonmilitary vessels, but in January 1917, Germany resumed its earlier practice. After the Germans sunk seven American merchant ships, Wilson declared war.

There were many other possible ways that the man who was reelected boasting that he kept us out of war could have approached the problem of the sinking of the ships, and since Germany posed no immediate or obvious threat to the United States, he had to sell the war to the American people. Speaking before a joint session of Congress on April 2, 1917, Wilson famously declared: "The world must be made safe for democracy. Its peace must be planted upon the tested foundations of political liberty. We have no selfish ends to serve. We desire no conquest, no dominion. We seek no indemnities for ourselves, no material compensation for the sacrifices we shall freely make. We are but one of the champions of the rights of mankind. We shall be satisfied when those rights have been made as secure as the faith and the freedom of nations can make them."

In January 1918, Wilson sought to codify and secure this vision with his "Fourteen Points" about the ordering of the

postwar world, including numerous specific recommenda-
tions about the borders of various European states. He also
called for the establishment of a League of Nations that would
prevent further conflicts. In 1919, he traveled to Europe for
the Paris Peace Conference, which resulted in the Treaty of
Versailles. That treaty dictated such punitive and destructive
terms for a defeated Germany that it planted seeds of resentment that would contribute, before two decades were out, to
the rise to power of Adolf Hitler. Wilson and the other allied
leaders, however, saw it as just and necessary, particularly in
establishing the League of Nations. For his efforts, Wilson was
awarded the 1919 Nobel Peace Prize.

Returning home, the president traveled the nation advocating adoption of the treaty and entry into the League.
In doing so, he destroyed his health, suffering a stroke that
incapacitated him to the extent that his wife Edith severely
restricted access to him; many believe she herself was making
executive decisions during this period. While Wilson was
severely ill, the treaty was defeated.

2. *The Espionage Act of 1917 and the Sedition Act of 1918.*
Wilson's second term saw a serious erosion of the freedom of
speech under the pretext of protecting the nation against the
enemies it was fighting in the Great War. The Espionage Act
of 1917 criminalized attempting to induce "insubordination,
disloyalty, mutiny, or refusal of duty in the military or naval
forces of the United States."[333]

---

333   "Primary Documents—U.S. Espionage Act, 7 May 1918," FirstWorldWar.com,
       http://www.firstworldwar.com/source/espionageact1918.htm.

While some were arrested and prosecuted (in the infamous raids carried out under the leadership of Attorney General A. Mitchell Palmer) under these acts for genuine sedition, others ran afoul of the government simply for opposing the war. Charles Schenck, general secretary of the Socialist Party of America, was accordingly imprisoned for anti-draft leaflets. Schenck appealed on First Amendment grounds, but the Supreme Court, in a unanimous vote, upheld his conviction. Justice Oliver Wendell Holmes, Jr., who was named to the high court by Theodore Roosevelt, explained: "The question in every case is whether the words used are used in such circumstances and are of such a nature as to create a clear and present danger that they will bring about the substantive evils that Congress has a right to prevent."[334]

The following year, Socialist Party leader Eugene V. Debs gave a speech in which he praised three "comrades" who had been "convicted of aiding and abetting another in failing to register for the draft."[335] Debs, too, was then imprisoned under the Espionage Act, as the Supreme Court deemed his speech to have a "natural tendency and reasonably probable effect to obstruct the recruiting service."[336]

3. *Latin American interventions*. Wilson intervened militarily in Cuba, the Dominican Republic, Haiti, Honduras, Mexico, and Nicaragua, explaining: "We are friends of constitutional government in America; we are more than its friends,

---

334   *Schenck v. United States*, 249 U.S. 47 (1919), Legal Information Institute, Cornell University, https://www.law.cornell.edu/supremecourt/text/249/47.

335   *Debs vs. U.S*, 249 US 211 (1919), FindLaw, http://caselaw.findlaw.com/us-supreme-court/249/211.html.

336   Ibid.

we are its champions. I am going to teach the South American republics to elect good men."[337]

4. *Expansion of government segregation.* Wilson was born in Virginia and moved north in the course of his academic career. Throughout his life, he retained the racist attitudes he learned in his youth, and when he became president, he made them U.S. government policy. In 1915, the notorious film *The Birth of a Nation* became the first motion picture to get a screening in the White House; the film portrayed the Ku Klux Klan as heroes, denigrated blacks in numerous ways, and quoted Wilson as a respected authority. Wilson was quoted decrying the supposed "policy of congressional leaders" to "put the white South under the heel of the black South."[338] In response, Wilson went on, as quoted in the film: "The white men were roused by a mere instinct of self-preservation... until at last there had sprung into existence a great Ku Klux Klan, a veritable empire of the South, to protect the Southern country."[339]

The showing of *The Birth of a Nation* was indicative of Wilson's attitudes: during his administration, government departments in Washington were segregated.

5. *Lowering tariffs.* In his first inaugural address on March 4, 1913, Wilson decried a list of "the things that ought to be

---

337   G. John Ikenberry, Thomas J. Knock, Anne-Marie Slaughter, and Tony Smith, *The Crisis of American Foreign Policy: Wilsonianism in the Twenty-First Century*(Princeton, NJ: Princeton University Press, 2009), 14.

338   Peter C. Rollins and John E. O'Connor, eds., *Hollywood's White House: The American Presidency in Film and History* (Lexington: University Press of Kentucky, 2005), 116.

339   Ibid.

altered," including "a tariff which cuts us off from our proper part in the commerce of the world, violates the just principles of taxation, and makes the Government a facile instrument in the hand of private interests."[340] Thus he made clear that he meant to work against the "private interests" that were the engine of the American economy, the business owners who provided jobs for ordinary Americans. The Revenue Act of 1913 lowered import tariff rates and reinstituted a federal income tax, which had been declared unconstitutional in 1895; the Sixteenth Amendment to the Constitution, ratified a month before Wilson took office, declared such taxes acceptable. By the time Wilson left office, the economy was mired in a recession.

6. *Establishing the Federal Reserve.* Late in the Roosevelt administration, the Knickerbocker Trust Company was failing, leading to a significant economic downturn, the Panic of 1907. Banking baron J. P. Morgan stepped in to aid banks that were failing and thus minimize the crisis. Princeton University President Wilson, showing again his taste for authoritarian government, wrote: "All this trouble could be averted if we appointed a committee of six or seven public-spirited men like J. P. Morgan to handle the affairs of our country."[341]

In establishing the Federal Reserve System, the first central bank in the country since the demise of the Second Bank of the United States at the hands of Andrew Jackson

---

340   Woodrow Wilson, "First Inaugural Address," March 4, 1913, Avalon Project, Yale Law School, https://avalon.law.yale.edu/20th_century/wilson1.asp.

341   David Usborne, "JP Morgan Hailed Again as 'Saviour of Wall Street,' " *Independent*, March 18, 2008.

in 1836, the nation went a long way toward doing just that. The Federal Reserve was officially established on December 23, 1913, but had been in the offing before Wilson took office. It had his full support, despite the fact that, during his 1912 campaign, Wilson had said that he was opposed to a central bank. He declared:

> A great industrial nation is controlled by its system of credit. Our system of credit is privately concentrated. The growth of the nation, therefore, and all our activities are in the hands of a few men who, even if their action be honest and intended for the public interest, are necessarily concentrated upon the great undertakings in which their own money is involved and who necessarily, by very reason of their own limitations, chill and check and destroy genuine economic freedom.[342]

Yet Wilson's opposition to a central bank proved to be as hollow a claim as "He Kept Us out of War" would prove to be in 1917. The Federal Reserve Act placed various regional Federal Reserve banks in private hands, controlled by a central board that was appointed by the president. The central board was supposed to prevent the growth of a moneyed oligarchy that would exercise undue control over the American political process, which was exactly what Jackson and Tyler had decried about the nineteenth-century bank. But the board itself came

---

342   Woodrow Wilson, *The New Freedom: A Call for the Emancipation of the Generous Energies of a People* (New York: Doubleday, 1913), 185.

to be dominated by those oligarchs, and once again, the public funds were in the control of a small number of people who had not been elected by the American people. If anyone was responsible for an enormous concentration of power "in the hands of a few men," it was Wilson.

Why his presidency was disastrous for America

William Gibbs McAdoo, who was Wilson's treasury secretary when the Federal Reserve came into existence, warned in his 1931 memoir: "The fact is that there is a serious danger of this country becoming a plutodemocracy; that is, a sham republic with the real government in the hands of a small clique of enormously wealthy men, who speak through their money, and whose influence, even today, radiates to every corner of the United States."[343] For this, he could thank Wilson and the Federal Reserve Act.

Wilson likewise abandoned the interests of the American people in his embrace of racism and segregation, which only prolonged the injustices done to black Americans and contributed to making the race issue the national trauma and a bleeding sore that will not heal to this day.

Wilson's foreign interventionism was just as bad. Why he believed it America's responsibility to teach the South American republics "to elect good men" by use of American military force he did not explain, and this paternalism has created resentments that have been detrimental to American interests.

---

343   William G. McAdoo, *Crowded Years: The Reminiscences of William G. McAdoo* (Boston: Houghton Mifflin, 1931), 165.

And World War I was the first war America would fight for principle alone, particularly in order to "make the world safe for democracy," rather than for self-defense, territorial expansion, or for the benefit of any American interests. It was not fought for the good of America as such; it was instead the first great crusade to defend civilization.

It would not be the last. In recent years, this idea informed the U.S. actions in Iraq and Afghanistan after the jihad terror attacks on September 11, 2001. American troops went to both countries not just to try to end the terror threat against the United States, but to establish both as stable, Western-style democracies that protected the rights of all citizens. The problem with this was that neither country had a democratic tradition nor any significant number of people who wanted such a government rather than one governed by Islamic law, which denies basic rights to women, non-Muslims, and others. Democracy led to the installation of Sharia constitutions and regimes that hated America, not to the creation of reliable American allies in the Islamic world.

Congress rejected the Treaty of Versailles and entry into the League of Nations, but Wilson had started the ball rolling toward the creation of an international organization that would challenge national sovereignty in numerous ways, although it would take another world war to induce the United States to join.

Not only was American participation in the war a sharp departure from the America-first principle; the war also came at an immense cost to American principles. The Sedition Act was repealed the day before Wilson left office, but the Espionage Act remains to this day; the Supreme Court upheld its constitutionality in 1919, but it has been challenged numerous times since then. While actively working to overthrow the government is clearly speech that should not enjoy First Amendment protection, Holmes's "clear and present danger" criterion was too elastic and subjective. It gave the federal government a means to silence its critics if it wished to do so and has been challenged on those grounds.

It nonetheless stands and illustrates the grim reality that the government has placed severe restrictions on the First Amendment's protection of the freedom of speech in the past and has justification ready if it chooses to do so in the future. If a government with a compliant Supreme Court determines that a "clear and present danger" is constituted by speech rejecting present-day leftist pieties such as the idea that advocacy of border control constitutes "white supremacism" and "racism," such speech could conceivably be proscribed. It's ironic that so racist a president as Woodrow Wilson set key precedents that can now be used to destroy First Amendment protections and extinguish the freedom of speech.

Wilson also lowered tariffs and began collecting income taxes based in part on his internationalist vision, in service to the idea of allowing America to play its "proper part in the commerce of the world," which in practice would mean making foreign-made products cheaper and more plentiful in the United States, providing a short-term benefit to American consumers while undermining the industries on which they depended for their livelihood. As always for progressives, Wilson couched this in the language of concern for the common man, posing as his savior from rapacious capitalist robber barons, as Theodore Roosevelt had before him and as another Roosevelt and many others would after him.

Woodrow Wilson merits the title of the first internationalist president, who put the interests of the world ahead of the interests of his country. As Donald Trump might put it, Wilson was president of the world more than he was president of the United States. Consequently, his presidency was an unmitigated disaster for the country he had been elected to govern.

TWENTY-NINE

WARREN G. HARDING

Library of Congress[344]

---

344   *Senator Warren G. Harding, Head-and-Shoulders Portrait, Facing Front*, ca.
1920, photograph, Library of Congress, https://www.loc.gov/item/96522644/.

Full name: Warren Gamaliel Harding
Lived: November 2, 1865–August 2, 1923
Presidency: March 4, 1921–August 2, 1923
Party: Republican
Evaluation: Very Good for America
Rating: 9

What qualified him to be president

Warren G. Harding had been lieutenant governor of Ohio and was a well-liked senator from Ohio of modest accomplishment when the deadlocked Republican National Convention of 1920 began. The front-runner, General Leonard Wood, was the progressive candidate, but conservatives abhorred him; his principal challenger, Illinois Governor Frank Lowden, was as unacceptable to progressives as Wood was to conservatives. Finally, after a meeting in a "smoke-filled room," a term that became legendary in American politics as referring to back-door dealing, the convention turned to the amiable Harding, with whom both factions thought they could deal. He was nominated for president on the tenth ballot.

How he won

Harding's campaign promised a "return to normalcy." In a speech on May 14, 1920, Harding articulated his opposition to Wilsonian utopianism and foreign interventionism: "America's present need is not heroics, but healing; not nostrums, but normalcy; not revolution, but restoration; not agitation, but adjustment; not surgery, but serenity; not the dramatic, but the dispassionate; not experiment, but equipoise; not submergence in internationality, but sustainment in triumphant nationality."[345] This message resonated powerfully with war-weary Americans, who wanted nothing more than to get things back to normal.

Harding also called for "an end to false economics which lure humanity to utter chaos" and added: "The world needs to be reminded that all human ills are not curable by legislation, and that quantity of statutory enactment and excess of government offer no substitute for quality of citizenship."[346] One Harding poster featured the slogan "America First."

Running against Harding was Ohio Governor James M. Cox, who bore Wilson's mantle, and all his baggage. But the nation had had enough of Wilson's quest to save the world, opting instead to save America. Harding was elected with over 60 percent of the popular vote, the largest margin in American history up to that time. He trounced Cox in the Electoral College as well, 404 to 127.

Notable accomplishments as president and events of his presidency

1. *Disarmament.* The global situation after World War I did not call for the maintenance of America's large wartime military force, but Harding was not so unwise as to pursue the unilateral disarmament that globalists and socialists have

---

345   Warren G. Harding, "Return to Normalcy," May 14, 1920, Teaching American History, https://web.archive.org/web/20061003192206/https://teachingamericanhistory.org/library/index.asp?document=954.

346   Ibid.

urged upon the republic in subsequent years. He convened the first arms control conference in American history, the Washington Naval Conference, which met from November 1921 to February 1922. American delegates met with representatives from Belgium, Britain, China, France, Italy, Japan, the Netherlands, and Portugal and hammered out a number of treaties that headed off an arms race between the victors in the Great War (Germany was already disarmed under the terms of the Treaty of Versailles, and Soviet Russia, then still widely regarded as a criminal rogue state, was not invited).

2. *Lowering taxes and raising tariffs.* President Harding moved decisively to end a postwar recession. He called a special joint session of both houses of Congress on April 12, 1921, and told the assembled representatives: "I know of no more pressing problem at home than to restrict our national expenditures within the limits of our national income"—that line drew applause, a sign that these were times very different from our own—"and at the same time measurably lift the burdens of war taxation from the shoulders of the American people."[347] He got income taxes cut by about 40 percent and tariffs raised, and the American economy responded quickly: the twenties began roaring.

3. *Lowering the national debt and implementing the Bureau of the Budget.* In his address to Congress on April 12, 1921, Harding denounced "the unrestrained tendency to heedless expenditure and the attending growth of public indebtedness."[348] On

---

347   Warren G. Harding, *Address of Warren G. Harding, President of the United States: Delivered at a Joint Session of the Two Houses of Congress, April 12, 1921* (Washington, D.C.: U.S. Government Printing Office, 1921), 3.

348   Ibid.

June 10, 1921, Harding signed the Budget and Accounting Act, which was designed to provide oversight that would make federal spending more efficient and prevent it from spiraling out of control. It hasn't always done this job, but the Harding administration slashed $2 billion from the national debt and cut federal spending nearly in half.

4. *Lowering unemployment.* Harding's mix of higher tariffs, lower taxes, and restraints on spending led to a boom for American business, and thus also for the American workers those businesses employed. Unemployment dropped from 12 percent in 1921 to 2.4 percent in 1923, when Harding died in San Francisco while on a speaking tour.

5. *Repairing relations with Latin America.* Harding did a great deal to roll back Wilson's imperious and paternalistic policies toward Latin America. He denounced Wilson's interventions in Haiti and the Dominican Republic and withdrew American troops from Cuba. He also extended recognition to the Mexican government of Álvaro Obregón, which Wilson had refused to do. He concluded the Thomson-Urrutia Treaty with Colombia, paying $25 million (equivalent to $325 million today) for Theodore Roosevelt's adventurism that detached Panama from Colombia to allow for the construction of the Panama Canal.

6. *The Teapot Dome Scandal* involved Harding's secretary of the interior, Albert Fall, accepting bribes in exchange for leases to drill at the Teapot Dome oil reserve in Wyoming. Fall ultimately went to prison, becoming the first former member of a president's Cabinet to serve time for crimes he committed while in office. Yet while this scandal overshadows by far

everything else about Harding's presidency, it actually only broke after his death, and it remains unclear how much he knew about it.

Why his presidency was very good for America

Warren G. Harding gets scant respect; his presidency is generally ranked as a failure.

About the only things that Americans today remember about him, if they remember anything at all, are that he had a mistress, his presidency was engulfed in scandal, and he was out of his depth as president, winning the election only because he was handsome and women had just been given the right to vote.

There is no doubt that Harding was no straitlaced Puritan, and he does appear to have had more than one extramarital affair. Insofar as the president should be a moral exemplar for the nation, he did fail, but that is not a constitutional duty, and his affairs did not become known until after his death. Regarding the Teapot Dome Scandal, Harding's responsibility for it lies only in the fact that he appointed and trusted Fall in the first place. One may fault him for being such a poor judge of men as to have thought Fall would be honest and upright, but that is the sort of misjudgment that can befall anyone, and there is no guarding against it.

The idea that Harding was not capable of being a competent president stems largely from his own statements. Harding himself abetted the impression that he was overmatched in the presidency with several self-deprecating expressions of frustration, including: "I am not fit for this office, and should never have been here."[349] And at one point, he told a friend: "I can't make a damn thing out of this tax problem. I listen to one side, and they seem right, and then—God!—I talk to the other side, and they seem just as right."[350]

Adding to the impression that President Harding had risen to the level of his incompetence was the wicked fun that journalist and satirist H. L. Mencken, among others, made of him. Mencken set the tone for how Harding would be regarded both during his presidency and afterward when he published a scalding appraisal of Harding's inaugural address, which he termed a "harangue."

Pointing out numerous grammatical and logical infelicities, Mencken wrote that Harding "writes the worst English I have ever encountered. It reminds me of a string of wet sponges; it reminds me of tattered washing on the line; it reminds me of stale bean soup, of college yells, of dogs barking idiotically through endless nights. It is so bad that a sort of grandeur creeps into it. It drags itself out of the dark abysm (I was about to write *abscess!*) of pish, and crawls insanely up the topmost pinnacle of posh. It is rumble and bumble. It is flap and doodle. It is balder and dash."[351]

But the fact that Harding was not a great thinker or inspiring speaker does not mean that he was an ineffective

---

349   Nicholas Murray Butler, *Across the Busy Years: Recollections and Reflections*, vol. 1 (New York: Charles Scribner's Sons, 1939), 411.

350   Robert K. Murray, *The Politics of Normalcy: Governmental Theory and Practice in the Harding–Coolidge Era* (New York: W. W. Norton & Company, 1973), 54–55.

351   H. L. Mencken, "Gamalielese," *Baltimore Sun*, March 7, 1921, http://deadlineartists.com/contributor-samples/h-l-mencken-%E2%80%93-gamalielese-%E2%80%93-baltimore-sun-%E2%80%93-3721/.

president. Nor does the fact that he was a humble man who was keenly aware of his limitations. The treaties resulting from the Washington Naval Conference eased postwar tensions and allowed America time to rebuild after the war. What Harding did for the economy ensured that the rebuilding was undertaken with enthusiasm. Eight years of Wilson had sapped the nation's energy and burdened it with taxes and regulations. Harding got the economy going again—indeed, booming, with policies that ushered in the Roaring Twenties, a time of prosperity and national exuberance after the grim and pious internationalism of the Wilson years. The country was much better off with the simple and humble Harding in the White House than it was when the renowned intellectual and crusader for civilization Wilson was there.

Harding's presidency deserves an honest reassessment, but that is unlikely to happen given the fact that most historians today share Wilson's messianic globalism and visions of massive state control.

THIRTY

CALVIN COOLIDGE

Library of Congress[352]

352　*Calvin Coolidge, Head-and-Shoulders Portrait, Facing Right*, ca. 1923,
photograph, Library of Congress, https://www.loc.gov/item/96522645/.

Full name: John Calvin Coolidge
Lived: July 4, 1872–January 5, 1933
Presidency: August 3, 1923–March 4, 1929
Party: Republican
Evaluation: Great for America
Rating: 10

What qualified him to be president

Calvin Coolidge shot to national fame in 1919, when, as governor of Massachusetts, he moved quickly and decisively to end a strike by policemen in Boston. In a telegram to Samuel Gompers, the president of the American Federation of Labor, he wrote: "There is no right to strike against the public safety by anyone, anywhere, any time."[353] Coolidge brushed aside Gompers's claim that the strike was justified because the Boston police commissioner had acted improperly: "Your assertion that the Commissioner was wrong cannot justify the wrong of leaving the city unguarded. That furnished the opportunity; the criminal element furnished the action."[354] He assured Gompers: "You can depend on me to support you in every legal action and sound policy."[355] However, he added: "I am equally determined to defend the sovereignty of Massachusetts and to maintain the authority and jurisdiction over her public officers where it has been placed by the Constitution and laws of her people."[356]

---

353   Calvin Coolidge, *Have Faith in Massachusetts: A Collection of Speeches and Messages* (Boston: Houghton Mifflin, 1919), 223.
354   Ibid.
355   Ibid.
356   Coolidge, 223–224.

The following year, Coolidge's strong action to end the police strike helped propel him to the Republican vice-presidential nomination.

How he won

When Harding died, Coolidge was visiting his family in rural Vermont. When the news finally reached him, he had his father, a justice of the peace, administer the oath of office in the early morning hours of August 3, 1923. It was a modest beginning to the presidency of a modest man whose accomplishments as president were anything but modest.

America was enjoying the prosperity that had resulted from Harding's economic policies; Coolidge stayed on course, and so he easily won the nomination in his own right in 1924. The Republicans suffered another progressive/conservative schism, with Wisconsin Senator Robert M. La Follette forming a new Progressive Party, calling for a broad expansion of government power, including federal takeover of the railroads and electric companies, in the name of caring for the common man.

The split raised Democratic hopes for another 1912, when Wilson was elected because of the war between Roosevelt and Taft. But Robert M. La Follette was no Theodore Roosevelt, and the Democrats were hopelessly split themselves. It took them a record 103 ballots to nominate the bland and colorless John W. Davis of West Virginia, a one-term congressman and former ambassador to Britain. Davis was known as a conservative, so the Democrats chose Charles W. Bryan, the brother of their famous three-time presidential candidate William

Jennings Bryan, as their vice-presidential candidate, as a sop to their progressive wing. Charles Bryan could not compete in appeal with Republican vice-presidential candidate Charles G. Dawes, who wrote the music that ended up, in the 1950s, becoming the pop hit "It's All in the Game."

Davis alienated his Democratic base in the South by denouncing the Ku Klux Klan and defending black Americans' right to vote, and, in the end, went down to a historic defeat with only 28.8 percent of the popular vote, the smallest percentage any Democrat has ever received. La Follette carried only Wisconsin, and President Coolidge kept the nation on its prosperous course.

Notable accomplishments as president and events of his presidency

1. *Lowering taxes.* Andrew W. Mellon, secretary of the treasury in the Harding and Coolidge administrations (and the subsequent Hoover administration as well), advocated lowering taxes to increase revenues. The idea was that allowing people to keep more of their own money, rather than confiscating it for taxes, would encourage individual initiative which would increase incomes, since the taxpayer would be able to keep the extra money he earned by working harder, rather than see it all taken by the tax collector. Lowering taxes would therefore increase the amount of money the government collected from a wealthier populace.

President Coolidge followed this advice. On January 25, 1925, speaking at the American Association of Newspaper Editors' annual convention, he enunciated what became his most famous adage: "The chief business of the American people is business."[357] This didn't mean just big business, but everyone's ability to engage in enterprise and benefit from the proceeds. He explained in another address five months later: "We are seeking to let those who earn money keep more of it for themselves and give less of it to the Government. This means better business, more of the comforts of life, general economic improvement, larger opportunity for education, and a greater freedom for all the people. It is in essence restoring our country to the people of our country. It reendows them not only with increased material but with increased spiritual values."[358]

The Revenue Act of 1926 cut taxes substantially, and these cuts were not the Left's proverbial Republican "tax cuts for the rich": by 1928, Coolidge's last full year in office, only the wealthiest two percent of the population paid any income tax at all.

2. *Reducing the national debt and federal spending.* Coolidge cut a good bit of fat from federal spending: it fell from $3.14 billion in 1923 to $2.96 billion in 1928. At the same time, under Harding and Coolidge, the national debt went from $23.9 billion in 1921 to $17.3 billion in 1929.

3. *Refusing to join the League of Nations.* Coolidge stood firm against ongoing pressure to join the new international body. In his first annual message to Congress on December 6, 1923,

---

357   Amity Shlaes, *Coolidge* (New York: HarperCollins, 2013), 323.
358   *Addresses of the President of the United States and the Director of the Bureau of the Budget at the Regular Meeting of the Business Organization of the Government at Memorial Continental Hall, June 22, 1925* (Washington, D.C.: U.S. Government Printing Office, 1925), 1.

he declared: "Our country has definitely refused to adopt and ratify the covenant of the League of Nations.... The League exists as a foreign agency. We hope it will be helpful. But the United States sees no reason to limit its own freedom and independence of action by joining it. We shall do well to recognize this basic fact in all national affairs and govern ourselves accordingly."[359]

4. *The Dawes Plan.* In 1924, Dawes developed, with Coolidge's approval, a plan to relieve Germany from the crushing burden of reparations called for under the Treaty of Versailles. These financial obligations had led to rampant inflation that destroyed the life savings of innumerable Germans and wrecked the German economy. The resulting social unrest became a recruiting tool for the likes of Adolf Hitler, who made his first attempt to take power in Germany in November 1923.

The Dawes Plan called for the withdrawal of Allied occupation troops from Germany and for a large loan to the German government, along with a payment plan that made it possible for Germany to meet its reparations obligations without impoverishing its people.

5. *The Kellogg-Briand Pact.* Coolidge's secretary of state, Frank B. Kellogg, was a principal author of this international agreement, which he and representatives of other great powers signed on August 27, 1928. The powers agreed to "condemn recourse to war for the solution of international

---

359   Calvin Coolidge, "First Annual Message" (speech, December 6, 1923), UVA
       Miller Center, https://millercenter.org/the-presidency/presidential-speeches/
       december-6-1923-first-annual-message.

controversies, and renounce it, as an instrument of national policy in their relations with one another."[360] They declared that "the settlement or solution of all disputes or conflicts of whatever nature or of whatever origin they may be, which may arise among them, shall never be sought except by pacific means."[361]

6. *Insisting on assimilation as a condition of immigration.* In his December 6, 1923 message to Congress, Coolidge said:

> American institutions rest solely on good citizenship. They were created by people who had a background of self-government. New arrivals should be limited to our capacity to absorb them into the ranks of good citizenship. America must be kept American. For this purpose, it is necessary to continue a policy of restricted immigration. It would be well to make such immigration of a selective nature with some inspection at the source, and based either on a prior census or upon the record of naturalization. Either method would insure the admission of those with the largest capacity and best intention of becoming citizens. I am convinced that our present economic and social conditions warrant a limitation of those to be admitted. We should find additional safety in a law requiring the immediate registration of all

---

360   Kellogg-Briand Pact, August 27, 1928, Avalon Project, Yale Law School, https://avalon.law.yale.edu/20th_century/kbpact.asp.

361   Ibid.

aliens. Those who do not want to be partakers of the American spirit ought not to settle in America.[362]

7. *Standing for civil rights.* President Harding supported a law making lynching a federal crime; it passed in the House in 1922, but Senate Democrats blocked it from becoming law. Coolidge wanted it revived, telling Congress in December 1923: "Numbered among our population are some 12,000,000 colored people. Under our Constitution their rights are just as sacred as those of any other citizen. It is both a public and a private duty to protect those rights. The Congress ought to exercise all its powers of prevention and punishment against the hideous crime of lynching, of which the negroes are by no means the sole sufferers, but for which they furnish a majority of the victims."[363] However, Senate Democrats blocked it again in 1924.

Coolidge was strong believer in the equality of rights of all people. In 1924, he received a letter complaining about a black man running for Congress. "I was amazed to receive such a letter," Coolidge remarked. "A colored man is precisely as much entitled to submit his candidacy in a party primary as is any other citizen."[364] In 1924, with the Democrats continuing to block the anti-lynching law and firmly ruling a segregated South, Coolidge demonstrated his support for the rights and advancement of black Americans by giving

---

362   Coolidge, "First Annual Message."

363   Ibid.

364   "Is It Time for Coolidge?" Calvin Coolidge Presidential Foundation, https://www.coolidgefoundation.org/is-it-time-for-coolidge/.

the commencement address at the predominantly black Howard University.

Why his presidency was great for America

The impotence of the League of Nations and the sorry record of its successor, the United Nations, prove that Coolidge was correct not to commit the United States to joining. Neither organization was ever genuinely capable of maintaining peace; the UN in particular has become a nest of corruption and hostility toward the United States and its allies, even while owing its existence largely to American patronage, and Coolidge was right that such organizations posed a threat to the "freedom and independence" of the nation.

Meanwhile, Coolidge's statements that "new arrivals should be limited to our capacity to absorb them into the ranks of good citizenship" and that "those who do not want to be partakers of the American spirit ought not to settle in America" would be reviled as "racist" today, but the president was simply putting America first and insisting on what should be an elementary principle of immigration wherever and whenever it occurs, in America or anywhere else: if someone has no intention of becoming a loyal citizen and obeying the laws of the new country, he or she ought not to be allowed in, or swiftly expelled. Why should the United States or any other country have any obligation to admit large numbers of people, or even one person, whose intention is to harm and weaken it, or at the very least to flout its laws and customs?

Coolidge was also a lifelong opponent of the now-fashionable idea that it is the government's responsibility to ensure not just equality of access to services and opportunities, but equality of outcomes despite differences in individual interests, abilities, and aptitudes. He would have opposed his successor Barack Obama's claim that "when you spread the wealth around, it's good for everybody."[365] Said Coolidge, "Don't expect to build up the weak by pulling down the strong."[366] Indeed. The history of totalitarian regimes throughout the twentieth and twenty-first centuries shows Coolidge to have been correct: state-enforced egalitarianism is not actually good for everybody, or anybody; it only makes everyone poor, with the exception of the elites that hold political power, and creates a gargantuan government that oppresses its own people.

Coolidge is often derided as an "isolationist" for refusing to bring the United States into the League of Nations, but, in reality, his intent was not to turn the nation's back on the world, but to protect American sovereignty. The Dawes Plan demonstrated the Coolidge administration's commitment to playing the role of the great power that America had become on the world stage, but without compromising the well-being of Americans or entangling the nation in self-defeating foreign adventures. And it worked for a while: Hitler's National Socialist Movement began to lose steam until its fortunes rose with the advent of the Great Depression.

The other major Coolidge administration foray into foreign affairs, however, was not so successful. In fact, it was Coolidge's only misstep. The Kellogg-Briand Pact was derided

---

365   David R. Francis, "How Obama's Tax Plans Would 'Spread the Wealth Around,'" *Christian Science Monitor*, October 27, 2008.
366   "Is It Time for Coolidge?"

in its time, and still is by some today, as naïve. It was actually worse than that. In "outlawing war," as it has often been characterized as doing, it didn't prevent nations from resorting to violence to achieve their ends. What it did accomplish, however, was a general renaming of the phenomenon of war itself, allowing signatory states to claim they aren't in violation of the agreement (which remains in effect to this day) even when they are. The United States now engages in "police actions" and "interventions" and the like, but hasn't fought an actual war since World War II. The Kellogg-Briand Pact opened the door for the United States to fight endless undeclared wars that had no clear purpose, goal, or end point, and were in no conceivable sense in line with American interests. Coolidge did not foresee and could not have foreseen this, but it is nonetheless the fruit of his administration's high-minded adventure on the international stage.

On August 2, 1927, the fourth anniversary of his becoming president, Coolidge called a press conference. Slips of paper were distributed, reading, "I do not choose to run for President in nineteen twenty eight."[367] The man known as "Silent Cal" declined to comment further, although he explained on other occasions that if he ran again, he would be president for nearly ten years, and that was too long for any man and bad for the republic. Another statement circulated, attributed to Coolidge's wife Grace: "Papa says there's going to be a depression."[368]

---

367   Shlaes, 381.
368   William C. Spragens, ed., *Popular Images of American Presidents* (Westport, CT: Greenwood Publishing Group, 1988), 327.

Whether or not she said it, and whether or not he said it, it was true, and that depression became the occasion for a massive upheaval in American politics. Those who benefited politically from the depression frequently blamed it on Coolidge, when (as we shall see) the responsibility for it can be much more accurately attributed to the policies of his two immediate successors.

THIRTY-ONE

HERBERT HOOVER

Library of Congress[369]

---

369   Underwood & Underwood, *Herbert Hoover, Head-and-Shoulders Portrait, Facing Slightly Right* [1928?], photograph, Washington, Library of Congress, https://www.loc.gov/item/96522651/.

Full name: Herbert Clark Hoover
Lived: August 10, 1874–October 20, 1964
Presidency: March 4, 1929–March 4, 1933
Party: Republican
Evaluation: Disastrous for America
Rating: 0

What qualified him to be president

Calvin Coolidge disliked Herbert Hoover, whom he nick-named "wonder boy."[370] The moniker was apt: Hoover's entire career was one of "progressive" activism, and before he became president, he had gained an international reputation as a champion of the downtrodden and needy, one who was indeed a wonder-worker. When World War I broke out and Germany occupied Belgium, the British blockaded Belgian ports, leading the Germans to announce that they were not responsible for feeding Belgian civilians when the British would not allow foodstuffs to reach them. Hoover, who was then a mining executive and financier living in London, organized (with the approval of the Wilson administration) the Commission for Relief in Belgium and worked tirelessly with the British, German, and Belgian governments to make sure the Belgians didn't starve.

Impressed, Wilson in April 1917 appointed Hoover the director of the U.S. Food Administration, which ensured that

---

370   Larry Schweikart and Michael Allen, *A Patriot's History of the United States: From Columbus's Great Discovery to America's Age of Entitlement, Revised Edition* (New York: Penguin, 2014), 569.

Americans had adequate food supplies during World War I. After the war, Hoover's organization was renamed the American Relief Administration and dedicated itself to providing food for Europeans in areas ravaged by the war, including Soviet Russia and defeated Germany.

Hoover was an international hero by the time of the 1920 presidential campaign and was touted as a presidential candidate in both parties. He declared himself a Republican not out of any rejection of state control over the economy or low tariffs, or for a concern for civil rights or any other issue, but because he thought the Democrats had little chance of winning after eight years of Wilson's pious internationalism. However, his association with Wilson's administration torpedoed his chances, and he had to settle for serving as secretary of commerce in both the Harding and Coolidge administrations. In that capacity, Coolidge later remarked, Hoover gave him "unsolicited advice for six years, all of it bad."[371]

The core difference between the two men was that Hoover believed that a large, activist government could and would solve the problems of ordinary citizens. Coolidge saw such a government as a threat to individual liberty. But Hoover was popular with "progressives": one of the nation's leading "progressives," who was another advocate of big government, echoed Coolidge in calling Hoover a "wonder," but without Coolidge's irony. Before Hoover entered the White House, this leading "progressive" added: "I wish we could make him President.... There couldn't be a better one."[372]

---

371   Ibid.
372   Ibid.

That "progressive" was Franklin D. Roosevelt, whose views on Hoover would evolve, as would Hoover's on big government.

How he won

As the 1928 campaign approached, Republicans asked, "Who but Hoover?"[373] With Coolidge's withdrawal, there was no one on the scene with anything approaching Hoover's stature, and he coasted to the nomination. The Republican platform called for continued low taxes and high tariffs, promising continued prosperity. The Hoover campaign promised "A Chicken for Every Pot," boasting: "Republican prosperity has *reduced* hours and *increased* earning capacity, silenced *discontent*, put the proverbial chicken in every pot. And a car in every back-yard, to boot."[374] The message was simple: "Wages, dividends, progress and prosperity say, 'Vote Hoover.' "[375]

The Democrats countered with New York Governor Al Smith, the first Roman Catholic to receive a major party's nomination. About the only thing Smith had going for him was that he was gregarious and charming where Hoover was austere and humorless, heavy with the consciousness of his responsibility to aid struggling humanity. The Smith-versus-Hoover personality contrast might have made a significant difference in the television age, but in 1928, it wasn't enough.

Smith was widely unpopular in the Democrats' lone stronghold, the Solid South, which not only disliked him

---

373   Boller, loc. 3008.

374   "A Chicken for Every Pot," Hoover campaign advertisement, *New York Times*, October 30, 1928, https://catalog.archives.gov/id/187095.

375   Ibid.

for being Catholic, but for being "wet," that is, supporting the repeal of the Eighteenth Amendment, which banned the manufacture, sale, and transportation of alcoholic beverages. Hoover and the Republicans were firmly in the "dry" camp, and Hoover gained even more support in the South by seeing to the removal of several blacks from leadership roles in local Republican Party organizations.

His betrayal paid off: the Solid South was broken, with Hoover carrying Texas, Florida, Tennessee, Kentucky, Virginia, and North Carolina on the way to a smashing victory, with 444 electoral votes to Smith's 87.

In his acceptance speech after winning the nomination, Hoover said grandly: "We in America today are nearer to the final triumph over poverty than ever before in the history of this land.... We shall soon with the help of God be in sight of the day when poverty will be banished from this land."[376]

History is full of surprises.

Notable accomplishments as president and events of his presidency

1. *The Great Depression.* Hoover's presidency was entirely dominated and ultimately destroyed by the economic emergency that began when the stock market crashed on October 29, 1929, just under eight months into his presidency.

The Great Depression was the result of several interlocking factors. Among them were the fact that businesses

---

376   Brian Loveman, *No Higher Law: American Foreign Policy and the Western Hemisphere since 1776* (Chapel Hill: University of North Carolina Press, 2010), 238.

were producing far more goods than American consumers could conceivably buy, while rich industrialists were investing huge sums in the stock market, paying massively over-inflated prices for stock in companies whose revenues could never have justified those prices. Prices fell as a result of the over-production, causing lenders to call in their loans to make up for their revenue shortfall; then, to pay the loans, investors sold off their stock. Finally, the whole house of cards came tumbling down, as international developments exacerbated the problem: stock prices, already artificially high, fell steeply, banks couldn't cover their loans and went out of business, and numerous businesses folded, leading to catastrophic and rapidly increasing unemployment.

Wonder Boy acted quickly to use the power of the federal government to reverse the economic downturn. In his memoirs, he recounted how his actions to alleviate the Depression were unprecedented in American history:

> With the October-November stock-market crash the primary question at once arose as to whether the President and the Federal government should undertake to mitigate and remedy the evils stemming from it. No President before had ever believed there was a governmental responsibility in such cases. No matter what the urging on previous occasions, Presidents steadfastly had maintained that the Federal government was apart from such eruptions; they had always been left to blow themselves out. Presidents Van Buren, Grant, Cleveland

and Theodore Roosevelt had all remained aloof. A few helpful gestures, however, had been made in the past. On one such occasion it was in the form of a little currency relief; on another, the deposit of Federal money in some banks; and there was the crisis when Cleveland announced his fidelity to the gold standard to steady a panicky public. Because of this lack of governmental experience, therefore, we had to pioneer a new field.[377]

President Hoover took on the role of pioneer energetically. Federal spending increased from $3.1 billion in 1929 ($45.5 billion today) to $4.7 billion ($69 billion today) when he left office, the highest level it had ever reached when there wasn't a war going on. He pressured business owners to keep wages at pre-Depression levels, despite the immense reductions in revenue that they were experiencing. He also pressured the Federal Reserve to make it easier for Americans to get credit. On June 17, 1930, Hoover signed the Smoot-Hawley Tariff Act, which raised tariff rates significantly, intending to protect American businesses and farmers from foreign competition and thereby alleviate the economic crisis.

Above all, it was Hoover, not Roosevelt, who initiated a massive program of public works that was intended to ease unemployment. He created a new government agency to deal with the economy, the Reconstruction Finance Corporation,

---

377   Herbert Hoover, *The Memoirs of Herbert Hoover: The Great Depression, 1929–1941* (Ravenio Books, 1951), 29.

which provided federal money to state and local governments and financial aid to banks and other businesses to help them stay afloat.

Why his presidency was disastrous for America

The conventional wisdom is that the Great Depression was the fault of Coolidge and the Republicans. Big business was out of control, and big government should have reined it in with regulations that would have prevented the crash from happening in the first place. Hoover's disastrous presidency is generally presented as evidence of this: most establishment historians echo the charge that Franklin D. Roosevelt and the Democrats began making in 1932, that Hoover's inaction and trust in the power of the economy to right itself only deepened the crisis and lengthened the Depression. Then Roosevelt's New Deal smorgasbord of government programs put Americans back to work and finally provided the economy the stimulus it needed to recover.

Virtually every aspect of that conventional wisdom is false. Had Coolidge been president in October 1929, he would have without any doubt followed the precedent established by Van Buren, Grant, Cleveland, and Theodore Roosevelt that Hoover explicitly rejected: do nothing, recognizing that economic relief was not the federal government's responsibility, and let market forces heal the economy. What Hoover doesn't mention in his memoirs is that in all four of those earlier cases, the president's policy worked, and the economy eventually righted itself, although in some cases it took longer to do so than some would have liked.

In contrast, Hoover and then Roosevelt oversaw the massive expansion of the federal government in response to the Great Depression, and it became the longest-lasting economic crisis in American history, not definitively ending until 1941. Government intervention didn't end the Depression; it prolonged it. Hoover's programs only added to the burden ordinary Americans had to carry, especially when he increased taxes in 1932. The tax increases were unavoidable, however: contrary to the assumptions of many Americans today, big government programs don't magically pay for themselves.

President Hoover's programs didn't accomplish anything, either. They didn't prevent banks from going out of business: over five thousand closed between 1929 and 1932. Hoover's programs didn't put Americans back to work: unemployment rose from 3.3 percent in 1929 to nearly 25 percent in 1933. The Smoot-Hawley Tariff Act had just the opposite of its intended effect: It raised consumer prices, increasing the burden on Americans who were already suffering from the effects of the economic crisis. It also diminished the global market for American farm products and led to retaliatory high tariffs from other countries that hurt American businesses. Smoot-Hawley, in fact, so closely associated high tariffs with economic disaster that the very mention of the act has sufficed in recent years to shoot down all protectionist proposals, even if they involve rates much lower than those of Smoot-Hawley. This ignores the fact that earlier high tariff rates, notably the 1897 Dingley Act, helped usher in long periods of prosperity. The Smoot-Hawley Tariff Act came at a time when the economy was already so weak that American businesses were unable to capitalize on the advantages thus afforded them.

Smoot-Hawley was just one of the many reasons why the dour and unapproachable Hoover was increasingly blamed for the Great Depression. Many of the unemployed lost their homes; they began camping out and establishing shanty towns in large cities—these came to be known as "Hoovervilles." When Hoover called in the military to disperse the Bonus Army, a gathering of veterans who were camping in Washington and asking for economic relief, Hoover's popularity fell lower than ever. A joke circulated that Hoover asked someone for a nickel so that he could call a friend. "Here's a dime," the man told the president. "Call both of them."[378]

The popular perception that Hoover was responsible for the Depression was largely correct, but his failure was in doing too much, not in not doing enough. Yet after resoundingly defeating Hoover in 1932, Roosevelt didn't reverse his predecessor's policies; he continued and expanded them. Raymond Moley, a charter member of FDR's "Brain Trust" of key advisors aiding him to develop the New Deal, recounted that "when we all burst into Washington after the inauguration, we found every essential idea enacted in the 100-day Congress [the Roosevelt administration's first flurry of activity to end the Depression] in the Hoover Administration itself."[379] Another member of the "Brain Trust," Rexford Tugwell, noted that, in his policies, Roosevelt bore an "amazing resemblance to Hoover" and observed that "practically the whole New Deal was extrapolated from programs that Hoover started."[380]

---

378   Matuz, 499.

379   Davis W. Houck, *Rhetoric As Currency: Hoover, Roosevelt and the Great Depression* (College Station: Texas A&M University Press, 2001), 9.

380   Ibid.

Hoover, meanwhile, became a vociferous critic of the Roosevelt administration and grew increasingly disenchanted with the power of the massive federal government apparatus that he had done so much to create. His repentance, however, was not total. In February 1939, nearly six years after leaving office, Hoover boasted that the Republicans, not the Democrats, pioneered big government: "It was the Republican Party that first established the concept that business must be regulated by government if the freedom of men was to be preserved. Indeed, it was the Republican Party that first initiated regulation against monopoly and business abuse in the states. Over the last fifty years it created seven out of the ten great Federal regulating agencies of today. It was Republicans who created the income and estate taxes that fortunes might not accumulate so as to oppress the nation and that there might be relief of tax burdens upon the poor."[381]

On the other hand, during a 1928 campaign speech, Hoover said: "Bureaucracy is ever desirous of spreading its influence and its power. You cannot extend the mastery of the government over the daily working life of a people without at the same time making it the master of the people's souls and thoughts."[382] Indeed. And it was he who started the ball rolling in that direction.

---

381   Herbert Hoover, "The Real State of the Union: Address Delivered to Fifty-Third Annual Lincoln Day Dinner of the National Republican Club" (speech, February 13, 1939), Pepperdine School of Public Policy, https://publicpolicy. pepperdine.edu/academics/research/faculty-research/new-deal/hoover-speeches/hh021339.htm.

382   Herbert Hoover, "Principles and Ideals of the United States Government," October 22, 1928, Teaching American History, https://teachingamericanhistory.org/library/document/principles-and-ideals-of-the-united-states-government/.

THIRTY-TWO

FRANKLIN D. ROOSEVELT

Library of Congress[383]

---

383   Elias Goldensky, *Franklin Delano Roosevelt, Head-and-Shoulders Portrait, Facing Slightly Left*, ca. 1933, photograph, Library of Congress, https://www.loc.gov/item/96523441/.

Full name: Franklin Delano Roosevelt
Lived: January 30, 1882–April 12, 1945
Presidency: March 4, 1933–April 12, 1945
Party: Democratic
Evaluation: Disastrous for America
Rating: 1

What qualified him to be president

Franklin D. Roosevelt had the good fortune to become the Democratic nominee for president at a time when the nation was suffering its worst fortunes. He had built a solid reputation as a "progressive" as governor of New York and was a longtime Democratic Party regular, having served as assistant secretary of the navy in the Wilson administration and the Party's candidate for vice president in 1920.

Even more importantly, during a time of nationwide misery, Roosevelt had a legendarily sunny personality and an inspiring personal story. He had battled back from polio to continue his political career despite being confined to a wheelchair. This was widely known although he took pains never to be photographed in the chair and wore heavy metal braces on his legs to give occasional speeches while standing. His tenacity, perseverance, and optimism made him a symbol of what Americans could accomplish if they put their minds to it.

At the Democratic National Convention, Roosevelt won the nomination on the fourth ballot after overcoming weak and halfhearted opposition from Al Smith and John Nance Garner, who became his first vice president. Roosevelt broke with tradition and appeared at the convention in person, entering while the band played "Happy Days Are Here Again." In his acceptance speech, he uttered the famous words: "I pledge you, I pledge myself, to a New Deal for the American people."[384] He sounded messianic "progressive" themes that had been familiar since the days of William Jennings Bryan: "This is more than a political campaign; it is a call to arms! Give me your help, not to win votes alone, but to win this crusade to restore America to its own people."[385]

During the 1932 campaign, Roosevelt made it clear that his crusade was, in part, against American business, which during previous economic downturns had been seen as an engine of economic recovery. In a major speech on September 23, 1932, he came out against business and for the redistribution of wealth, saying:

> A mere builder of more industrial plants, a creator of more railroad systems, an organizer of more corporations, is as likely to be a danger as a help.... Our task now is not discovery or exploitation of natural resources, or necessarily producing more goods. It is the soberer, less dramatic business of administering resources and plants already in hand...of distributing wealth and products more equitably.[386]

---

384   Lorant, 593–594.
385   Lorant, 594.
386   Franklin D. Roosevelt, "Commonwealth Club Address" (speech, September 23, 1932), Teaching American History, https://teachingamericanhistory.org/library/document/commonwealth-club-address/.

Roosevelt grandly concluded: "The day of enlightened administration has come."[387] He would not be the last "progressive" president to cast the forced redistribution of wealth and massive expansion of state control as "enlightened."

How he won

The Democratic candidate wasn't alone in seeing this election as a watershed moment. On October 21, 1932, two and a half weeks before the election, Herbert Hoover gave a major speech at Madison Square Garden in New York City, saying:

> This campaign is more than a contest between two men. It is more than a contest between two parties. It is a contest between two philosophies of government....

> The primary conception of this whole American system is not the regimentation of men but the co-operation of free men.... It is founded on a peculiar conception of self-government designed to maintain this equal opportunity to the individual, and through decentralization it brings about and maintains these responsibilities. The centralization of government will undermine responsibilities and will destroy the system.[388]

---

387   Ibid.
388   Herbert Hoover, "The Consequences of the Proposed New Deal" (speech, October 21, 1932), Pepperdine School of Public Policy, https://publicpolicy. pepperdine.edu/academics/research/faculty-research/new-deal/hoover-speeches/hh102132.htm.

These were grand words, but hollow: Hoover didn't really offer an alternative to Roosevelt's program. In fact, his administration was its precursor. Unlike Hoover, however, Roosevelt was popular. With the economy in the tank and a widely hated president running for reelection, Roosevelt was a shoo-in. The campaign was long on ballyhoo and short on genuine substance; it was Tippecanoe and Tyler Too all over again, with a tinge of class warfare. A cigar-store Indian could have beaten Hoover in 1932, and it was a bonus that Roosevelt was much more appealing personally than Hoover. He trounced Hoover with 472 electoral votes to the incumbent's 59. The New Deal was underway.

Roosevelt remained popular throughout his presidency. He outdid Grant and his own fifth cousin Theodore, becoming the first president to be elected to more than two terms. FDR won four terms in all. Nineteen years after his death, a Republican presidential candidate, Barry Goldwater, would offer voters "a choice, not an echo," that is, not just a "me-too" response to the Democratic agenda, but a genuine alternative. After Hoover, however, the Republicans continued to offer an echo, not a choice, nominating three "progressives" who never challenged the basic premises of the New Deal but just claimed that they could do its job more efficiently than the Democrats: Kansas Governor Alf M. Landon, businessman and lawyer Wendell Willkie, and New York Governor Thomas E. Dewey. Not surprisingly, Roosevelt won in a landslide every time.

Notable accomplishments as president and events of his presidency

1. *The Great Depression.* In his first inaugural address, Roosevelt proclaimed that "the only thing we have to fear is fear itself," which made little sense and wasn't true at a time when so many Americans were facing imminent financial ruin, but it sounded good and reassured people.[389] The Roosevelt administration compounded the impression that it had matters well in hand when it charged out of the gate in its first hundred days with a large number of initiatives designed to end the Great Depression. The Emergency Banking Act was the first federal bailout of the nation's banks and gave the federal government massive new power to regulate the banking system.

On April 5, 1933, Roosevelt signed an executive order forbidding the hoarding of gold. This was a time of economic panic, with people withdrawing gold from the banks at a phenomenal rate. By ending the massive run on gold, Roosevelt saved the banks, and the American economic system (which was still on the gold standard), from wholesale collapse.

President Roosevelt also established a number of new federal agencies designed to provide relief for the poor, get the unemployed working, enable American businesses to get on their feet, and more. These included the Federal Emergency Relief Administration (FERA), the Civilian Conservation Corps (CCC), the Agricultural Adjustment Administration (AAA), the Public Works Administration (PWA), the National Recovery

---

389   Franklin D. Roosevelt, "First Inaugural Address" (speech, March 4, 1933), Avalon Project, Yale Law School, https://avalon.law.yale.edu/20th_century/froos1.asp.

Administration (NRA), and the Tennessee Valley Authority (TVA). More of these new agencies and initiatives followed. The Social Security Act of 1935 established a plan to tax Americans to provide pensions for the aged.

All this and other New Deal initiatives made Roosevelt more popular than ever: it gave the impression that the administration was tackling the Depression with tremendous energy and would soon have America back on its feet.

2. *Ending Prohibition.* On March 22, 1933, Roosevelt signed the Cullen-Harrison Act, which legalized beer and wine with low alcohol content. On December 5, 1933, the Twenty-First Amendment, repealing the Eighteenth, which had outlawed alcoholic beverages, was ratified. At very least, in the midst of all their economic misery, Americans could enjoy an occasional drink.

3. *Changing the character of the Supreme Court.* As the Supreme Court struck down some of his New Deal organizations as unconstitutional, Roosevelt and his allies castigated the justices as "nine old men," obstructionists who didn't care if Americans suffered. Finally, Roosevelt had had enough. On February 5, 1937, he unveiled a scheme to add as many as six new justices to the Supreme Court and more to lower courts, on the pretext that dockets were overcrowded and the claim that older judges had lost their powers of judgment.

The "court-packing plan" became one of Roosevelt's few legislative defeats, but it proved unnecessary anyway. The Supreme Court made a sudden turn to the left in March 1937 and began declaring New Deal programs to be constitutional despite having previously struck down quite similar programs.

The ever-resourceful president also found another way to work around the obstacles that the Supreme Court placed in front of his agenda: he was careful to appoint justices who shared his vision for the country and who weren't excessively bothered by legal minutiae such as adherence to the letter of the Constitution. The activist Supreme Court, willing to bend or ignore constitutional restraints, was born during the Roosevelt administration.

4. *World War II.* When war in Europe began in September 1939, the United States stayed neutral. This was a popular position: the anti-war America First Committee had eight hundred thousand members at its peak, including future presidents John F. Kennedy and Gerald Ford. Roosevelt recognized that most Americans wanted to stay out of the war, and in an October 30, 1940 campaign speech, he sought to reassure them: "I have said this before, but I shall say it again and again and again; your boys are not going to be sent into any foreign wars."[390]

At the same time, Roosevelt aided Britain as much as he could, developing the Lend-Lease program to supply war matériel to the United States' Great War ally. He took increasingly belligerent stances toward the Axis powers and disparaged foes of the war as isolationists, blind to genuine international threats and unwilling to support America acting in the world as a great power.

All that changed on December 7, 1941. The next day, President Roosevelt told Congress: "Yesterday, December 7, 1941—a date which will live in infamy—the United States of America

---

390   William D. Pederson, *The FDR Years* (New York: Infobase Publishing, 2009), 391.

was suddenly and deliberately attacked by naval and air forces of the Empire of Japan."[391]

The Great Depression was finally over. Unemployment fell from 17 percent in 1939 to 1 percent in 1944 as millions of Americans went to work for the war effort. Roosevelt oversaw extraordinarily rapid production of military matériel that quickly made the American Armed Forces the most powerful fighting force in the world. World War II was an unquestionably just war against two implacable and inhumane enemies, and for many Americans, Roosevelt's very presence in the White House became the assurance that the good would ultimately prevail over evil.

5. *The United Nations.* The structure and goals of a new international organization to replace the moribund League of Nations were formulated at the Dumbarton Oaks Conference in September and October 1944. In the midst of World War II, the Roosevelt administration argued that such an international organization was necessary to prevent future wars. Anxious that his new international body would be viable, Roosevelt agreed to give the Soviet Union three votes at the United Nations, while all other countries would have only one, by treating the Soviet provinces of Ukraine and Byelorussia as if they were independent states.

In a harbinger of things to come, the executive secretary of the Dumbarton Oaks Conference was the Roosevelt State Department's director of the Office of Special Political Affairs,

---

391 Franklin D. Roosevelt, "Pearl Harbor Speech" (December 8 1941), American History from Revolution to Reconstruction and Beyond, http://www.let. rug.nl/usa/presidents/franklin-delano-roosevelt/pearl-harbor-speech-december-8-1941.php.

Alger Hiss. A few years later, Hiss would be famously revealed to be a spy for the Soviet Union, amid strenuous denials from the leftist establishment, which quickly made Hiss into a "progressive" martyr, a role he played indefatigably until his death in 1996.

Why his presidency was disastrous for America

In his first inaugural address, Roosevelt not only declared that fear was all that Americans should fear; he also attempted to lower expectations for an economic recovery by trying to convince the nation that material prosperity wasn't all it was cracked up to be. "Happiness," he declared sonorously, "lies not in the mere possession of money; it lies in the joy of achievement, in the thrill of creative effort." He continued, "The joy and moral stimulation of work no longer must be forgotten in the mad chase of evanescent profits...." He called on Americans to recognize "the falsity of material wealth as the standard of success."[392]

During the 1936 campaign, Roosevelt reiterated his determination to redistribute wealth, adapting the Marxist slogan "From each according to his ability, to each according to his needs" in saying: "Here is my principle: Taxes shall be levied according to ability to pay. That is the only American principle."[393] As was so often the case with Roosevelt, this sounded better than it was. A graduated income tax has been in place

392   Roosevelt, "First Inaugural Address."
393   Franklin D. Roosevelt, *Public Papers of the Presidents of the United States: F.D. Roosevelt, 1936, Volume 5* (Best Books, 1938), 525.

in America for many years, but that doesn't negate the fact that penalizing wealthier Americans by forcing them to pay higher taxes only decreases their ability and reduces their incentive to maintain businesses that provide jobs for ordinary citizens. A genuine "American principle" would be to tax everyone equally, which would naturally result in the wealthy paying more anyway.

As the Great Depression dragged on, perhaps there were some Americans who comforted themselves with the realization that they were not corrupted by "the falsity of material wealth." They had scant other comfort. In May 1939, halfway through Roosevelt's lengthy presidency, Secretary of the Treasury Henry Morgenthau went before the House Ways and Means Committee and frankly admitted that the New Deal had been an abject failure. "We have tried spending money," declared Morgenthau. "We are spending more than we have ever spent before and it does not work.... I want to see this country prosperous. I want to see people get a job. I want to see people get enough to eat. We have never made good on our promises.... I say after eight years of this Administration we have just as much unemployment as when we started...and an enormous debt to boot!"[394]

Morgenthau was right. The economy recovered more slowly during the Great Depression than it did from any other economic crisis in the nation's history. Nor was the New Deal's damage limited solely to the fact that it didn't work. From the empty sagacity of proclamations like "the only thing we have

---

[394]   Burton W. Folsom, *New Deal Or Raw Deal?: How FDR's Economic Legacy Has Damaged America* (New York: Simon and Schuster, 2009), 2.

to fear is fear itself" to his fireside chats, in which he explained his policies and reassured listeners about the Depression and the war, Roosevelt brought the full force of his considerable personal charm to give Americans the impression that, in the midst of its two worst-ever crises, the nation was in the care of a calm, competent leader who would see them through. His avuncular and patrician public persona, combined with the New Deal's complex of social programs, gave tremendous impetus to the assumption that if George Washington was the Father of His Country, Franklin D. Roosevelt was the Nation's Dad: calming, in control, and offering comprehensive care for the basic needs of his children, the citizens of the republic. Radio offered him the chance to speak directly to the American people as they sat in their living rooms. For the first time, the president of the United States became a local politician, as close as the local city councilman. This contributed a great deal to the sense that he was the kindly national father figure.

Because of the example FDR set, his successors were widely considered to be responsible for national morale to a much greater extent than were his predecessors. And Americans began, more than ever, to look to the federal government to solve all their problems—not only to help them make ends meet, but to carry them through an ever-increasing range of life's difficulties. The line is direct from the New Deal to the Ohio woman who cried out during the 2012 election, "Keep Obama in president, you know! He gave us a phone, he's gonna do more."[395]

---

395   Kelly Phillips Erb, "Crazy for 'Obama Phones'—but Are They for Real?," Forbes, September 28, 2012.

Numerous commentators at that time pointed out that there was no government free-phone program; the phones were actually reduced to bargain-basement prices for those on the welfare rolls. They were both splitting hairs and missing the point. The Obama-phone woman provided evidence of the fact that by 2012, eighty years after Roosevelt was elected, many Americans took for granted that one of the government's primary functions was to bestow various forms of largesse upon the American people, using money taken from productive Americans to do so. That is Franklin Delano Roosevelt's most enduring, and most damaging, legacy.

It does not, however, represent the full extent of the damage he did to the country. Many found the proliferation of New Deal agencies, all known by their three initials, bewildering, and ridiculed them as "alphabet agencies." Al Smith, Roosevelt's old rival in the Democratic Party, said that the government during the Roosevelt administration was "submerged in a bowl of alphabet soup."[396]

Smith was making light of a situation that was actually quite serious: the New Deal was the impetus for a massive expansion of government regulation and federal bureaucracy. By mid-1934, the National Recovery Administration had added nearly five hundred new laws to the statute books; during the first year of the Roosevelt era, ten thousand new pages had been added to federal law books, tripling them in size—which meant that one year of Roosevelt was responsible for three times the legal output of the previous thirty-one presidential

---

396   William Safire, *Safire's Political Dictionary* (Oxford: Oxford University Press, 2008), 15.

administrations. This rapid growth of regulations inevitably stifled initiative and began to make it harder for businesses to get started and become prosperous. This, in turn, slowed down the economy and hurt the Americans who would have found gainful employ in those businesses had they not been spending so much time and money making sure they were in compliance with arcane and picayune federal rules.

Meanwhile, the justices Roosevelt appointed to the Supreme Court set the stage for a politicized court that legislated from the bench, overseeing a huge expansion of federal power by approving measures that more constitutionally minded justices would have struck down. This threatened the very foundation of the American republic: if the nation's highest judges often allowed themselves a very broad view of what the Constitution permitted, then there were no constraints to the government's power. The door was open to tyranny. Franklin D. Roosevelt opened it.

President Roosevelt's leadership during World War II is one of the cornerstones of his reputation as one of America's greatest presidents, and there is no doubt that his calm demeanor, determination, and optimism were just what the nation needed in one of its darkest hours. But Roosevelt made drastic mistakes in his handling of the war at its beginning, middle, and end, needlessly prolonging the conflict, condemning untold numbers of people to unimaginable suffering and death, and consigning whole nations to slavery in totalitarian systems when that fate could have been avoided.

Although Pearl Harbor was a surprise attack, there were numerous signs in 1941 that an attack of its kind was in the works. Roosevelt ignored them to the extent that both the army and the navy were drastically unprepared for war on December 7, 1941, and that unpreparedness led to many catastrophic American defeats in 1942. Exacerbating the ill effects of this lack of readiness was Roosevelt's frivolous and cavalier handling of negotiations with Japan in the fall of 1941, which many thought made the war inevitable. While some believed that Japanese militarism was implacable and war inevitable, George Kennan, a State Department analyst and architect of the postwar containment strategy that was utilized against the Soviet Union and its allies, stated that "surely it cannot be denied that had FDR been determined to avoid war with the Japanese, he would have conducted American policy quite differently."[397]

Others objected to Roosevelt's pursuance of a belligerent stance toward Japan and Germany before Pearl Harbor. "Inevitably, we had to get into it," observed historian Merlo Pusey. "I just wish we had done it honestly and openly in our constitutional way of doing things instead of...by the back door.... If he had been less of a politician and more of a statesman, he would have taken a stand instead of trying to do it covertly."[398] Roosevelt became a model for emulation for legions of politicians who were not statesmen by any stretch of imagination. Yet even with all his belligerence toward the Axis before Pearl Harbor, the U.S. military still wasn't ready for war.

Also, the interventionist equation of an America-first stance with irresponsible isolationism before Pearl Harbor

---

397   Thomas Fleming, *The New Dealers' War: FDR and the War within World War II* (New York: Basic Books, 2001), 47–48.

398   Ibid., 48.

has led to an enduring caricature of those who want to put the nation first as selfish, shortsighted fools with their heads in the sand regarding international problems. Or worse: some members of the America First Committee were undoubtedly anti-Semites with fascist sympathies, but it was also undeniable that many Americans who were neither anti-Semitic nor fascist were among its members. This has made it extremely difficult since World War II to oppose any American intervention anywhere for any reason: interventionists all too easily charge their foes with isolationism and the discussion is over. In reality, a genuine concern for the nation and desire to defend it will sometimes lead to opposition to rash international adventurism, and this opposition is not isolationism; but Franklin D. Roosevelt muddled that distinction.

World War II is frequently remembered today as a great struggle against one of the most evil regimes in human history, that of Adolf Hitler, and his allies in Japan and Italy. Roosevelt, however, acted more than once to obscure the moral aspect of the conflict. Even as evidence mounted of horrifying Nazi atrocities against the Jews of Europe, he steadfastly refused to take in Jewish refugees in any significant numbers. Infamously, the German ship *St. Louis*, carrying nine hundred Jews on what became known as "the Voyage of the Damned," was turned away from Miami and forced to return to Europe, where most of the people on board were murdered in the Holocaust. Assistant Secretary of State Breckinridge Long warned that the activities of the World Jewish Congress "may lend color to the charges of Hitler that we are fighting this war on account of and at the instigation of and direction of our Jewish citizens.... It might easily be a detriment to our war effort."[399] For those optics, untold numbers of European Jews died.

The same concerns led Roosevelt to reject calls to bomb the railroad lines leading to Auschwitz, which could have saved millions of Jewish lives. Assistant Secretary of War John McCloy successfully argued that U.S. military resources should be used only for military purposes. McCloy also recalled later that Roosevelt didn't think such a bombing would achieve its purpose: "I remember talking one time with Mr. Roosevelt about it, and he was irate. He said, 'Why, the idea!... They'll only move it down the road a little way.' "[400] However, no alternative plan to save Europe's Jews was ever devised.

Roosevelt likewise obscured the character of the war as a moral crusade on February 19, 1942, albeit on a much less horrifying scale, when he signed an executive order mandating the evacuation of Japanese Americans on the West Coast to internment camps farther inland, based on the concern that some of them could be working for the enemy. Opponents of this measure included FBI Director J. Edgar Hoover, Attorney General Francis Biddle, and Secretary of the Interior Harold Ickes, who called it "stupid and cruel."[401] It was also a violation of the cardinal principle of innocent until proven guilty, on a scale comparable to the forced relocation of the Indians during the administrations of Andrew Jackson and Martin Van Buren. There has been a great deal of hysteria about these internment camps in recent years; in reality, they were not

---

399   Ibid., 265.
400   Michael Beschloss, "FDR's Auschwitz Secret," *Newsweek*, October 13, 2002.
401   Fleming, 110.

"concentration camps." Nobody was killed, tortured, or even imprisoned in them; they had churches, schools, and stores. They were not remotely comparable to the Nazi death camps in which millions of Jews and others perished. They were, nonetheless, a needless deprivation of the civil liberties of numerous loyal Americans.

Meanwhile, many analysts believe that President Roosevelt prolonged the war unnecessarily and may even have helped keep Hitler in power when in January 1943, at a conference with British Prime Minister Winston Churchill in Casablanca, Roosevelt announced (to Churchill's dismay) that nothing would be acceptable from Germany except unconditional surrender. This stymied the efforts of the German opposition to Hitler, for many who might otherwise have joined the resistance reasoned that there was no point, as Germany would be forced to fight to the death anyway. It appeared to substantiate Hitler's claim that the Allies were fighting in order to destroy Germany utterly, and that if the Nazis lost the war, there would simply be no more German nation.

Germany was finally defeated anyway, and with that defeat looming in February 1945, a gravely ill Roosevelt flew all the way to Yalta in the Crimea to confer with Churchill and Soviet Premier Joseph Stalin about the nature of the postwar world. At Yalta, Roosevelt effectively agreed to Soviet domination of Eastern Europe, acquiescing to the Soviet annexation of eastern Poland and the Soviet seizure of the homes of thousands of Polish soldiers. The war began with the invasion of Poland; thanks to Roosevelt, it ended with Poland's betrayal. Many have argued that there was little else Roosevelt could have done without embroiling the U.S. in a new war against its World War II ally, the Soviet Union. There is no doubt, however, that Roosevelt was naïve in his assessment of Stalin, leading to a prolonging of this alliance of convenience in ways that were detrimental to the U.S. in the early days of the Cold War.

Franklin D. Roosevelt died on April 12, 1945, eleven weeks into his fourth term. He had been extremely ill for a year and had run for reelection in 1944 while his doctors lied to the American people about the seriousness of his condition. This was an appropriate end to an administration of deceptions, which had an effect on many Americans akin to a narcotic: it felt good but was ultimately dangerous to one's health.

In light of that, it is also fitting that one of the Roosevelt administration's lasting legacies is the United Nations, which for seventy years now has deceived the world into thinking that it is an instrument of peace. In reality, although its record is not entirely negative, the UN has ultimately proven many of those who doubted its viability to be correct. It has been responsible for an ongoing drain of America's resources to perpetuate an organization that became first a useful forum for the Soviet Bloc and then served the same purpose for the fifty-six-nation Organization of Islamic Cooperation; in both cases, it was steadfastly and consistently anti-American. Nor has it prevented numerous armed conflicts from breaking out all over the world. But the United States can't get out of it and expel it from New York City: to do so would be to turn one's back on efforts to bring peace to the world.

Franklin D. Roosevelt, that master manipulator, would smile at the near-total success of this propaganda that he did so much to further.

THIRTY-THREE

HARRY S. TRUMAN

Library of Congress[402]

---

402   *Harry Truman, Half-Length Portrait, Facing Front*, ca. 1945, photograph, Library of Congress, https://www.loc.gov/item/96523444/.

Full name: Harry S. Truman
Lived: May 8, 1884–December 26, 1972
Presidency: April 12, 1945–January 20, 1953
Party: Democratic
Evaluation: Did Good Things but Also Significant
  Damage
Rating: 6

What qualified him to be president

Harry Truman had been a senator from Missouri, known during the war for his efforts to combat corruption in military production, for nine years when he was chosen to be Roosevelt's running mate in 1944. He was FDR's third vice president. The first, John Nance Garner, served for Roosevelt's first two terms but grew increasingly opposed to the statist thrust of the New Deal and went off into grumpy retirement in 1941. Replacing him was Henry Wallace, a socialist dreamer whose naïve leftism alarmed many in the Democratic Party (which was different in those days). With Roosevelt quite obviously seriously ill, despite his doctors' denials, the vice-presidential nomination in 1944 was crucial, as it was widely believed that whoever was elected vice president would become the next president.

On April 12, 1945, when Roosevelt died of a cerebral hemorrhage, that belief proved true. Truman, who had gotten the vice-presidential nod for being a reliable party man and not as trusting as Wallace toward the Soviet Union, was suddenly president. Truman recounted, "I felt as though the moon, the stars, and all the planets had fallen upon me."[403] When a colleague addressed him as "Mr. President," he replied, "I wish you didn't have to call me that."[404]

How he won

By 1948, Truman had warmed to the job, although the American people had not exactly warmed to having him in it. As the campaign season began, his approval ratings were in the thirties. The Democrats suffered the defection of not one, but two significant party factions: the "progressives," led by Henry Wallace, who didn't think Truman was friendly enough to the Soviets and in favor of enough government control at home, and Southern Democratic segregationists, under the leadership of South Carolina governor Strom Thurmond, who were enraged at Truman for integrating the armed forces and fighting for the voting rights of black Americans.

With the Democratic vote split among three candidates and Truman unpopular, Republican candidate Thomas E. Dewey, who had lost to Roosevelt in 1944, looked to be a lock. He led comfortably in all the polls, so much so that his relatives began writing to him about when would be a good time to visit him in the White House. The *New York Times* declared: "Thomas E. Dewey's election as President is a foregone conclusion."[405] Just before the election, *Life* magazine ran a photo of

---

403   Lorant, 683.
404   Ibid.
405   Boller, loc. 3621.

Dewey captioned: "The next President of the United States."[406] Virtually everyone, except Harry Truman, seemed to agree.

Since Dewey and his team ascribed their 1944 defeat to being overly aggressive and partisan, they opted this time around to deal in vague, soothing platitudes and not engage Truman. Dewey's determination to be inoffensive left him with nothing but bromides and meaningless verbiage. In a speech in Phoenix, he intoned: "America's future—like yours in Arizona—is still ahead of us."[407] The *Louisville Courier Journal* ridiculed him: "No presidential candidate in the future will be so inept that four of his major speeches can be boiled down to these historic four sentences: Agriculture is important. Our rivers are full of fish. You cannot have freedom without liberty. Our future lies ahead."[408]

Truman, in contrast, went vigorously on the offensive. He raced around the country excoriating the Republican-controlled Eightieth Congress as "the worst in history" and the Republicans themselves as "gluttons of privilege."[409] He asked, after the manner of "progressives" since William Jennings Bryan, "Is the government of the United States going to run in the interest of the people as a whole or in the interest of a small group of privileged big businessmen?"[410]

The crowds loved it, and exhorted him to "Give 'em hell, Harry!"[411] He did. The *New York Times* headlined its coverage

---

406   Boller, loc. 3626.
407   Lorant, 716.
408   John Baldoni, "Why Hillary Clinton Is Reminiscent of President Dewey," Forbes, August 29, 2016.
409   Boller, loc. 3672.
410   Ibid.
411   Ibid.

of one Truman speech as "PRESIDENT LIKENS DEWEY TO HITLER AS FASCISTS' TOOL."[412] Even then, Dewey wouldn't respond.

Harry gave 'em hell again on election night, confounding all the pundits by soundly defeating Dewey. After the election, he was photographed jubilantly holding the *Chicago Tribune*'s early edition, featuring the headline "DEWEY DEFEATS TRUMAN." The president had proven the whole world wrong.

Notable accomplishments as president and events of his presidency

1. *The atomic bomb.* The atomic bomb had been in development, in the strictest secrecy, for a considerable period: as a senator and then vice president, Truman knew nothing about it, only finding out when he became president. Germany surrendered in May 1945, but the war in the Pacific continued. After much consideration, President Truman decided to use it in order to bring the war with Japan to an end. On August 6, 1945, the U.S. dropped the first atomic bomb on the Japanese city of Hiroshima; another was dropped on Nagasaki on August 9. These were the most devastating weapons in human history: with just these two bombs, 105,000 Japanese were killed. The Japanese announced their surrender on August 15.

2. *The Berlin Airlift and the Cold War.* In the aftermath of World War II, Germany was divided into four occupation zones: American, British, French, and Soviet. The city of Berlin,

---

412   David Pietrusza, *1948: Harry Truman's Improbable Victory and the Year That Transformed America's Role in the World* (New York Union Square Press, 2011), 371.

which lay deep within the Soviet zone, was also divided into four parts.

On June 24, 1948, as tensions were rising between the U.S. and the Soviets, Stalin blockaded Berlin, closing access to the American, British, and French zones. Truman acted quickly and decisively. The Berlin Airlift began the following day, bringing food, medical supplies, and other necessary goods to Berliners. In May 1949, the Soviets ended the blockade, although the Airlift continued. At this point, it was clear to the entire world that the wartime alliance between the U.S. and the Soviet Union was not going to continue in peacetime.

The original goal had been to unite the four zones into a single state. The antagonism between the Soviets and the U.S., however, made this impossible. In May 1949, the American, British, and French zones were combined to create the Federal Republic of Germany. The Soviets countered in October of that year with the establishment of a Communist state in their zone, the German Democratic Republic. The Cold War, a decades-long competition in the international arena between the United States and the Soviet Union, had begun.

3. *The Marshall Plan.* In light of the new tensions with the Soviet Union, Secretary of State George Marshall devised this program to help rebuild western Europe, so as to reduce the appeal of Communism. The U.S. spent over $12 billion ($125 billion today) on this plan.

4. *Recognition of Israel.* Unlike Roosevelt and his own State Department, Truman strongly supported the Zionist effort to establish a Jewish state in the region of Palestine. Secretary of State Marshall warned him that the Muslim Arabs of the

area would be enraged, but Truman thought that the case for Israel was a matter of simple justice. At midnight on May 14, 1948, the State of Israel declared its independence. The United States recognized it eleven minutes later, at 12:11.

5. *The Korean War.* On August 10, 1945, with the Japanese on the verge of surrender, the U.S. divided Korea at the thirty-eighth parallel, into Soviet and American occupation zones. No one expected this arrangement to continue indefinitely, but the U.S. was entirely unprepared when, on June 25, 1950, the Communists of North Korea invaded the South. The United Nations condemned the invasion and sent troops to Korea to counter the invaders.

Most of the troops were American; General Douglas MacArthur, a World War II hero, commanded them. President Truman, however, did not ask Congress for a declaration of war; this was the first of a huge number of "police actions" that the U.S. military would pursue.

MacArthur achieved great early success, but then the Communist Chinese invaded in November 1950 and threw the UN forces back. MacArthur wanted to attack Chinese bases, which Truman would not allow, as he did not want to escalate the conflict. MacArthur began acting unilaterally until Truman summarily fired him. This was a tremendously unpopular move at the time, as the American people understood MacArthur as trying to win the war and liberate the Communist North, with Truman stymieing him. Reality was more complicated: the Chinese forces were significantly stronger than the U.S. had anticipated, and Truman worried that getting involved in a direct conflict with them could provoke World War III.

This undeclared war went on inconclusively until after Truman was out of the White House.

6. *Standing for civil rights.* Truman moved to protect the voting rights of black Americans. In July 1948, he signed an executive order mandating equal opportunity in the armed forces, which had been largely segregated before then. For this, Truman suffered politically, with many Southern Democrats bolting from the party in 1948.

7. *Creation of the CIA.* On July 26, 1947, Truman signed the National Security Act, which provided for the creation of a foreign intelligence service, the Central Intelligence Agency (CIA). This shadowy agency was immediately involved in unsuccessful actions in Korea and subsequently in numerous clandestine operations around the world. Given the highly secretive nature of its work, the extent of its activity may never be fully known. That also made its accountability to the president and Congress an ongoing problem.

Why his presidency did good things but also significant damage

The atomic bomb killed over a hundred thousand Japanese civilians; for that reason, many have classified it as a war crime and harshly criticized Truman for using it. On October 14, 1948, in a campaign speech in Milwaukee, Truman offered a simple explanation for his decision: "I decided that the bomb should be used in order to end the war quickly and save countless lives—Japanese as well as American."[413] The alternative to the atomic bomb was a ground invasion of Japan that could have taken the lives of untold numbers of Americans as well as tens of thousands of Japanese civilians, many more than the number who died at Hiroshima and Nagasaki, not because Americans would have targeted civilians in that context, but because of the total militarism and mobilization of Japanese society.

Wars are full of hard choices. In the heat of the conflict, it is seldom easy to make a clear moral choice. Truman did not face a choice between dropping the bomb and not harming Japanese civilians; the way the Axis fought World War II, refraining from harming civilians was not an option (although that is not to say that every Allied action was justified).

President Truman also faced criticism in his own time and to this day for recognizing Israel, but as far as he was concerned, on this issue the right choice was clear: "Hitler had been murdering Jews right and left. I saw it, and I dream about it even to this day. The Jews needed some place where they could go. It is my attitude that the American government couldn't stand idly by while the victims [of] Hitler's madness are not allowed to build new lives."[414]

The Marshall Plan, meanwhile, helped innumerable people build new lives in Europe. This was decisive in preventing Soviet Communist influence from growing in

---

413   Harry S. Truman, "Address in Milwaukee, Wisconsin" (speech, October 14, 1948), American Presidency Project, https://www.presidency.ucsb.edu/documents/address-milwaukee-wisconsin.

414   Norman Berdichevsky, "Israel: From Darling of the Left to Pariah State," *New English Review*, May 2012.

western Europe. Unfortunately, however, it became a feature of the American way of warfare. The U.S. spent far more to rebuild Iraq and Afghanistan in the first two decades of the twenty-first century than it did on achieving the actual aims of the war. The Marshall Plan ethos boosted the idea that the United States was not just the world's policeman, but the world's hospital, responsible for getting troubled areas of the world back on their feet, even if doing so had nothing to do with American interests.

Secretary of State Marshall did have American interests in mind when he devised the plan in the first place, as he did when he argued against recognizing Israel. He pointed out that doing so would enrage the neighboring Muslim Arab states. That was true, but he was essentially arguing that the United States should bow to violent intimidation and tailor its foreign policy accordingly. Truman, unlike many of his successors, showed that he was not susceptible to this bullying.

Was recognizing Israel really what was best for America? Many have insisted, and have continued to insist, that it was not, as it earned the U.S. the everlasting antagonism of numerous Arabs and Muslims and involved America in conflicts that did not serve its own interests. However, these arguments involve bowing to a force that will never be friendly on a lasting basis to a non-Muslim polity no matter what and overlook the fact that a genuine America-first policy does not mean that America will not have allies. As the lone free republic in the Middle East and the primary target of the global jihad that struck America on September 11, 2001, Israel is a valuable ally to the U.S. as an embodiment of the principles that animate both countries and an important strategic ally in the defense against that jihad, however ineptly that defense has been pursued.

The Korean War, by contrast, was disastrous for the United States in a number of ways. In bypassing congressional approval, Truman set a precedent for a myriad of undeclared military interventions that have sapped America's strength in ill-defined conflicts where American involvement does not serve American interests. Placing American troops under UN auspices was another negative precedent, for although Americans commanded the UN troops in the Korean conflict, the door was opened to American troops being commanded by foreigners who did not have America's best interests at heart.

It was not necessarily contrary to American interests to get involved militarily in Korea; there was ample justification for trying to defend free societies and beat back Communist aggression. However, it was extremely unwise of Truman to commit U.S. forces to a conflict for which the military was unprepared and that it was unable to win. Truman's firing of MacArthur was entirely correct: the president is the commander in chief of the armed forces, and no general should ignore or countermand his orders. However, drawing back when MacArthur had a chance to win the war set yet another bad precedent. Truman's desire to avoid a global conflict was certainly realistic and prudent, but the inconclusiveness of the Korean War set the stage for the involvement of the U.S. in conflicts in which victory was not the goal and in which there was no clear goal at all.

The Korean War also gave rise to the Cold War situation of a more or less permanent mobilization. For the first time in American history, the U.S. began to maintain a large military force in what was supposed to be peacetime. With Communism growing increasingly aggressive worldwide, particularly in Eastern Europe and China, this situation was unavoidable. However, Truman's successor, Dwight D. Eisenhower, would warn of its inherent pitfalls. His warning has not been heeded.

Truman didn't foresee the ill effects of America's intervention in Korea, but he did come to see the dangers of the CIA—ten years after he left the White House. On December 22, 1963, Truman wrote in the *Washington Post* that "for some time I have been disturbed by the way [the] CIA has been diverted from its original assignment. It has become an operational and at times a policy-making arm of the Government. This has led to trouble and may have compounded our difficulties in several explosive areas."[415]

With the CIA by that time having intervened in the internal affairs of Iran, Guatemala, Indonesia, the Democratic Republic of the Congo, the Dominican Republic, South Vietnam, and elsewhere, Truman wrote: "I never had any thought that when I set up the CIA that it would be injected into peacetime cloak and dagger operations. Some of the complications and embarrassment I think we have experienced are in part attributable to the fact that this quiet intelligence arm of the President has been so removed from its intended role that it is being

---

415   Harry S. Truman, "Limit CIA Role to Intelligence," *Washington Post*, December 22, 1963.

interpreted as a symbol of sinister and mysterious foreign intrigue—and a subject for cold war enemy propaganda."

Truman concluded: "We have grown up as a nation, respected for our free institutions and for our ability to maintain a free and open society. There is something about the way the CIA has been functioning that is casting a shadow over our historic position and I feel that we need to correct it." He was right. But nothing was done.

Truman is also to be recognized for the fact that he suffered financial difficulties after he left office, which he no doubt considered nothing to be proud of. However, given the pattern of public servants today, his post-presidential financial woes are commendable for demonstrating that he did not fatten himself at the public trough. Truman left office before the age when politicians of modest means would go to Washington, serve in Congress for a few years, and return home millionaires. Nor did he receive outrageously inflated fees for speaking. He stayed home. His financial straits, however, led to the Former Presidents Act of 1958, which transformed former presidents into the nation's foremost, and best-paid, wards of the state.

THIRTY-FOUR

DWIGHT D. EISENHOWER

Library of Congress[416]

416   Fabian Bachrach, *Dwight D. Eisenhower, Head-and-Shoulders Portrait, Facing Slightly Left*, 1952, photograph, Library of Congress, https://www.loc.gov/item/96523445/.

Full name: Dwight David Eisenhower
Lived: October 14, 1890–March 28, 1969
Presidency: January 20, 1953–January 20, 1961
Party: Republican
Evaluation: Did Good Things but Also Significant
    Damage
Rating: 6

What qualified him to be president

It had been a long time since America elected a war hero president, but Dwight D. Eisenhower revived the old practice when he swept to victory in the 1952 election. Eisenhower was a five-star general and had been the supreme commander of the Allied Expeditionary Force in Europe during World War II. He had never held public office; before he was elected president of the United States, he served as president of Columbia University. In December 1950, he took an extended leave from Columbia to become the first supreme commander of the North Atlantic Treaty Organization (NATO). In May 1952, he returned to the university.

No one was sure what kind of president he would be, but he was overwhelmingly popular. Both parties courted him. His choice of the Republicans was not entirely surprising, as he had been raised in a Republican family; it also reflected his internationalism: Republican presidential hopeful Robert Taft, the son of the twenty-seventh president, opposed American involvement in NATO, and Eisenhower wanted the U.S. in NATO. A principal reason why he ran as a Republican was to stop Taft.

How he won

Eisenhower, known affectionately as "Ike," could have stood for virtually anything in 1952 and won the presidency. The Democrats countered with Adlai E. Stevenson, the governor of Illinois, who had impeccable "progressive" credentials and the enthusiastic support of Eleanor Roosevelt, the widow of the thirty-second president and godmother of American "progressives." Stevenson was respected for his great erudition. This was the first campaign to feature what became a recurring media caricature: the intellectual but somewhat remote Democrat versus the amiable Republican dunce.

The year 1952 was also the first TV-age campaign. The Republicans ran thirty-second TV ads featuring a catchy "I Like Ike" jingle. The Democrats responded with a song of their own, "I Love the Gov," which proclaimed, "Adlai, love you madly," but it just wasn't as catchy. The modern packaging of presidential candidates in what later came to be known as sound bites had begun.

America really did like Ike and didn't like Truman at all. Stevenson, even though he had not been part of the Truman administration and was himself likeable enough, was saddled with its baggage. Eisenhower promised to "clean up the mess in Washington," counter Communist influence at home as well as abroad, and even to go to Korea in order to find a way to end that conflict.[417] His campaign only hit one snag, when his vice-presidential candidate, a youthful congressman named Richard M. Nixon, was accused of benefiting improperly from

---

417   Michael S. Mayer, *The Eisenhower Years* (New York: Infobase Publishing, 2009), 188.

a campaign expense fund. Eisenhower was considering dropping him from the ticket, but Nixon went on national television and delivered an emotional defense of his actions. He strenuously denied using the fund to enrich himself personally, and maintained that his family lived modestly on his salary as a senator. He did insist, however, that he was going to keep one gift that his family had received from a well-wisher: a little dog, Checkers, that his daughters loved.

This folksy touch saved Nixon's candidacy and future in American public life. Eisenhower won with 442 electoral votes to Stevenson's 89.

Apparently, the Democrats, as the old quip goes, thought it would be a good idea to keep on hitting themselves over the head with a hammer because it felt so good when they stopped. They decided that 1956 was not the time to stop. They ran Stevenson against Eisenhower again, and predictably, Eisenhower's margin of victory this time was even larger: 457 electoral votes for the president. Stevenson received 73.

Notable accomplishments as president and events of his presidency

1. *Ending the Korean War*. An armistice took effect in Korea in July 1953, with the boundary between the Communist North and the free South much the same as it had been before the war began. Neither side could be said to have won, an outcome that, after the Korean War, would be repeated in many military engagements in which the U.S. would be involved.

2. *Keeping the New Deal in place*. The Republicans in 1952 not only won the presidency for the first time since 1928;

they also won control of both houses of Congress for the first time since 1946 (the Eightieth Congress that Truman had so relentlessly and successfully assailed during the 1948 campaign). Many Republicans wanted to roll back some of the Roosevelt-era programs that had expanded federal government control over so many areas of American life. Eisenhower, however, would not hear of this. He asserted: "Should any party attempt to abolish social security and eliminate labor laws and farm programs, you would not hear of that party again in our political history. There is a tiny splinter group, of course, that believes you can do these things.... Their number is negligible and they are stupid."[418]

The Eisenhower administration backed up these harsh words with actions that would have pleased FDR. It expanded the social security program and supported a bill raising the hourly minimum wage from seventy-five cents ($7 today) to a dollar ($9.50 today). It tried, but failed, to get a bill passed requiring the federal government to underwrite private health insurance policies, which was the beginning of the long push for government control over the health care system.

3. *Establishing the interstate highway system.* Eisenhower's largest New Deal-style program was the Federal Aid Highway Act, which he signed on June 29, 1956. It covered the nation with highways that enabled long-distance travel to be more convenient, if not more interesting, than it had ever been before. Eisenhower saw the highways as having a military as well as a civilian use, allowing for the rapid movement of troops and even serving as landing strips for airplanes. But the highway

---

418   Ibid., xii.

system also revolutionized the nation, bringing it closer in one way just as television was doing in another. Eisenhower was the first president to utilize TV to reach the American people, introducing the president (among much else) into American living rooms. The interstate highway system brought those living rooms much closer than they had ever been to one another, at the cost of $25 billion ($237 billion today) in taxpayer money, the largest domestic expenditure in U.S. history.

4. *The Warren Court*. The politicization of the Supreme Court that began with Franklin D. Roosevelt's abortive court-packing plan picked up speed when Eisenhower appointed Earl Warren as chief justice in 1953. The Warren Court's unanimous decision against segregation in *Brown v. Board of Education of Topeka* in 1954 was just and necessary, but too many of its other decisions were based on constitutional foundations that were dubious at best.

5. *The Cold War*. The Cold War with the Soviet Union was a matter of ongoing anxiety during the Eisenhower administration, with Senator Joseph McCarthy of Wisconsin charging that there had been extensive Communist infiltration of the U.S. government. Eisenhower privately deplored McCarthy's activities, which he and many others considered reckless and featuring accusations made on insufficient evidence. McCarthy was eventually condemned by the Senate. The perceived injustice of his actions made "McCarthyism" a byword that was used to discredit all efforts against Communist infiltration, as well as infiltration by other entities.

Eisenhower was firmly committed to the principle that Communism must be countered everywhere. Speaking specifically of the Middle East on January 5, 1957, Eisenhower enunciated what has become known as the Eisenhower Doctrine, which recommended "the employment of the armed forces of the United States to secure and protect the territorial integrity and political independence of such nations, requesting such aid, against overt armed aggression from any nation controlled by International Communism."[419]

And not just the armed forces, and not always upon request. The CIA helped overthrow left-leaning governments in Iran and Guatemala. Eisenhower also sent marines to Lebanon in 1958 to stave off a pro-Communist revolution. He pursued the containment of Communism in other ways as well: after the French defeat in Vietnam, Eisenhower founded the Southeast Asia Treaty Organization (SEATO) to stop the spread of Communism in that region.

At the same time, President Eisenhower made overtures to the Soviet Union, inviting it to join him in finding peaceful uses for atomic energy (the "Atoms for Peace" program) and meeting with Soviet premier Nikita Khrushchev. Tensions nonetheless remained high, and went even higher on May 1, 1960, when the Soviets shot down an American U-2 spy plane and paraded its pilot, Francis Gary Powers, before the television cameras while demanding that the Americans apologize. Eisenhower refused, and a planned summit to discuss mutual arms reductions and other issues was derailed.

6. *The Suez Crisis.* On July 26, 1956, Egyptian President Gamal Abdel Nasser nationalized the Suez Canal. Britain

---

419   Dwight D. Eisenhower, "Eisenhower Doctrine Speech" (speech, January 5, 1957), UVA Miller Center, https://millercenter.org/the-presidency/presidential-speeches/january-5-1957-eisenhower-doctrine.

and France subsequently began planning operations to seize the canal and overthrow the Nasser regime; they reluctantly included Israel in their plans, and ultimately it was decided that Israel would invade first, which it did on October 29, 1956.

The Israelis hoped to stop the Egyptian raids and murders of civilians in Israel and open up the Suez Canal to Israeli shipping. Israeli diplomat Abba Eban also told U.S. Secretary of State John Foster Dulles: "As a result of what Israel has done, Nasser is going to lose all his credit. A more moderate government will replace his. Possibly Israel and other countries will be able to make peace at last in the Middle East."[420] Eisenhower, however, had other ideas. He warned that Israel's actions could mean the end of "friendly cooperation between our two countries."[421] The U.S. even sponsored a UN resolution calling upon Israel to withdraw from the Sinai, although the British and French vetoed it. The Israeli government withdrew its forces from the Sinai, after obtaining Eisenhower's promise that the U.S. would ensure that its ships could make use of the Suez Canal.

7. *The space race.* On October 4, 1957, the Soviets launched an artificial satellite, Sputnik, into orbit. There was widespread shock in the U.S., as this was regarded as a Soviet victory in the Cold War and a possible threat to the U.S. from a weaponized satellite. On January 31, 1958, the U.S. responded with its own satellite, Explorer 1, and later that year, Eisenhower established the National Aeronautics and Space Administration (NASA). The U.S. and the Soviet Union would vie throughout

---

420   Howard M. Sachar, *A History of Israel from the Rise of Zionism to Our Time*, 2nd ed. (New York: Alfred A. Knopf, 2001), 503.

421   Ibid., 506.

the sixties for preeminence in space exploration, which Eisenhower later came to see as a waste of taxpayer money.

8. *Working for civil rights.* When Secretary of the Navy Robert Anderson advised Eisenhower not to press the South to accept the integration of the armed forces, the president shot back: "We have not taken and we shall not take a single backward step. There must be no second class citizens in this country."[422] He signed the Civil Rights Acts of 1957 and 1960, which encountered firm resistance in the South. After the Supreme Court ruled in *Brown v. Board of Education of Topeka* that segregation in schools was unconstitutional, he sent the National Guard to Arkansas to make sure that segregationist Governor Orval Faubus would not be able to block the entry of black students into a public high school in Little Rock.

9. *Warning against the military-industrial complex.* In his farewell address on January 17, 1961, Eisenhower stated, "We must guard against the acquisition of unwarranted influence, whether sought or unsought, by the military-industrial complex. The potential for the disastrous rise of misplaced power exists and will persist. We must never let the weight of this combination endanger our liberties or democratic processes. We should take nothing for granted. Only an alert and knowledgeable citizenry can compel the proper meshing of the huge industrial and military machinery of defense with our peaceful methods and goals, so that security and liberty may prosper together."[423]

---

422   Jean Edward Smith, *Eisenhower: In War and Peace* (New York: Random House, 2012), 711.

423   Dwight D. Eisenhower, "Military-Industrial Complex Speech" (January 17, 1961), Avalon Project, Yale Law School, https://avalon.law.yale.edu/20th_century/eisenhower001.asp.

Why his presidency did good things but also significant damage

Dwight D. Eisenhower's presidency was largely a time of peace and stability for the United States, amidst immense international tension and ferment. He successfully kept the peace with the Soviet Union through numerous crises when it seemed as if nuclear war was imminent. His commitment to civil rights was consistent; at a time of increasing racial strife, he did all he could to undo the wrongs of nearly a century since the abolition of slavery.

For all that, President Eisenhower is undeniably to be commended. The devil, however, is in the details.

One of the most damaging aspects of Eisenhower's presidency was his refusal to challenge the basic premises of the New Deal. The Eisenhower administration was generally a period of great prosperity. However, in the year after Eisenhower implemented his minimum wage increase, unemployment jumped from 4.2 percent to 5.2 percent, and the economy went into a recession. This was entirely predictable: faced with larger operating expenses, many business owners will cut costs by laying off workers. When the government mandates those larger operating expenses, unemployment will rise, and the economy will suffer. The interstate highway system, meanwhile, effectively destroyed the passenger railroad industry, although there is no doubt that it also was a tremendous boon to the automobile industry.

With the Republicans implementing large government programs, and the Democrats remaining the standard-bearers for an expanded federal government, voters had no choice but to accept it. Even Eisenhower realized this. In 1964, three years out of office and a popular and respected elder statesman, he wrote an article for the *Saturday Evening Post* entitled "Why I Am a Republican." In it, he declared: "I am increasingly disturbed by the steady, obvious drift of our nation toward a centralization of power of the Federal Government. And in this fact is found the primary reason why I sincerely urge all voters, no matter their present political affiliations, to take a fresh, thoughtful look at the basic Republican philosophy and Republican performance as compared to that of the Democrats. For the hard fact is that under many years of Democratic Party leadership our country has been lured into the 'easy way,' a path of federal expediency which, like a narcotic, may give us a false sense of well-being, but in the long run is dangerous to our future, our basic rights, our moral fiber and our individual freedom."[424]

This was no doubt true. But as president, Eisenhower had done little to halt the expansion of federal power. He resisted numerous measures that would have repealed or rolled back New Deal programs. He was determinedly bipartisan, going along with numerous Democratic initiatives, even when they involved the centralization that he warned against. In 1954, he stated his guiding philosophy: "I have just one purpose, outside of the job of keeping this world in peace...and that is to build up a strong progressive Republican Party in this country. If the right wing wants a fight, they are going to get it. If they want to leave the Republican Party and form a third party, that's their

---

424   Dwight D. Eisenhower, "Why I Am a Republican," *Saturday Evening Post*, April 11, 1964.

business, but before I end up, either this Republican Party will reflect progressivism or I won't be with them anymore."[425]

That meant that both parties endorsed a rapidly expanding federal government, higher taxes, and more state interference in the daily lives of Americans. His 1964 article suggests that, by then, he had seen the error of his ways. But by then, it was too late.

Eisenhower's "Modern Republicanism" reduced the Republican Party to a faint echo of the Democrats. Democrats would formulate grand proposals that generally involved a massive expansion of government spending and control, and instead of challenging these proposals at their foundations and arguing against them on principle, Republicans would merely quibble that they could be implemented more cheaply and efficiently. Eisenhower ensured that even when Republicans were in the majority, they continued to have a minority mentality: the Democrats were setting the agenda for the country.

There would be pushback against this assumption within the Republican Party, but the dominant mainstream of Republicanism ever since Ike has been to say "Me too" to the Democrats, rather than "I object." Eisenhower didn't originate the idea of making the Republican Party a pale copy of the Democratic Party, rather than a genuine principled opposition: Landon, Willkie, and Dewey would likely have done much the same thing, but they lost and he won, so Eisenhower must be credited as the primary architect of what is

---

425   Stephen E. Ambrose, *Eisenhower the President*, vol. 2 (New York: Simon and Schuster, 2014), 220.

essentially a single party in two factions that has, for the most part, governed America since the 1950s.

In the Suez Crisis, meanwhile, Eisenhower backed an adversary, Egypt, over an ally, Israel, and forced it to abandon tangible military gains in exchange for intangible assurances. Once again, an example was set that other presidents would follow, to the detriment of everyone involved.

Nuclear weapons had changed the very nature of warfare. Like Truman, Eisenhower didn't want to use nuclear weapons in Korea but believed that he could not take control of the entire peninsula and put an end to the Communist regime there without risking nuclear war. So the Korean War ended up being fought for nothing at all, as the *status quo ante* was restored, with the country remaining divided at the thirty-eighth parallel. The Communist aggression, however, was successfully turned back.

The downside of this was that it established the practice of fighting wars without attempting to win them. The Communists were fighting for total control of Korea, as they would later in Vietnam; America, by contrast, was fighting a limited war, afraid to do what victory would require. While it may have been that victory in Korea could mean nuclear war, it certainly wasn't true in other interventions later. The Korean War established the paradigm for the United States fighting limited wars that it could not or would not win, including some with no clear goal or end point.

In light of these undeclared, unfocused, unending wars, Eisenhower's warning about the military-industrial complex was prophetic. Balancing the genuine requirements of the national defense against the temptation to engage in military action for less than noble purposes, including the profit motive, was not done nearly as often as it should have been by Eisenhower's successors. Had the United States been consistent in requiring a declaration of war, and in fighting wars only when there was a clear national interest and a ready definition of victory, it would have prevented a great deal of this.

The Cold War made it harder to distinguish acting in the genuine national interest from unrestrained and irresponsible adventurism. The CIA operations in Iran and Guatemala helped overthrow popular regimes, which was against the stated American commitment to political freedom and self-determination. These regimes were also, however, left-leaning ones that could have led to governments that were far more repressive and posed a real danger to the United States. It would be facile, and require a blind eye to the manifest inhumanity of every Communist regime the world has ever seen, to fault Eisenhower for authorizing actions against pro-Communist regimes because they enjoyed some transient popularity among populations that were not fully aware of the dangers they represented. At the same time, such operations gave ammunition to those who charged that the U.S. was hypocritical and antidemocratic, a chorus that has increased in volume and influence up to this day.

Even worse, after the Cold War ended, the United States continued to act as if it were still going on and applied, notably in Iraq and Afghanistan, its Cold War policies as a template for dealing with conflicts that were actually markedly different in character. The results, predictably, were disastrous.

THIRTY-FIVE

JOHN F. KENNEDY

Library of Congress[426]

---

426   *President John F. Kennedy, Head-and-Shoulders Portrait, Facing Front*, 1961,
       photograph, Library of Congress, https://www.loc.gov/item/96523447/.

Full name: John Fitzgerald Kennedy
Lived: May 29, 1917–November 22, 1963
Presidency: January 20, 1961–November 22, 1963
Party: Democratic
Evaluation: Did Little Good but Not Much Damage
Rating: 5

What qualified him to be president

John F. Kennedy had served for six years in the House and six more in the Senate when he became the Democratic Party's presidential nominee in 1960, but his record in both the House and Senate was undistinguished. He was widely considered a lightweight, known more for his looks, his glamorous wife Jacqueline, and his friendships with the stars than for his legislative accomplishments. However, he was also the son of Joseph P. Kennedy, who had been ambassador to Great Britain during the Franklin D. Roosevelt administration, and who was determined to make him president.

Kennedy commanded a navy patrol boat, PT 109, during World War II, which a Japanese destroyer cut in half. Kennedy injured his back swimming with his crewmen to safety and was awarded the Purple Heart. With an eye toward a future political career, his father did all he could to portray his son as a war hero. Joe Kennedy also applied pressure to get his son awarded the Pulitzer Prize for his 1956 book, *Profiles in Courage*, which was actually ghostwritten by the man who became Kennedy's presidential speechwriter, Ted Sorensen.

With the candidate's résumé thus artificially padded, the handsomely financed Kennedy machine steamrolled through the Democratic primaries. Kennedy's principal primary challenger, Senator Hubert Humphrey, quipped, "I feel like an independent merchant competing against a chain store."[427] Kennedy's Catholicism was a big issue, as was his statement declaring: "I am not the Catholic candidate for President. I am the Democratic Party's candidate for President who happens also to be a Catholic."[428]

That appeared to settle the matter, putting to rest the concerns of some Protestants that Kennedy in the Oval Office would be taking orders from the Pope in Rome. However, one Associated Press reporter observed that "the Kennedy people seemed determined to make a bigger thing out of the religious issue than it really was" by portraying their man as the continuing victim of religious prejudice, wildly exaggerating the attacks on his religion in order to do so.[429] John F. Kennedy was the first, but by no means the last, presidential candidate to position himself as the underdog candidate of the broadminded and enlightened, fighting against the dark forces of prejudice and bigotry.

How he won

The Republican candidate was Richard M. Nixon of California. There was little that distinguished Kennedy's views from his, and so the 1960 campaign became one of personalities. Nixon was only forty-seven (Kennedy was forty-three) but had been

---

427 David Pietrusza, *1960: LBJ vs. JFK vs. Nixon* (New York: Union Square Press, 2008), 86.
428 Ibid., 256.
429 Ibid., 117.

vice president since 1953 and campaigned as the candidate of experience and continuity with Eisenhower's successful presidency.

The campaign is famous for the televised debates between Nixon and Kennedy, the first debates between the presidential candidates of each major party. The effect of television may have decided the election. A majority of those who listened to the first debate on the radio thought Nixon had won, but on television, he had unwisely eschewed makeup and sweated profusely under the hot lights, making him look nervous and shifty. Most TV viewers thought Kennedy had won.

Eisenhower also may have torpedoed Nixon's chances when he was asked during a nationally televised press conference to name a "major idea" that Nixon originated and Eisenhower adopted. "If you give me a week," Ike replied, "I might think of one. I don't remember."[430] Eisenhower called Nixon and apologized, but the damage was done: the Democrats made a campaign commercial out of the president's remark, mocking Nixon's claim that he had been influential in the Eisenhower administration.

Even after all that, the election itself was extremely close, with Kennedy winning only 112,000 more popular votes than Nixon. Illinois and Texas decided the contest. Both were quite close themselves: if Nixon had won forty-seven thousand more votes in Texas (the home state of Democratic vice-presidential candidate Lyndon B. Johnson) and ten thousand in Illinois (where Democratic machine boss Richard Daley, the mayor of

---

430   Stephen E. Ambrose, *Eisenhower: Soldier and President* (New York: Simon and Schuster, 1991), 525.

Chicago, held sway), he would have become president. There was significant evidence that the Kennedy machine had committed voter fraud in both states, but Nixon declined to contest the election, saying that he did not wish to plunge the country into a crisis with the Cold War raging.

Notable accomplishments as president and events of his presidency

1. *Affirming internationalism.* In his inaugural address, Kennedy issued a ringing declaration that expanded the Eisenhower Doctrine regarding the Middle East to an explicit avowal that the United States would do whatever was necessary to combat Communism around the world: "Let every nation know, whether it wishes us well or ill, that we shall pay any price, bear any burden, meet any hardship, support any friend, oppose any foe, in order to assure the survival and the success of liberty."[431]

Kennedy followed up his famous admonition in that same address—"And so, my fellow Americans: ask not what your country can do for you—ask what you can do for your country"—with another affirmation of internationalism: "My fellow citizens of the world: ask not what America will do for you, but what together we can do for the freedom of man."[432]

2. *Working for civil rights.* In his first State of the Union message on January 30, 1961, Kennedy said: "The denial of

---

431   John F. Kennedy, "Inaugural Address" (speech, January 20, 1961), Avalon Project, Yale Law School, https://avalon.law.yale.edu/20th_century/kennedy.asp.

432   Ibid.

constitutional rights to some of our fellow Americans on account of race—at the ballot box and elsewhere—disturbs the national conscience, and subjects us to the charge of world opinion that our democracy is not equal to the high promise of our heritage."[433]

On March 6, he signed an executive order establishing the President's Committee on Equal Employment Opportunity, which stipulated that government contractors must "take affirmative action to ensure that applicants are employed, and that employees are treated during employment, without regard to their race, creed, color, or national origin."[434]

In June 1963, when Alabama Governor George Wallace blocked a doorway at the University of Alabama to prevent black students from entering, Kennedy sent the National Guard; Wallace moved away from the doors. Kennedy set the wheels in motion for new legislation to guarantee blacks' voting rights and access to schools; after his assassination, it became the Civil Rights Act of 1964.

3. *The Bay of Pigs invasion.* Executing a plan that Eisenhower had approved, the CIA trained a force of 1,500 Cuban exiles to invade their home country and lead the Cuban people to depose the Communist dictator Fidel Castro. When the invasion began on April 17, 1961, however, the Cuban people did not rise up to support the invaders. Kennedy also declined

---

433   John F. Kennedy, "State of the Union Address" (speech, January 30, 1961), UVA Miller Center, https://millercenter.org/the-presidency/presidential-speeches/january-30-1961-state-union.

434   John F. Kennedy, "Executive Order 10925 Establishing the President's Committee on Equal Employment Opportunity," March 6, 1961, Wikisource, https://en.wikisource.org/wiki/Executive_Order_10925.

to give them U.S. air support, apparently so as to be able to maintain that the U.S. was not involved and keep tensions as low as possible with the Soviets.

About a third of the invaders were killed; the rest were captured. Castro demanded, and received, $53 million ($456 million today) in food and medicine in exchange for the captured men. Kennedy took full responsibility for the fiasco, and the impression began to grow that he was indeed a light-weight playboy who was too weak and distracted to do his job properly.

4. *The Cuban Missile Crisis.* Soviet Premier Nikita Khrush-chev certainly thought Kennedy was weak, particularly after meeting and browbeating him on June 4, 1961. Khrushchev saw Kennedy's weakness as an opportunity. On October 14, 1962, U2 spy planes conducting reconnaissance over Cuba discovered the existence of a number of Soviet-built ballistic missile sites, from which nuclear missiles could easily have been launched into the United States.

For two weeks, the world held its breath, fearful that nuclear war would break out any minute. Finally, on October 28, Khrushchev blinked and agreed to remove the sites, although it came to light later that Kennedy had privately agreed to the reciprocal action of removing American missiles from Turkey and Italy. Although Khrushchev had outsmarted the youthful president and received a reward for his aggres-sive action, the world, including the Soviet Politburo, viewed Kennedy as the victor in the confrontation, and the Cuban Missile Crisis precipitated Khrushchev's removal from power in 1964.

5. *The Berlin Wall.* Another manifestation of Khrushchev's perception that Kennedy was weak was the construction of the Berlin Wall. In July 1961, Kennedy warned that an attack on West Berlin would be considered an attack on the United States. Building a wall was not an attack, but the Communists were clearly contemptuous of his threats. East German leaders just a few weeks later began building a barrier between East Berlin and West Berlin in order to stop citizens of East Germany from fleeing to freedom in the West.

Beyond reinforcing the American brigade that was guarding West Berlin, Kennedy did nothing. He did, however, always have an eye for the theatrical. On June 26, 1963, before a tumultuous crowd in West Berlin, Kennedy proclaimed:

> Two thousand years ago the proudest boast was "civis Romanus sum." Today, in the world of freedom, the proudest boast is "Ich bin ein Berliner...."[435]

> There are many people in the world who really don't understand, or say they don't, what is the great issue between the free world and the Communist world. Let them come to Berlin. There are some who say that Communism is the wave of the future. Let them come to Berlin. And there are some who say in Europe and elsewhere we can work with the Communists. Let them come to Berlin. And there are even a

---

435   "I am a Roman citizen" and "I am a Berliner."

few who say that it's true that Communism is an evil system, but it permits us to make economic progress. *Lass' sie nach Berlin kommen.* Let them come to Berlin.

Freedom has many difficulties and democracy is not perfect, but we have never had to put a wall up to keep our people in, to prevent them from leaving us.[436]

6. *The space program.* On May 25, 1961, President Kennedy told Congress, "I believe that this nation should commit itself to achieving the goal, before this decade is out, of landing a man on the moon and returning him safely to the earth."[437] NASA's 1962 budget more than doubled in 1963 as the Space Age went into full swing.

7. *Intervention in Vietnam.* Kennedy increased the American military presence in South Vietnam in its escalating conflict with the Communist North. America would not leave Vietnam until ten years after Kennedy was killed.

8. *Moving to reduce taxes.* In January 1963, Kennedy unveiled a proposal that would significantly lower federal income tax rates, as well as corporate tax rates. Unlike later Democratic presidents, he believed these cuts would spur

---

436   John F. Kennedy, "Remarks of President John F. Kennedy at the Rudolph Wilde Platz" (speech Berlin, June 26, 1963), John F. Kennedy Presidential Library and Museum, https://www.jfklibrary.org/archives/other-resources/john-f-kennedy-speeches/berlin-w-germany-rudolph-wilde-platz-19630626.

437   John F. Kennedy, "Address to Joint Session of Congress" (speech, May 25, 1961), https://www.jfklibrary.org/learn/about-jfk/historic-speeches/address-to-joint-session-of-congress-may-25-1961.

economic growth. The Revenue Act of 1964, as it ultimately came to be known, wasn't passed until after his death, but it proved him correct: unemployment fell from 5 percent in 1964 to 4 percent in 1965 and 3.8 percent in 1966.

Why his presidency did little good but not much damage

Kennedy's assassination on November 22, 1963 led to an unprecedented adulation and idolization of the martyred president. His brief presidency is consistently ranked among the greatest, and Kennedy himself has become a hero of myth and legend.

Reality was more prosaic. Kennedy was an inspiring speaker during the height of the Cold War and made a strong impression on screen in the still-infant TV age. Meanwhile, the Kennedy administration was a time of great confidence in America. The centerpiece of this confidence was the space program; the Space Race was about more than just competing with the Soviets—it was a key source of the feeling that the nation was on the brink of immense technological breakthroughs that would transform society for the better. Nonetheless, Khrushchev outmaneuvered Kennedy over the Berlin Wall and the Cuban Missile Crisis, and the internationalism of the Kennedy administration kept the nation on the road to carrying a sense of responsibility for the world at the expense of its own citizens.

Hardly any of President Kennedy's domestic agenda was completed at the time of the assassination. His efforts to secure civil rights for black Americans were laudable, but his use of the term "affirmative action" in his executive order regarding equal employment opportunity was a dark hint of how the struggle for civil rights would soon become the province of race hucksters who had no actual interest in making sure, as Martin Luther King, Jr. put it on August 28, 1963, that Americans "will not be judged by the color of their skin but by the content of their character."[438]

By the time the Kennedy administration began, America was already well on the way to steadily increasing federal control, unending international commitments, and relentless exacerbation of racial tensions by those who claimed to be in the business of calming them. Kennedy did little to buck those trends.

438   Martin Luther King, Jr., "I Have a Dream" (speech, Washington, D.C., August 28, 1963), King Institute, Stanford University, https://kinginstitute.stanford. edu/king-papers/documents/i-have-dream-address-delivered-march-washington-jobs-and-freedom.

LYNDON B. JOHNSON

Library of Congress[439]

---

439   Lyndon B. Johnson, Head-and-Shoulders Portrait, Facing Left, 1964, photograph,
       Library of Congress, https://www.loc.gov/item/96522661/.

Full name: Lyndon Baines Johnson
Lived: August 27, 1908–January 22, 1973
Presidency: November 22, 1963–January 20, 1969
Party: Democratic
Evaluation: Disastrous for America
Rating: 1

What qualified him to be president

Lyndon B. Johnson was the quintessential Washington insider. He was a congressman from Texas from 1937 to 1949. In 1948, he was elected to the Senate after narrowly losing: over two hundred ballots were miraculously discovered six days after the election and gave the Senate seat to Johnson. He kept it until 1961. As Senate majority leader from 1955 to 1961, he burnished the reputation he already had as a canny operator and unscrupulous wheeler-dealer who could wheedle or strong-arm virtually anyone to get what he wanted.

Johnson mounted a late challenge to Kennedy for the 1960 Democratic presidential nomination. Over the objections of his team, which was bitter over Johnson's attacks on Kennedy and didn't consider the Texan "progressive" enough, Kennedy offered LBJ the vice-presidential slot to help ensure that the ticket would carry Texas. Kennedy overruled the naysayers by telling them: "I'm forty-three years old, and I'm the healthiest candidate for President in the United States.... I'm not going to die in office. So the vice presidency doesn't mean anything."[440]

As it turned out, it did.

---

440   Robert A. Caro, *The Passage of Power: The Years of Lyndon Johnson*, vol. IV (New York: Vintage Books, 2012), loc. 3307, Kindle.

How he won

When Kennedy was assassinated, it was just a year before the 1964 election. It was virtually inconceivable that a grieving nation would turn out the man who had served as his vice president so soon after that national trauma; Johnson was, therefore, a lock to win election in his own right.

Nonetheless, the 1964 election was one of the most hotly contested in American history. For the first time since 1924, the Republicans nominated a candidate who actually dissented from the now-dominant idea that federal government power must forever expand and take control over progressively more of Americans' daily lives. Senator Barry Goldwater of Arizona had, in 1957, criticized the Eisenhower administration as a "dime-store New Deal."[441] In 1964, he offered, in the words of one campaign slogan, "A Choice, Not an Echo," and asserted in another, "In Your Heart, You Know He's Right."[442] A Hollywood actor, Ronald Reagan, made a popular television speech for Goldwater that launched his own political career.

The Johnson campaign countered by charging that Goldwater was an extremist, not a respectable conservative, and they were right: a respectable conservative, by this time, was a Republican who wanted to do what the Democrats did, only more slowly and efficiently. Goldwater, said the Democrats, would exacerbate racial strife and risk plunging the country into nuclear war. One infamous Johnson ad showed a three-year-old girl picking the petals from a daisy before being

---

441   Niels Bjerre-Poulsen, *Right Face: Organizing the American Conservative Movement 1945–65* (Copenhagen: Museum Tusculanum Press, 2002), 210.
442   Boller, loc. 4161.

obliterated by a nuclear explosion. Then Johnson intoned: "These are the stakes. To make a world in which all of God's children can live, or to go into the dark. We must either love each other, or we must die."[443]

Goldwater, according to one thousand psychiatrists in a widely publicized poll, was unstable and unfit to be president. The senator successfully sued for libel, but the Democrats had discovered another tactic: as far as Democratic strategists were concerned, the Republicans would never again nominate a candidate who was psychologically fit.

Johnson swamped Goldwater with 486 electoral votes to the Republican's 52. Besides his native Arizona, Goldwater carried only the Deep South states that, up until then, had been the heart of the Democrats' Solid South. Goldwater won them by opposing the Civil Rights Act of 1964 on constitutional grounds (he had voted for the Civil Rights Acts of 1957 and 1960). A cartoonist depicted Goldwater driving a car onto a sidewalk and into a light pole labeled "Election Results." Richard Nixon, in the passenger seat, tells him, "You're too far to the right."[444]

That seemed to be the lesson of the 1964 campaign. But the Johnson administration was its own car wreck: LBJ was too far to the left.

---

443 "Peace Little Girl (Daisy)," 1964 Johnson vs. Goldwater, video, Living Room Candidate, Museum of the Moving Image, http://www.livingroomcandidate.org/commercials/1964/peace-little-girl-daisy#3983.

444 Lorant, 901.

Notable accomplishments as president and events of his presidency

1. *The Civil Rights Act of 1964* prohibited racial discrimination in education, employment, and public facilities, as well as in voter registration. There were already laws on the books prohibiting most of this, but Democratic officials in the South had successfully ignored them for nearly a hundred years. The Civil Rights Act of 1964 had more teeth and soon brought segregation in the South, the immense injustice that had been in place since Reconstruction, to a definitive end.

2. *War on Poverty.* It was the age when administrations had slogans: FDR had the New Deal, Truman the Fair Deal, and Kennedy the New Frontier. Johnson, not to be outdone, proclaimed that his administration would create the Great Society. In pursuit of that, in his State of the Union address on January 8, 1964, Johnson said, "This administration today, here and now, declares unconditional war on poverty in America."[445] He proposed a broad range of social programs to accomplish this, including youth employment legislation, food stamps, expanded minimum wage laws, health insurance for the elderly, and housing and urban renewal programs. Much of this ambitious program was enacted and implemented. Federal spending rose to levels that had not been seen since World War II and continued to rise ever after.

3. *Eliminating racial and ethnic quotas in immigration laws.* The Immigration and Nationality Act, which Johnson signed

---

445   Lyndon B. Johnson, "State of the Union Address" (speech, January 8, 1964), UVA Miller Center, https://millercenter.org/the-presidency/presidential-speeches/january-8-1964-state-union.

on October 3, 1965, set aside restrictions on immigration that had been in place since the 1920s, which had limited the numbers of Asians, Southern Europeans, and Eastern Europeans who could come to the U.S. Johnson proclaimed: "For over four decades the immigration policy of the United States has been twisted and has been distorted by the harsh injustice of the national origins quota system.... Only 3 countries were allowed to supply 70 percent of all the immigrants.... This system violated the basic principle of American democracy—the principle that values and rewards each man on the basis of his merit as a man."[446]

Immigration into the United States began to increase steadily. In 1965, 4.8 percent of the people in the United States had been born somewhere else. By 2016, it was 14 percent.

4. *Griswold v. Connecticut.* The apex of this tendency to play fast and loose with the letter of the Constitution, and to treat the document as if it were a gnomic oracle into which one could read virtually any meaning, came on June 7, 1965, when the Supreme Court in *Griswold v. Connecticut* struck down a law prohibiting contraceptives. Justice William O. Douglas, a Roosevelt appointee, discovered in the Constitution a "right of marital privacy," explaining away the absence of this phrase in the Constitution by claiming that "specific guarantees in the Bill of Rights have penumbras, formed by emanations from those guarantees that help give them life and substance."[447]

---

446   Lyndon B. Johnson, "Remarks at the Signing of the Immigration Bill" (speech, Liberty Island, New York, October 3, 1965), https://arquivo.pt/wayback/20160516063650/http://www.lbjlib.utexas.edu/Johnson/archives.hom/speeches.hom/651003.asp.

447   *Griswold v. Connecticut*, 381 U.S. 479 (1965), Legal Information Institute, Cornell Law School, https://www.law.cornell.edu/supremecourt/text/381/479.

This essentially meant that enterprising and politically motivated justices could find anything they wanted in the Constitution, as long as they could argue that it was an "emanation" of a "penumbra."

5. *The Vietnam War.* President Johnson oversaw a huge escalation of the American military presence in Vietnam, from 16,000 troops in 1963 to 536,000 in 1968. The goal of the war was to prevent the Communist North from conquering the South, but it went on long after it became clear that this would not be accomplished within the parameters of the limited war the U.S. was fighting.

After the Communist North Vietnamese fired upon an American destroyer in the Gulf of Tonkin on August 2, 1964, and was reported to have launched a second attack, although this was later proven to be false (and Johnson and his staff knew it was false), Congress passed the Gulf of Tonkin Resolution. This allowed Johnson to use armed force to "promote the maintenance of international peace and security in southeast Asia," until such time as "the President shall determine that the peace and security of the area is reasonably assured by international conditions created by action of the United Nations or otherwise."[448] How exactly he was to make such a determination was not explained.

The war grew increasingly unpopular throughout the Johnson administration. By 1968, there were antiwar demonstrations all over the country, featuring chants of "Hey,

---

[448] Eighty-Eighth Congress of the United States of America, "Gulf of Tonkin Resolution," August 10, 1964, Our Documents, https://www.ourdocuments.gov/doc.php?flash=true&doc=98&page=transcript.

hey, LBJ, how many kids did you kill today?"[449] The virtually unknown Senator Eugene McCarthy of Minnesota, running on an antiwar platform, nearly defeated Johnson in the New Hampshire primary on March 12, 1968. Seeing that he could not be reelected, Johnson withdrew his candidacy on March 31.

Why his presidency was disastrous for America

The Civil Rights Act of 1964 is often cited as the beginning of a switch of the parties, as the Republicans began to pursue a "Southern strategy," abandoning their longtime support for civil rights and embracing white pro-segregation Southerners, while the Democrats repudiated their sorry history of exacerbating racial hatred and became the party of equal rights for all. Goldwater's opposition to the act supports this analysis. However, Republicans in both the House and Senate voted for the act in higher percentages than did Democrats. The growing Republican support in the South in the 1960s and thereafter is frequently attributed to the supposed racism of the party, but in reality, segregation and Jim Crow ended at the same time that Republican support was growing, and no Republicans campaigned on bringing them back. The "Southern strategy" was not a Republican embrace of racism, but of social conservatism and greater economic freedom than the Democrats offered, both of which had great appeal in the South.

What no one expected in 1964, in any case, was that the Civil Rights Act would herald not the end of racial tensions in

---

449   "Remembering 1968: How an Upstart Primary Challenge Ended a Presidency," CBS News, March 11, 2018.

the United States, but their aggravation. Segregation ended in the South and equality of opportunity was virtually assured, with stiff penalties for those who denied it. Yet civil rights activists began to insist that racism was so deeply embedded in the psyche of the nation that had done more than any other to eradicate it that much more legislation was required, including measures giving not just equality of opportunity, but special boosts and privileges to minorities. This all but guaranteed that racial friction would remain a feature of the American landscape.

The War on Poverty didn't help, either. It has been a gargantuan exercise in applying the wrong solution to problems and only making them worse rather than solving them, yet the Democratic Party to this day is full of leaders who refuse to admit that it has been a defeat and a disaster and keep pushing to repeat its mistakes on an even larger scale. The War on Poverty has cost over $22 trillion since 1964, over three times the cost of all the actual wars that the U.S. has ever fought. All that has resulted from it, however, is urban blight, nagging minority unemployment, and above all, more poverty. Poverty levels were falling sharply before Johnson declared war on poverty; in 1950, 32 percent of Americans were considered to be living below the poverty line. By 1965, when the War on Poverty was just getting started, the poverty level had been cut nearly in half and was down to 17 percent. But by 2014, after trillions had been spent in the War on Poverty, it was at 14 percent, nearly the same as it had been when the War on Poverty began.

The War on Poverty failed because it ignored a basic law of economics: if you pay for something, you'll get more of it, not less. As the government expanded welfare programs that subsidized food, housing, and health care for the poor, it got more poor people, not fewer, as the Johnson administration had created an economic incentive to remain poor. The Great Society ended segregation in the South and replaced it with nationwide programs that were even worse for the poor, as they took away incentives to work and created a permanent unemployed underclass in which an ever-larger group of people were essentially wards of the state.

That may have been the idea all along. The famously coarse Johnson is said to have boasted about the Civil Rights Act of 1964: "I'll have those niggers voting Democratic for two hundred years."[450] Between that act and the War on Poverty, he certainly did create a bloc of black Americans who could be counted on to vote Democratic. Whether or not those votes were in the best interests of those who cast them was highly debatable, but they did contribute mightily to the perpetuation and expansion of the welfare state.

When Johnson signed the Immigration and Nationality Act, he said: "This bill that we will sign today is not a revolutionary bill. It does not affect the lives of millions. It will not reshape the structure of our daily lives, or really add importantly to either our wealth or our power."[451] Yet this bill was revolutionary, and it did affect Americans as much or more than anything any president has ever done. As it was being

---

450   Ronald Kessler, *Inside the White House: The Hidden Lives of the Modern Presidents and the Secrets of the World's Most Powerful Institution* (New York: Pocket Books, 1996), 33.

451   Johnson, "Remarks at the Signing of the Immigration Bill."

debated, Senator Robert Kennedy of New York, brother of the slain president, sought to "set to rest any fears that this bill will change the ethnic, political or economic makeup of the United States."[452] Another Kennedy brother, Senator Ted Kennedy of Massachusetts, promised that "our cities will not be flooded with a million immigrants annually.... The ethnic mix of this country will not be upset."[453]

It took a while. The first time the annual immigration rate topped a million was in 1990, and the U.S. began to take in an average of over a million people a year early in the twenty-first century. Immigrants streamed in from all over the world. Johnson's direct attack on national quotas as un-American lent gravity to the claim that any suggestion that they be brought back was "racist," even when they were motivated by a desire to preserve the United States as a cohesive culture with common values. Any suggestion that immigration be limited in any way, meanwhile, was condemned as "xenophobic." The earlier assumption that immigrants should assimilate and adopt American values was lost. Only "racists" were concerned that the U.S. might be bringing in large numbers of people who had vastly different priorities and perspectives, which would gravely threaten the continued existence of the nation as a free society.

Forces unleashed during the Vietnam War proved devastating to national cohesion. The youth movement that arose in the 1960s transformed American culture, as the hippies grew

---

452   Bill Ong Hing, *Defining America: Through Immigration Policy* (Philadelphia: Temple University Press, 2012), 95.

453   Ibid.

up, cut their hair, and began to assume positions of power. That movement was not only antiwar; it was deeply contemptuous of American values, which it saw as hollow and hypocritical, and of American patriotism, which it caricatured as a blind loyalty to rapacious politicians and military men. The assumption that to be patriotic and wish to defend America is either a manifestation of stupidity or a cynical attempt to manipulate the easily led for nefarious purposes has become deeply ingrained. Since the Vietnam War, popular culture has relentlessly inculcated Americans with the assumption that American patriotism is cruel and sinister.

This is the most lasting and damaging legacy of the extraordinarily harmful presidency of Lyndon B. Johnson.

THIRTY-SEVEN

RICHARD M. NIXON

Library of Congress[454]

---

454   *Richard M. Nixon, Head-and-Shoulders Portrait, Facing Front,* 1969–1974,
       photograph, Library of Congress, https://www.loc.gov/item/96522669/.

Full name: Richard Milhous Nixon
Lived: January 9, 1913–April 22, 1994
Presidency: January 20, 1969–August 9, 1974
Party: Republican
Evaluation: Very Damaging for America
Rating: 2

What qualified him to be president

Richard Milhous Nixon was a man of many paradoxes, including one that ran through his long and tumultuous political career: he was, in his domestic policies as president, a man of the Left, but because of his anticommunism, he was identified with conservatives and hated with passionate intensity by other people of the Left.

After serving in the navy and being commended by the secretary of the navy during World War II, Nixon entered politics. At the very beginning of his political career, he became a focus of leftist loathing. As a first-term congressman from California in 1947, he joined the House Un-American Activities Committee and co-sponsored the Mundt-Nixon Bill to fight against Communism in the United States. The following year, he stoutly defended former Communist spy Whittaker Chambers in his accusations that State Department official Alger Hiss was a spy who had been in his circle. Chambers, and Nixon, were vindicated when Chambers produced microfilm of State Department documents that Hiss had passed to him and that Chambers had hidden in a hollowed-out pumpkin on his farm. Hiss and his leftist defenders, however, maintained his innocence for decades thereafter, and the Left's hatred for Nixon became more intense.

Then, in 1950, he ran for the Senate against Rep. Helen Gahagan Douglas, whom he dubbed "the Pink Lady," painting her as a Communist sympathizer. Douglas, taking note of his tactics, retaliated by giving him a name that stuck for the rest of his career: "Tricky Dick." Nixon won handily, and the leftist animus against him grew still more.

Through it all, Nixon remained a "progressive" Republican, and so, in 1952, at the age of thirty-nine, he became Eisenhower's running mate. As vice president in 1958, he courageously stood down a mob in Venezuela while on a goodwill tour in South America. In July 1959, he was in Moscow for the opening of the American National Exhibition and engaged in an impromptu debate with Soviet Premier Nikita Khrushchev in the kitchen of a model home. The "Kitchen Debate" sealed Nixon's status as the front-runner for the 1960 Republican presidential nomination.

After his narrow loss to Kennedy, Nixon ran for governor of California in 1962 and lost again. At a press conference right after the election, he excoriated the press for its leftist bias and said, "You won't have Nixon to kick around anymore, because, gentlemen, this is my last press conference."[455]

It wasn't. Nixon quietly rebuilt his standing within the Republican Party and, by 1968, was the only candidate in the field with international stature. He was nominated on the first ballot.

---

455   Richard Nixon, "Richard Nixon Following His Loss in the 1962 California Gubernatorial Election," Beverly Hilton Hotel, November 7, 1962, YouTube video, https://www.youtube.com/watch?v=JA1edgj1U5E.

How he won

The Democratic National Convention of 1968 took place in Chicago amid violent riots that mirrored the strife in the country at large. The Democrats nominated Vice President Hubert Humphrey to run against Nixon and faced yet another schism as former Alabama Governor George Wallace led the pro-segregation South out of the party once again.

The year 1968 was one of civil strife, highlighted by the assassinations of Martin Luther King, Jr. and Robert Kennedy. The antiwar hippie youth movement that cheerfully flouted social conventions and norms of decent behavior was in full swing, warning young people not to trust anyone over thirty. Amid widespread disgust over all this, Nixon ran on a law-and-order platform. Humphrey, meanwhile, was saddled with being seen as Lyndon Johnson's political heir and defending a war that was growing more unpopular by the day. And although the charismatic and plain-spoken Wallace had been a Democrat and would be again, his candidacy appealed to some people in both parties. "There ain't a dime's worth of difference between the Democratic and Republican parties," he thundered, and he certainly had a point.[456] His bluntness and honesty gained him appeal among people who had not supported his segregationist stand but were fed up with politicians who didn't say a word before checking its appeal with focus groups.

With Wallace drawing support from both parties, Nixon won a narrow victory, gaining five hundred thousand more

---

456   Justin D. Lamb, "Kentucky's Connection to George Wallace," Walk through History, Marshall County Daily, Grand Rivers, KY, WCBL-FM, December 12, 2016.

popular votes than Humphrey, albeit fewer than he had received in 1960. Wallace won five Southern states for forty-six electoral votes, which, along with his nearly ten million popular votes, was one of the best showings ever for a third-party candidate.

The election in 1972 was a much easier campaign for Nixon, as he carried forty-nine states against far-left Democrat George McGovern of South Dakota. A break-in at the Democratic Party Headquarters in a Washington, D.C., hotel was a minor news item that didn't receive significant notice until after the election, in which the nation decisively rejected the candidate of "acid, amnesty and abortion."[457] The Republicans were still the minority party, however, as the Democrats retained the majorities in the House and Senate they had held since 1954. The "progressive" Republicans' practice of echoing the Democratic agenda, rather than providing a genuine alternative, clearly wasn't working, but no one dared challenge it.

Notable accomplishments as president and events of his presidency

1. *Drawing down the American presence in Vietnam.* Nixon entered the White House under intense pressure to bring the troops home. Amid harsh criticism that his pledges to do so were insincere and that he wasn't moving quickly enough, Nixon reduced the number of American troops in Vietnam from 475,000 in 1969 to 24,000 in 1972, pursuing a policy

---

457   Timothy Noah, "'Acid, Amnesty, and Abortion': The Unlikely Source of a Legendary Smear," New Republic, October 22, 2012.

he called "Vietnamization," that is, turning the resistance to Communism over to the South Vietnamese. On January 27, 1973, the U.S. and North Vietnam, after peace talks in Paris, signed the Agreement on Ending the War and Restoring Peace in Viet-Nam, or the Paris Peace Accords, and all but a handful of the remaining U.S. troops there were withdrawn.

2. *Establishing the Environmental Protection Agency (EPA)*. Nixon signed an executive order establishing this watchdog agency on December 2, 1970. This was part of an ambitious program that Nixon had devised to clean up the nation's air and water and monitor the state of the environment, and the agency took immediate action to solve several nagging and large-scale pollution problems.

3. *Taking America off the gold standard and imposing wage and price controls*. On August 15, 1971, in response to rising inflation, Nixon took the nation's currency off the gold standard, under which a paper note was a certificate that could be turned in for a certain amount of gold. Instead, America has ever since issued fiat currency, that is, a dollar is a dollar because the government says it is, not because the paper dollar has any relation to any amount of precious metal.

That same day, Nixon also became the first president in American history to impose wage and price controls during peacetime. In a nationally televised address, he explained that his freeze on wages and prices was "temporary": "To put the strong, vigorous American economy into a permanent strait-jacket would lock in unfairness; it would stifle the expansion of our free enterprise system." And while he threatened "government sanctions" on those who violated the freeze, he maintained: "It will not be accompanied by the establishment of a huge price control bureaucracy. I am relying on the voluntary cooperation of all Americans—each one of you: workers, employers, consumers—to make this freeze work. Working together, we will break the back of inflation, and we will do it without the mandatory wage and price controls that crush economic and personal freedom."[458]

The freeze helped stabilize inflation rates for a brief period, but as many did all they could to get around the freeze, prices started rising again.

4. *The oil crisis.* In October 1973, the Organization of Petroleum Exporting Countries (OPEC) imposed an embargo on oil in retaliation for the United States' support of Israel in the Yom Kippur War. This led to spiraling gasoline prices and huge lines at gas stations. Nixon told a group of American governors: "The only way we're going to solve the crisis is to end the oil embargo, and the only way we're going to end the embargo is to get the Israelis to act reasonable. I hate to use the word blackmail, but we've got to do some things to get them to behave."[459] Nixon did not realize, or care, that the OPEC oil states were entirely dependent upon oil sales and thus could not have maintained the leaky embargo. He sided with states that were hostile to America rather than with America's ally.

5. *Roe v. Wade.* The most notorious of the constitutional "emanations" that the Supreme Court had begun to find in the

---

458   Richard Nixon, "The Challenge of Peace" (speech, August 15, 1971), CVCE, https://www.cvce.eu/content/publication/1999/1/1/168eed17-f28b-487b-9cd2-6d668e42e63a/publishable_en.pdf.

459   William B. Quandt, *Peace Process: American Diplomacy and the Arab-Israeli Conflict Since 1967* (Washington, D.C.: Brookings Institution Press, 2001), 465, n. 23.

Constitution was the *Roe v. Wade* decision of January 22, 1973, in which the Supreme Court voted 7–2 that there was a right to abortion in the Constitution and struck down all state laws that restricted the practice. The Left fanatically defended this decision, asserting that it was the centerpiece of equality of rights for women and ignoring the biological evidence that abortion actually involved putting a human being to death.

6. *Overture to Communist China.* On July 15, 1971, President Nixon shocked the world by announcing that he, who had built his political reputation on fighting Communism, would become the first president to visit Communist China. The visit took place in February 1972 and led, several years after Nixon was out of office, to U.S. recognition of the Beijing government as the sole legitimate government of China and the withdrawal of that recognition of the Taiwanese government.

7. *Overture to the Soviet Union.* Nixon followed up his visit to Beijing with a trip to Moscow in May 1972. This heralded the era of "détente" between the two superpowers. On May 26, 1972, Nixon and Soviet Premier Leonid Brezhnev signed the Strategic Arms Limitation Talks (SALT) agreement, beginning an era of arms control initiatives designed to decrease Cold War tensions. The underlying assumptions of these talks were that the arms race was madness, that it would ultimately destroy the economies of both countries, and that it could end up destroying the world altogether. The Soviet Union was here to stay, and consequently, the U.S. had to come to some accord with it. Nixon, as a veteran anti-Communist and Cold Warrior, was generally perceived as being uniquely positioned to bring about this accord, as he was considered to be tough, free of illusions, and unwilling to make harmful concessions to the Soviets.

8. *Watergate.* The seeds of the destruction of Nixon's presidency were planted on June 17, 1972, when Nixon was coasting to victory in the November election. Five men were caught breaking into Democratic Party Headquarters at the Watergate Hotel in Washington, D.C. The story got little attention at first, but gradually began to grow as reporters linked the Nixon White House to the cover-up that followed the break-in. Nixon disclaimed knowledge of the cover-up, saying on November 17, 1973: "People have got to know whether or not their President is a crook. Well, I'm not a crook."[460] He acknowledged that he had "made a mistake" in not keeping a closer eye on the actions of his campaign team, but that did not defuse the situation. Eventually, through secret tapes Nixon had recorded of Oval Office meetings, it became clear that he had known about and approved the cover-up. After learning that he would almost certainly be impeached in the House and convicted and removed from office by the Senate, Nixon on August 9, 1974, became the first (and, so far, the only) president to resign from office.

Why his presidency was very damaging for America

Nixon was right to withdraw U.S. troops from Vietnam. It would never have been possible for the U.S. to guarantee the freedom of South Vietnam on an indefinite basis; at some point, "Vietnamization" would have had to have been undertaken. Nixon

---

460   Carroll Kilpatrick, "Nixon Tells Editors, 'I'm Not a Crook,'" *Washington Post*, November 18, 1973.

insisted that had the terms of the Paris Peace Accords been honored, South Vietnam would have been able to continue in existence as a free state. That may be, but when the North Vietnamese almost immediately began violating the agreement, Nixon, by this time increasingly preoccupied with Watergate, did nothing. Vietnam continued to be a wound in the national psyche and a kneejerk reproach to the prospect of any military intervention anywhere, even when such interventions were warranted. That was not Nixon's fault: he inherited the problem of Vietnam and did his best to extricate the U.S. from it gracefully. His failure in this followed Johnson's.

Nixon's response to the oil crisis led to more bad precedents. After the Muslim Arab nations surrounding Israel started an aggressive war against the Jewish State, he declared his intention to pressure *Israel* to "act reasonable"[461] and "behave."[462] Although the vaunted and wholly unsuccessful "Middle East Peace Process" hit its apogee after Nixon had left the White House, Nixon's victim-blaming set a pattern for future presidents to pressure Israel to make disastrous concessions to fanatically intransigent Palestinian Arab jihadis.

The outreach to China was another exercise in abandoning allies and embracing enemies. It may have been historically inevitable in the sense that Communists controlled the entirety of mainland China, with the Republic of China restricted only to a small island. The Communist government was indeed the ruler of most Chinese; it was, however, also a repressive totalitarian state that was viciously hostile to the U.S. and American

461   Quandt, 465, n. 23.
462   Ibid

interests, whereas Nationalist China had been a reliable ally of the United States since the end of World War II.

The United Nations expelled Nationalist China, a founding member, on October 25, 1971. The world body may have been emboldened to do this by Nixon's imminent visit to Red China and the legitimization it represented. In any case, the Nixon administration, although it voted no on the expulsion resolution, did nothing to counter the acceptance of the Communist regime, and quickly jumped on the bandwagon. When the UN resolution passed, the Albanian ambassador to the UN, Reis Malile, hailed it as a "great victory" for "peace-loving Member States" and "a great defeat for the United States of America."[463] Yes. Could Nixon have reached out to Communist China without betraying Taiwan? We will never know.

The overture to the Soviet Union was less damaging, but it was not entirely the diplomatic victory that Nixon made it out to be. To reduce the tensions of the Cold War was all to the good. However, the arms limitation talks were widely perceived as lopsided in favor of the Soviet Union, with Nixon and his immediate successors anxiously making concessions to the Soviets in order to keep the process alive. Many Nixon critics also pointed out that the trade deals he made with the Soviets only helped keep the Communist regime in power, when otherwise its own people might have overthrown it when it failed to meet their basic needs. Nixon contributed to the legitimization of yet another monstrous regime when he had no real need to do so: in just a few short years, one of Nixon's successors, Ronald Reagan, would show the hollowness of the

---

463   United Nations General Assembly, 1976th plenary meeting, October 25, 1971, 41.

détente approach and the utility of the arms race in destabilizing and destroying the totalitarian dictatorship that Nixon had so vigorously opposed for most of his political career, only to bring it in from the cold as president of the United States.

At home, like Eisenhower ratifying and continuing the New Deal, the Nixon administration was, in many ways, a continuation of the Great Society. The EPA was established in order to deal with genuine problems, and it did some real good, but it quickly became a massive, multi-tentacled monster that would exercise all manner of interference in the lives of Americans, often in pursuit of a nebulous economic goal that was based on poorly supported or politically motivated scientific findings.

Nixon's wage and price controls, meanwhile, were initially popular; they gave the impression that the president was acting boldly to meet a crisis. He would have done better to have emulated all the presidents who faced economic crises before Hoover and done nothing, knowing that the economy would recover quickly. After some immediate success, the wage and price controls illustrated the wisdom of this yet again, as inflation began to spiral upward again. Nixon reimposed the wage and price controls in June 1973, making the situation even worse.

The wage and price controls were damaging for many reasons but especially for two: they represented an expansion of federal power over the national economy, and they reduced supplies of goods, as cash-strapped businesses cut production rates to meet expenses. This resulted in shortages and the rise in prices that the controls had been meant to prevent. Some farmers even killed their own chickens rather than sell them at artificially fixed prices that were lower than the cost of raising them.

The abandonment of the gold standard likewise worked against Nixon's stated goal of ending inflation. Tying paper money to the gold supply limited the amount of paper money that could be produced; once that tie was removed, money could be printed at will. With more money in circulation, prices rose, and the savings of millions of Americans were steeply devalued.

Watergate overshadows everything in Nixon's presidency. In one sense, it was an example of the system working: President Nixon was demonstrably guilty of obstruction of justice, and so his resignation, forestalling his impeachment, conviction, and removal from office, was just.

At the same time, partisan politics couldn't help but play a part. Nixon's short-sightedness and irresponsibility handed his enemies, who had hated him ever since the days of Helen Gahagan Douglas and Alger Hiss, the weapon they used to destroy him. He himself pointed it out in 1977: "I brought myself down. I gave them a sword, and they stuck it in. And they twisted it with relish. And, I guess, if I'd been in their position, I'd have done the same thing."[464]

It worked once; Democrats reasoned that it could work again. Ever since Watergate, the Democratic Party has made the threat of impeachment a key element of their arsenal when they are not in the White House: they have continuously portrayed Republican presidents as corrupt, usually on the thinnest of pretenses, and have introduced impeachment

---

464   Elizabeth Drew, *Richard M. Nixon* (New York: Times Books, 2007), 138.

proceedings against every one of them except Gerald Ford, although most of these efforts didn't get very far, being voted down by large margins in the House of Representatives and never coming to trial in the Senate. The Republicans, meanwhile, tried ineptly and failed to use the same weapon against Bill Clinton. What was supposed to be a tool of last resort to try presidents accused of "high crimes and misdemeanors" became a weapon in partisan jockeying for power.[465] The legacy of the president who insisted that he was not a crook was that every president is under the shadow of being considered a crook.

The incandescent hatred that Nixon's enemies had for him was not sated with his political downfall. All the Republican presidents after him except Ford and George H. W. Bush would be the objects of the same vituperation. The worst aspect of the aftermath of Watergate has been the poisoning of the American political discourse. Presidents have always been hated, reviled, excoriated, and lied about. The strange roller-coaster career of Richard Nixon made all that even worse.

---

465   Constitution, art. 2, sec. 4.

GERALD R. FORD

Library of Congress[466]

---

466   *Gerald R. Ford, Half-Length Portrait, Facing Front, with Arms Crossed*, 1974,
photograph, Library of Congress, https://www.loc.gov/item/96522670/.

Full name: Leslie Lynch King, Jr., then Gerald Rudolph
Ford, Jr. from 1916
Lived: July 14, 1913–December 26, 2006
Presidency: August 9, 1974–January 20, 1977
Party: Republican
Evaluation: Did Little Good but Not Much Damage
Rating: 5

What qualified him to be president

Gerald R. Ford famously said he was "a Ford, not a Lincoln," but in the beginning, he wasn't even a Ford, but a King.[467] His original name was Leslie King, Jr., but the elder King was alcoholic and abusive. When the baby was two, his parents divorced; the next year, his mother married Gerald Ford, Sr., and the boy became known to the world as Gerald Ford, Jr., although his name was not legally changed.

The future president only was told about all this when he was seventeen, and just a few months later, a man he had never met came into a restaurant where he was working and said to the startled young man, "Leslie, I'm your father."[468] Ford recalled that his father was "a carefree, well-to-do man who didn't really give a damn about the hopes and dreams of his firstborn son."[469] A few years later, after Ford turned twenty-one, he made his name change official.

---

467   "A Common Man on an Uncommon Climb," *New York Times*, August 18, 1976.
468   Ibid.
469   Gerald R. Ford, *A Time to Heal: The Autobiography of Gerald R. Ford* (New York: Harper & Row, 1979), 48.

Ford never showed scars from the chaotic circumstances of his earliest days. An affable, good-natured, self-effacing man, he was a superb athlete, a college football player who received offers to join the Green Bay Packers and Detroit Lions of the National Football League. But he opted to go to Yale Law School instead. He served in the navy and saw action in the Pacific during World War II.

When he was tapped to be vice president, Ford had been a congressman from Michigan for twenty-four years (1949–1973), and House minority leader for the last eight of those. He described himself as "a moderate in domestic affairs, a conservative in fiscal affairs, and a dyed-in-the-wool internationalist in foreign affairs."[470] Above all, he was friendly and easygoing, able to get along with most everyone on both sides of the aisle.

Ford did annoy President Johnson, however, when he and Senator Everett Dirksen offered a series of proposals countering Johnson's policies. "Gerry Ford is so dumb he can't fart and chew gum at the same time," quipped Johnson in a quote that would be frequently repeated in a sanitized form.[471] Ford, said Johnson, "played football too long without his helmet."[472] The impression that he was an amiable dunce lingered throughout Ford's presidency. He wasn't. Although he was, despite his disagreements with Johnson, just another "progressive" Republican.

---

470   "Gerald R. Ford," Obama White House, https://obamawhitehouse.archives. gov/1600/presidents/geraldford.

471   Harold Jackson, "Gerald Ford: Former U.S. President Who Entered the White House after the Watergate Scandal without Receiving a Single Electoral Vote," *Guardian*, December 27, 2006.

472   Brock Brower, "Under Ford's Helmet," *New York Times*, September 15, 1974.

How he became president

Nixon wasn't the only crook in his administration. On October 10, 1973, Vice President Spiro Agnew resigned after pleading no contest to a charge of tax evasion. The new Twenty-Fifth Amendment provided for the appointment of a new vice president when the office became vacant. Nixon tapped Ford, who had fewer enemies than other candidates; he was overwhelmingly confirmed and took the oath of office as vice president on December 6, 1973. Eight months later, when Nixon himself resigned, Ford was president of the United States.

Notable accomplishments as president and events of his presidency

1. *Pardoning Nixon.* When Ford took office on August 9, 1974, he declared: "My fellow Americans, our long national nightmare is over. Our Constitution works; our great Republic is a government of laws and not of men. Here the people rule. But there is a higher Power, by whatever name we honor Him, who ordains not only righteousness but love, not only justice but mercy."[473]

Ford explicitly endeavored to be an agent of that mercy when, on September 8, 1974, he pardoned Nixon, explaining: "I do believe, with all my heart and mind and spirit, that I, not as President but as a humble servant of God, will receive justice without mercy if I fail to show mercy."[474] It was the right thing

---

473 Gerald R. Ford, "Remarks upon Taking the Oath of Office as President" (speech, August 9, 1974), Gerald R. Ford Presidential Library & Museum, https://www.fordlibrarymuseum.gov/library/speeches/740001.asp.

474 Gerald R. Ford, "Pardoning Richard Nixon" (speech, September 8, 1974), History Place, http://www.historyplace.com/speeches/ford.htm.

to do, he said, in light of the fact that "many months and perhaps more years will have to pass before Richard Nixon could obtain a fair trial by jury in any jurisdiction of the United States."[475] But above all, it was for the good of the nation that had been riven by Watergate for too long: "My conscience tells me clearly and certainly that I cannot prolong the bad dreams that continue to reopen a chapter that is closed. My conscience tells me that only I, as President, have the constitutional power to firmly shut and seal this book. My conscience tells me it is my duty, not merely to proclaim domestic tranquility but to use every means that I have to insure it."[476]

2. *Inflation and recession.* The economy was mired in a recession throughout the Ford administration, with unemployment exceeding 8 percent in 1975. On October 8, 1974, Ford announced the Whip Inflation Now (WIN) campaign; this amounted to little more than bright red buttons that said "WIN." Beyond that, President Ford seemed uncertain what to do, although, by this time, doing nothing and letting the economy right itself was not on the table. He called first for raising taxes, then for lowering them. Because federal spending continued to increase, the tax cuts resulted in a growing federal deficit.

Ford called for cuts in federal spending, but the Democratic-controlled Congress was loathe to accommodate him. However, when New York City Mayor Abraham Beame asked the federal government to take on his bankrupt, spendthrift city as a welfare case, Ford refused. Reporting the news,

475   Ibid.
476   Ibid.

the *New York Daily News* ran the headline "FORD TO CITY: DROP DEAD."[477]

Ford's reasoning, however, was sound. On October 29, 1975, he listed a number of programs that New York City maintained that were a clear waste of taxpayer money. He said that if he bailed out New York, "the primary beneficiary would be the New York officials who would thus escape responsibility for their past folly and be further excused from making the hard decisions required now to restore the city's fiscal integrity."[478] And he explained: "If we go on spending more than we have, providing more benefits and more services than we can pay for, then a day of reckoning will come to Washington and the whole country just as it has to New York City. And so, let me conclude with one question of my own: When that day of reckoning comes, who will bail out the United States of America?"[479]

3. *Détente.* Ford continued Nixon's foreign policy, keeping the renowned Secretary of State Henry Kissinger on the job and visiting China and the Soviet Union himself. The recognition of Communist China and arms reduction talks with the Soviets stayed on track. The Helsinki Accords with the Soviet Union recognized the post-World War II boundaries

---

477 Frank Van Riper, "Ford to City: Drop Dead," *New York Daily News*, October 30, 1975.

478 Gerald R. Ford, "Remarks at a Question-and-Answer Session at the National Press Club on the Subject of Financial Assistance to New York City" (speech, October 30, 1975), in *Gerald R. Ford: Containing the Public Messages, Speeches, and Statements of the President,* book 2 (Washington, D.C.: U.S. Government Printing Office, 1977), 1733.

479 Ford, *Public Messages,* 1735.

of Europe, which made official U.S. acceptance of the Soviet seizure of the eastern half of Poland and other territories.

4. *The end of the Vietnam War.* In April 1975, South Vietnam fell to the Communist North Vietnamese. South Vietnamese President Nguyen Van Thieu blamed the U.S. for abandoning his country. That abandonment was vividly illustrated at the end of April, when Americans and South Vietnamese were evacuated from Saigon just ahead of the arrival of the North Vietnamese Army.

Why his presidency did little good but not much damage

Ford's address on August 9, 1974, included this plea: "As we bind up the internal wounds of Watergate, more painful and more poisonous than those of foreign wars, let us restore the golden rule to our political process, and let brotherly love purge our hearts of suspicion and of hate."[480] His call was not heeded. His pardon of Nixon didn't bind up the nation's wounds; instead, it destroyed the feeling of goodwill that had surrounded Ford since he had assumed the presidency and gave rise to persistent suspicions that Nixon had only resigned in exchange for Ford's assurance that he would be pardoned. Many ascribed Ford's narrow loss to Jimmy Carter in the 1976 election to continuing anger over the pardon.

There is no doubt, however, that Ford was correct in saying that it would have been extremely difficult for Nixon to get a fair trial, and that the Watergate affair would drag

---

480   Ford, "Remarks upon Taking the Oath of Office as President."

on for years to come if he didn't act to put an end to it. While Nixon was guilty of obstruction of justice, the proceedings against him had always been tainted by more than a tinge of the hatred the Democrats had held for him ever since he first called Helen Gahagan Douglas "the Pink Lady" and defended Whittaker Chambers in his accusations that Alger Hiss was a Communist spy. The determination to see Nixon not just driven from office, but languishing in prison, stemmed largely from this. Ford was wise to put a cap on this loathing, though it would reappear when later Republican presidents had the temerity to cross the Democrats.

The economy, meanwhile, almost certainly also contributed to Ford's loss in 1976. His refusal to bail out New York City earned him the scorn and rage of the news media, and he had no economic successes of his own to which he could point in defense of his reasoning. Nonetheless, his reasoning was sound and should have been heeded in his own day, as well as by future presidents and Congresses, as federal spending continued to mount ever higher.

Foes of the Vietnam War claimed vindication when Saigon fell, claiming that this illustrated the folly of all American interventions; Vietnam has been used ever after as a counter to interventionist arguments encapsulated in a single word. And certainly, it showed how interventions should not be pursued. Those who were actually vindicated were defenders of the war, who had warned about the reign of terror that followed the fall of South Vietnam. Those defenders also blamed the foes of the war in the media and the political arena, as well as the antiwar protesters, for making it impossible to pursue the war successfully.

These points were well taken, but there were also additional reasons why the U.S. venture failed. After the manner of Korea, actual victory was not contemplated. The U.S. was fighting to defend the division of the country into a Communist section and a free section, while the North Vietnamese were fighting to gain control of the whole thing. When one side fights an all-out war and the other is waging only a limited conflict, the outcome is inevitable, even if delayed. What's more, the North Vietnamese could simply bide their time, knowing that the U.S. could not remain there forever.

The Vietnam War thus demonstrated the inherent limitations of a foreign policy that depended heavily on military intervention. There was no doubt that Communism was a menace, and that the United States, as the world's leading power after World War II, had either to counter it or surrender to it. The question was whether it was wise, or even possible, to counter each of its encroachments with an American military presence, or if there might be another way to counter it. Gerald Ford had been out of the White House for several years when that other way was implemented under President Reagan. Even after that, no lessons were learned. America would, once again, wage undeclared wars with no clear goal or end point that threatened to go on indefinitely. Neither Ford nor any president after him for decades would dare challenge the wisdom of waging such wars.

THIRTY-NINE

JIMMY CARTER

Library of Congress[481]

---

481   Karl Schumacher, *Jimmy Carter, Head-and-Shoulders Portrait, Facing Front, Next to an American Flag*, 1977, photograph, Library of Congress, https://www.loc.gov/item/96522672/.

Full name: James Earl Carter, Jr.
Lived: October 1, 1924–
Presidency: January 20, 1977–January 20, 1981
Party: Democratic
Evaluation: Disastrous for America
Rating: 0

What qualified him to be president

Jimmy Carter's appeal to voters in 1976 was that he was *not* qualified to be president in the conventional sense. He was not and had never been a senator or congressman. He had served in the navy but was no war hero. For one term, he was governor of Georgia, where he attracted little attention before he began his run for president. In the aftermath of Watergate, when voters had had their fill of corruption from Washington insiders, Carter's slight résumé was a selling point. He was just a humble peanut farmer with a toothy grin, a devout Christian coming to Washington to clean up the place.

How he won

Carter began his outsider campaign for the 1976 Democratic presidential nomination on October 12, 1974, earlier than all of his competitors. When the media noticed his efforts at all, he was seen as a curiosity or a regional favorite son; no one thought he had a chance. But as the other Democratic candidates presented themselves as alternatives to Republican corruption, Carter was able to outflank them. He wasn't just a Washington politician whose hands were cleaner than

Richard Nixon's; he wasn't a Washington politician at all. By the spring of 1976, he was the front-runner and coasted to the nomination.

That nomination virtually assured Carter the presidency. Republicans in the aggregate were blamed for Watergate, and Ford had dispelled the goodwill that accompanied his accession to the presidency when he pardoned Nixon. Ford barely even won the nomination. Former Hollywood actor and California Governor Ronald Reagan showed that the Goldwater wing of the party was not dead when he nearly took the nomination away from the largely "progressive" sitting president.

Carter began with a substantial lead over Ford in the polls: in mid-July, he led by 62 percent to 29 percent. Unexpectedly, however, the upstart turned out to be an exceptionally weak candidate. With a huge lead, the media in his pocket, and considerable popular ill will toward the opposition party, which was itself deeply split, Carter couldn't seal the deal. The president slowly and steadily began closing the gap. Even when Ford shot himself in the foot—as he did in his debate with Carter on October 6, 1976, when he declared that "there is no Soviet domination of Eastern Europe and there never will be under a Ford administration"—he lost little ground to the untainted Washington outsider.[482] (That statement has become the media's favorite example of a candidate destroying his chances with a "gaffe," but reality, as is so often the case, was otherwise.)

As weak a candidate as he was, Carter won the election by a hair and set out to become a weak president.

---

482   David A. Graham, "The Myth of Gerald Ford's Fatal 'Soviet Domination'
       Gaffe," *Atlantic*, August 2, 2016.

Notable accomplishments as president and events of his presidency

1. *The energy crisis.* On April 18, 1977, with inflation and unemployment spiraling ever upward, Carter went on television in the guise of an apocalyptic prophet crossed with a scolding schoolmarm, telling Americans with a touch of condescension: "Tonight I want to have an unpleasant talk with you about a problem that is unprecedented in our history. With the exception of preventing war, this is the greatest challenge that our country will face during our lifetime."[483] He was speaking of the energy crisis, which, he warned, "has not yet overwhelmed us, but it will if we do not act quickly."[484]

Carter the prophet of doom informed Americans that the sky was falling: "The oil and natural gas that we rely on for 75 percent of our energy are simply running out.... Unless profound changes are made to lower oil consumption, we now believe that early in the 1980's the world will be demanding more oil than it can produce.... World consumption of oil is still going up. If it were possible to keep it rising during the 1970's and 1980's by 5 percent a year, as it has in the past, we could use up all the proven reserves of oil in the entire world by the end of the next decade."[485]

Carter the peevish schoolmarm told Americans it was all their fault: "We must not be selfish or timid if we hope to have a decent world for our children and our grandchildren.... Each

---

483   Jimmy Carter, "Address to the Nation on Energy" (speech, April 18, 1977), UVA Miller Center, https://millercenter.org/the-presidency/presidential-speeches/april-18-1977-address-nation-energy.

484   Ibid.

485   Ibid.

American uses the energy equivalent of 60 barrels of oil per person each year. Ours is the most wasteful nation on Earth. We waste more energy than we import. With about the same standard of living, we use twice as much energy per person as do other countries like Germany, Japan, and Sweden."[486]

Echoing Lyndon Johnson's War on Poverty, Carter created another unwinnable war against a nebulous foe: "This difficult effort will be the 'moral equivalent of war,' except that we will be uniting our efforts to build and not to destroy."[487]

Carter moved quickly to save the world, counterintuitively prohibiting exploration to find new sources of oil and gas in the Western states. He also ordered oil producers to focus on home heating oil rather than on gasoline; Americans consequently had to wait in lengthy lines, often for hours on end, to get gas. Adding insult to injury, President Carter proposed a stiff new federal tax on gasoline of fifty cents on the gallon, but wasn't able to get this through Congress. He was able to get through his National Energy Act, though, which taxed low-mileage cars and gave tax credits to people for using solar and other alternative forms of energy (Carter did his part, having solar panels installed in the White House). On July 10, 1979, he even ordered that public buildings not set their air conditioners below a sweltering seventy-eight degrees and, in the next winter, not to raise their heat above sixty-five degrees.

Above all, Carter faced this supposedly civilization-threatening crisis by creating yet another federal agency, the Cabinet-level Department of Energy, to coordinate further

---

486   Ibid.
487   Ibid.

action to save the nation and the world from the catastrophe Carter sketched out in April 1977.

2. *The Department of Education.* Carter lowered taxes in 1978 and proposed cuts in federal spending but contradicted his efforts to bring fiscal responsibility to the enormous and ever-growing federal government by creating a second new Cabinet-level agency: the Department of Education. This new agency introduced the federal government into areas that had hitherto been under private control, and constitutional literalists pointed out that there was no mention of education in the nation's founding document, and hence no clear warrant for the federal government to get involved in it. But few were concerned about such details.

3. *The Camp David Accords.* In September 1978, President Carter invited Egyptian President Anwar Sadat and Israeli Prime Minister Menachem Begin to the presidential retreat of Camp David to end the protracted conflict between the two countries. Sadat told his aides: "What we are after is to win over world opinion. President Carter is on our side. This will end in Begin's downfall!"[488] He was right. Carter told Sadat: "I will represent your interests as if they were my own. You are my brother."[489] A jubilant Sadat told his aides that "poor naïve Carter" was ready to pressure Begin into giving Egypt everything it wanted.[490]

---

488   Lawrence Wright, *Thirteen Days in September: The Dramatic Story of the Struggle for Peace* (New York: Vintage Books, 2014), 68.

489   Zbigniew Brzezinski, *Power and Principle: Memoirs of the National Security Adviser 1977–1981* (New York: Farrar Straus Giroux, 1983), 284.

490   Mohamed Ibrahim Kamel, *The Camp David Accords: A Testimony by Sadat's Foreign Minister* (London: KPI, 1986), 302.

Sadat was right. "Mr. Prime Minister," Carter told Begin icily after Sadat presented his proposals "that is not only the view of Sadat, it is also the American view—and you will have to accept it."[491] Angrily he repeated, "You will have to accept it."[492] These included Israel's withdrawal from the Sinai Peninsula, which Israel had occupied after Egypt attacked it in 1967. While territorial expansion at the expense of an aggressor nation had been recognized as a right of the victor in a war from time immemorial, Carter was determined that it would not apply to Israel. He also wanted Israel to acknowledge that it was carrying out an illegitimate occupation of Palestinian land. He complained to Begin: "Listen, we're trying to help you bring peace to your land. You would have us feel that we are going out of our way deliberately to be as unfair to Israel as possible."[493] Indeed.

4. *Betraying the shah of Iran.* As protests against the rule of another American ally, the shah of Iran, engulfed that country, Carter abandoned the shah to his fate. Many in the Carter administration admired the Ayatollah Khomeini, the Islamic leader who was at the center of the protests. Andrew Young, Carter's ambassador to United Nations, said, "Khomeini will eventually be hailed as a saint."[494] The U.S. ambassador to Iran, William Sullivan, said, "Khomeini is a Gandhi-like figure."[495] Carter advisor James Bill declared the Ayatollah a

---

491   Ibid., 332.

492   Ibid.

493   Wright, *Thirteen Days in September,* 226.

494   Oliver North, "Avoiding a Jimmy Carter Moment," Townhall, February 4, 2011; Sheda Vasseghi, "Where's Jimmy? A Past President Goes Silent on His Iran Legacy," *World Tribune,* August 6, 2009.

495   Ibid.

"holy man" of "impeccable integrity and honesty."[496] The shah later recounted: "The fact that no one contacted me during the crisis in any official way explains everything about the American attitude.... It is clear to me now that the Americans wanted me out."[497]

On January 4, 1979, Carter told French President Valéry Giscard d'Estaing that the U.S. was abandoning its ally, withdrawing all support from the shah and backing Khomeini. "I was horrified," recalled Giscard. "The only way I can describe Jimmy Carter is that he was a 'bastard of conscience.' "[498] On January 16, 1979, the shah and his family left Iran. The Islamic Republic of Iran was established soon after.

5. *The Iran hostage crisis.* On October 23, 1979, Carter reluctantly allowed the gravely ill shah to enter the U.S. for medical treatment. On November 4, a group calling itself Muslim Student Followers of the Imam's Line (that is, Khomeini's line) retaliated by entering the U.S. embassy compound in Tehran and taking hostage the skeleton staff of sixty-six that was still serving there after the fall of the shah.

Khomeini sneered, "Jimmy Carter is too much of a coward to confront us militarily."[499] Carter did, however, mount Operation Eagle Claw to rescue the hostages in April 1980, which was a miserable failure; a crash killed eight U.S. military personnel. Fifty-two hostages remained in captivity for 444

---

496 Ibid.

497 Mehran Kamrava, *The Modern Middle East: A Political History since the First World War*, 3rd ed. (Berkeley: University of California Press, 2013), 150.

498 Michael D. Evans, "35 Years Ago: An Iranian Revolution Thanks to Jimmy Carter," Blaze, February 11, 2014.

499 Korey Willoughby, "Temptation," *Daily Iowan*, November 28, 1979.

days. They were freed on January 20, 1981, the day Ronald Reagan took office.

6. *Arming jihadis against the Soviets in Afghanistan.* Backing Khomeini was not Carter's only foray into assisting the global Islamic jihad, which was just beginning its resurgence during his presidency. In July 1979, Carter authorized Operation Cyclone, a covert CIA operation to arm jihad warriors in Afghanistan who were fighting against the Soviets. This became an extremely lengthy and expensive CIA operation, continuing long after Carter left the White House. Meanwhile, when the Soviets invaded Afghanistan, Carter did nothing publicly beyond boycott the Moscow Olympics, only enhancing his reputation for weakness and pusillanimity.

7. *Giving away the Panama Canal.* On September 7, 1977, Carter and Panamanian strongman Omar Torrijos signed treaties that mandated the transfer of the Panama Canal to Panamanian sovereignty. The move was unpopular in the U.S., with critics including Carter's 1980 opponent Ronald Reagan noting that Torrijos was not friendly to the United States and arguing that the U.S. was giving away an important strategic asset.

Why his presidency was disastrous for America

The Departments of Energy and Education were another manifestation of the assumption, by now taken for granted by nearly everyone, that if the nation faced a problem, the best way to solve it was to unleash a new army of federal bureaucrats. Neither department has any significant accomplishments to justify their existence. Even worse, the massive expenditures both required undermined and contradicted Carter's stated goal of reducing federal spending.

President Carter's scolding of Americans for using too much energy, combined with his new department, heralded a new proliferation of government regulation in order to make Americans become more energy-conscious and less wasteful. And of course, these regulations did come.

But the whole endeavor was built on sand: there was actually no energy crisis. The world's oil reserves did not run out in the 1980s, and not because Jimmy Carter saved the day by winning his "moral equivalent of war." The real problem was one that Carter only made worse: oil companies were so beset with restrictions and regulations that they couldn't take adequate steps to find new oil supplies. Carter's successor changed that, and the days of the energy crisis were over, at least until apocalyptic climate hysteria of a different kind became the centerpiece of later Democratic presidents' efforts to assert even more federal control over the lives of Americans.

The Department of Education is another failure. Despite pouring tens of billions into U.S. public schools, student performance has not improved. Even worse, the federal bureaucrats who oversee the Department of Education have created national standards and curricula that are frequently tendentious and politicized, with a pronounced leftist bias. In our own day, this has taken the form of an almost manic attention to race and diversity, at the expense of giving children a basic education. Ronald Reagan and other presidents have vowed to abolish this massive boondoggle, but it still exists, as part of the unremittingly devastating legacy of President Carter.

Carter has received a great deal of praise, as well as a Nobel Peace Prize, for the Camp David Accords, but in reality, they accomplished little. The final agreement had Israel making substantial territorial concessions in exchange for promises that Egypt would not attack Israel, which the Egyptians kept because U.S. foreign aid was made contingent upon peace. Other than that, the Accords brought no peace to the Middle East. They legitimized the existence of the "Palestinian" people, a propaganda invention of the KGB in the 1960s, and advanced the claim that Israel was occupying Palestinian territory to which only Israel had a legitimate claim. Carter, after his presidency, has written several books about the Israeli-Palestinian conflict that have brought him charges of anti-Semitism; the deep bias of the Camp David Accords strongly suggests that, even at that time, he had an animus toward Israel. His palpable lack of sympathy for the Jews of Israel, who are permanently under siege, continues to this day.

Meanwhile, the hostage crisis, as well as the abject failure and apparent amateurishness of the rescue operation, epitomized the Carter administration's impotence in the face of repeated provocations from the nascent Islamic Republic of Iran. One of Reagan's campaign themes in the 1980 election was that he would deal with the Iranians much more firmly than Carter had, and the Iranians clearly respected Reagan in a way they did not respect Carter. This was ironic in light of the fact that the Islamic Republic owed its very existence to Carter's betrayal of the shah. In a very real sense, Jimmy Carter is the Father of the Islamic Republic of Iran, a rogue regime that has viciously oppressed its own people while allying with and financing jihad terror groups around the world.

Carter also bears partial responsibility for the 1992 take-over of Afghanistan by Islamic jihadis. The jihadis had defeated the Soviet Union with matériel and other aid supplied by the United States. But they had no gratitude for the United States; their theology dictated that they see America as an infidel nation, as an enemy, and the aid they received from it didn't change that. The folly of the policy Carter initiated became clear to the entire world on September 11, 2001, when jihadis trained in Afghanistan murdered three thousand Americans in jihad attacks in New York and Washington.

Jimmy Carter was as sanctimonious as he was inept. America is still paying the price for the damage he wrought during his presidency. He effectively lost his bid for reelection on July 15, 1979, when he once again commandeered the nation's television screens in order to scold and hector Americans in what came to be known as his "malaise" speech, although he did not use that word. "It's clear," Carter claimed, "that the true problems of our Nation are...deeper than gasoline lines or energy shortages, deeper even than inflation or recession."[500] He asserted, "All the legislation in the world can't fix what's wrong with America."[501] What was really threatening the nation, he said, was "a crisis of confidence": "It is a crisis that strikes at the very heart and soul and spirit of our national will. We can see this crisis in the growing doubt about the meaning of our own lives and in the loss of a unity

---

500   Jimmy Carter, "Energy and the National Goals—A Crisis of Confidence" (speech, July 15, 1979), American Rhetoric, https://www.americanrhetoric. com/speeches/jimmycartercrisisofconfidence.htm.
501   Ibid.

of purpose for our nation. The erosion of our confidence in the future is threatening to destroy the social and the political fabric of America."[502]

What he did not address was the extent to which his maladroit handling of the presidency was responsible for that crisis. The malaise began to lift when he was voted out of office.

---

502   Ibid.

FORTY

RONALD REAGAN

Library of Congress[503]

---

503   *Ronald Reagan, Head-and-Shoulders Portrait, Facing Front*, 1981, photograph,
       Library of Congress, https://www.loc.gov/item/96522678/.

Full name: Ronald Wilson Reagan
Lived: February 6, 1911–June 5, 2004
Presidency: January 20, 1981–January 20, 1989
Party: Republican
Evaluation: Very Good for America
Rating: 9

What qualified him to be president

Ronald Reagan was a Hollywood actor of some success and initially a man of the Left who admired Franklin Roosevelt and consistently voted Democratic. But over the years, he became increasingly concerned about Communism and the freedom of American workers from state and union interference; he joined the Republican Party in 1962. Years later, he stated: "Now, I'm a former Democrat, and I have to say: I didn't leave my party; my party left me."[504]

In 1964, he made a televised speech for Barry Goldwater, warning about the dangers of federal control over the economy; the speech attracted so much favorable attention that Reagan began to be considered a political figure in his own right. Two years later, he was elected governor of California, serving two terms and acquiring a reputation as a firm supporter of limited government and individual freedom, such as had not been seen since the days of Calvin Coolidge. He mounted a maverick challenge to Gerald Ford for the 1976 Republican presidential nomination and came close to

---

504   Ronald Reagan, "Remarks at a Republican Campaign Rally in Mount Clements, Michigan" (speech, November 5, 1988), Ronald Reagan Presidential Library & Museum, https://www.reaganlibrary.gov/research/speeches/110588b.

winning. By 1980, he was the Republican front-runner, even as establishment "progressive" Republicans including Ford warned that he was a reckless cowboy who was much too far to the right to be an effective president. He nonetheless won the nomination easily.

Reagan considered placating the "progressives" by naming Ford as his running mate, and establishment Republicans were thrilled at the prospect. Ford spoke excitedly in an interview about being "co-president" with Reagan so that the establishment party men could control the candidate who dared to want to control the growth of federal power.[505] That was enough for Reagan, who intended to be president in his own right. He chose George H. W. Bush instead, who was another "progressive" Republican but at least would accept that Reagan, not he, was the man in charge.

How he won

Jimmy Carter was so unpopular by 1980 that he faced an unusual and strong challenge for renomination from Senator Ted Kennedy of Massachusetts, the brother of two Democratic Party heroes, President John F. Kennedy and Senator Robert Kennedy. Ted Kennedy criticized Carter for not being "progressive" enough, which played well among Democrats. Kennedy was, however, damaged by charges that he had not done anything to save the life of a woman, Mary Jo Kopechne, who was riding in his car when he drove off a bridge on Chappaquiddick Island in Massachusetts in July 1969. Subsequently lying

---

505   John Kreiser, "From Ike to Jerry Ford," CBS News, December 27, 2006.

about the incident also didn't help. Carter defeated Kennedy in the primaries, but not decisively enough to stave off a challenge at the Democratic National Convention, where Kennedy delivered a stem-winding speech defending "liberalism," that is, massive state control in the guise of a fair shake for working people, and played hard to get as Carter followed him around on the convention stage trying to get a handshake. His failure to get Kennedy to stand with him before the convention was yet another sign of Carter's endemic weakness.

That weakness carried through to the general election campaign. Reagan bested Carter decisively in a debate on October 28, 1980, winning over Americans by appearing in cool, confident command, chuckling gently and saying "There you go again" when Carter misrepresented his positions, while Carter came off as angry, stiff, self-righteous, and arrogant. In his closing statement, Reagan asked Americans: "Are you better off than you were four years ago? Is it easier for you to go and buy things in the stores than it was four years ago? Is there more or less unemployment in the country than there was four years ago? Is America as respected throughout the world as it was? Do you feel that our security is as safe, that we're as strong as we were four years ago?"[506]

The answers were clear. Reagan made them even clearer on the night before the election, when he challenged the defeatism of Carter's infamous "malaise" speech: "For the first time in our memory many Americans are asking: does

---

506 "October 28, 1980 Debate Transcript," Commission on Presidential Debates, https://www.debates.org/voter-education/debate-transcripts/october-28-1980-debate-transcript/. https://www.youtube.com/watch?v=qN7gDRjTNf4.

history still have a place for America, for her people, for her great ideals? There are some who answer no; that our energy is spent, our days of greatness at an end, that a great national malaise is upon us.... I find no national malaise, I find nothing wrong with the American people. Oh, they are frustrated, even angry at what has been done to this blessed land. But more than anything they are sturdy and robust as they have always been."[507]

Reagan's optimistic message resonated with voters. He won by a huge electoral margin, with 489 votes to Carter's 49. Reagan was six years older than John F. Kennedy and, at sixty-nine, became the oldest man to become president. He retained many of his old Hollywood connections and used them to bring a glamor back to the White House that had not been seen since the Kennedy days. Reagan was aware of the power of modern-day presidents to set the national mood; his humor and optimism quickly dispelled the gloom of the Carter years.

Many, however, were not amused. In 1984, Ted Kennedy illustrated the depths of the American Left's hatred and fear of Reagan when he tried to head off his reelection by reaching out to the Soviets. According to a KGB memo, Kennedy said he was "impressed" with Soviet leader Yuri Andropov and recommended "steps to counter the militaristic politics of Reagan."[508] Nothing seems to have come of this bizarre appeal, and with the country benefiting from the prosperity his policies had

---

507   Ronald Reagan, "Election Eve Address: A Vision for America" (speech, November 3, 1980), Ronald Reagan Presidential Library & Museum, https://www.reaganlibrary.gov/11-3-80.

508   Paul Kengor, "The Kremlin's Dupe: Ted Kennedy's Russia Romance," *American Spectator*, April 12, 2018.

made possible, Reagan was returned to the White House with the highest electoral vote total in American history, 525, to 13 for Walter Mondale, who had been Carter's vice president.

Notable accomplishments as president and events of his presidency

1. *Fighting against the growth of the federal government.* In his first inaugural address, Reagan became the first president since FDR began the New Deal to challenge its central assumption, that the unrestricted growth of the federal government was good for Americans. "It is time," Reagan said, "to check and reverse the growth of government which shows signs of having grown beyond the consent of the governed. It is my intention to curb the size and influence of the Federal establishment."[509]

He didn't. Reagan failed to convince a Democrat-controlled Congress to go along with his endeavor to stop the out-of-control growth of the federal government, as he himself acknowledged in his biography: "I'd argued for years that if you cut tax rates, government revenues would go up because lower rates would stimulate economic growth. Well, in the first six years after tax rates started coming down in late 1981, the federal government, despite the lower rates, experienced an increase of $375 billion in tax revenues—more than four times greater than the amount projected before the cuts.... But, during this same period, Congress increased

---

509   Ronald Reagan, "First Inaugural Address" (speech, January 20, 1981), Avalon Project, Yale Law School, https://avalon.law.yale.edu/20th_century/reagan1.asp.

spending by $450 billion. So, we lost our chance to slash the deficit."[510]

2. *Reaganomics.* Reagan stated his guiding philosophy succinctly in his autobiography: "I believed that if we cut tax rates and reduced the proportion of our national wealth that was taken by Washington, the economy would receive a stimulus that would bring down inflation, unemployment and interest rates, and there would be such an expansion of economic activity that in the end there would be an increase in the amount of revenue to finance the important functions of government."[511]

Reagan vividly illustrated the real cost of high taxes when he explained that when he was a movie actor, he paid so much in taxes that he actually had an incentive to work less so as to fall into a lower tax bracket. He pointed out that the less he worked, the less the movie studio staff, which was made up of people in lower tax brackets, also worked, and everyone suffered. Contrary to Democrats' claims that Reagan's tax cuts benefited only the wealthy, they actually increased prosperity across the board. In 1982, with the economy still largely mired in Carter's malaise, unemployment was 10.8 percent; by 1988, it was 5.3 percent.

3. *Ending the energy crisis.* Reagan understood that the energy crisis of the Carter years was a problem of overregulation, not of diminishing supplies. On January 29, 1981, just nine days after taking office, he issued an executive order

---

510   Ronald Reagan, *An American Life: The Autobiography* (New York: Simon and Schuster, 1990), 335–336.

511   Reagan, *An American Life*, 231.

removing restrictions on the price of gasoline and heating oil. Establishment economists warned that this would send gas prices skyrocketing and cripple the economy, but instead, the oil companies began, once again, competing with one another, prices dropped, and since restrictions on exploring for new oil sources were also removed, supplies soon became plentiful. The energy crisis became a bad memory and a warning against federal overreach.

4. *Breaking the air traffic controllers' strike.* In August 1981, the Professional Air Traffic Controllers Organization (PATCO) began a strike. Air traffic controllers were federal government employees, and so they could not lawfully strike, but no one expected Reagan to enforce this law. Reagan, however, dared to do what no president of the twentieth century had done: he dared to face down the union, firing the air traffic controllers, breaking PATCO's power, and providing a basis for non-union workers to find employment, and employers to hire them, without fear of reprisals from the unions.

5. *The War on Drugs.* Reagan greatly expanded the anti-drug program that the Nixon administration began. His Anti-Drug Abuse Act in 1986 devoted $1.7 billion ($4 billion today) to anti-drug efforts. Drug use was not appreciably affected.

6. *The Bork debacle.* Ever since *Roe v. Wade*, every new Supreme Court appointment has occasioned a fierce confirmation battle in Congress. Reagan succeeded in appointing constitutional loyalist Antonin Scalia, but when another vacancy opened up and Reagan chose Judge Robert Bork, an erudite legal scholar who was, like Scalia, faithful to the actual words of the Constitution, Democrats worried that *Roe v.*

Wade would be overturned. Bork was accordingly subjected to a vicious campaign of character assassination led by Senator Ted Kennedy, who charged hysterically and counterfactually that "Robert Bork's America is a land in which women would be forced into back-alley abortions, blacks would sit at segregated lunch counters, rogue police could break down citizens' doors in midnight raids, and schoolchildren could not be taught about evolution, writers and artists could be censored at the whim of the Government, and the doors of the Federal courts would be shut on the fingers of millions of citizens."[512]

It worked. Bork was defeated. Reagan offered him scant support when he was under fire. Reagan ultimately chose Anthony Kennedy, who was more acceptable to Senate Democrats.

7. *Amnesty for illegal immigrants.* On November 6, 1986, Reagan signed the Immigration Reform and Control Act of 1986, also known as the Simpson-Mazzoli Act. This act made it unlawful to hire people who had come into the country illegally, but also granted amnesty to virtually all illegal immigrants who had entered before 1982—some three million people.

8. *Arming the Afghan jihadis.* Reagan continued and greatly expanded the CIA's Operation Cyclone to arm and train Afghan jihadis who were fighting against the Soviet Union. The Soviets' ignominious withdrawal from Afghanistan in February 1989, just after Reagan left office, can be attributed in large part to this aid. However, aiding the jihadis would prove to have disastrous consequences for the United States.

---

512   James Reston, "Washington; Kennedy and Bork," *New York Times*, July 5, 1987.

9. *Ending the Cold War*. Reagan became president in the era of détente, when it was generally agreed that the best way to deal with the Soviet Union and global Communism in general was to play down differences, turn a blind eye to the human rights abuses endemic to socialist states, seek accords that would ease tensions, prevent the use of nuclear weapons, and allow the two sides to continue in much the same way indefinitely. The détente era reached its apex on June 18, 1979, when Jimmy Carter and Soviet Premier Leonid Brezhnev signed the SALT II Treaty, and then, as the world watched agog, Carter embraced and kissed the Communist despot.

President Reagan set a different tone. He was a public critic of détente as disadvantageous to American interests. On June 8, 1982, in a speech before the British House of Commons, he contradicted the conventional wisdom that the Soviet Union was here to stay and boldly predicted its demise. Reagan said, "The march of freedom and democracy...will leave Marxism-Leninism on the ash-heap of history, as it has left other tyrannies which stifle the freedom and muzzle the self-expression of the people."[513]

He went even further on March 8, 1983, in a speech to Christian leaders, when he called the Soviet Union an "evil empire."[514] He warned them against the temptation to "simply call the arms race a giant misunderstanding and thereby

---

513   Ronald Reagan, "Address to British Parliament" (speech, June 8, 1982), History Place: Great Speeches Collection, https://www.historyplace.com/speeches/reagan-parliament.htm.

514   Ronald Reagan, "Evil Empire Speech" (March 8, 1983), Voices of Democracy: The U.S. Democracy Project, https://voicesofdemocracy.umd.edu/reagan-evil-empire-speech-text/.

remove yourself from the struggle between right and wrong and good and evil."[515] The international media, as well as many foreign policy "experts" within the Reagan administration, were aghast, charging that Reagan's rhetoric was reckless, destroyed the possibility for further détente accords with the Soviets, and greatly increased the possibility of nuclear war.

In calling the Soviet Union an "evil empire," however, Reagan rejected the moral equivalency that had become fashionable during the era of détente and restored the idea of the Cold War as not just a jockeying for interests between two superpowers but a just and necessary moral crusade against a monstrous regime that victimized its own people. This heartened and emboldened Soviet dissidents and residents of Soviet satellites who had been dismayed to see the leading nation in the free world begin to treat the Soviet Union as if it were anything but a cruel totalitarian state.

At the same time, Reagan began a massive military buildup, again to the consternation of the foreign policy establishment, which again warned that he was risking a nuclear war. But Reagan's remark that Marxism-Leninism would be relegated to the "ash-heap of history" was not just a rhetorical flourish; Reagan discerned what the establishment analysts missed: détente was allowing the Soviet economy breathing room, and the Soviets would not be able to keep up with the new arms race. Reagan calculated that the strain of trying to do so would weaken the Soviet economy, and that would lead to the end of the Soviet Union as a Communist superpower.

---

515   Ibid.

Reagan also directly challenged Soviet propaganda, which often found echoes in the Western media, claiming that the Soviet bloc was working for peace against a warmongering, imperialist United States. On June 12, 1987, at the Brandenburg Gate in West Berlin, Reagan addressed Soviet Premier Mikhail Gorbachev: "There is one sign the Soviets can make that would be unmistakable, that would advance dramatically the cause of freedom and peace. General Secretary Gorbachev, if you seek peace, if you seek prosperity for the Soviet Union and Eastern Europe, if you seek liberalization: Come here to this gate! Mr. Gorbachev, open this gate! Mr. Gorbachev, tear down this wall!"[516]

Two years later, the Communists could contain their peoples' desire for freedom no longer. On November 9, 1989, East German authorities, under immense pressure, announced that their borders were open; hundreds of thousands of East Germans massed at the Wall, vastly outnumbering the guards, who ultimately let them through. The Berlin Wall, where so many people had been gunned down making a desperate rush for freedom, soon afterward began to be torn down. The Soviet Union dissolved in 1991.

Why his presidency was very good for America

President Reagan's failure to stop the growth of the federal government was unfortunate on many levels, not least because

---

516   Ronald Reagan, "Tear Down This Wall," June 12, 1987, History Place: Great Speeches Collection, https://www.historyplace.com/speeches/reagan-tear-down.htm.

it reinforced the "progressive" notion that massive state control over the ordinary lives of Americans was a historical inevitability toward which the nation was inexorably "progressing," and nothing could be done about it. His War on Drugs was also a curious departure from his guiding beliefs: Reagan, of all people, should have known that throwing billions of dollars and new government regulations at a problem doesn't solve it. Still, even just by raising the issue of the growth of the federal government and making efforts to reduce its size a centerpiece of his presidency, Reagan dealt a serious blow to New Deal orthodoxy and awakened in many people the idea that the galloping horse of federal spending could one day be reined in, even if Reagan was unable to accomplish this.

Reagan's breaking of the air traffic controllers' strike was a genuine defense of working people. The power and influence of labor unions had grown throughout the twentieth century. Many unions became monopolies in their own right, and so could make increasingly unreasonable demands and call strikes when they were not met. At times, they acted against the interests of the workers they were pledged to protect and defend by calling strikes over relatively trivial matters when it would have been more profitable for the workers to keep working, as strikes often led cash-strapped companies to lay off workers in large numbers.

Unions didn't disappear after Reagan acted against PATCO, but workers became much freer not to join them if they chose and gained much more control over their own destiny than they had enjoyed before the air traffic controllers' strike. Businesses benefited from this as well, as Federal

Reserve Chairman Alan Greenspan explained in 2003. Reagan's action, noted Greenspan, "gave weight to the legal right of private employers, previously not fully exercised, to use their own discretion to both hire and discharge workers": "There was great consternation among those who feared that an increased ability to lay off workers would raise the level of unemployment and amplify the sense of job insecurity. It turned out that with greater freedom to fire, the risks of hiring declined."[517] Thus, more people were hired, unemployment went down, businesses prospered, and wages increased. This was a significant element of the economic boom of the latter portion of the twentieth century.

On the other side of the ledger, however, is the Simpson-Mazzoli Act, which heralded a massive influx of illegal immigrants into the United States, thereby harming the employment prospects of American citizens and legal immigrants.

In the foreign policy realm, President Reagan was trying to bring the Cold War to a victorious conclusion. In that regard, he saw the Afghans who were fighting against the Soviet Union as useful and greatly boosted their ability to disrupt the Soviet attempts to subdue the country and make it a Communist state. Neither Reagan nor anyone in the State Department had studied the Islamic doctrine of jihad; no one understood that American aid to Afghan jihadis would not win their friendship and loyalty, for it would not change the fact that the United States was a non-Muslim country, and the Qur'an

---

517   Alan Greenspan, "The Reagan Legacy" (speech, Simi Valley, CA, April 9, 2003), Federal Reserve Board, https://www.federalreserve.gov/boarddocs/speeches/2003/200304092/default.htm.

commanded Muslims to wage war against and subjugate unbelievers. Because he continued and expanded Operation Cyclone, Reagan bears more responsibility than Carter for the jihad attacks on September 11, 2001, and the general resurgence of the global jihad in the twenty-first century.

Reagan is seldom given credit today for ending the Cold War, which was clearly in America's best interests in removing its biggest adversary of the time from the world stage. Analysts prefer to give the credit to Gorbachev for relaxing the restrictions on Soviet citizens, and to Pope John Paul II for inspiring and encouraging Polish shipyard workers to resist the Communist government's iron fist. But Gorbachev's liberalization was a response to the tremendous economic pressure that the Soviets were experiencing as a result of Reagan's arms buildup, and if the Pope's words played a role in inspiring resistance to Communism, so did Reagan's when he dared to cast the Cold War as a struggle of freedom versus slavery and good versus evil. President Reagan deserves immense credit for the collapse of the Soviet bloc and the end of the Cold War.

Reagan's last years in the White House, however, were dogged by scandal, when it was discovered that his administration sold arms to the Islamic Republic of Iran, in violation of an embargo on such sales, in order to finance the activities of the Contras, a group fighting against Communism in Nicaragua. The Democrats were working from their post-Nixon playbook, trying to portray the affair as a new Watergate and hoping to implicate Reagan in wrongdoing and force his resignation or impeachment. They failed, however, to demonstrate that he had any knowledge of, much less involvement in, any illegal activity, and the whole thing fizzled out.

The worst aspect of the Iran-Contra Affair was little remarked: the Reagan administration was aiding a regime in Iran that considered America an enemy and had vowed to destroy it. It was as shortsighted, and shortsighted in the same way, as arming jihadis in Afghanistan. While Reagan could not have known that anything on the order of 9/11 was in the offing, the hostility and repression of the Islamic Republic of Iran were well known. Reagan's aides made the overtures to Iran without his knowledge, but he was the president and rightly took full responsibility.

Nevertheless, the presidency of Ronald Reagan stands out brilliantly in American history. When the country was mired in malaise, in decline economically, and adrift internationally, Reagan was able, despite fierce resistance and the undying contempt and hostility of the Washington establishment, to restore it to being what he termed "this place called America, this shining city on a hill, this government of, by, and for the people."[518]

---

518   Ronald Reagan, "State of the Union Address" (speech, January 25, 1988), Ronald Reagan Presidential Library & Museum, https://www.reaganlibrary. gov/research/speeches/12488d.

GEORGE H. W. BUSH

Library of Congress[519]

---

519   David Valdez, *George Bush, Half-Length Portrait, Facing Front*, 1989, photograph, Library of Congress, https://www.loc.gov/item/89715763/.

Full name: George Herbert Walker Bush
Lived: June 12, 1924–November 30, 2018
Presidency: January 20, 1989–January 20, 1993
Party: Republican
Evaluation: Very Damaging for America
Rating: 2

What qualified him to be president

Ronald Reagan was a genial but unmistakably defiant outsider who challenged the Washington establishment in numerous ways. His vice president, however, was a career Washington insider who during the campaign for the 1980 Republican presidential nomination had derided Reagan's economic program as "voodoo economics."[520]

After an unexceptional four years as a congressman from Texas, George Herbert Walker Bush served as ambassador to the United Nations and then chairman of the Republican National Committee during the Nixon administration, followed by stints as chief of the U.S. Liaison Office in Beijing and director of the CIA during the Ford administration. He became Reagan's running mate to placate the establishment Republicans whom Reagan made nervous. By the end of Reagan's second term, he was his heir apparent and overcame a crowded field of challengers with relative ease.

---

520   George H. W. Bush, "Voodoo Economics" (speech, Pittsburgh, PA, April 10, 1980).

How he won

To oppose Bush, the Democrats put up Massachusetts Governor Michael Dukakis, whose chief claim to fame was the so-called Massachusetts Miracle, which Dukakis effected by behaving in a decidedly non-New Dealish way, lowering taxes and making the state more attractive to business. Bush, meanwhile, set out immediately to distance himself from Reagan, saying in his acceptance speech at the Republican National Convention: "I want a kinder, gentler nation," which strongly implied that the nation under Reagan's leadership was unkinder and harsher than it need have been.[521]

Bush did not hesitate, however, to get into the trenches. His campaign ran a TV commercial calling attention to the fact that Dukakis had overseen a prison furlough program in Massachusetts that allowed a convicted murderer named Willie Horton to leave prison on a weekend pass, during which he committed armed robbery and rape, and disappeared. The Bush campaign justly portrayed Dukakis as weak and soft on crime; this ad has been frequently characterized since 1988 as "racist," but Horton's race was never mentioned (although he was pictured) and the facts of the case were not in question. Another Bush ad also mocked Dukakis for donning a helmet and riding in a tank, which both belied his Democratic commitment to slashing military spending and made him look silly.

Above all, Bush ran on Reagan's record. In his acceptance speech, he proclaimed: "My opponent won't rule out raising

---

521   George H. W. Bush, "1988 Acceptance Speech" (August 18, 1988), C-Span, https://www.c-span.org/video/?3848-1/george-hw-bush-1988-acceptance-speech.

taxes. But I will. And the Congress will push me to raise taxes and I'll say no. And they'll push, and I'll say no, and they'll push again, and I'll say to them, 'Read my lips: no new taxes.'"[522]

Americans believed him. Bush's margin of victory was not as large as Reagan's, but he still overwhelmed Dukakis, with 426 electoral votes to the Democrat's 111. Bush became the first sitting vice president to be elected president since Martin Van Buren.

Bush was elected on the Reagan legacy. Four years later, he was defeated for reelection because he did not uphold that legacy.

Notable accomplishments as president and events of his presidency

1. *Raising taxes.* With congressional Democrats continuing to refuse to cut federal spending, the federal deficit grew ever larger. With the economy in a mild recession, Bush, on November 5, 1990, signed the Omnibus Budget Reconciliation Act of 1990, which raised income taxes and other taxes as well. This was unnecessary, as the growth of the economy occasioned by Reagan's tax cuts would continue, with some pauses, and wipe out the deficit within a decade. But President Bush was under heavy pressure from Democrats and the media to renege on his campaign promise, and in the manner of establishment Republicans since the Eisenhower administration, he gave in.

---

522   George H. W. Bush, "1988 Acceptance Speech."

2. *Diversity Immigrant Visas.* The Immigration Act of 1990 established the Diversity Immigrant Visa program, which admitted immigrants into the United States in order to enhance the nation's ethnic, racial, and cultural diversity. The watchword was "Diversity is our strength," which was seldom, if ever, questioned.

3. *Appointing Clarence Thomas to the Supreme Court.* Bush's first Supreme Court appointment was David Souter, a quintessential establishment Republican who quickly began voting with the court's Democrats. For the next court vacancy, Bush chose Clarence Thomas, a relatively youthful black judge known for his disdain for creative interpretations of the Constitution, including *Roe v. Wade.* Thomas's nomination faced passionate opposition from the start, which became even more strident when a former employee of Thomas's at the Equal Employment Opportunity Commission, Anita Hill, charged him with sexual harassment. Hill could not convincingly explain why she had waited ten years to make her allegations publicly despite Thomas's prominence as a judge or why she had followed him to a second job after the harassment supposedly took place.

Thomas, meanwhile, indignantly denied all the allegations and declared: "This is not an opportunity to talk about difficult matters privately or in a closed environment. This is a circus. It's a national disgrace. And from my standpoint, as a black American, as far as I'm concerned it is a high-tech lynching for uppity blacks who in any way deign to think for themselves, to do for themselves, to have different ideas, and it is a message that unless you kowtow to an old order, this is what will happen to you. You will be lynched, destroyed, caricatured by a committee of the U.S. Senate rather than hung from a tree."[523]

Indeed. He was narrowly confirmed, but the Democratic Party had discovered another new tactic.

4. *The fall of the Berlin Wall and the dissolution of the Soviet Union.* The destruction of the Berlin Wall and the demise of the Soviet Union were world-historical events that brought the Cold War to a close and transformed the global political landscape. Bush had nothing to do with any of this; these were the results of forces that Reagan had set in motion.

5. *Invading Panama.* Bush took Reagan's War on Drugs to a whole new level. Panamanian dictator Manuel Noriega engaged in drug trafficking and annulled an election to keep himself in power. In December 1989, he announced that Panama was in a "state of war" with the U.S. and had a U.S. marine murdered.[524] Bush responded by sending American troops to invade Panama and topple Noriega's regime. Noriega was brought to the U.S., imprisoned, and convicted on drug trafficking charges.

6. *Invading Iraq.* In August 1990, Iraqi President Saddam Hussein invaded and quickly occupied the neighboring nation of Kuwait. Bush said, "This will not stand, this aggression

---

523 "Hearing of the Senate Judiciary Committee on the Nomination of Clarence Thomas to the Supreme Court," September 13, 1991, Electronic Text Center, University of Virginia Library, https://web.archive.org/web/20130913093438/ http://etext.lib.virginia.edu/etcbin/toccer-new-yitna?id=UsaThom&images =images%2Fmodeng&data=%2Flv6%2Fworkspace%2Fyitna&tag=public& part=24.

524 Stewart Brewer, *Borders and Bridges: A History of U.S.-Latin American Relations* (Westport, CT: Greenwood Publishing Group, 2006), 146.

against Kuwait."[525] After economic sanctions didn't force Saddam to withdraw, Bush asked Congress in January 1991 to approve military intervention. Congress did so. Bombing in Iraq began shortly thereafter, followed by a ground invasion on February 23. By February 27, American and allied troops had driven the Iraqi army out of Kuwait. Bush declined, however, to pursue the war until Saddam Hussein was removed from power.

The Gulf War was extraordinarily popular in the United States, and Bush's approval ratings soared. His reelection seemed assured. But the economy had other ideas.

7. *Invading Somalia.* On December 4, 1992, after he had already lost his bid for reelection, Bush announced that he was sending American troops to Somalia. The goal was to protect humanitarian missions in the East African nation, which was torn by civil war.

Why his presidency was very damaging for America

When Bush raised taxes in 1990, he set himself up for defeat in the 1992 election by allowing himself to appear, at best, vacillating and, at worst, untrustworthy. He also reinforced the tendency of Republicans to give in to the Democratic and media agenda, rather than standing firm on their own principles. Bush proved yet again the truth of George Wallace's adage

---

525   George H. W. Bush, "Remarks and an Exchange with Reporters on the Iraqi Invasion of Kuwait" (speech, August 5, 1990), Margaret Thatcher Foundation, https://www.margaretthatcher.org/document/110704.

that there was not a "dime's worth of difference" between the parties and robbed Americans of a genuine electoral choice.

The Diversity Immigrant Visa program, meanwhile, reinforced the idea that had been born during the late nineteenth-century controversies over the Chinese Exclusion Act and had taken root during the Lyndon Johnson administration: that any opposition to virtually unrestricted immigration was simply racist, xenophobic, and nativist, and did not need to be considered on any other terms. Yet foes of the program had valid concerns involving the necessity of requiring immigrants to assimilate, as well as the possibility that some immigrants might come with cultural assumptions that were incompatible with American values but never challenged during the immigration process. The charges of "racism," however, made it impossible for these concerns to be rationally evaluated.

On the other side of the ledger, Bush's appointment of Clarence Thomas to the Supreme Court was laudable and strengthened the opposition to the tendency to read into the Constitution whatever policy the Democratic Party wanted to enact. But there were then, and would be later, plenty of establishment Republicans on the court who would do everything they could to make sure that tendency remained dominant in the Supreme Court's jurisprudence.

In the foreign policy realm, Bush did a great deal to expand America's commitment to internationalism. On December 20, 1989, he explained his invasion of Panama by saying that America's goal was "to safeguard the lives of Americans," as well as "to defend democracy in Panama, to combat drug trafficking, and to protect the integrity of the Panama Canal

Treaty."[526] He declared: "The Panamanian people want democracy, peace, and a chance for better life in dignity and freedom. The people of the United States seek only to support them in pursuit of these noble goals."[527] Aside from safeguarding some individuals from possible violence by the Noriega regime and combating drug trafficking, it was hard to see how all this was in the best interests of the United States. While it would be good for Panamanians to enjoy a better life in dignity and freedom, it would be impossible for the United States to place troops in every country where citizens lacked dignity and freedom and ensure they had better governments.

Bush's statement was the apotheosis of Wilson's vow to "make the world safe for democracy," and Bush made matters much worse on January 17, 1991, when the U.S. began bombing Baghdad. He reaffirmed the nation's commitment to interventionism and internationalism, saying in another televised speech: "This is an historic moment. We have in this past year made great progress in ending the long era of conflict and cold war. We have before us the opportunity to forge for ourselves and for future generations a new world order—a world where the rule of law, not the law of the jungle, governs the conduct of nations. When we are successful—and we will be—we have a real chance at this new world order, an order in which a credible United Nations can use its peacekeeping role to fulfill the promise and vision of the U.N.'s founders."[528]

---

526   George H. W. Bush, "U.S. Military Action in Panama," December 20, 1989, in *American Foreign Policy Current Documents* (Washington, D.C.: Historical Division, Bureau of Public Affairs, 1990), 720.

527   Ibid., 721.

528   George H. W. Bush, "President George Bush Announcing War in Iraq" (speech, January 17, 1991), History Place, https://www.historyplace.com/speeches/bush-war.htm.

The "new world order" he had in mind was apparently much like the old one, in which the United States would serve as the world's policeman. But during the Cold War, it was not difficult to argue that various interventions served America's interests in resisting the spread of Communism. Bush, in contrast, justified his invasion of Iraq by stating explicitly that it was in the service of the United Nations, and was *not* a conflict between Iraq and the United States. Bush charged: "Saddam was warned over and over again to comply with the will of the United Nations: Leave Kuwait, or be driven out. Saddam has arrogantly rejected all warnings. Instead, he tried to make this a dispute between Iraq and the United States of America."[529] If it was not that, at least on some level, what business did he have sending American troops in? Some argued that the war was necessary in order to protect America's sources of oil. But the nation was buying oil from other nations besides Iraq and Kuwait, and if Iraq had absorbed Kuwait and made it into an Iraqi province, it would still have sold oil to the rest of the world anyway. Bush advanced the idea that many took for granted then and now, that it was the responsibility of the United States to solve the world's problems, even when those problems did not affect America itself.

President Bush brought this principle to its fullest fruition when he sent troops to Somalia. There was no conceivable American interest in protecting the delivery of humanitarian aid to Somalia. Somalia had no oil or any other significant products for export. It did not remotely threaten the U.S. or even nearby countries militarily. But the United States under

---

529   Ibid.

George H. W. Bush had become the world's strict but benevolent father, intervening wherever it deemed necessary for the good of its children. That these interventions could ultimately exhaust America's resources while accomplishing no good purpose (nearly thirty years after Bush's intervention, Somalia still has no stable central government that is recognized throughout that country) was not even considered.

Bush was frequently compared unfavorably to Ronald Reagan for lacking a grand vision for the nation, or what Bush himself dismissively called "the vision thing."[530] Those critics give Bush too little credit. He actually had quite a bit of "the vision thing": his vision was of the United States establishing and enforcing a "new world order" and sending troops to all corners of the world in order to ensure that the various members of the new world order enjoyed good government. It was a calamitous vision for America. But Bush also managed to get Clarence Thomas on the Supreme Court, and for that alone, his presidency was not a disaster on the order of Lyndon Johnson's or Jimmy Carter's.

---

530   Robert Ajemian, "Where Is the Real George Bush?" *Time Magazine*, January 26, 1987.

FORTY-TWO

BILL CLINTON

Library of Congress[531]

---

531   *Bill Clinton, Head-and-Shoulders Portrait, Facing Front*, 1992, photograph, Library of Congress, https://www.loc.gov/item/93505822/.

Full name: William Jefferson Blythe III, then William
    Jefferson Clinton from 1950
Lived: August 19, 1946–
Presidency: January 20, 1993–January 20, 2001
Party: Democratic
Evaluation: Disastrous for America
Rating: 0

What qualified him to be president

Bill Clinton was known as the "Man from Hope," that is, Hope, Arkansas, the hardscrabble little town where he was born and named William Jefferson Blythe III.[532] His father, William Jefferson Blythe, Jr., died in an automobile accident before he was born. When young Bill was four, his mother married Roger Clinton, and the boy became William Jefferson Clinton. Bill Clinton has described his stepfather as an abusive alcoholic whom he more than once had to threaten in order to keep him from harming his mother.

Clinton rose quickly from these humble and precarious beginnings. He won a scholarship to Georgetown University, and then a Rhodes Scholarship to Oxford, where he organized protests against the Vietnam War. From there, he went to Yale Law School. Then he became attorney general of Arkansas at the age of thirty and governor at the age of thirty-two. In twelve years as governor of Arkansas, Bill Clinton lowered some taxes and amassed a reputation as fiscally responsible, as well as of questionable ethical and moral standards.

---

532   "It All Began in a Place Called Hope: President Bill Clinton," Clinton White House, https://clintonwhitehouse2.archives.gov/WH/EOP/OP/html/Hope.html.

Democrats, who saw the electoral results in 1980 and 1984 of their party's steady move to the left, began to see Clinton as a possible presidential candidate in 1988, but Clinton decided not to run.

By 1992, however, the picture had changed considerably. Another far-left Democrat had lost decisively yet again, and the field seemed open to a Democrat who seemed less committed than most to expanding state control.

But when George H. W. Bush's approval ratings went through the roof after the invasion of Iraq, leading Democrats such as New York Governor Mario Cuomo and activist Jesse Jackson declined to run. The field was open to an apparently reasonable, centrist Democrat. And while Clinton faced some challengers in the Democratic primaries and had to address charges of marital infidelity and corruption as governor, he quickly emerged as the clear front-runner and had little trouble obtaining the nomination.

How he won

During the campaign, Clinton stole Bush's mantle as the political heir of Ronald Reagan, which Bush himself had made easy by squandering the Reagan legacy. Clinton cannily positioned himself as the choice of those who, like Reagan, favored small government. He promised tax cuts, a reduction of the federal deficit, and reform of the welfare system—a sensible Democratic candidate after a succession of irresponsible tax-and-spend statists. Bush's tax hike rendered him vulnerable to this kind of attack, and Clinton hit him hard for reneging on his "Read my lips, no new taxes" promise. Clinton and his staff adopted "It's the economy, stupid" as an internal slogan to remind themselves to keep hammering home the message they thought was most effective against Bush.[533]

Even so, Bush might have won reelection were it not for billionaire H. Ross Perot, who entered the race pledging to use his business acumen to wipe out the deficit and clean up other messes that the career politicians had made. His message resonated with a great many Americans, and he even led Bush and Clinton in a June 1992 Gallup poll. But he proved erratic, dropping out of the race and later reentering it, and his maverick appeal began to wear thin. Still, he received almost twenty million popular votes, nearly 19 percent. As his message was similar to Clinton's in its promises of fiscal responsibility, he almost certainly drew more voters away from Bush (who ran a campaign so lackluster that he often looked as if he didn't even want to be reelected) than from the Democrat. With just 43 percent of the popular vote, Bill Clinton became president.

Perot did it again in 1996, although he received over ten million fewer votes than he had in 1992. The Republicans ran another uninspiring establishment candidate, Kansas Senator Bob Dole, and Clinton became the first Democrat to be reelected since Franklin D. Roosevelt.

Notable accomplishments as president and events of his presidency

1. *Raising taxes.* Clinton said during the campaign that he would cut taxes on middle-class Americans and raise them only for

---

533   Matuz, 714.

the wealthy. On October 29, 1992, just five days before the election, he went further, promising to cut spending rather than renege on this pledge: "If the tax proposals I have made do not fund the spending levels I have proposed, then I will scale back the spending, cut other Government spending or both."[534] He didn't envision having to do this, as he said on October 31 that his economic estimates were "good and sound" and again pledged reductions in spending rather than tax hikes if those estimates proved to be erroneous after all: "We might have to phase in the health care program over a couple of more years; we might have to slow down the education programs."[535]

However, he reneged almost immediately. In a televised address on February 15, 1993, just three weeks after taking office, he claimed that despite his best efforts, keeping his promise had proved impossible: "I had hoped to invest in your future by creating jobs, expanding education, reforming health care, and reducing the debt without asking more of you, and I've worked harder than I've ever worked in my life to meet that goal. But I can't, because the deficit has increased so much beyond my earlier estimates and beyond even the worst official government estimates from last year."[536]

A pattern of disingenuousness was established that continued throughout the Clinton administration.

---

534   David E. Rosenbaum, "The 1992 Campaign: Taxes; Clinton Promises to Protect Middle Class on Taxes," *New York Times*, October 31, 1992.

535   Ibid.

536   Bill Clinton, "Address to the Nation on the Economic Program" (speech, February 15, 1993), in *Public Papers of the Presidents of the United States, William J. Clinton*, book 1 (Washington, D.C.: Office of the Federal Register, National Archives and Records Administration, 1994), 106.

2. *Balancing the budget.* The Clinton White House website boasts that he "signed the Balanced Budget Act of 1997, a major bipartisan agreement to eliminate the national budget deficit, create the conditions for economic growth, and invest in the education and health of our people."[537]

It seemed to work. In 1998, the federal government ran a surplus for the first time since 1969.

3. *Hillarycare.* During the 1992 campaign, Clinton touted the intelligence and acumen of his wife, Hillary, and said that if he was elected, America would be getting "two for one—buy one, get one free."[538] Hillary herself added, "If you vote for my husband, you get me. It's a two-for-one, blue plate special."

This was one promise on which he made good, quickly appointing Hillary to head his Task Force on National Health Care Reform, a responsibility for a First Lady that was unparalleled in American history.

Hillary Clinton came up with a health care proposal that was extraordinarily complicated, running over a thousand pages, and offering a predictable set of proposals for a colossal increase in government control over the health care system in the familiar "progressive" guise of fairness for ordinary people. The plan faced stiff opposition from the start, not just from Republicans, but from the health care industry, which included many who did not want to see the nation's medical system start down the road to nationalization. The plan was

---

537   "The Clinton Presidency: Historic Economic Growth," Clinton White House, https://clintonwhitehouse5.archives.gov/WH/Accomplishments/eightyears-03.html.

538   Bernard Ryan, *Hillary Rodham Clinton: First Lady and Senator* (New York: Infobase Publishing, 2009), 53.

ultimately defeated in the summer of 1994 and had made such a negative impression on Americans that the Democrats suffered crushing defeats in the 1994 elections, losing both the House and the Senate for the first time since 1952.

4. *Don't Ask, Don't Tell.* In December 1993, Clinton ordered the implementation of a policy known as "Don't Ask, Don't Tell," which allowed homosexuals to serve in the military as long as they weren't open about their sexuality, and which prohibited military officials from asking about it.

5. *NAFTA.* On December 8, 1993, President Clinton signed the North American Free Trade Agreement (NAFTA) with Canada and Mexico, which removed virtually all tariffs and other restrictions on trade between the three countries. Clinton boasted that the agreement would not only create "the world's largest trade zone," but also "200,000 jobs in this country by 1995 alone."[539]

6. *Desultory response to terrorism.* Islamic jihad terrorists began striking in the United States during the Clinton administration. On February 26, 1993, jihadis bombed the World Trade Center in New York, hoping to bring the complex's two towers down, murdering thousands. Their attack didn't go as planned, but it was a harbinger of things to come: the financier of the attack was Khalid Sheikh Mohammed, who would become a mastermind of the 9/11 attacks. Other jihad plotters planned to detonate bombs, all on the same day, at five key New York City locations, including the UN headquarters,

---

539   Bill Clinton, "Remarks on the Signing of NAFTA" (speech, December 8, 1993), UVA Miller Center, https://millercenter.org/the-presidency/presidential-speeches/december-8-1993-remarks-signing-nafta.

the George Washington Bridge, and the Holland and Lincoln Tunnels.

In April 1993, former president George H. W. Bush visited Kuwait. While he was there, Kuwaiti authorities arrested seventeen people for a plot to murder him. After it became clear that Saddam Hussein was behind the plot, Clinton had a building in Baghdad bombed, and as far as he was concerned, that was the end of the matter.

Even worse was President Clinton's reaction to the bombing at an Oklahoma City federal building on April 19, 1995. Two Americans, Timothy McVeigh and Terry Nichols, were found guilty of the bombing, which killed 168 people. Clinton used the bombing as a pretext to redirect the focus of the FBI and other intelligence agencies away from foreign terror threats and toward domestic ones. Yet the foreign threats were much larger, as became clear on September 11, 2001.

On June 25, 1996, jihadis bombed the Khobar Towers in Saudi Arabia, where many U.S. troops who were enforcing the no-fly zone in southern Iraq that resulted from the Gulf War were being housed. Twenty were killed. The Clinton administration had received warnings before the attack, but downplayed them, and did little after the attack. Then on October 12, 2000, jihadis bombed the USS *Cole*, a destroyer, while it was being refueled in the Yemeni port of Aden. Seventeen sailors were killed. The international jihad terrorist organization al-Qaeda claimed credit for the attack. Once again, Clinton offered only a token response.

7. *Withdrawing from Somalia.* In October 1993, Somali forces downed a pair of U.S. Black Hawk military helicopters;

several Americans were killed, and their corpses were dragged through the streets of Mogadishu as crowds cheered the defeat of the Americans. Clinton thereupon decided to end the U.S. operation in Somalia.

8. *Intervening in Kosovo.* In 1999, Clinton spearheaded a campaign of airstrikes against Serbia in defense of the breakaway province of Kosovo. In June 2019, Clinton visited Kosovo, where its president, Hashim Thaçi, told him: "We thank you for the just decision to stop the Serbian genocide during 1999. We are very grateful for the support of the US to Kosovo. The story of Kosovo is a story of joint success. You are our hero."[540] Clinton replied: "I will always be proud of the fact that I happened to be the president of the United States when you needed someone to stand up and say no more ethnic cleansing, no more people running out of their homes, no more killing innocent civilians, there's got to be another way."[541] Clinton's action paved the way for Kosovo's declaration of independence in 2008.

9. *Expanding NATO.* The Cold War was over; Russian President Boris Yeltsin came to Washington in 1998 to try to establish a friendlier relationship with the United States. The next year, however, Clinton oversaw the admission of two former Soviet satellites, Poland and the Czech Republic, into NATO. Some in the Kremlin saw this as an unwarranted provocation. The chilly relationship between the two countries would continue.

---

540   Blerta Begisholli, "Kosovo Honours Bill Clinton for NATO Intervention in 1999 War," Balkan Insight, June 11, 2019.
541   Ibid.

10. *Aiding China.* After the People's Republic of China had stolen many U.S. military secrets due to lax Clinton-era security controls, Clinton gave the Chinese even more, including advanced missile technology, allegedly in return for campaign contributions. The *Washington Post* noted in an editorial that "in the first three quarters of 1998 nine times as many [supercomputers] were exported [to China] as during the previous seven years."[542] Yet this was three years after the Chinese spying operation had been discovered, and with no indication that China would not continue to be generally hostile to American interests.

11. *Impeachment.* Before, during, and after his presidency, Clinton was dogged by accusations of marital infidelity. In 1997, allegations surfaced that he had carried on a sexual relationship with a young White House intern, Monica Lewinsky. The establishment media initially spiked the story, but it stayed alive on a new medium, the internet, and finally began to draw enough attention that Clinton had to respond. Full of indignation and righteous anger, the president wagged his finger at the press corps and the television cameras during a January 1998 press conference and defiantly declared, "I did not have sexual relations with that woman, Miss Lewinsky."[543] He later said much the same thing under oath. House Republicans charged him with perjury, and on December 19, 1998, Clinton became the second president to be impeached. The Senate acquitted him two months later.

---

542   Matthew Vadum, "Flashback: Bill Clinton Gave China Missile Technology," *FrontPage Magazine*, December 21, 2016.

543   "What Clinton Said," *Washington Post*, September 2, 1998.

Clinton's defense revolved around hairsplitting distinctions regarding what constituted sexual relations and what did not. The media, meanwhile, insisted that the impeachment was a partisan farce, motivated by a vindictive desire to get back at the Democrats for Watergate, and claimed that it was all about sex and enforcing a puritanical moral code, not about perjury.

12. *Corruption.* The Lewinsky affair was just one of many Clinton scandals. Not long after he took office, Clinton fired the staff of the White House travel office; critics said he did so in order to fill the office with his cronies, and he ultimately had to reinstate those who were fired. White House counsel Vince Foster committed suicide in July 1993, giving rise to a flurry of theories trying to make sense of the incident. Suspicions persisted that the Clintons had profited illegally in real estate and related deals involving the Whitewater Development Corporation in Arkansas.

On August 20, 1998, Clinton sent cruise missiles to destroy the al-Shifa pharmaceutical company, explaining that he did so because the factory was producing chemical weapons and was linked to Osama bin Laden. American officials later acknowledged that there was no evidence that the factory really was producing chemical weapons. Some even charged that Clinton ordered the bombing to distract attention from the Lewinsky scandal.

On his last day in office, Clinton pardoned international financier Marc Rich, allegedly in exchange for large contributions to the Democratic Party. But neither this nor any of the other suspicions surrounding Clinton ever stuck. Hillary

Clinton dismissed the allegations as a "vast right-wing conspiracy" to discredit her husband.[544]

Why his presidency was disastrous for America

Clinton's impeachment overshadowed his second term, and his disingenuous, Jesuitical response to questions ("It depends on what the meaning of the word 'is' is") made him a deeply polarizing figure at the time he left the White House, although his approval ratings were high.[545] Despite his enduring popularity, offending the dignity of his office and getting away with committing perjury by confusing the issue at hand and engaging in reckless partisanship were the least of the damage Bill Clinton did to America.

On January 23, 1996, during his annual State of the Union address, President Clinton proclaimed, "The era of big government is over."[546] But even the most cursory look at his administration showed that he didn't really believe that. It was just another disingenuous statement from this outstandingly dishonest president.

During Clinton's presidency, the federal deficit was finally wiped out. That was not accomplished, however, by Clinton following through on his pledge to reduce federal spending if his estimates proved inaccurate. In fact, he deserves little

---

544   Joe Carroll, "Hillary Condemns 'Right-Wing Conspiracy,'" *Irish Times*, January 28, 1998.

545   "Bill Clinton and the Meaning of 'Is,'" *Slate*, September 13, 1998.

546   Bill Clinton, "State of the Union Address" (speech, January 23, 1996), https://clintonwhitehouse4.archives.gov/WH/New/other/sotu.html.

or no credit for the budget surplus, although that has never stopped him from claiming it as his handiwork.

In reality, Clinton opposed efforts to reduce the deficit by cutting government spending. He opposed the 1993 Penny-Kasich Deficit Reduction Act, which proposed the elimination of numerous useless and wasteful government agencies. He also opposed the balanced budget amendment, a measure that would have prohibited deficit spending. In mid-1995, the Clinton administration made it clear: "Balancing the budget is not one of our top priorities."[547]

Clinton paradoxically became the principal beneficiary of the fact that his far-left policies lost both the House and the Senate for the Democrats in 1994. The Republican Congress was determined to restore some semblance of fiscal responsibility to the federal government. And it ultimately did so with the aid of an economy that was still booming (with a few downturns) since the Reagan era. Bill Clinton's foremost accomplishment was primarily the handiwork of his political adversaries.

NAFTA, meanwhile, ensured that the deleterious effects of the Clinton administration would be felt for years after the Man from Hope left the Oval Office. When he signed the agreement, Clinton admonished those who weren't entirely on board with the internationalist program, saying: "We cannot stop global change. We cannot repeal the international economic competition that is everywhere. We can only harness the energy to our benefit. Now we must recognize

---

547   Stephen Moore, "No, Bill Clinton Didn't Balance the Budget," Cato Institute, October 8, 1998.

that the only way for a wealthy nation to grow richer is to export, to simply find new customers for the products and services it makes. That, my fellow Americans, is the decision the Congress made when they voted to ratify NAFTA."[548]

Yet NAFTA did not enable a wealthy nation to grow richer; its effect was just the opposite. In the first twenty years after it was signed, the U.S. lost over 850,000 jobs and suffered ballooning trade deficits with both of its NAFTA partners, Canada and Mexico. Even worse, while most of those jobs went to Mexico because workers there could be paid less than they had to be paid in the United States, the massive increase of employment opportunities in Mexico did not bring about prosperity there, as wages were kept low to undercut American workers, and contributed to the huge increase of illegal immigration from Mexico into the U.S.

Clinton was damaging to America in numerous other ways as well. With the "Don't Ask, Don't Tell" policy, Clinton tried to bridge the gap between two opposing camps: those who wanted homosexuals to continue to be banned from the military and those who insisted that open homosexuals should be admitted without any reservations. This policy hastened the abuse of the military as a forum for social engineering rather than a fighting force. Those who had objected to homosexuals in the military did so not solely on moral grounds but also opposed Clinton's measure for the pragmatic reason that having homosexuals in military units could be distracting and disruptive to the unit's morale and cohesion. Such concerns were swept aside, however, in the service of presenting a

---

548   Clinton, "Remarks on the Signing of NAFTA."

military that was an expression of the Left's agenda. The door was now open, and much more of this would come.

Much more jihad terrorism would come as well. On September 10, 2001, just hours before the jihad attacks of September 11 that murdered nearly three thousand people, Clinton, just eight months out of office, told a group of Australian businessmen that Osama bin Laden, the chief architect of the 9/11 attacks and head of al-Qaeda, was a "very smart guy," further saying, "I've spent a lot of time thinking about him— and I nearly got him once.... And I could have killed him, but I would have to destroy a little town called Kandahar in Afghanistan and kill 300 innocent women and children, and then I would have been no better than him. And so I didn't do it."[549]

Clinton's concern for those three hundred Afghan civilians was laudable, but it was bitterly ironic that the next day, the man whose life he spared out of concern for those civilians brought about the murder of ten times that number of American civilians. The National Commission on Terrorist Attacks upon the United States, which investigated the 9/11 attacks, also found that Clinton had other chances to kill bin Laden but passed up all of them. In 1999, bin Laden was spotted in a hunting camp in Afghanistan, but several officials from the United Arab Emirates were there as well, and so Clinton declined to strike, and the terror mastermind cheated death once again.

Meanwhile, his weak response to jihad terror activity throughout his administration, and concentration on

---

549   Dan Good, "Bill Clinton, Hours before 9/11 Attacks: 'I Could Have Killed' Osama bin Laden," ABC News, August 1, 2014.

domestic terror threats after the Oklahoma City bombing, considerably emboldened the jihadis worldwide. Bin Laden himself pondered the implications of the U.S. withdrawal from Somalia and decided the time was right to strike America hard. In his 1996 "Declaration of Jihad against the Americans Occupying the Land of the Two Holiest Sites" (that is, Saudi Arabia), he wrote: "When dozens of your troops were killed in minor battles, and one American pilot was dragged in the streets of Mogadishu, you left the area defeated, carrying your dead in disappointment and humiliation. Clinton appeared in front of the whole world threatening and promising revenge. But these threats were merely a preparation for withdrawal. God has dishonored you when you withdrew, and it clearly showed your weaknesses and powerlessness."[550]

U.S. troops never should have been in Somalia in the first place. There was no American interest involved. But the haste of Clinton's withdrawal and its direct connection to the Black Hawk incident encouraged bin Laden to plan more jihad terror attacks against the United States. It is also worth noting that while Islam has doctrines mandating warfare against unbelievers, the immediate pretext of bin Laden's anger was the stationing of U.S. troops in Saudi Arabia. Muhammad, the prophet of Islam, had said that in Arabia, no religion other than Islam should be allowed to be practiced (bin Laden either didn't know or didn't care about the U.S. military's strict prohibition on non-Muslim religious practice among U.S. troops in Saudi Arabia). The U.S. only had troops in Saudi

---

550   Osama bin Laden, "Declaration of Jihad against the Americans Occupying the Land of the Two Holiest Sites," Combating Terrorism Center, September 2, 1996.

Arabia because of the Gulf War, which was yet another unnecessary foreign intervention. Bad policy has bad consequences that reverberate beyond the initial sphere of action. This is by no means to say that there would have been no jihad activity in the U.S. if there had been no Americans in Saudi Arabia; another pretext would have been found. It is virtually certain, however, that no one in the Clinton State Department had the slightest inkling of what the consequences would be of putting them there.

More unintended consequences resulted from Clinton's actions in Kosovo. The violence and ethnic cleansing were not all on one side; Orthodox Christian Serbs were also expelled or massacred and numerous churches were destroyed as Muslim Kosovars endeavored to efface all traces of Kosovo's lengthy Christian history. Bill Clinton enabled the creation of a Muslim state in southern Europe that was host to numerous jihad terrorists. A great deal of the problems that twenty-first century presidents have had to confront—jihad terrorism, tensions with China and Russia, a sluggish economy, trade deficits, and more—have their seeds in the Clinton administration.

Bill Clinton's life has been full of good fortune. The biggest of his many lucky breaks were the ability to enjoy and take credit for the fruits of Reagan economic policies and the relative peace of the immediate aftermath of the Cold War, neither of which he had anything to do with bringing about, as well as the evasion of responsibility for later economic downturns and national security disasters, despite having done so much to make both inevitable. His morally unacceptable behavior, from Arkansas to Washington, involving both money and sex, is also an enduring part of his legacy.

GEORGE W. BUSH

Library of Congress[551]

---

551   Eric Draper, *President Bush Poses for His Official Portrait in the Roosevelt Room (Blue Tie) / Official Portrait of President George W. Bush*, 2003, photograph, Library of Congress, https://www.loc.gov/item/2011645073/.

Full name: George Walker Bush

Lived: July 6, 1946–

Presidency: January 20, 2001–January 20, 2009

Party: Republican

Evaluation: Disastrous for America

Rating: 1

What qualified him to be president

Ann Richards was a popular governor of Texas and a hero among Democrats for her famous gibe at George H. W. Bush at the 1988 Democratic National Convention: "Poor George, he can't help it—he was born with a silver foot in his mouth."[552] Richards was a rising star in the Democratic Party until 1994, but then the son of the target of her scorn, George W. Bush, decided to settle the score, as he would nine years later against another famous foe of his father, Saddam Hussein. Bush was well known in Texas as the managing general partner of the Texas Rangers baseball team, and he defeated Richards running on a platform of fiscal responsibility and welfare reform.

Bush was a popular Texas governor as well. In 1998, he was reelected with a staggering 69 percent of the vote and became a prime contender for the 2000 Republican nomination. Bush maintained his front-runner status against a crowded Republican field and won the nomination easily.

---

552 "Transcript of the Keynote Address by Ann Richards, the Texas Treasurer," *New York Times*, July 19, 1988.

How he won

The Democrats nominated Vice President Al Gore of Tennessee, who ran on the Clinton administration's record of apparent but not real achievement. Bush ran as a "compassionate conservative," that is, a conservative who accepted much of the fundamental leftist premise that massive government programs and handouts under the guise of aiding the needy, and ever-expanding government control over people's lives, were beneficial for the nation. Bush had, however, imbibed the Reagan-era lesson that tax cuts aided the economy, and appealed to conservatives by going on the *Rush Limbaugh Show*, a radio talk show that became hugely popular for dissenting from the leftist line of the establishment news media.

Ultimately, however, there was little to distinguish the candidates. Like other establishment Republicans, Bush endorsed most of the Democratic program, but just insisted that the Republicans could do a better job implementing that program.

One issue on which Bush and Gore did disagree was whether the U.S. should expend its resources to improve the governments of other countries. In their second debate on October 11, 2000, Bush said that the incursion into Somalia "started off as a humanitarian mission and it changed into a nation-building mission, and that's where the mission went wrong." He continued: "The mission was changed. And as a result, our nation paid a price. And so I don't think our troops ought to be used for what's called nation-building. I think our troops ought to be used to fight and win war."[553]

Bush's personal story of overcoming alcoholism and turning his life around humanized him, especially in contrast to the relatively wooden Gore. However, just days before the election, the media attempted to weaponize Bush's past against him, as the news broke that he had been arrested for drunk driving in 1976. He readily acknowledged this, adding that the timing of the story's release was "interesting."[554] It was. Bush and other Republican candidates in the late twentieth and early twenty-first centuries had to run against not only their Democratic opponents, but against the supposedly objective news services.

Nevertheless, on election night, November 7, 2000, it looked to the world as if Bush had won, although he had lost the popular vote. Gore even made the customary call to him to concede defeat. An hour later, however, Gore called back to withdraw his concession: the situation in Florida was unclear and would decide the election. The completed Florida count on the day after the election showed Bush the winner by 1,784 votes, close enough to require a mandatory recount under Florida law. That recount on November 15 again showed Bush the winner, albeit by a reduced margin of only 327 votes. Gore refused to accept this and successfully appealed to the Florida Supreme Court for more recounts. On November 26, Florida

---

553   "The Second Gore-Bush Presidential Debate," October 11, 2000, Commission on Presidential Debates, https://www.debates.org/voter-education/debate-transcripts/october-11-2000-debate-transcript/.

554   "Bush Acknowledges 1976 DUI Charge," CNN, November 2, 2000.

officials certified Bush the winner by a margin of 537 votes, but Gore and his team pressed on, pushing for more recounts. Florida officials were closely scrutinizing spoiled and poorly marked ballots for any sign of the voter's will, in a process that Republicans criticized as a Lyndon Johnson-style attempt to steal the election. On December 12, the U.S. Supreme Court voted 5–4 that the endless recounting should stop. Bush was at last officially declared the winner.

In 2004, Bush, still riding a wave of popularity he had enjoyed since 9/11 and the beginning of the American incursions into Iraq and Afghanistan, won a close but undisputed victory over Senator John Kerry. Some excitement was injected into the campaign on September 8, 2004, when *CBS Evening News* anchor Dan Rather claimed that several 1973 memos from Lieutenant Colonel Jerry Killian, Bush's commanding officer in the Texas Air National Guard, showed Bush to be lazy, lackadaisical, and protected from the consequences of his actions by powerful friends of his father. The documents, however, were forgeries: while the forgers clearly attempted to make them look decades old, their typographic features were identical to those of a 2000-era computer, not a 1970s typewriter. Rather nevertheless insisted they were authentic, even claiming that typography experts had authenticated them, which some of those experts then denied. CBS retracted the story, and Rather was fired.

Despite the firing, however, the episode showed that the establishment media had gone to a new level of bias. As far back as 1960, Richard Nixon had complained that the media was opposed to him and other Republican candidates and slanted their coverage to portray Democrats favorably and Republicans unfavorably. This charge persisted over the years, with media figures always hotly denying it, although surveys showed that journalists were overwhelmingly Democrats. The Killian/Rather memos refuted all those denials. They showed that the establishment media outlets were actually less news sources than press agencies for the Democratic Party. This problem would only grow worse in later years.

Notable accomplishments as president and events of his presidency

1. *Cutting taxes, increasing government spending.* With the federal government still enjoying a budget surplus, Bush, on June 7, 2001, signed the Economic Growth and Tax Relief Reconciliation Act of 2001 into law, which provided for the largest tax cut in U.S. history. Congress, meanwhile, did its part to fritter away the surplus with enormous increases in federal spending, much of it going to defense in the "War on Terror," but a great deal also to Medicare, social security, and other government programs.

2. *9/11.* On September 11, 2001, Islamic jihadis hijacked jetliners and flew them into the Twin Towers of the World Trade Center in New York City and the Pentagon in Washington, D.C. Passengers resisted on a fourth jet and managed to bring it down in rural Pennsylvania, far from its intended Washington target, which may have been the White House or the Capitol Building. Nearly three thousand people were killed.

In his "Letter to the American People" on November 24, 2002, Osama bin Laden made it clear that the war against the United States would end only with America's submission to Islam: "The first thing that we are calling you to is Islam."[555] Other al-Qaeda plotters involved in planning the September 11 attacks, including Khalid Sheikh Mohammed, agreed, writing in 2009: "It would have been the greatest religious duty to fight you over your infidelity. However, today, we fight you over defending Muslims, their land, their holy sites, and their religion as a whole."[556]

Bush didn't agree that the attacks had any Islamic component. On September 17, 2001, he went to the Islamic Center of Washington, D.C., in the company of several prominent Muslim leaders, and said: "These acts of violence against innocents violate the fundamental tenets of the Islamic faith. And it's important for my fellow Americans to understand that...the face of terror is not the true faith of Islam. That's not what Islam is all about. Islam is peace."[557] He warned Americans not to think ill of Muslims, as if the 9/11 attacks had been perpetrated by Americans targeting Muslims, despite the fact that Muslims were not being subjected to wholesale vigilante

555   Ibid.

556   Khalid Sheikh Mohammed, Walid bin Attash, Ramzi bin As-Shibh, Ali Abd Al-Aziz Ali, and Mustafa Ahmed Al-Hawsawi, "The Islamic Response to the Government's Nine Accusations," Jihad Watch, March 11, 2009, https://www.jihadwatch.org/2009/03/911-defendants-we-ask-to-be-near-to-god-we-fight-you-and-destroy-you-and-terrorize-you-the-jihad-in.

557   " 'Islam Is Peace' Says President: Remarks by the President at Islamic Center of Washington, D.C.," George H. W. Bush White House, September 17, 2001, https://georgewbush-whitehouse.archives.gov/news/releases/2001/09/20010917-11.html.

attacks at that time or at any point subsequently. His defense of the U.S. after 9/11 was known as the "War on Terror," that is, a war against a tactic of warfare, not a war against any particular foe.

This may have, at least in part, been because he was unwilling to identify not just the ideology behind the attacks, but the real attackers. Bush must have known what the world discovered in July 2016, when the twenty-eight-page section of the *9/11 Commission Report* detailing Saudi Arabia's involvement in 9/11, which Bush had ordered redacted, was finally released (albeit with substantial portions still kept secret). The section confirmed that the 9/11 jihadis had received significant help from people at the highest levels of the Saudi government.[558] Less noted but no less significant was the Islamic Republic of Iran's role in the September 11 attacks—also a subject of U.S. government cover-up attempts. On December 22, 2011, U.S. District Judge George B. Daniels ruled in *Havlish, et al. v. bin Laden, et al.* that the Islamic Republic of Iran and its Lebanese proxy Hizballah were liable for damages to be paid to relatives of the victims of the jihad attacks on September 11, 2001, in New York and Washington, as both Iran and Hizballah had actively aided al-Qaeda in planning and executing those attacks.[559]

---

558   Jim Sciutto, Ryan Browne, and Deirdre Walsh, "Congress Releases Secret '28 Pages' on Alleged Saudi 9/11 Ties," CNN, July 15, 2016; Fred Kaplan, "The Idealist in the Bluebonnets: What Bush's Meeting with the Saudi Ruler Really Means," *Slate*, April 26, 2005.

559   "U.S. District Court Rules Iran behind 9/11 Attacks," PR Newswire, December 23, 2011, https://www.prnewswire.com/news-releases/us-district-court-rules-iran-behind-911-attacks-136148008.html.

Bush maintained the friendliest of relations with the Saudis throughout his presidency, even holding hands with the Saudi king during an April 2005 meeting. He never publicly confronted the Saudis about their role in 9/11.

3. *Infiltration.* Bush's denial regarding the ideological roots of 9/11 and his failure to confront the nations that were its chief perpetrators may have been due, at least in part, to the infiltration of the U.S. government. Shortly after 9/11, Muslim cleric Anwar al-Awlaki, who soon emerged as an international jihad terror mastermind, was invited to a private luncheon at the Pentagon to discuss how the nation should defend itself against the jihad al-Awlaki was working to advance.

Also, right after 9/11, influential Republican power broker Grover Norquist set up a meeting for fifteen Muslim leaders with President Bush. The fruit of that meeting was Bush's appearance at the mosque, where Bush stood with Abdurahman Alamoudi, a prominent Muslim leader who, during the presidency of Bill Clinton, served as a State Department "goodwill ambassador" to Muslim lands.[560] Alamoudi was ultimately unmasked as a senior al-Qaeda financier.

Norquist also introduced Bush to Nihad Awad, the co-founder and executive director of the Council on American-Islamic Relations (CAIR), who was also in the mosque with Bush on September 17, 2001. Awad declared in 1994, "I am in support of the Hamas movement."[561] Hamas styles itself in its 1988 charter as "one of the wings of the Muslim Brothers

---

560   Helen Kennedy, "Israel Foe's Donation Draws Flak," *New York Daily News*, January 10, 2002.

561   Joe Kaufman, "A Night of Hamas 'Heroes,'" *FrontPage Magazine*, March 8, 2004.

in Palestine."[562] The Muslim Brotherhood spelled out its goals for the United States in an internal document seized by the FBI in 2005, saying that Muslim Brotherhood members in the United States were told that they "must understand that their work in America is a kind of grand jihad in eliminating and destroying the Western civilization from within and 'sabotaging' its miserable house by their hands and the hands of the believers so that it is eliminated and Allah's religion is made victorious over all other religions."[563]

Although this same Muslim Brotherhood was and is the moving force behind virtually all of the mainstream Muslim organizations in America, Bush did nothing of significance to counter this "grand jihad"; his mosque speech in the presence of Alamoudi and Awad heralded the mainstreaming of key players in this initiative.

4. *Invasion of Afghanistan.* On September 20, 2001, Bush declared at a joint session of Congress: "Every nation, in every region, now has a decision to make. Either you are with us, or you are with the terrorists. From this day forward, any nation that continues to harbor or support terrorism will be regarded by the United States as a hostile regime."[564] This was

---

562   "The Charter of Allah: The Platform of the Islamic Resistance Movement (Hamas)," trans. and annot. by Raphael Israeli, the International Policy Institute for Counter-Terrorism, April 5, 1998, http://www.ict.org.il/documents/documentdet.cfm?docid=14.

563   Mohamed Akram, "An Explanatory Memorandum on the General Strategic Goal for the Group in North America," May 22, 1991, government exhibit 003-0085, *U.S. vs. HLF, et al.*, 3:04-CR-240-G, 7 (21) .

564   George W. Bush, "Address to a Joint Session of Congress and the American People" (speech, September 20, 2001), George W. Bush White House, https://georgewbush-whitehouse.archives.gov/news/releases/2001/09/20010920-8.html.

not true of Saudi Arabia, but it was of Afghanistan, where many of the 9/11 hijackers had trained in al-Qaeda training camps. Osama bin Laden was living there with the protection of Afghanistan's pro-jihad Taliban government, which refused to hand him over to the U.S. On October 7, 2001, the U.S. invaded Afghanistan.

The goals of the invasion were to topple the Taliban from power and destroy the al-Qaeda bases. Yet even as the U.S. oversaw the installation of a new government in Kabul and largely ended the training of jihad terrorists from around the world in Afghanistan, American troops remained in the country. The war in Afghanistan became the longest military engagement in American history. When Barack Obama succeeded George W. Bush, they were still there. When Donald Trump succeeded Obama, they were still there. As the 2020 election year began, they were still there, and the Taliban controlled 70 percent of the country, more than it did before the invasion.

5. *Invasion of Iraq.* The Bush administration charged that Iraqi President Saddam Hussein was stockpiling weapons of mass destruction and that he had aided Osama bin Laden with the 9/11 attacks. The U.S. invasion began on March 20, 2003, and advanced quickly. In mid-April, Saddam went into hiding, and on May 1, Bush declared that the fighting was over.

That should have been the day the troops began to come home. Instead, as in Afghanistan, the Americans stayed in order to make sure that the Iraqis ratified a constitution and elected a government, and they remained beyond that as well. On January 20, 2009, when Bush left office, U.S. troops were still in Iraq. Bush initially refused to say when they would leave, arguing that to do that would give an opportunity to America's adversaries. But in December 2008, he gave on this, agreeing to a withdrawal date of no later than December 31, 2011.

6. *The surveillance state.* Bush authorized the National Security Agency to place suspected terrorists under surveillance, which involved monitoring their electronic communications without a search warrant. This opened the door to the creation of a huge surveillance apparatus, much of which is still shrouded in secrecy and which has been accused of monitoring the communications of people who aren't terrorists at all.

7. *Increasing immigration rates.* During the Bush administration, there was a sharp increase in the number of immigrants to the United States, with nearly half of those coming in doing so illegally. Instead of confronting illegal immigration and moving to stop it, Bush proposed measures that would eventually lead to granting the illegals citizenship.

8. *Recession.* A financial crisis began in 2007, in large part because of irresponsible practices by two federal agencies designed to enable poor people to buy houses: the Federal National Mortgage Association (Fannie Mae), a New Deal-era program, and the Federal Home Loan Mortgage Corporation (Freddie Mac), which was established during the Nixon administration. To his credit, Bush had tried to reform those agencies early in his administration but was blocked by congressional Democrats. When the recession hit, however, Bush's response was straight out of the Hoover/FDR playbook: he pushed a

$700 billion bailout plan through Congress. It didn't work, and the economic downturn, as well as the public's weariness with the ongoing wars in Iraq and Afghanistan, played a large role in the defeat of Republican candidate John McCain in 2008.

Why his presidency was disastrous for America

President Bush's tax cuts gave Americans some real economic relief, and for that, he should be commended, but he did not follow through by cutting government spending. Yet although Bush was an establishment Republican with no significant commitment to reducing the size of the federal government, leftists hated him as much as they had hated Nixon and Reagan. The Democrats and the media vehemently criticized Bush's handling of the aftermath of Hurricane Katrina in 2005, but the real responsibility for the failure of rescue efforts lay with the state and local governments; the blaming of Bush was opportunistic, and a reflection of the ever-growing tendency to see the president as having power over everything and responsible for all things. The Left also hated Bush because of the wars, but more precisely because he was a Republican president fighting wars. There were real reasons to deplore the presidency of George W. Bush, but they were generally other than what led leftists to dub him "Bushitler."

Osama bin Laden boasted that it was "easy for us to provoke and bait this administration" because: "All that we have to do is to send two mujahedeen to the furthest point east to raise a piece of cloth on which is written al Qaeda, in order to make generals race there to cause America to suffer human, economic and political losses without their achieving anything of note other than some benefits for their private corporations."[565] He explained: "We are continuing this policy in bleeding America to the point of bankruptcy," and noted happily that America had suffered "the loss of a huge number of jobs," while "as for the economic deficit, it has reached record astronomical numbers estimated to total more than a trillion dollars.... And it all shows that the real loser is you. It is the American people and their economy.... So the war went ahead, the death toll rose, the American economy bled, and Bush became embroiled in the swamps of Iraq that threaten his future."[566]

This was, unfortunately, an accurate analysis. The "War on Terror" cost trillions, for very little reward. The weapons of mass destruction that the Bush administration told the world Saddam had were never found. Debate continues over whether they were moved, possibly to Syria, or never existed at all, with Bush lying about them in order to take revenge on Saddam Hussein for trying to assassinate his father. In any case, after Hussein was toppled, the U.S. presence in Iraq lost all focus and any semblance of a goal, and like the invasion of Afghanistan, threatened to drag on for generations. Bush's father ran for president vowing not to raise taxes; yet he raised them. The second President Bush ran for president vowing to fight wars to win them and not engage in nation-building; yet he got the U.S. involved in its two lengthiest and costliest nation-building endeavors.

---

565   "Bin Laden: Goal Is to Bankrupt U.S.," CNN, November 1, 2004.
566   Ibid.

If the U.S. was in both countries for the Wilsonian goal of ensuring they had good governments, both incursions were dismal failures, especially Iraq, where what followed Saddam was worse than Saddam. Vice President Dick Cheney said on March 16, 2003: "I think things have gotten so bad inside Iraq from the standpoint of the Iraqi people, my belief is we will, in fact, be greeted as liberators."[567] He was wrong. Most people in Iraq (and Afghanistan as well) believed that Islamic law was the immutable law of Allah, infinitely superior to a law based on human consensus, and hence regarded America's democratic enterprise with suspicion at best. On April 13, 2004, Bush said: "America's objective in Iraq is limited and it is firm. We seek an independent, free and secure Iraq."[568] Iraq became none of those things. It instead degenerated into a chaotic mess. U.S.-supervised elections in this majority Shi'ite nation led inevitably to a majority Shi'ite government in Baghdad that behaved increasingly like a satellite of the Islamic Republic of Iran. Sunnis refused to accept this government, and Sunni jihad groups vied for hegemony in the northern part of the country, while all sides brutalized and victimized Christians and other religious minorities.

By the time Bush took office, the idea that wars were fought in order to be won and end a threat to the nation seemed to be entirely gone, replaced by airy notions of "nation-building" involving trying to plant democratic

---

567   Dick Cheney, interview by Tim Russert, *Meet the Press*, September 14, 2003; transcript at http://www.nbcnews.com/id/3080244/ns/meet_the_press/t/transcript-sept/#.WpYG-hPwaV4.

568   "Transcript of Bush's Remarks on Iraq: 'We Will Finish the Work of the Fallen,'" *New York Times*, April 14, 2004.

governments in areas that not only had no democratic traditions, but where operations in both Afghanistan and Iraq became quagmires, immense drains on American personnel, money, and matériel, with little to no upside.

Meanwhile, Bush's speech at the Islamic Center of Washington on September 17, 2001, crippled counterterror efforts both at home and abroad, as it made it difficult and ultimately impossible to fulfill that oldest adage of warfare, "Know your enemy." Political leaders all over the West echoed his words about Islam's being a religion of peace, having nothing to do with terrorism. This became a commonplace of the Western political discourse, rejected only by a small minority, who were quickly stigmatized as racists and bigots with an irrational animus against Islam and Muslims.

The refusal to name the enemy properly, or even to call him what he called himself, also augmented the dangers of the Bush administration's surveillance measures. If the National Security Agency can monitor the communications of suspected terrorists, that means it can monitor the communications of any and all people for whom such suspicions can be devised. The Left increasingly terms patriotic Americans with no intention whatsoever of contravening the rule of law "extremists," which was originally an Obama-era euphemism for terrorists. Simply opposing various aspects of the leftist agenda can earn one this term. Labeling jihadis "extremists" opened the door to Bush-era surveillance procedures being used against ordinary Americans solely because of their political views. Bush made that possible.

Bush's "compassionate conservatism" was on abundant display, meanwhile, in his stance toward illegal immigration. But he did not appear to have the same compassion for the American citizens who had to compete with those illegals for jobs. He also showed no concern whatsoever for the possibility that American society could ultimately suffer massive unrest due to the admittance of large numbers of people who had no intention of adopting American values or respecting American culture. Such concerns were, as always, drowned out with charges of "racism" and "Islamophobia."

After the presidency of George W. Bush, America was poorer, more threatened, and less free than it had been before. Yet Bush's successor made his presidency look successful by comparison.

FORTY-FOUR

BARACK OBAMA

Library of Congress[569]

---

569   Pete Souza, *Official Portrait of President-Elect Barack*, 2009, photograph,
       Library of Congress, https://www.loc.gov/item/2010647151/.

Full name: Barack Hussein Obama II
Lived: August 4, 1961–
Presidency: January 20, 2009–January 20, 2017
Party: Democratic
Evaluation: Disastrous for America
Rating: 0

What qualified him to be president

The Vietnam War and the hippie generation of Bill Clinton and his peers brought about the mainstreaming of a virulent anti-Americanism among American youth. Many young people regarded their own country as a militaristic, racist, imperialist power; every generation since the late sixties has been subjected to this perspective in public schools. On January 20, 2009, one of the people educated in this way became president of the United States for the first time.

On July 27, 2004, a candidate for the Senate from Illinois named Barack Obama delivered a ringing call for national unity in his keynote address at the Democratic National Convention, declaring: "There's not a liberal America and a conservative America—there's the United States of America. There's not a black America and white America and Latino America and Asian America; there's the United States of America."[570]

Obama's speech electrified the crowd and made him a national figure. He won his Senate election by a huge margin.

---

[570] "Barack Obama's Keynote Address at the 2004 Democratic National Convention" (speech, July 27, 2004), PBS.

To many, he seemed to promise a new era of national reconciliation, bridging the political and racial divide. He even personified that unity by being of mixed race himself: he was born in Hawaii to a black exchange student from Kenya who was in a bigamous marriage with a white teenage girl from Kansas.

Others, however, found a great deal suspicious about Obama, including the fact that he refused for years to produce his birth certificate, fueling speculation that he was not born in the United States or that some other aspect of his official biography was false. This was not just wild speculation, as Obama's literary agency, Acton & Dystel, in a 1991 booklet promoting him as a writer, said that Obama was "born in Kenya and raised in Indonesia and Hawaii."[571] There was no doubt about the fact that he had a classic late twentieth-century upbringing, being raised by a single mother (his parents divorced when he was two) and, in high school, being much more concerned with smoking marijuana than pursuing any serious studies.

Of greater concern to numerous Americans was the fact that he had early associations with Communists such as black activist Frank Marshall Davis, whom Obama described in his first autobiography *Dreams from My Father* as something of a mentor, and Bill Ayers of the 1960s terror group the Weather Underground, who hosted Obama's 1995 entry into politics, his announcement that he was running for the Illinois State Senate. Many Americans were appalled that Obama

---

571   Dylan Stableford, " 'Born in Kenya': Obama's Literary Agent Misidentified His Birthplace in 1991," ABC News, May 17, 2012.

had been a member of Trinity United Church of Christ in Chicago for years and was close to its pastor, the Reverend Jeremiah Wright. Wright frequently incited race hatred and hatred of America, even once going so far as to cry out, "God damn America!"[572]

Obama's supporters were not concerned about the radicalism of his politics at all; his far-left positions had become mainstream in the Democratic Party. The fact that he had only been a senator for two years (and had a slight résumé before that) when he announced his candidacy for president on February 10, 2007 was one indication that he was widely valued more as a symbol—of America's finally healing its racial traumas and stepping into a new age of national harmony—than for his actual record.

It also helped that he was immensely more likeable than the presumptive 2008 nominee, former First Lady and senator Hillary Clinton. Obama's victory over Clinton was an upset, but it nonetheless had an air of inevitability about it: even though he was running against the woman who would have been the first female candidate of a major party, the Democrats were not going to reject their first viable black presidential candidate.

How he won

Obama's victory over the 2008 Republican candidate, Senator John McCain of Arizona, seemed inevitable as well. McCain was seventy-two and white; Obama was forty-seven and half

---

572   Roland S. Martin, "The Full Story behind Rev. Jeremiah Wright's 9/11 Sermon," *Anderson Cooper 360*, CNN, March 21, 2008.

black, living proof that America had cast off its past and had truly become the land of opportunity for all people. McCain was gruff and irascible; Obama was smooth and collected. Obama offered a program of expanding government intervention and control; McCain countered with much the same, just a bit less of it. Obama won convincingly, with 365 electoral votes to McCain's 173.

Obama's campaign rallies were charged with a messianic excitement that the candidate himself did nothing to dampen. On October 30, 2008, just before he was first elected president, Obama grandly proclaimed that "we are five days away from fundamentally transforming the United States of America."[573]

This wasn't just campaign rhetoric. Internationalists in the U.S. and around the world knew this: on October 9, 2009, Obama was awarded the Nobel Peace Prize for little more than being the first black president and a deeply committed leftist.

By 2012, the American people knew much more about Barack Obama than they had before; many didn't like what they saw. But the Republicans put up yet another weak candidate, former Massachusetts governor Mitt Romney, who squandered numerous opportunities to establish a sharp contrast between his proposals and Obama's. Obama received over 3.5 million fewer popular and 33 fewer electoral votes than he had in 2008, but it was still enough.

---

573   Barack Obama, "Obama Rallies Columbia, Missouri," Real Clear Politics, October 30, 2008.

Notable accomplishments as president and events of his presidency

1. *Exacerbating racial and religious tensions.* Throughout his tenure, Obama stoked racial tensions rather than calming them. When he took office, the Justice Department was pursuing a case against the New Black Panther Party for voter intimidation in Philadelphia. Obama's attorney general, Eric Holder, abruptly dropped the case in May 2009 and refused to cooperate with further investigations, giving the impression that the Black Panthers were getting away with voter intimidation because of their race.

Obama's response to several widely publicized incidents exacerbated racial tensions. On July 16, 2009, black intellectual Henry Louis Gates found himself locked out of his Massachusetts home and began trying to force his way in. An officer arrived to investigate a possible break-in; Gates began berating him and was arrested for disorderly conduct. Obama claimed that the police "acted stupidly" and noted the "long history in this country of African-Americans and Latinos being stopped by police disproportionately," although there was no indication of racial bias in this case.[574] He invited Gates and the police officer to the White House for a "beer summit," which the media hailed as a manifestation of his determination to heal racial divisions, when in fact it was just the opposite: he was taking a case of misunderstanding and disorderly conduct and portraying it as a racial incident requiring presidential reconciliation.

---

574   Helene Cooper, "Obama Criticizes Arrest of Harvard Professor," *New York Times,* July 22, 2009.

Obama also made matters worse when a young Hispanic, George Zimmerman, on February 26, 2012, shot dead a young black man, Trayvon Martin, in what was widely reported as a racial hate crime. NBC edited a recording of Zimmerman's call to the police to give the false impression that Zimmerman was suspicious of Martin solely because he was black. Instead of trying to calm the situation, Obama stoked the idea that Zimmerman acted out of racial hatred and said, "If I had a son, he'd look like Trayvon."[575] Yet Zimmerman was acquitted of murder and the Justice Department declined to prosecute him for a hate crime.

Obama made a similar rush to judgment in the case of Ahmed Mohamed, a Muslim high school student who was arrested in September 2015 after bringing what appeared to be a suitcase bomb to his Texas high school. Mohamed claimed it was a homemade clock and that he was a victim of "Islamophobic" bigotry. Obama invited him to the White House, making the boy a symbol of the nation's "Islamophobia" and the need to overcome it. Mohamed's father filed a lawsuit against the school district, which was dismissed when he failed to establish that the school had engaged in any prejudice or discrimination.

2. *The "apology tours."* Shortly after taking office, Obama embarked upon two world tours that critics quickly dubbed the "apology tours," as at every stop Obama had some negative words for the U.S. He had little to say about America being the most generous, and most free, nation on earth.

---

575   Byron Tau, "Obama: 'If I Had a Son, He'd Look like Trayvon,'" Politico, March 23, 2012.

3. *Appeasing Russia.* On March 6, 2009, Secretary of State Hillary Clinton gave Russian Foreign Minister Sergey Lavrov a red button saying "Reset," as a symbol of the Obama administration's desire to improve U.S.-Russia relations, although the button didn't actually say "Reset" in Russian, but "Overload."[576] In pursuit of this elusive reset, Obama approved a deal in 2010 that gave Russia 20 percent of America's capacity to mine uranium and ordered investigators looking into Russian cyberattacks involving the 2016 election (which were not, as is commonly claimed, directed to electing Donald Trump) to "stand down."[577]

4. *Covering up Islamic jihad.* Obama, like Bush, denied that Islamic texts and teachings had any role in inciting jihad terrorists to commit acts of violence, but he took this denial to ridiculous extremes. He frequently criticized Christianity, while repeatedly praising Islam and touting the great contributions of Muslims to U.S. history, which were entirely fictional. Obama's Homeland Secretary Janet Napolitano scrupulously avoided calling jihad terror attacks "terrorism"; she preferred the term "man-caused disasters."[578] When Army Major Nidal Malik Hasan, screaming "Allahu akbar," murdered thirteen people and wounded thirty at Fort Hood on November 5, 2009, he consistently explained that his shootings were an Islamic jihad attack.[579] Yet Obama's Defense Department

---

576   Mark Landler, "Lost in Translation: A U.S. Gift to Russia," *New York Times*, March 6, 2009.
577   Michael Isikoff, "Obama Cyber Chief Confirms 'Stand Down' Order against Russian Cyberattacks in Summer 2016," Yahoo News!, June 20, 2018.
578   " 'Away from the Politics of Fear,' " *Spiegel International*, March 16, 2009.
579   Helen Pidd and Ewen MacAskill, "Fort Hood Gunman Shouted 'Allahu Akbar' as He Opened Fire," *Guardian*, November 6, 2009.

classified Hasan's shootings not as a terrorist act but as "workplace violence."[580]

On October 19, 2011, Islamic groups demanded that the Obama administration adopt this denial and willful ignorance as official policy, scrapping all counterterror training materials that made any mention of Islam. Obama readily agreed. The "Countering Violent Extremism" program studiously avoided making any mention of Islam in connection with terrorism. The entire American law enforcement and intelligence apparatus was made to go along with the fiction that when Islamic terrorists themselves explained their motivating ideology, they were misunderstanding their religion, and the real cause of their behavior had to be found elsewhere.

5. *Obamacare.* On March 23, 2010, Obama signed the Affordable Care Act, which was supposed to make it possible for all Americans, even the poorest, to afford health insurance. He had promised repeatedly that his plan would not interfere with existing health plans, insisting, "If you like your doctor, you will be able to keep your doctor."[581] That did not turn out to be true. Obamacare also included the notorious individual mandate, which required Americans to buy health insurance and set fines for not doing so.

The individual mandate was challenged from all sides on constitutional grounds, as critics pointed out that while the Commerce Clause gave the federal government the authority

---

580   Susan Crabtree, "Fort Hood Victims See Similarities to Benghazi," *Washington Times*, October 18, 2012.

581   Mary Lu Carnevale, "Obama: 'If You Like Your Doctor, You Can Keep Your Doctor,' " *Wall Street Journal*, June 15, 2009.

to *regulate* commerce, it did not give it the power to *require* commerce by forcing people to buy something. Obamacare went to the Supreme Court, where on June 28, 2012, the court voted 5–4 in *National Federation of Independent Business v. Sebelius* that it was constitutional, as the individual mandate was essentially a tax. Chief Justice John Roberts, a Bush appointee, was the deciding vote.

6. *Illegal and legal immigration.* Throughout the Obama administration, illegal immigrants crossed more or less freely into the United States across the border from Mexico. Epitomizing the failure of the Obama administration's immigration policies was the killing of a young woman named Kate Steinle on July 1, 2015, in San Francisco. The killer was an illegal immigrant, José Inez García Zárate, who had seven felony convictions and had been deported five times.

Meanwhile, the Obama administration brought in entire communities of people from countries such as Bosnia and Somalia and placed them in small and medium-sized American cities, where predictable civil strife ensued: the Somali community in Minneapolis became the nation's leader in the recruitment of jihad terrorists. And from October 2015 to October 2016, as civil war raged in Syria, the Obama administration admitted 12,587 Syrian refugees into the country. Of those, 12,363 were Sunni Muslims and 68 were Christians, despite the fact that the Christians of Syria were targeted by the Islamic State (ISIS) and other jihad groups far more than Sunni Muslims were. While Christians still outnumbered Muslims in the total number of refugees admitted during the Obama administration, the figures from that single year regarding Syrian refugees were an indication of Obama's lack of awareness of or indifference to the suffering of Christians in Muslim lands.

7. *Operation Fast and Furious* was a sting operation designed to flush out drug cartels in Mexico by selling weapons to buyers who would then sell them to the drug operations, enabling drug enforcement agents to locate the cartels. The Obama administration sent two thousand guns into Mexico, and the plan quickly went wrong. One of the weapons was used to kill a border agent. Even worse, Attorney General Eric Holder then falsely claimed that he knew nothing about the whole scheme, and Obama claimed executive privilege to withhold pertinent documents from Congress. Congress voted to hold Holder in contempt of Congress.

8. *Weaponizing the IRS against political opponents.* Obama oversaw the rapid politicization of the supposedly apolitical civil service, including targeted Internal Revenue Service harassment of groups with "tea party" or "patriot" in their names, as the director of the IRS Exempt Organizations division, Lois Lerner, admitted in 2013.[582]

9. *Betraying allies.* In 2009, Obama abandoned plans for a missile defense system in Poland and the Czech Republic. But the most notorious example of his betrayal of allies was his treatment of Israel. Obama had thinly veiled contempt for the Jewish State and its prime minister, Benjamin Netanyahu, and constantly worked from the presumption that the Jewish

---

582   Zachary A. Goldfarb and Karen Tumulty, "IRS Admits Targeting
       Conservatives for Tax Scrutiny in 2012 Election," *Washington Post*, May 10,
       2013.

State was the sole obstacle to peace and the sole party that had to make concessions.

In November 2011, Obama's view of Israel and Netanyahu was revealed to the world when French President Nicolas Sarkozy, unaware that the microphone in front of him was on, said to the president, "I cannot bear Netanyahu, he's a liar," and Obama replied, "You're fed up with him, but I have to deal with him even more often than you."[583]

10. *Killing Osama bin Laden.* The al-Qaeda leader was killed on May 2, 2011, in an American raid on the compound in Pakistan where he had been living for several years.

11. *Enabling the rise of ISIS and aiding jihadis in Syria.* Obama stuck to the December 2011 date George W. Bush had set for the withdrawal of U.S. troops from Iraq. Sunnis were unwilling to accept the rule of the weak Shi'ite government that resulted from elections held after the toppling of Saddam; some of these joined a vicious and inhumane jihad group known as the Islamic State (ISIS), which quickly took control of large portions of Iraq and Syria, controlling at its height a territory larger than Britain. Obama dismissed ISIS as "a jayvee team."[584]

Yet ISIS proved so formidable that American troops returned to Iraq in 2014 to fight it and other jihad groups but made little headway. This may have been because the Obama administration actively aided the rise of jihad groups that were allied with ISIS. In an August 2015 interview, former

---

583   Yann Le Guernigou, "Sarkozy Tells Obama Netanyahu Is a 'Liar,'" Reuters, November 8, 2011.

584   David Remnick, "Going the Distance," *New Yorker*, January 27, 2014.

director of the Defense Intelligence Agency (DIA) Michael Flynn revealed that ISIS's rise was not an accidental result of Obama's policies. "I think it was a willful decision," said Flynn.[585] Flynn read from a declassified 2012 DIA report that suggested "establishing a declared or undeclared Salafist principality in Eastern Syria...in order to isolate the Syrian regime." ISIS ended up establishing that Salafist principality.

Obama also wanted American troops in Syria. In 2013, he charged that Syrian President Bashar al-Assad had used chemical weapons against his own people in the course of the Syrian civil war and began an energetic push for American military intervention to remove Assad from power. It wasn't clear that Assad had been the one who actually used the chemical weapons, and the only beneficiaries of the removal of Assad would have been Sunni jihad groups including ISIS, but that didn't stop the Obama administration from advocating that America send troops. Their motivation seemed at least in part to be pecuniary; Secretary of State John Kerry revealed in September 2013 that "Arab countries" had offered "to bear costs."[586] The world's proudest military force would have been reduced to the status of mercenaries.

That plan didn't come to fruition, but the U.S. did arm jihad groups in Syria. "We have a Free Syrian Army and a moderate opposition that we have steadily been working with that we have vetted," Obama said in September 2014, ignoring

---

585   Brad Hoff, "Rise of Islamic State Was 'a Willful Decision': Former DIA Chief Michael Flynn," *Foreign Policy Journal*, August 7, 2015.

586   Aaron Blake, "Kerry: Arab Countries Offered to Pay for Invasion," *Live Blog, Washington Post*, September 4, 2013.

the fact that in July 2014 several Free Syrian Army factions had pledged allegiance to ISIS.[587]

12. *Aiding jihadis in Libya and Egypt.* Obama was enthusiastic about the "Arab Spring" uprisings of 2011. The establishment media backed him up by claiming that they were democratic revolutions. Reality was, as always, different: the "rebels" were generally Sharia supremacists and often outright jihadis. The U.S. backed the Muslim Brotherhood regime that came to power in Egypt in 2012, despite the Brotherhood's dedication to jihad for the implementation of Sharia. The Brotherhood regime was overthrown in 2013, as protesters held signs in Cairo denouncing Obama for supporting terrorism.

In Libya, meanwhile, Obama-backed jihadis overthrew and murdered strongman Muammar Qaddafi in October 2011, to the delight of Hillary Clinton, who chortled, "We came, we saw, he died!"[588] Clinton would discover that the jihadis were not grateful for the American help they received.

13. *The Benghazi jihad massacre.* On September 11, 2012, Islamic jihadis stormed the U.S. diplomatic compound in Benghazi, Libya, and murdered the U.S. ambassador to Libya, Chris Stevens, and three other Americans. The Obama State Department had done nothing when Stevens repeatedly requested additional security.

Hillary Clinton's initial statement suggested that the massacre was a spontaneous reaction to a YouTube video,

---

587   Jordan Schachtel, "Daily Jihad: Obama's 'Vetted' Free Syrian Army Joining Forces with Islamic State Terror Group," Breitbart, September 9, 2014.

588   Corbett Daly, "Clinton on Qaddafi: 'We Came, We Saw, He Died,' " CBS News, October 20, 2011.

"Innocence of Muslims," which was critical of Muhammad, the prophet of Islam. Other administration officials would make that claim outright. Clinton declared: "Some have sought to justify this vicious behavior as a response to inflammatory material posted on the Internet. The United States deplores any intentional effort to denigrate the religious beliefs of others."[589]

Yet Clinton told Egypt's prime minister and member of the Muslim Brotherhood, Hesham Kandil, the next day, "We know that the attack in Libya had nothing to do with the film. It was a planned attack—not a protest.... We believe the group that claimed responsibility for this was affiliated with al Qaeda."[590] Yet administration officials kept repeating the lie that the massacre was because of a video. Obstructing the investigation, Hillary Clinton deleted thousands of emails related to her handling of the crisis.

14. *Attacking the freedom of speech.* In July 2012, Representative Trent Franks of Arizona asked Thomas Perez, the assistant attorney general for the Civil Rights Division to pledge that "this administration's Department of Justice will never entertain or advance a proposal that criminalizes speech against any religion."[591] Perez refused to answer, claiming that it was a "hard question."[592] But the Obama administration ultimately

---

589   Hillary Rodham Clinton, "Statement on the Attack in Benghazi," U.S. Department of State, September 11, 2012.

590   "The Secretary's Call with Egyptian PM Kandil," September 12, 2012 (email released by U.S. Department of State to Benghazi Select Committee), http://benghazi.house.gov/sites/republicans.benghazi.house.gov/files/documents/Tab%2079.pdf.

591   Trent Franks, "High Ranking DOJ Official Refuses to Affirm 1st Amendment Rights," YouTube, July 26, 2012.

592   Ibid.

made clear what it thought of the freedom of speech. After the Benghazi massacre, Clinton said, "We're going to have that person arrested and prosecuted."[593] "That person" was a Christian from Egypt who had produced the video that the administration had scapegoated for the attack.

On September 25, 2012, thirteen days after the massacre, Obama stated at the United Nations General Assembly, "The future must not belong to those who slander the prophet of Islam."[594] Two days after Obama said this, Hillary Clinton made good on her promise to Woods: the filmmaker was arrested on the pretext of a minor probation violation and imprisoned for several months.

15. *The Iran nuclear deal.* On July 14, 2015, the U.S., along with Russia, China, Britain, and the European Union concluded an agreement with the Islamic Republic of Iran that Obama promised would bring peace. He said that Iran's "every pathway to a nuclear weapon" had been blocked and boasted: "We have stopped the spread of nuclear weapons in this region."[595]

Why his presidency was disastrous for America

As he forbade law enforcement and intelligence agencies from understanding the motivating ideology behind jihad

---

593   Robert Spencer, "Hillary Clinton on Muhammad Filmmaker: 'We're Going to Have That Person Arrested and Prosecuted,' " Jihad Watch, October 25, 2012.

594   "Remarks by the President to the UN General Assembly," White House, September 25, 2012.

595   Andrea Mitchell, Cassandra Vinograd, and Abigail Williams, "Iran Nuclear Deal: Tehran, World Powers Agree to Historic Pact," NBC News, July 14, 2015.

terrorism, Obama created an institutional culture of denial that became deeply embedded. All too many FBI agents and others who should have known better thought that the best thing they could do when confronted with a terror-tied mosque was conduct "outreach" and reassure Muslims of their goodwill. This policy bore lethal consequences in April 2013, when two jihadis set off bombs at the Boston Marathon, killing three people and injuring several hundred, and FBI Director Robert Mueller admitted that the agency had visited the bombers' mosque only for "outreach," not to investigate.

The FBI was not just full of useful idiots with no knowledge of the ideology of those they were trying to oppose; it was also likely infiltrated by people with that same ideology. The infiltration had already started during the George W. Bush administration, but under Obama, it galloped ahead, with all concerns about it dismissed as "Islamophobic." When Representative Michele Bachmann of Minnesota called in 2012 for an investigation into Muslim Brotherhood infiltration into the U.S. government, she also was decried as "Islamophobic," and no investigation was conducted.

Meanwhile, the IRS targeting of conservative groups was a prelude to many more revelations about how the civil service had become a corrupt and compromised stronghold of the Left while Obama was president. And *National Federation of Independent Business v. Sebelius* was the most ill-advised Court ruling since *Plessy v. Ferguson*, which allowed for racial segregation, and the Dred Scott decision. Chief Justice Roberts's vote and opinion showed yet again how establishment Republicans constantly affirmed, rather than challenged, the Democrats' statit agenda. Obamacare gave the federal government a huge role in health insurance and, not coincidentally, caused more trouble than it solved. Millions of people lost plans that were working and had to pay more for other plans, or in fines for not having insurance, than they would have paid previously. And the federal government continued its seemingly inexorable advance toward control of every aspect of citizens' lives.

Shortly before Obama was elected in 2008, he said, "When you spread the wealth around, it's good for everybody."[596] In December 2013, he said that the fact that some people made much more money than others was the "defining challenge of our time."[597] He believed not in equality of opportunity but equality of outcome, which could only be enforced by the state powers exercised in socialist states. He didn't make America a socialist state, but with Obamacare and more, he put it firmly on the socialist path, as both Mexico, because of NAFTA, and the People's Republic of China drew millions of jobs out of the U.S.

Obama's foreign policy was just as disastrous, although in Iraq the responsibility was not wholly Obama's. While Obama repeatedly took credit for the killing of Osama bin Laden, efforts to find and kill him had been going on for years before he became president. If anything, the raid on bin Laden's hideout, which was just down the street from a major Pakistani military installation, highlighted the failure of both

---

596   Susan Jones, "'Spread the Wealth around' Comment Comes Back to Haunt
         Obama," CNS News, October 15, 2008.
597   Jim Kuhnhenn, "Obama: Income Inequality a Defining Challenge,"
         Associated Press, December 4, 2013.

Bush and Obama to reevaluate and reconfigure America's alliance in light of the new realities of the global jihad. Pakistan may have been an ally during the Cold War, but it certainly was not by the twenty-first century.

Bush's policies left Iraq in chaos; Obama inherited the mess. His keeping to the public timetable for withdrawal allowed jihad groups to plan for offensives to begin when the Americans were gone. ISIS was the biggest beneficiary of America's absence. Then when ISIS did arise, Obama's response was feeble. However, his withdrawal from Iraq epitomized another problem with America's undeclared, goalless wars: American troops couldn't stay in Iraq forever, and anytime they left, the jihadis would take advantage. Obama could have spearheaded the formulation of a new strategy to contain the jihad threat without committing American troops, but since his administration was committed to unreality regarding that threat, that possibility was out of the question.

The Iran nuclear deal was dramatically flawed. It even allowed the Iranians under some circumstances to inspect their own nuclear sites and report to the UN on whether or not they were in compliance with the deal. Aside from that, it mandated so much advance notice before anyone from outside could come inspect the sites that the Iranians would have plenty of time to hide anything that was in violation of the deal. And after just ten years, it removed all restrictions on Iran's ability to construct nuclear weapons.

Even worse, Obama removed economic sanctions on Iran, allowing for a massive cash inflow into the mullahs' coffers at a time when the nation's economic instability was threatening the very foundations of the Islamic Republic. He also sent Iran $1.7 billion, in pallets of cash delivered under the cover of night, that the shah's government had sent to Washington as part of a canceled arms deal in the 1970s, and that Carter, Reagan, George H. W. Bush, Clinton, and George W. Bush had all thought improper to return to the Islamic Republic. Obama broke ranks with them and sent the money to Iran, which promptly used it to finance the activities of the jihad terror group Hizballah and other jihad groups around the world.

When Obama left the White House, he was hailed and lionized as much as he had been when he took office. But he had done nothing but weaken the United States on virtually all fronts. Only a courageous leader with a strong capacity for independent thought could even begin to undo the havoc Obama wrought.

FORTY-FIVE

DONALD TRUMP

Library of Congress[598]

---

598   *Portrait of President-Elect Donald Trump*, 2016, photograph, Library of
         Congress, https://www.loc.gov/item/2017645723/.

Full name: Donald John Trump
Lived: June 14, 1946–
Presidency: January 20, 2017–
Party: Republican
Evaluation: Great for America
Rating: 10

What qualified him to be president

Other men besides Donald Trump had no political experience before running for president of the United States, but none had as improbable a background for a chief executive. Trump was a billionaire real estate developer, a playboy whose name was more often mentioned in gossip columns than in political analysis, and the host of a popular reality TV show.

Throughout his career, however, Trump had an eye on politics. When asked in a 1990 interview if he would consider running for president, he answered: "I'd do the job as well as or better than anyone else.... I don't want to be President. I'm 100 percent sure. I'd change my mind only if I saw this country continue to go down the tubes."[599]

When the country continued to go down the tubes and Trump decided to run, the political and media elites mocked him. As late as August 2016, when Trump wrote on the social media site Twitter that Obama would "go down as perhaps the

---

599   Glenn Plaskin, "The Playboy Interview with Donald Trump," *Playboy*, March 1, 1990.

worst president in the history of the United States," Obama responded, "At least I will go down as a President."[600]

Obama would by no means be the only one who would have to eat his words. Trump stood out amid a crowded field of twelve Republican candidates for the 2016 nomination in large part because he was not a politician. His positions weren't poll-tested or approved by focus groups. His speeches were off the cuff, funny, and honest, and addressed the real concerns of many Americans. Despite being a billionaire, he appeared to those he won over to be a common man, an ordinary American who loved his country and didn't want to see it "continue to go down the tubes."

How he won

Opposing him was a Democratic candidate who had done a great deal to send America down the tubes: Hillary Clinton, who had been Bill Clinton's proactive First Lady, the architect of his failed health care plan, and then a senator from New York and Obama's first secretary of state, in which capacity her negligence enabled the murder of American diplomatic personnel at Benghazi. She had also grown fabulously wealthy in public service and was thus emblematic of the corrupt political establishment against which Trump was running.

Her election as president, however, seemed to have the same aura of inevitability that Obama had enjoyed in 2008.

---

600   Donald Trump (@DonaldTrump), Twitter, August 2, 2016, https://twitter.com/realDonaldTrump/status/760552601356267520; "Trump can't WIN!," YouTube video, November 22, 2016, https://www.youtube.com/watch?v=YZ46I3kMOr0.

Obama claimed at the Democratic National Convention that "there has never been a man or a woman, not me, not Bill, nobody more qualified than Hillary Clinton to serve as president of the United States of America."[601]

This wasn't even close to true: numerous presidents had better résumés than Hillary Clinton, but it nonetheless became an oft-repeated Clinton talking point. In their third and final debate, Clinton said: "And on the day when I was in the Situation Room, monitoring the raid that brought Osama bin Laden to justice, [Trump] was hosting *The Celebrity Apprentice*. So I'm happy to compare my 30 years of experience, what I've done for this country, trying to help in every way I could, especially [helping] kids and families get ahead and stay ahead, with your 30 years, and I'll let the American people make that decision."[602]

Clinton was dogged by suspicions that she had acted improperly as secretary of state in storing her emails, including some containing classified information, on an unsecured private server in her home, in violation of government regulations. The FBI, however, declined to prosecute, and the media downplayed the matter. Clinton was also intensely unlikeable, but to many, so was Trump, whose bluster and braggadocio balanced her icy arrogance. Trump ran on a promise to "Make America Great Again," clean up corruption in Washington ("Drain the Swamp"), and put "America First" in a way it had

---

601   Libby Nelson, "Is Hillary Clinton Really the Most Qualified Candidate Ever? An Investigation," Vox, August 1, 2016.

602   "October 19, 2016 Debate Transcript," Commission on Presidential Debates, https://www.debates.org/voter-education/debate-transcripts/october-19-2016-debate-transcript/.

not been by recent presidents. Clinton ran offering more of the drift toward internationalism and socialism that had characterized the last few presidencies.

Hardly anyone thought Trump had a chance. All the polls showed Clinton with a comfortable lead. Political "experts" explained that it wasn't even possible for Trump to capture enough traditional Democratic strongholds to amass enough electoral votes to win. The week of the election, *Newsweek* published a keepsake edition featuring a smiling Clinton and the triumphant headline "MADAM PRESIDENT."[603]

It turned out to be a latter-day "DEWEY DEFEATS TRUMAN": Trump won a decisive victory, with 304 electoral votes to Clinton's 227. He lost the popular vote, but Clinton's huge victory margins in densely populated areas of Los Angeles and New York accounted entirely for that, and served as a new reminder of why the Electoral College was necessary, ensuring that the presidential choice was truly national, and preventing a small number of high-population areas from dominating the election.

Immediately after Trump won, some Democrats began a campaign to compel enough electors to break their pledges to vote for him and vote for Clinton instead. When that failed, the talk of impeaching Trump began, before he had even been sworn in. The partisan divide in America had often been bitter, and presidents had always been a focus of hatred from some of their opponents, but when Donald Trump became president, the hatred reached an unprecedented level.

---

603   *Newsweek*, November 8, 2016.

In his inaugural address, Trump announced that "today we are not merely transferring power from one Administration to another, or from one party to another—but we are transferring power from Washington, D.C., and giving it back to you, the American People. For too long, a small group in our nation's Capital has reaped the rewards of government while the people have borne the cost. Washington flourished—but the people did not share in its wealth. Politicians prospered—but the jobs left, and the factories closed. The establishment protected itself, but not the citizens of our country.... That all changes—starting right here, and right now, because this moment is your moment: it belongs to you."[604]

Unlike numerous other presidents who had spoken in the past about taking the government from the oligarchs who controlled it and giving it back to the people, Trump's words didn't herald a push to expand government power under the guise of working for the people. On the contrary, he was determined to expand the freedom Americans enjoyed and roll back government power.

A new era had begun in American politics. But the guardians of the old order were not going to give way easily.

Notable accomplishments as president and events of his presidency

1. *Fighting the "deep state."* Most Americans assumed that when Trump became president, he would be able to implement his

---

604   Donald J. Trump, "Inaugural Address" (speech, January 20, 2017), White House, https://www.whitehouse.gov/briefings-statements/the-inaugural-address/.

own agenda insofar as he could secure the cooperation of Congress, as other presidents had done. But Trump encountered an entrenched coterie of bureaucrats at all levels who were determined to thwart his every move.

While the media dismissed talk of a "deep state" as a conspiracy theory, the *New York Times* admitted its existence on September 5, 2018, when it published an anonymous op-ed that proclaimed, "I work for the president but like-minded colleagues and I have vowed to thwart parts of his agenda and his worst inclinations."[605] The *Times* elaborated on these foes of Trump within his own administration in October 2019: "President Trump is right: The deep state is alive and well. But it is not the sinister, antidemocratic cabal of his fever dreams. It is, rather, a collection of patriotic public servants—career diplomats, scientists, intelligence officers and others—who, from within the bowels of this corrupt and corrupting administration, have somehow remembered that their duty is to protect the interests, not of a particular leader, but of the American people."[606]

Obama's CIA Director John Brennan also all but admitted its existence in October 2019, when he tweeted, "As in previous times of National peril, we rely on our military, diplomats, intelligence officials, law enforcement officers, & other courageous patriots to protect our liberties, freedom, & democracy."[607] In this case, however, the diplomats, intelligence officials, and

---

605   "I Am Part of the Resistance inside the Trump Administration," *New York Times,* September 5, 2018.

606   Michelle Cottle, "They Are Not the Resistance. They Are Not a Cabal. They Are Public Servants," *New York Times,* October 20, 2019.

607   John Brennan (@JohnBrennan), Twitter, October 29, 2019, https://twitter.com/JohnBrennan/status/1189182527136813056.

law enforcement officers in question were not protecting the nation from foreign enemies, but from what they considered to be the misguided policies of the man whom they were supposed to be serving, the president of the United States.

While this sounded high-minded, there is no doubt whatsoever that the *New York Times* and Brennan would have taken the opposite position if the federal bureaucracy had dared interfere with the Obama agenda.

2. *Impeachment.* The apex of the deep state coup was the Democrats' attempt to make Trump appear guilty of various misdeeds, which would lead to his impeachment. Before he was inaugurated, he began to be charged with being a tool of Russian President Vladimir Putin and colluding with Russia to fix the 2016 election. Trump agreed to appoint a special counsel, former FBI director Robert Mueller, to investigate this.

After a two-year investigation, Mueller found nothing for which Trump could be impeached. The Democrat-controlled House didn't give up, however; it then fastened on a phone call Trump had in the summer of 2019 with Ukrainian President Volodymyr Zelensky, claiming that Trump had threatened to withhold U.S. aid to Ukraine until Zelensky agreed to investigate Joe Biden, a front-runner for the 2020 Democratic nomination. The transcript of the call showed this was not the case, Zelensky denied it, and Ukraine received the aid. But the Democrats charged ahead anyway, impeaching Trump on two counts, one of abuse of power for the Ukraine matter and one of obstruction of Congress, which wasn't a crime in any code of law, for not cooperating with the sham investigation.

3. *Restoring the Supreme Court.* Trump made two Supreme Court appointments, of Neil Gorsuch and Brett Kavanaugh, that went a long way toward restoring the Supreme Court to fidelity to the Constitution, lessening the likelihood that the court would continue to rubber-stamp the ever-spiraling expansion of federal power that threatened the freedom of Americans. The Kavanaugh confirmation hearings were a circus, as the Democrats focused their opposition to him on unsubstantiated charges that he had attempted rape decades earlier. The shameful episode was an additional illustration, besides the deep state's attempted coup against Trump, of the fact that the Left would stop at nothing to retain power.

4. *Cutting regulations and lowering taxes.* In June 2016, Obama ridiculed Trump's pledge to attract U.S. companies that had moved out of the country back to the United States, asking Trump, "What magic wand do you have?"[608] Trump's magic wand was an unprecedented initiative to cut regulations on businesses and drastically lower taxes. It began to work immediately. Harry Moser of the Reshoring Initiative, which tracks jobs returning to the U.S. from companies that had relocated elsewhere, stated, "I'd say 300, 400 [companies], at least, announced in 2017" that they were returning.[609]

They brought jobs with them. In 2019, unemployment was at 3.5 percent, the lowest it had been since 1968. The Trump administration also set record lows for unemployment among

608   Rebecca Savransky, "Obama to Trump: 'What Magic Wand Do You Have?'" Hill, June 1, 2016.
609   Jason Margolis, "Trump Hypes Jobs Relocating Back to the U.S. Are They?" PRI, December 26, 2018.

blacks and Hispanics and record highs for the stock market. Trump proved the point that had been made in the 1920s and subsequently forgotten: lower taxes and fewer regulations mean that businesses can prosper, and when businesses prosper, so do the Americans whom they employ.

The Trump-era economy boomed until the coronavirus pandemic wiped out the gains that had been made; there was no doubt, however, that it would have been even weaker still had the steps Trump took to get it going again not been taken in the first place.

5. *Trade deal to replace NAFTA.* During the 2016 campaign, Trump called the North America Free Trade Agreement (NAFTA) "the worst trade deal ever made" and vowed to replace it. He did: in November 2018, he signed the United States-Mexico-Canada Agreement (USMCA), which mandated much more favorable terms for the United States than NAFTA did. Democrats in the House, however, true to their internationalist commitments and disdain for Trump's America-First ethos, refused to ratify it.

6. *Ending the individual mandate.* Trump vowed to repeal and replace Obamacare, but establishment Republicans in the Senate, including 2008 Republican nominee John McCain, voted with the Democrats to preserve the drastically flawed program. However, Trump was able to remove the individual mandate, the Obamacare provision that forced people to buy health insurance and fined them if they didn't.

7. *The travel ban and the wall.* During the campaign, Trump called for a moratorium on Muslim immigration to the United States in light of ongoing jihad terror attacks. He never made

any attempt as president to implement this, but he did place temporary restrictions on immigration from five Muslim countries—Iran, Libya, Somalia, Syria, and Yemen—along with Venezuela and North Korea, in light of the fact that they could not or would not provide U.S. immigration officials with adequate documentation about prospective immigrants, thus making it possible that terrorists or other criminals would attempt to enter the U.S. from those countries and be undetected. Emblematic of the overheated rhetoric of the opposition to Trump was the fact that Islamic advocacy groups in the U.S. called this a "Muslim ban" even though it wasn't, as immigration from fifty-one Muslim countries remained unrestricted.

Trump also famously pledged during the 2016 campaign to build a wall along the U.S.-Mexico border to stymie illegal immigration. Democrats derided this plan as impractical as well as racist, but Americans who faced losing their jobs to illegal immigrants or who were suffering the effects of migrant crime applauded it. Amid frenzied opposition, Trump was able to secure some funding, and construction of the wall began, albeit more slowly than many Trump backers had hoped. Meanwhile, stricter enforcement of existing laws led to a sharp decline in illegal immigration.

8. *Energy independence.* For decades, the United States had relied on imported oil to meet its energy needs, creating a dependence on Saudi Arabia that had deleterious effects on the U.S. in both the foreign and domestic spheres. The full extent of the Saudi role in the 9/11 attacks has never been revealed, and it was largely Saudi pressure that led to George H. W. Bush's incursion into Iraq, the consequences of which

are still reverberating. In November 2019, however, because of Trump's rollback of restrictions on energy exploration, the U.S. became a net exporter of oil. This created jobs for Americans and heralded a new era of freedom in American foreign policy.

9. *Withdrawing from the Paris Climate Agreement.* The agreement had pledged the U.S. to reduce carbon emissions and take other steps to reduce the threat of "climate change," which Democratic leaders described in apocalyptic terms, but which was actually based on highly dubious and politically motivated scientific studies. Obama signed the agreement in 2015; Trump announced on June 1, 2017, that he was withdrawing the U.S. from it, explaining: "The Paris Climate Accord is simply the latest example of Washington entering into an agreement that disadvantages the United States to the exclusive benefit of other countries, leaving American workers—who I love—and taxpayers to absorb the cost in terms of lost jobs, lower wages, shuttered factories, and vastly diminished economic production."[610]

10. *Withdrawing from the UN Human Rights Council.* Trump became the first post-World War II president to strike a blow against the internationalism that had led the United States into the blind alley of the United Nations, which for decades had been a platform—and funding source—for entities that were openly and unapologetically hostile to the United States. Trump withdrew the U.S. from the UN Educational, Scientific,

---

610   Donald Trump, Statement on the Paris Climate Accord (speech, Washington, D.C., June 1, 2017), White House, https://www.whitehouse.gov/briefings-statements/statement-president-trump-paris-climate-accord/.

and Cultural Organization (UNESCO) in October 2017 and from the UN Human Rights Council (UNHRC) in June 2018. UN Ambassador Nikki Haley explained: "I want to make it crystal clear that this step is not a retreat from human rights commitments. On the contrary, we take this step because our commitment does not allow us to remain a part of a hypocritical and self-serving organization that makes a mockery of human rights."[611]

After the U.S. had played along with and actively funded the UN's relentless enabling of totalitarian states and demonization of the United States for decades, this was a breath of fresh air.

11. *Destroying ISIS.* When Barack Obama left office, the Islamic State looked as if it was going to be able to hold territory in Iraq and Syria indefinitely. But by March 2019, virtually all of the terror state's former domains had been recaptured. ISIS remained a threat in several countries around the world, but its caliphate was no more.

12. *Recognizing Jerusalem as Israel's capital and cutting aid to the Palestinians.* On December 6, 2017, Trump fulfilled another campaign promise and shocked the world by recognizing Jerusalem as Israel's capital, and announcing that the U.S. embassy would move there. "When I came into office," Trump said, "I promised to look at the world's challenges with open eyes and very fresh thinking. We cannot solve our problems

---

611   Nikki Haley, "Speech Announcing U.S. Withdrawal from the
        United Nations Human Rights Council" (June 19, 2018), American
        Rhetoric, https://www.americanrhetoric.com/speeches/
        nikkyhaleyunhumanrightscouncilwithdrawl.htm.

by making the same failed assumptions and repeating the same failed strategies of the past. Old challenges demand new approaches."[612]

Trump continued, "My announcement today marks the beginning of a new approach to conflict between Israel and the Palestinians."[613] He pointed out that the U.S. Congress passed the Jerusalem Embassy Act in 1995, asking that the U.S. recognize Jerusalem as Israel's capital and move the embassy there. Bill Clinton, George W. Bush, and Barack Obama had all promised to do so but signed a waiver every year postponing the recognition and the move. This was a clear capitulation to jihad terrorist intimidation: Clinton, Bush, and Obama were allowing jihad terrorists' threats to dictate American policy. Trump would allow for no more American capitulation. The new U.S. embassy in Jerusalem opened on May 14, 2018, the seventieth anniversary of Israel's independence.

Trump also stopped enabling and abetting the Palestinian jihad against Israel, ending the pretense that the Palestinian Authority was a "peace partner" although it had taken no genuine steps to a peaceful accord with Israel. In 2018, the U.S. cut hundreds of millions of dollars of aid to the Palestinians and ended all funding for the United Nations Relief and Works Agency for Palestine Refugees in the Near East (UNRWA), to which it had donated $360 million in 2017 alone, despite the fact that the agency had been found on several occasions to be aiding Palestinian terrorists.

---

612   Donald Trump, "Statement by President Trump on Jerusalem" (speech, Washington, D.C., December 6, 2017), White House.

613   Ibid.

13. *Withdrawing from the Iran nuclear deal.* Trump vowed during the 2016 campaign to end the Iran nuclear deal. His multitude of critics responded with claims that the deal was working, that Iran was more peaceful than it had been, and that it was rejoining the family of nations. This was not true and never had been true. The deal had just been concluded when the Islamic Republic's supreme leader, Ayatollah Ali Khamenei, reaffirmed his nation's hostility toward the U.S.: "Even after this deal our policy towards the arrogant U.S. will not change."[614] Two days later, Khamenei said in a speech, "According to Qur'anic principles, fighting against arrogance and global imperialism is never-ending and today, America is the very epitome of arrogance."[615] Just four days after the JCPOA agreement was signed, Khamenei praised the Iranian people for screaming "Death to America" and "Death to Israel" at nationwide rallies. The Iranian regime spent a great deal of the money Obama gave it on jihad terror groups, as Obama and John Kerry had acknowledged they were likely to do.

On May 8, 2018, Trump announced that he was withdrawing the U.S. from the Iranian nuclear deal, explaining: "This was a horrible one-sided deal that should have never, ever been made. It didn't bring calm, it didn't bring peace, and it never will."[616] He placed new sanctions on Iran that immediately began to have an effect: as the Iranian economy suffered,

614   Ali Wambold, "Fatal Flaw in the Iran Deal," *New York Sun*, August 11, 2015.
615   "Iran's Khamenei Hails His People for Demanding Death to America and Israel," Times of Israel, July 18, 2015.
616   Mark Landler, "Trump Abandons Iran Nuclear Deal He Long Scorned," *New York Times*, May 8, 2018.

the Iranian people increasingly turned against the regime, and there were demonstrations all over the country.

Why his presidency was great for America

Donald Trump became president when the nation had lost its way. He made herculean efforts to bring it back to what the Founding Fathers had intended it to be: a bastion of freedom.

Yet in his efforts to "Drain the Swamp," Donald Trump faced fierce pushback from the swamp itself. Establishment media coverage of his presidency was uniformly negative and frequently outrageously inaccurate. The media had been biased against foes of big government and appeasement of America's enemies for decades, but against Trump, this bias reached unprecedented levels of unanimity—virtually *all* the news coverage Trump received was negative—and vituperation. Meanwhile, the Democrats in the House and Senate did everything they could to obstruct his agenda and impugn him personally. Yet he was still able to accomplish in the first three years of his presidency more that was beneficial for Americans than many presidents were able to accomplish in eight.

One of the most important results of the Trump presidency was not one anyone intended: it revealed the deep corruption and politicization of the civil service, and the crying need to reform it. The deep state coup attempt, as many Republicans characterized the proceedings against Trump, should lead to civil service reform that undoes much of what was done in the 1880s and that makes it possible for a president to remove various officers and appoint people in their place who will implement his agenda. Democrats should support this as well as Republicans: no elected president should be impeded by unelected bureaucrats. But it is likely that the Democrats have too much to lose if the full story of the deep state were revealed to support such a move.

The impeachment of Trump was a serious abuse of what the Framers of the Constitution had intended to be a measure of last resort to remove a president guilty of "high crimes and misdemeanors." It was telling that many of the witnesses the House called to discuss the Ukraine phone call were bureaucrats and diplomats who had no knowledge of any Trump wrongdoing but simply disagreed with his policies. Telling also was the fact that the Trump impeachment vote in the House, in a sharp departure from the votes in the Andrew Johnson and Bill Clinton impeachments, was strictly along party lines, with no Republicans voting for impeachment and two Democrats breaking ranks. In contrast to earlier impeachments, there was no bipartisan support for the Democrats' evidence-free case against the president; only establishment Republican Mitt Romney voted with the Democrats in the Senate to convict Trump. It was an indication of how the Democrats had made impeachment a weapon of partisan politics, as they had been attempting to do since Watergate.

The Trump impeachment was a dark day for America and a sign of how shockingly corrupt and self-serving the American Left had become. If Hillary Clinton had been elected president, the people who engineered it would have enjoyed unfettered power. Their actions against Trump, however, exposed and discredited them. Accomplishing so much despite the unparalleled obstacles he faced places Trump in the first rank of American presidents.

The coronavirus pandemic destroyed the Trump administration's economic achievements, and gave the Democrats a new pretext for charging him with malfeasance, although Trump moved quickly and efficiently to marshal the nation's resources to combat the virus. The crisis itself was in many ways a vindication of points Trump had been making for years, including his repeated assertion that China (where the virus originated) was no friend of the United States, and constituted an economic threat—not an ally. Trump and George Washington were proven correct about avoiding foreign entanglements: the nation was unwise to outsource so much of its manufacturing to the People's Republic or to any other foreign country. The crisis showed that Trump was also correct that strong border controls were essential for national security, as one of his earliest responses to the crisis was to restrict travel from China to the United States, for which the Democrats, predictably focused on destroying his presidency and not on what was best for Americans, charged him with "racism."

The coronavirus crisis demonstrated anew why Trump is a great president: because he puts America first. After a long line of internationalists occupied the White House since 1933, with the sole and partial exception of Ronald Reagan, Trump unashamedly made America first, a principle that had been discredited as "isolationist" since the bombing of Pearl Harbor, not just a slogan, but the cornerstone of his administration. This should have been taken for granted: putting America first is actually the central duty of the president, as encapsulated in his oath of office, in which he solemnly swears to "preserve, protect and defend the Constitution of the United States."

As Trump said: "I never forget, that I am not President of the world, I am President of the United States of America. We reject globalism and we embrace patriotism. We believe that every American citizen, no matter their background, deserves a government that is loyal to them. The Democrat Party and the extreme radical left are trying to abolish the distinction between citizens and non-citizens."[617]

Indeed. But it is, or ought to be, simple common sense: every head of government the world over should make his or her top priority the protection and strengthening of his or her own nation, not the interests of some other nation or group of nations.

Trump is not a great president solely for restoring this principle. He also inherited from Obama an economy that was worse off than it had been since the Great Depression, with spiraling unemployment, rapidly expanding welfare rolls, and job growth at record lows. Trump, cutting taxes and discarding miles of red tape that were hampering American businesses, immediately began to turn the economy around, overseeing an unprecedented rise in the stock market, record growth in wages, and decreases in unemployment to levels not seen in nearly fifty years.

Trump also did all he could to protect American citizens from a tidal wave of illegal, unvetted immigrants that threatened the American economy and the safety of American citizens. In this, however, he encountered fierce resistance

---

617   Donald Trump, "Political Rally in Lake Charles, Louisiana" (speech, October 10, 2019), https://factba.se/transcript/donald-trump-speech-kag-rally-lake-charles-la-october-11-2019.

from a cadre of bureaucrats and judges appointed by Bill Clinton and Barack Obama, who challenged his attempts to put America first at every turn.

Trump vowed during his campaign to Make America Great Again—a slogan that the Democrats tried to portray as racist and hateful. Even as he faced vociferous and relentless opposition from a supposedly objective mass media and unremitting hostility from the allegedly loyal opposition, Donald Trump made good on that promise.

He became president when internationalism and the steady decline of America was taken for granted. In less than three years, Donald J. Trump, against extraordinary odds, turned that around, and in doing so, became nothing less than one of the greatest presidents in American history. After a long string of internationalist mediocrities, the presidency was once again occupied by a man who put America first.

ACKNOWLEDGMENTS

Over the years, I've encountered many people who assume that the scope of a writer's published work is the extent of his or her knowledge and expertise, and so I'm grateful to David S. Bernstein of Bombardier Books for giving me the opportunity to write this book, which is nothing like my previous nineteen books, but is a topic with which I've been fascinated for no less than five decades now. Thanks also to Heather King for making the proceedings move along so efficiently.

Although he didn't agree with many of my conclusions, Hugh Fitzgerald, whom I am proud to call my fellow writer at Jihad Watch, gave me a great deal of valuable direction and correction as I put this book together, reining in my rhetorical excesses, asking me hard questions about many of my statements, and overall making this a much better book than it would have been. It's an old Acknowledgments cliché to say that the merit in the book is owed to someone else while its defects are all the author's, but in this case, it's really true. Thanks again, Hugh.

Meanwhile, Hugh and Christine Douglass-Williams, along with the mysterious tech expert Marc, have helped me keep things going at Jihad Watch while I hobnobbed with Millard Fillmore and Franklin Pierce.

And, of course, none of this would be possible had I not the indefatigable support of the great David Horowitz, as well as Mike Finch and everyone at the David Horowitz Freedom Center, along with others who prefer not to be named; as always, you all know who you are, and you know I love you.

And, once again, I must thank the man without whom I may not have published any books at all: the visionary Mr. Jeffrey Rubin.